JOE JOYCE

THE
GUINNESSES

The Untold Story of Ireland's
Most Successful Family

POOLBEG

Published 2009
by Poolbeg Books Ltd
123 Grange Hill, Baldoyle
Dublin 13, Ireland
E-mail: poolbeg@poolbeg.com
www.poolbeg.com

© Joe Joyce 2009

Copyright for typesetting, layout, design
© Poolbeg Books Ltd

The moral right of the author has been asserted.

1 3 5 7 9 10 8 6 4 2

A catalogue record for this book is available from the British Library.

ISBN 978-1-84223-403-7

Typeset by Patricia Hope in Sabon
Printed by Litographia Rosés, S.A., Spain
Cover design by Glen McArdle

www.poolbeg.com

ABOUT THE AUTHOR

Joe Joyce is a writer and journalist who has worked for *The Irish Times* and *The Guardian*. He is the co-author, with Peter Murtagh, of *The Boss*, the classic account of Charles Haughey in government, and the author of two thrillers, *Off The Record* and *The Trigger Man*, and a play, *The Tower*.

CONTENTS

GUINNESS FAMILY TREE

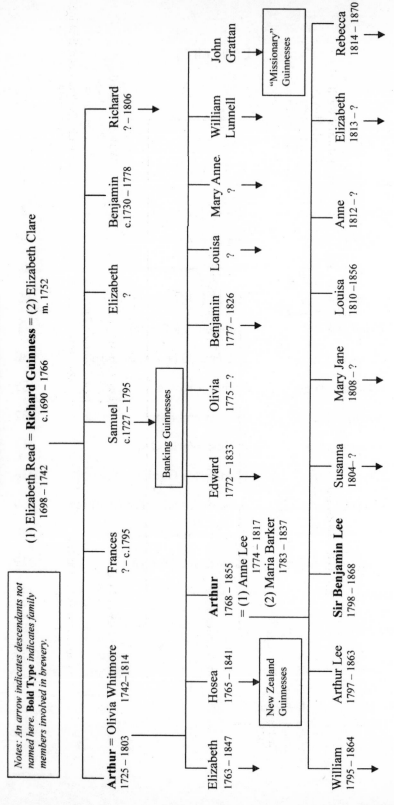

Notes: *An arrow indicates descendants not named here.* **Bold Type** *indicates family members involved in brewery.*

(1) Elizabeth Read = **Richard Guinness** = (2) Elizabeth Clare
     1698 – 1742   c.1690 – 1766   m. 1752

Arthur = Olivia Whitmore
1725 – 1803   1742–1814

Frances
? – c.1795

Samuel
c.1727 – 1795

Elizabeth
?

Benjamin
c.1730 – 1778

Richard
? – 1806

Banking Guinnesses

Elizabeth
1763 – 1847

Hosea
1765 – 1841

New Zealand Guinnesses

Arthur
1768 – 1855
= (1) Anne Lee
1774 – 1817
(2) Maria Barker
1783 – 1837

Edward
1772 – 1833

Olivia
1775 – ?

Benjamin
1777 – 1826

Louisa
?

Mary Anne.
?

William Lunnell

John Grattan

"Missionary" Guinnesses

William
1795 – 1864

Arthur Lee
1797 – 1863

Sir Benjamin Lee
1798 – 1868

Susanna
1804–?

Mary Jane
1808 – ?

Louisa
1810 –1856

Anne
1812 – ?

Elizabeth
1813 – ?

Rebecca
1814 – 1870

GUINNESS FAMILY TREE

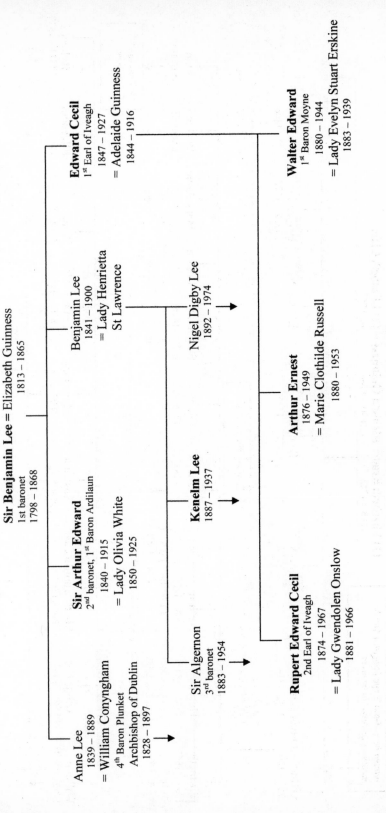

Sir Benjamin Lee = Elizabeth Guinness
1st baronet   1813 – 1865
1798 – 1868

Anne Lee
1839 – 1889
= William Conyngham
4th Baron Plunket
Archbishop of Dublin
1828 – 1897

Sir Arthur Edward
2nd baronet, 1st Baron Ardilaun
1840 – 1915
= Lady Olivia White
1850 – 1925

Benjamin Lee
1841 – 1900
= Lady Henrietta
St Lawrence

Edward Cecil
1st Earl of Iveagh
1847 – 1927
= Adelaide Guinness
1844 – 1916

Sir Algernon
3rd baronet
1883 – 1954

Kenelm Lee
1887 – 1937

Nigel Digby Lee
1892 – 1974

Rupert Edward Cecil
2nd Earl of Iveagh
1874 – 1967
= Lady Gwendolen Onslow
1881 – 1966

Arthur Ernest
1876 – 1949
= Marie Clothilde Russell
1880 – 1953

Walter Edward
1st Baron Moyne
1880 – 1944
= Lady Evelyn Stuart Erskine
1883 – 1939

GUINNESS FAMILY TREE

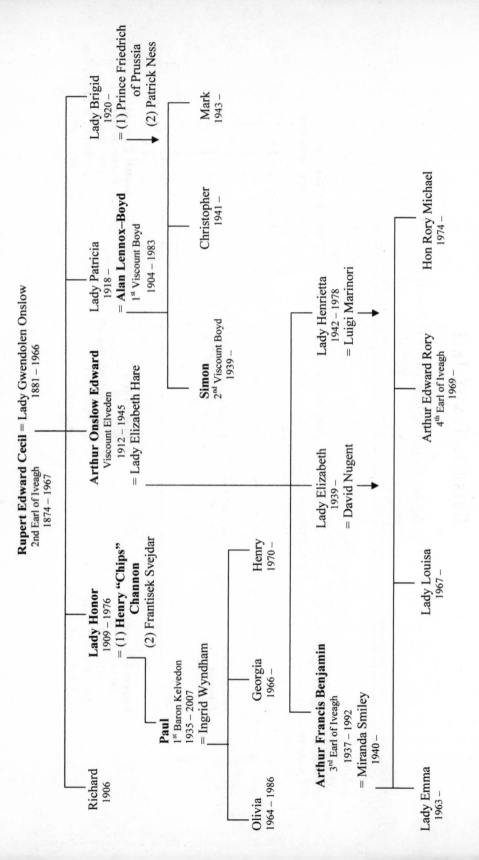

GUINNESS FAMILY TREE

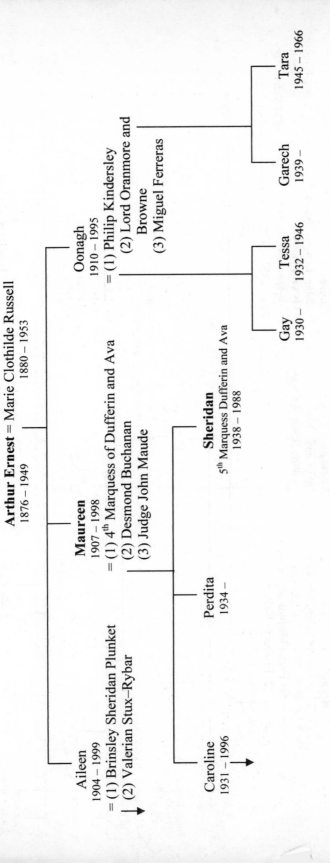

Arthur Ernest = Marie Clothilde Russell
1876 – 1949   1880 – 1953

Aileen
1904 – 1999
= (1) Brinsley Sheridan Plunket
(2) Valerian Stux–Rybar

Maureen
1907 – 1998
= (1) 4th Marquess of Dufferin and Ava
(2) Desmond Buchanan
(3) Judge John Maude

Oonagh
1910 – 1995
= (1) Philip Kindersley
(2) Lord Oranmore and Browne
(3) Miguel Ferreras

Caroline
1931 – 1996

Perdita
1934 –

Sheridan
5th Marquess Dufferin and Ava
1938 – 1988

Gay
1930 –

Tessa
1932 – 1946

Garech
1939 –

Tara
1945 – 1966

GUINNESS FAMILY TREE

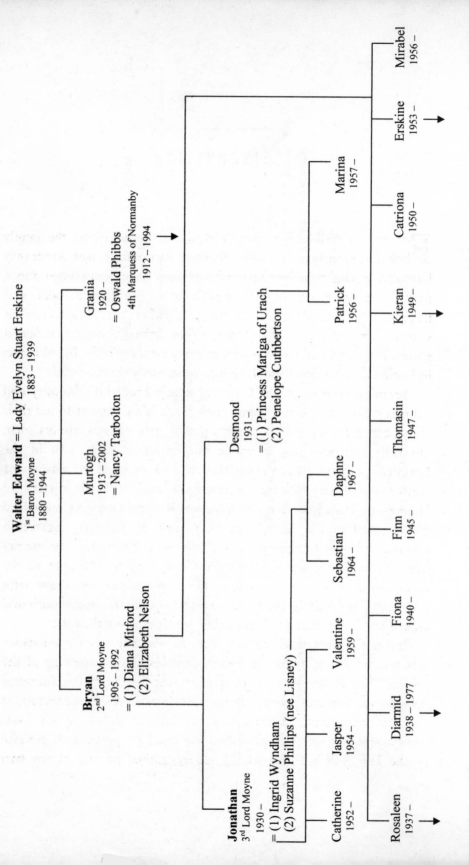

INTRODUCTION

For such a well-known, even ubiquitous, brand name, the family behind Guinness is curiously unknown. Part of the reason is that they have rarely sought the limelight although they have been pushed into it now and then because of their wealth, social positions, scandals and tragedies. "Guinness" means "stout" everywhere and is synonymous with Dublin and Ireland but it also means different things in different places. In Ireland and elsewhere its primary meaning is the brand name; in England, on the other hand, Guinness primarily means wealth.

Seven generations of the Guinness family headed the brewery and company that carries their name. This book is an attempt to tell their story, concentrating on the main man or men (it was always men, although Guinness women made an impact of their own in the twentieth century) in each generation, and to tease out the reasons for their extraordinary success. It does not deal with the myriad of Guinnesses who also descended from one Richard Guinness, who lived and worked in Celbridge, County Kildare in the early eighteenth century, and went on to be successful bankers or Protestant missionaries over the following centuries. Neither does it try to deal with all the descendants of Arthur Guinness, but concentrates on those with responsibility for the brewery, the ones who amassed huge wealth and picked up an earldom and three other peerages along the way.

It is not an authorised history of the family; a request for assistance was refused promptly by the Iveagh Trustees at the beginning of the project. No assistance was sought or received from the Guinness company or its current owner, Diageo plc. Instead, it is based mainly on primary sources, on contemporary accounts of events, mostly from newspapers, and on other published sources. I am particularly grateful to the late Professor Patrick Lynch, co-author of one of the two

1

authorised histories of Guinness, *Guinnesses Brewery in the Irish Economy 1759–1876*, for his advice and guidance and helping me to read between some of the lines in his book. In spite of his wide knowledge of the subject, some of the things that emerged from the research came as surprises to him.

I am also particularly grateful to the members of the Guinness family who spoke to me, especially Patrick Guinness (who has finally resolved the questions of where the Guinnesses came from originally through DNA tests, as outlined in his own book on Arthur Guinness, *Arthur's Round*), Desmond Guinness and Garech de Brún. I know they will not agree with all my interpretations and conclusions but they were generous with their time and set no conditions on their assistance. Many others assisted me in one way or another, including Lena Boylan, Stephen Collins, Maurice Craig, Louis Cullen, Noeleen Dowling, Michael Duggan, Finbarr Flood, the Knight of Glin, David Hearst, Simon Hoggart, Ann Kennedy, Des Lennon, Seán Ó Riain, and Padraic Yeates. My thanks also to the staffs of the National Library and the RDS library in Dublin, the National Archives in Dublin and London, the British Library and the Parliamentary Archives in London. I am also grateful for those who gave permission to reproduce photographs and portraits, especially the Guinness family members and *The Irish Times*.

This book has been a very long time in the making, mostly for involuntary reasons. I am glad that it has come together with Poolbeg Press, through the agency of Jonathan Williams, and would like to thank my sharp-eyed editor Brian Langan, as well as Kieran Devlin and all the team at Poolbeg. My family has also lived with it for a long time and my wife, Frances O'Rourke, has been a model of patient encouragement. My daughters, Catherine, Joanna and Molly, however, will no longer be able to use their favourite riposte – "Have you written that book yet?" – when questioned about some omission on their part.

It is inevitable that errors and misinterpretations will have crept into the book since it attempts to cover three centuries of the one family and business and the changing social, economic and political backdrops of their times. I hope they have been kept to a minimum.

CHAPTER ONE

The End of an Era

"He felt it his duty to preserve the 200-year-old tradition of a family-led business although by nature ill-at-ease and reticent in boardroom and company chair."

VERY REVEREND VICTOR GRIFFIN

at the memorial service for Benjamin Guinness

On a Thursday afternoon in late July 1992, a dreary day of occasionally drenching rain, the Guinness family gathered in St Patrick's Cathedral in Dublin for a memorial service for the third Earl of Iveagh, Benjamin Guinness. Decked with old flags, its high stone walls dotted with plaques and memorials to the once-powerful, the church was full. The organ played a Bach fugue while the congregation waited for the late earl's family to arrive: his former wife Miranda, in whose London home he had died a month earlier after a short final illness, and his four children, two sons and two daughters.

It was the second memorial service for Benjamin, following a private funeral to the Iveagh's English seat at Elveden in Suffolk. The first had been held a week earlier in St Margaret's at Westminster in London and was attended by a long list of titled friends and relatives, illustrating their many marital links within the British aristocracy. The memorial service in St Patrick's was a kind of homecoming for the head of the family but the death of Benjamin Guinness also marked the end of an era. For the first time in seven generations, a Guinness was not in control, neither in reality nor in name, of the company and brewery that bore the family name.

The Guinnesses had built a family business in Dublin into a huge fortune and into one of the world's great brands. They were back in the city where they were once the largest employers but which they had left for the greater power and prestige of London. The third earl had reversed that trend, making his main home in Dublin, but their power and influence in Ireland had slipped away, replaced by a sentimental attachment on both sides.

Representatives of the new Irish establishment now took pride of place in St Patrick's over those of the old Protestant ascendancy, of which the family had once become prominent members. The presence of the four living former Taoisigh and a former President, plus representatives of the current office-holders, testified to how far the Guinnesses had risen above the old Anglo-Irish divisions. They had managed to steer a successful course through the treacherous political turbulence of the nineteenth and early twentieth centuries, not always certain whether they were Irish or English but able to drift with ease between both. Guinness and the independent Ireland whose birth the family had vigorously opposed shared the same symbol, the harp, albeit of slightly different designs and, appropriately, facing in opposite directions.

All around them in the cathedral were echoes of the family's past as Benjamin's sons read lessons from the Wisdom of Solomon ("the righteous live for evermore") and St John ("in my father's house are many mansions"). A large stained-glass window overlooked their pews, depicting Christ serving humanity, and dedicated to the memory of Edward Guinness, the first Earl of Iveagh and the man who took the family into serious wealth and high society. The gothic cathedral itself was a memorial to his father, Benjamin Lee Guinness, who designed and paid for the renovation which saved it from nineteenth-century dereliction. Nearby, the stolid red-bricked blocks of the Iveagh Trust flats and hostel for the homeless were darkened by the driving rain. Like their more extensive counterparts in London, they remained one of the main monuments to the family's famed philanthropy. Dotted around the city, around Ireland, and around England, were numerous other memorials to their wealth, their generosity, their power and their privileged lives.

Less than a mile away was St James's Gate with its mixture of industrial and Georgian architecture: huge vats, tangles of pipes, a power station, railway tracks through cobbled streets and, still, the greying brick of eighteenth-century houses from which the family's influence had once spread out like the distinctive smell of hops that pervaded the area as a tangible proof of their industry. It was there, six generations earlier, that Arthur Guinness leased an abandoned brewery and set his descendants on course to scale the heights of British society on the strength of a single product, porter. Along the way, they were noted for their enlightened employment practices as well as for their philanthropy; neither, however, got in the way of amassing great riches.

The secret of their commercial success was based on many factors: their business acumen, their religion, the size of their families, and their ability to pick key employees, especially a family of stout brewers from London, the Pursers, who played a major role in helping the company to emerge dominant from among the scores of breweries in late eighteenth- and early nineteenth-century Dublin.[1] They were good at what they did and, literally, at minding their own business. They were adept at looking after their commercial interests, no matter how the times and circumstances around them changed, and at seizing opportunities like those presented by the Great Famine. Long before the days of "spin doctors", they were good at public relations and weaving a successful path through the political and sectarian minefield of the Dublin of their times; they remained firmly attached to their minority religion and politics while satisfying customers who mainly followed the majority's rival creed and political faith. Their strong religious beliefs and attachment to the Church of Ireland underpinned their business endeavours, endorsing their pursuit of wealth which the first Arthur genuinely considered to be "a token of divine favour".[2] Not surprisingly, one line of the family went into religion, becoming as distinguished in their own field for missionary work around the globe as the brewers were in theirs.

Large families gave the early generations the option of handing over the brewery to the son who showed the greatest ability; until they joined the aristocracy and adopted the rigid rule of primogeniture, an eldest son had never ended up in control. They were good at wealth management long before that became an industry; each generation was encouraged to keep the business intact and their wealth within the family. It led, on the one hand, to frequent marriages between cousins and, on the other, to trusts which granted outside spouses the use of inheritances for their lifetimes only. In that, as in many other aspects of the family and the business, the founding Arthur set the model to be followed by his descendants.

The size of their families also created other tensions which continued and grew over the generations. Inevitably, there were "black sheep" who transgressed the sober family code by their unorthodox lifestyles, scandalous sexual liaisons, alcoholism, gambling and an ability to lose money at whatever business ventures they attempted. The second Arthur Guinness once bemoaned the number of individuals and families relying on him for support, "most of whom appear to have been fecund and many, especially the clergy, feckless".[3] By the time they came into the twentieth century, their wealth was at its height, allowing members of the family to indulge all their enthusiasms and eccentricities. These included everything from the intrigues of society and politics, to real-life Indiana Jones-style explorations of exotic and largely unknown territories in search of rare animals. Inevitably, as their daughters outnumbered their sons, their riches attracted a host of colourful characters in marriage, like the bisexual American adventurer "Chips" Channon, and as lovers and mistresses, like the beautiful Russian dancer and impresario Ida Rubinstein. Their paths also crossed those of many other famous people, from Winston Churchill to Alec Guinness, who was named after them because he was conceived on one of their yachts. Inevitably, too, their wealth attracted attention to their tragedies: tabloid newspapers decided the Guinnesses were the victims of an undefined "curse" which brought tragic deaths, both accidental and deliberate, to some of their heirs and heiresses (although it is a moot point whether they suffered a higher level of tragedy than other families of similar size).

Their clannishness was legendary, extending at times to include other branches of the family, like the banking Guinnesses who descended from the first Arthur's brother, Samuel. They were secretive in many ways; they rarely sought publicity and frequently tried to discourage it, not always successfully, especially when they became as famous for their wealth in Britain as they were for their stout in Ireland. They were not averse to encouraging myths about how their stout was created, by accidentally burning hops, secret formulas and recipes, special wells and Liffey water, or allowing other dubious claims to be repeated until they appeared to be facts.

They were deeply involved in politics, in Ireland particularly from the second half of the nineteenth century and in Britain for all the twentieth century, but managed to keep a relatively low political profile. They had an uncanny ability to appear in different guises to different people and surf the hostile historical currents sometimes flowing around them, whether it was the tide of Irish nationalism, land reform or the rise of trade unionism. Their detachment was often more apparent than real, more public relations than fact, and was undoubtedly facilitated by their generosity and philanthropy. On the other hand, their philanthropy was not entirely altruistic; it was part of the established path towards British high society which they trod successfully.

By the time of the third earl's death in 1992, much had changed in the family's fortunes. In the popular imagination it was known in equal measure for its eccentrics, socialites and scandals, all of which had increased in number in line with its enormous wealth in the twentieth century, but that wealth was in decline in relative terms and in terms of what was available to new generations from ageing trust funds. The family was also tarnished with financial scandal by the share-price rigging that went on during the Guinness company takeover of Distillers; by the early 1990s, as a result, "Guinness" and "scandal" were almost as commonly linked in the media as "Guinness" and "stout". The takeover, however, helped to boost the family's wealth at a time when it was waning. The value of its shares in Guinness, although greatly reduced in number over the years, increased significantly as the family faded from the picture and the Guinness company became an international conglomerate in which distilling rather than brewing became the dominant occupation. The *Sunday Times* Rich List for 1993 estimated the family's overall wealth at £560 million and ranked them the twelfth richest in Britain. It was something of a comedown from the turn of the twentieth century when the first Lord Iveagh was widely believed to be Britain's second richest man, but it was still a very considerable fortune.

And it had all been built on modest beginnings in Celbridge, County Kildare.

CHAPTER TWO

The First Arthur

". . . the labourers went on destroying the [water] course till the arrival of Mr Guinness, who violently rushed upon them, wrenching a pickaxe from one and declaring with very much improper language, that they should not proceed . . ."

Dublin Corporation report on a dispute with
Arthur Guinness over illegal water supplies to his brewery

B rewing was an attractive commercial activity in the eighteenth century: it involved a relatively simple technique and equally simple technology and there was always a good market for alcohol. All it required was a supply of barley to produce malt, water, minimal machinery and no power other than the force of gravity. Ale had been produced for centuries using malt alone; the addition of hops turned it into beer; and a switch to brown or roast malt produced the dark beer halfway in strength between the other two which came to be known as stout (from its greater strength) or porter (from its popularity among porters and other manual labourers in the markets of early eighteenth-century London).

Porter, meaning a dark beer, seems to have been first produced by a brewer named Harwood in Shoreditch in east London and sold in a local pub, The Blue Last, in 1722[1] – coincidentally the same year for which the earliest written record exists of one Richard Guinness of Celbridge, County Kildare. Far from inventing porter, the Guinnesses were relative late-comers to the business of brewing it. It was a popular drink in mid-eighteenth-century England and imported into Dublin at a low enough price and a high enough quality to make competition difficult for local brewers. Neither were the Guinnesses the first to brew it in Dublin: another brewer, Thomas Andrews of New Row, was awarded the Dublin Society's prize for selling the greatest quantity of Irish porter in 1765.[2] By then, Arthur Guinness had been brewing ale and beer for about ten years, six of them in Dublin, but he did not brew porter.

He began nearer home, in the village of Leixlip, ten miles upstream of Dublin on the River Liffey and three miles downstream of the village of Celbridge, where he was born in 1725, the eldest son of Richard Guinness. Details of Richard's life are sketchy: neither the date nor place of his birth nor the date or place of his death is known for certain. By the time of his death, generally believed to be about 1766, his son Arthur was a relatively successful merchant in Dublin, a rising figure among the city's brewers and a member of the city council. In such circumstances, the fact that almost all traces of Richard's existence have disappeared suggests that his sons, notably Arthur, deliberately destroyed all records of their father's antecedents.

Why this might have been done is not known but it was done quite effectively and would stymie research into the family's background for a long time: efforts by the family at the end of the nineteenth and early twentieth centuries to break through the wall of silence about their origins failed to reach any definitive conclusions. A common reason in earlier times for hiding one's antecedents was "illegitimacy" but there is no evidence that this was the case with the Guinnesses. One family tree, drawn up by Henry Seymour Guinness, the main twentieth-century researcher into the family history, undermines that theory by suggesting that Richard had a brother, William Guinness, who became a gunsmith in Dublin.[3] A direct descendant of Richard and Arthur, Patrick Guinness, says definitively that Richard's father was a tenant farmer called Eoin or Owen Guineas or Guinis of Dalkey, County Dublin, and later Simmonscourt, south of Dublin, who had three sons, George, William and Richard.[4]

From Arthur's time on, the family claimed to be descended from the old Irish family of Magennis which came from the Iveagh peninsula in

County Down. The first Arthur received a mug engraved with the Magennis coat of arms and those of his wife's family when they married in 1761.[5] A century and a half later, on joining the peerage, his great-grandson, Edward, took the title of Baron Iveagh, a claim to a Magennis inheritance that was vigorously disputed at the time (see Chapter Seven). The Magennis family remained Catholics after the Reformation and held the title of viscounts of Iveagh from the early seventeenth century until the Battle of the Boyne in 1690 when they fought in King James II's army. After its defeat by William of Orange, they went into exile in Austria and later in France and Spain. Although stripped of their title by King William, the family continued to use it both in Ireland and in exile on the continent.[6]

Another theory, supported by hearsay and anecdotal evidence from some of the nineteenth-century members of the family, suggested that Richard Guinness was descended from a soldier in Oliver Cromwell's army which went through Ireland with a fearsome fervour in 1649 and 1650. The soldier, it was speculated, may have come from the village of St Gynnys in Cornwall.

The question of the family's origins was cleared up only in the twenty-first century through the use of DNA tests on Patrick Guinness and other members of the family and comparisons with those of descendants of the Magennises and other families in the Iveagh peninsula. They found that the Guinnesses *did* come from County Down but were not Magennises: their closest DNA match was with another Iveagh family, the McCartans.[7] Thus, it appears that the Guinness antecedents came from the Iveagh peninsula, moved south to the Dublin area at some point in the mid- to late seventeenth century, changed religion and probably their surnames, and subsequently claimed a higher social status through the Magennis connection than they had actually occupied.

It is assumed that Richard was born about 1690 but nothing definite is known about him until 1722 when he came to work for the Reverend Arthur Price in the village of Celbridge. Price, whose portrait hangs in the examination hall of Trinity College Dublin, was a colourful character whose position as a pillar of the Church of Ireland did not always meet with universal approval. He came from a family of

11

Welsh clergymen and had succeeded his father as vicar of Celbridge in 1705. By 1722 he was the dean of Ferns and on his way to a successful career on the bench of bishops as, successively, Bishop of Clonfert and Kilmacduagh (1724), of Ferns and Leighlin (1730), of Meath (1733) and as Archbishop of Cashel (1744). His first appointment as a bishop caused the Irish chancellor, Lord Middleton, to swear and describe it as "most highly provoking". His firm attachment to the crown and his devotion to "the English interest" were cited as reasons for his appointment to Meath.

Price is not remembered primarily for his contribution to religion but, among other things, for his unrequited love for Esther Vanhomrigh, Jonathan Swift's "Vanessa", who lived at Celbridge between 1717 and her early death in 1723. Price (and another cleric) may have proposed to her but she was interested only in what she called her "unexpressible passion" for the more famous Dean Swift, who abandoned her for "Stella" (Esther Johnston). Price was again rejected when he offered to attend her as she was dying. She sent him back a message saying "No Price, No Prayers" along with a "scrap out of *The Tale of a Tub*", Swift's satire on religion.[8]

As Archbishop of Cashel, Price's main memorial was the destruction of the ancient cathedral on the famous Rock of Cashel under an act of parliament which he sought and obtained in 1749. He claimed it was necessary because the building was falling into decay but local tradition suggests that his real reason for having its roof removed and turning it into a ruin was that he was too fat to climb the rock to conduct services in the cathedral on its summit.

His most lasting claim to fame lies, however, in his role as a benefactor to the Guinness family.

When Richard Guinness began working for him in Celbridge in 1722, Price had bought a local house with three acres of land, a malt house, barn, stable, cowhouse, and garden. It lay to the east of the village and, about the same time, to the west one of the great Irish houses, Castletown, was under construction for William Conolly, the speaker of the Irish House of Commons. (Castletown, some 250 years later, was to be the headquarters of the Irish Georgian Society, founded by Desmond Guinness.) Although there is no comparison between them, tradition has it that Price's more modest mansion, Oakley Park,[9] was also designed by Castletown's Florentine architect, Alessandro Galilei, though this is unlikely. Price certainly remained deeply attached to it: in spite of his succession of episcopal appointments and several other building projects in his various dioceses, he retained Oakley Park as his main residence.

Richard Guinness and his family lived there too for the 30 years he continued to work for Price.[10] Around the time of his arrival in Celbridge, Richard married his first wife, Elizabeth Read, the daughter of a publican and farmer in the townland of Hutton Read, some five miles away. She was one of five children, three sons and two daughters, whose descendants also became well-known cutlers and jewellers in Dublin. The couple's marriage and arrival in Celbridge may have been connected: there is a tradition in the Read family that Richard was employed as the Read's groom and eloped with the eldest daughter, Elizabeth. If he did, the families seem to have been reconciled later in life, as Richard erected a headstone to Elizabeth and her parents, William and Catherine Read, after Elizabeth died in 1742 at the age of 44. The Guinnesses had four sons and two daughters. The eldest, Arthur, was born in 1725 and, apparently, was called after Arthur Price, who may also have been his godfather. Their second son, Samuel, remembered as the "goldbeater" (a step down from a goldsmith), from whom the banking Guinnesses are descended, may have been named after Price's father, also Samuel.

Richard's job in the Price household is as unclear as almost all the other details about him. Practically the only documentary evidence of his life rests in the numerous church leases and other legal documents which he, along with other of Price's servants, signed as witnesses. The first of these is dated from 1722, confirming his employment by Price in that year.[11] Other servants also witnessed Price's legal documents, including John Earsum (Price's butler and a shopkeeper in Celbridge) and the young Arthur Guinness from the time he was 18.

Richard has been variously described as a coachman, groom, maltster, butler and steward. There is a record of an exchequer bill which describes him as the "agent or receiver" of the Archbishop of Cashel and manages to spell his name in four different ways: Gunnis,

Gennis, Ginnis and "Richard Guinis, Gent". This persuaded Henry Seymour Guinness to reject suggestions that Richard was either a butler or coachman and to conclude: "All available evidence seems to indicate that he was steward to the Archbishop."[12] On the other hand, one of the main critics of Guinnesses in the next generation claimed that Richard's "humble condition . . . [was] that of driving other people's coaches instead of their own".[13] It is likely that Richard was, at different times, employed in some or all the different capacities ascribed to him. There is no doubt that he and his family ended up as Price's most important retainers.

The fact that Price's will left Richard and Arthur £100 each – the same amount as he bequeathed to all his "poor relations" in Wales – proves their final position in his household. His butler, John Earsum, and another couple, Thomas Jones and his wife, also received £100 each. By contrast, his coachman, John Holdship, got a mere 12 guineas while another servant with unspecified duties, Christopher Hanlan, was left only £10. In all, Price distributed £8,000 in cash among relatives, servants and colleagues, interspersed with occasionally acerbic comments on some of them ("£25 to James Price of Banagher and I forgive him all the money I have formerly advanced for him, and particularly for his law suit about his glebe at Banagher") and an instruction that all his sermons and writings be burned "and that no other be suffered to peruse any of them".

Arthur's role in the Price household is as unclear as his father's but, given his subsequent activities, there is inevitably speculation that he was the Archbishop's brewer or maltster. Like every substantial property at the time, Oakley Park had a malt house, and the Guinnesses turned to brewing almost immediately after Price's death, indicating that they had some knowledge of its procedures.

One can only speculate about the influences on Arthur of growing up in the environment in which he did. The twin pillars of the Protestant ascendancy, church and state, dominated Celbridge through Price and Speaker Conolly's family, who were the main employers in the area. Even though Price was not noted for his religious fervour, Arthur grew up in a religious household and religion played an important part in his life. He must also have been affected, on a personal level, by the early death of his mother in 1742 when he was 17.

Ten years later, Price's sudden death at his Dublin residence on 17 July 1752 left the Guinnesses without a home for the first time in 30 years. Richard moved to a house in the village owned by Richard Nelson, the administrator of Price's estate. Within months he married again, to Elizabeth Clare in St Mary's Church in Dublin on 19 October. A widow, she ran an inn in the main street of Celbridge called "The White Hart". It was next door to the house of John Earsum, Price's butler, and, on the other side, adjoined a brewery. There is no record of Arthur's movements immediately after Price's death. More than likely, he accompanied his father; whether they did any brewing or not in the inn – most innkeepers brewed their own beer at the time – is not recorded. Shortly afterwards, the extended family of Richard, his sons and Elizabeth Clare moved to the nearby village of Leixlip and went into brewing on a commercial scale.

In a valley where the River Liffey is joined by a tributary, the Rye, and on the main route from Dublin to the west, Leixlip was on the point of becoming a boom town in the mid-eighteenth century. Workmen digging the nearby Royal Canal hit a spring which turned it into a briefly fashionable spa. It was said in 1764 to be "one of the pleasantest villages in Ireland" and "much resorted to by the genteel company from Dublin and many parts of Ireland, to drink of the sulphurous spa that springs close to the edge of the Liffey, a little below the village".[14]

In April 1755, Arthur applied for membership of the guild of brewers in Dublin; by the end of the year he was being described as a brewer in Leixlip. In September 1756 he took a lease on a small brewery[15] which was clearly successful enough to encourage him to broaden his horizons. Three years later, at the age of 34, he set off for Dublin to start another new brewery, leaving his youngest brother, Richard, to run the Leixlip operation.

———⟨∞⟩———

Dublin in the middle of the eighteenth century was no place for the faint-hearted. It had all the characteristics of a frontier town and is frequently compared with those of the American Wild West a century later. Violence, rioting, murder and kidnapping were rife. A large number of English immigrants had come to the city to get rich quick, mixing with a volatile local strata of "bucks and rakes" who delighted in outrageous, and frequently violent, exploits. Stories of their doings have gone into the city's folklore, like that of Buck English, famous for shooting a waiter dead and having him charged at £50 on his bill, or the brothers known as Kilkelly and Kilcoachy, because one killed a man called Kelly and the other killed a coachman. Maurice Craig described the era in his classic history of the city:

> Immigrants who, had they stayed in England, would have behaved like normal Englishmen, found in Ireland an almost rootless society of speculators and go-getters. Many individuals adopted a violent habit of behaviour which brought them closer to the dispossessed helots than might have seemed possible . . . The immigrant Dubliners, like the immigrant New Yorkers of a later era, often adopted the gangster mentality as a rule of life in struggle. Men who would in happier circumstances have been English gentlemen, drifted into the habit of surrounding themselves with roughs and plug-uglies: the sensitivity of their touch upon the environment round them took the form of the trigger-finger.[16]

The contemporary records of Dublin Corporation are full of outrage over violent attacks, offers of rewards to catch those responsible, and regular riots. "Pinking dindies" – eighteenth-century muggers – roamed the evening streets, slashing or "pinking" passers-by with the tips of their swords, which stuck out of their scabbards, in order to extract money from them. In 1764, the corporation had to hire eight watchmen to guard Essex Bridge (now Capel Street Bridge), the central Liffey crossing, from eight o'clock in the evening until seven in the morning, because of the number of robberies and murders.

It was a time of rapid expansion in both the population and the physical city. Dublin had about 140,000 inhabitants in 1760, double the number at the start of the century.[17] The population of Ireland as a whole was also rising rapidly: by 1800 it was about five million, twice what it had been a century earlier and half that of Britain. But its economy was undeveloped, with activity concentrated almost exclusively on coastal areas and around Dublin. The city looked to England in trade and politics, though it had a parliament which flexed its muscles more and more as the century went on, until the fallout from the French Revolution, and the rebellion by its local followers, the United Irishmen, led to the integration of Ireland in the United Kingdom with the Act of Union in 1800. Although the population was predominantly Catholic, the Protestant ascendancy was in total, if often nervous, control since the Williamite victories of 1690 and 1691.

The presence of the parliament gave Dublin many of the attributes of a capital, notably the occasional presence of a large number of landed gentry. Up to 400 of them sat in the two houses of parliament, creating a layer of high society which gave the city an extra buzz, even if "the half-mounted gentlemen and barbarous squireens remained curiously close to the grand and polite society of the capital".[18] A contemporary anonymous traveller was more flattering: "On the whole the inhabitants are an agreeable medium between the English and the French, being neither so boorish and uncivil as the one nor so insincere as the other."[19]

It was also the period of development which gave Dublin its orderly Georgian character. The Commission for Making Wide and Convenient Streets was laying out the city centre; the front of Trinity College was being built, followed by the Custom House and Four Courts and the squares and streetscapes of the Gardiner estates, Merrion and Fitzwilliam. As the city and the fashionable moved east, the areas left behind to the west became the commercial centre.

Among them was St James's Gate, one of the traditional entrances to the city from the west, which was widely favoured by brewers, distillers and others whose enterprises relied on agricultural products and fresh water. Brewing was a popular and profitable activity, attracting the fly-by-nights as well as the more reputable. Although beer was neither as popular a drink as whiskey or even claret, there was still a ready market for it among the middle classes and, subsequently, the working class. One estimate in 1775 put the number of pubs in Dublin at 4,000. In spite of a 20-year period of stagnation around the middle of the century, brewing was one of the city's largest industries, with up to 70 breweries. The large number was undoubtedly influenced by the prospects of substantial profits: brewing was a lucrative business. While the brewers complained constantly about competition from England and sharp practices by their colleagues, the success of families like the Leesons illustrated what the ambitious could achieve. They had made a fortune from brewing since their arrival in Ireland at the end of the seventeenth century. Their experience also illustrated that brewing was not quite acceptable in better society; they felt obliged to give it up when they became earls of Milltown in the 1740s.[20]

The Arthur Guinness who entered this milieu in 1759 was clearly ambitious, had begun to develop his business expertise and was, as subsequent events demonstrated, very determined. He was 34 years old, unmarried, the owner of a brewery and several houses in Leixlip, and a firm believer in the religion in which he had grown up; he would be influenced strongly by John Wesley during his tours of Ireland. He was already a member of the brewers' guild, which made him a "free citizen" of Dublin and gave him trading privileges and the right to vote in municipal and parliamentary elections. Before leaving County Kildare, he had also been secretary of a local branch, or knot, of the Friendly Brothers of St Patrick, a strongly Protestant organisation whose aims included the discouragement of duelling.

The brewery he took over, on a 9,000-year lease at £45 a year, was on a reasonably large site and, crucially, alongside the city watercourse, on the other side of which there was another brewery, owned by a Mr Joyce. The brewery itself was small, badly equipped and had been out of use for several years. It had a copper kieve (described as in very bad condition), a mill, two malthouses, a brewhouse, stables for twelve horses and a loft that held 200 loads of hay. The site, which stretched back 400 feet from James's Street, also included a house and garden, with a fish pond, a summerhouse and out-houses.[21] Arthur lived there in the early years and family members continued to live in and beside the brewery well into the nineteenth century.

The brewery could produce about 200 hogshead (about 10,400 gallons) of beer a year and, for the first 15 years or more of Arthur's ownership, it brewed only ale and beer. Although the site was extensive compared to other breweries in the area, the Guinness output was considerably less than that of the largest producers in the·early years. Arthur began brewing stout only towards the end of the 1770s and had settled on it as his brewery's only product by the end of the century. His reason for switching was probably the fact that stout was the most successful brewery product in the eighteenth century. (It cannot be compared with today's Guinness; for one thing, the stout at the time was dark in colour but not black and its taste is unknown.)[22]

On his arrival in Dublin, Arthur wasted little time in trying to make his mark. He quickly became prominent within the brewers' guild, being elected its warden by 1763 and later its master. In the following years, he wore the buff and blue cockade of the group, the Guild of St Andrew, as one of the three representatives of the brewers who, with the other guilds, took part in the annual "riding the franchise" ceremony when they rode around the city's boundaries.[23] Within six years, he was representing the brewers on the common council of Dublin Corporation, which was made up of guilds' representatives and which, with the self-perpetuating aldermen, formed the municipal authority.

His shrewdest move, however, may have been in his choice of wife: two years after his arrival in Dublin, in June 1761, Arthur married Olivia Whitmore. She was 19, little more than half his age, and the daughter of a Dublin merchant, William Whitmore, and his County Kildare-born wife, Mary Grattan. Olivia was a ward of William Lunnell, a woollen merchant who married her aunt (his second wife) and had built up a successful export trade through smuggling. The son of a refugee Huguenot from France who fought at the Battle of the Boyne, William got around an English ban on the exports of Irish woollens by the simple expedient of dressing sailors in them. As his business expanded, however, he devised a system of smuggling with Scandinavian ships. After they had been checked out of Dublin port, they would send a boat ashore to Clontarf, on the north side of Dublin Bay, where William met them by prior arrangement with coachloads of contraband woollens. His trade was extensive enough to make him a fluent Danish speaker[24] and his importance to the Guinness family was evident by the frequency with which Lunnell became a second name in the succeeding generations.

Olivia also inherited £1,000 from her father and gave Arthur valuable connections with a number of influential families. Through her mother, she was connected to Henry Grattan, who dominated Dublin politics in subsequent decades and was a major champion of the interests of Dublin brewers. He later told the brewers' guild that he considered their prosperity and the health of Ireland to be intimately connected: a long time before Guinness advertised the wholesomeness of their porter, Grattan suggested that beer was a means of health and a cure for intoxication.[25] Olivia was also connected to some of the main movers in the Irish business world, including the La Touche family, who were prominent bankers and, along with William Lunnell's son, involved in the Bank of Ireland; the Darleys, speculative builders who built the front of Trinity College; and the Smyths, churchmen, merchants and architects.

Arthur and Olivia had a long and, by all appearances, happy marriage, even though it seems to have had more than its fair share of tragedy. She gave birth to 21 children, of whom only ten survived infancy, a high mortality even for the time. Their first child appears to have been a daughter, christened Olivia in St Catherine's Church in Dublin in 1762, who did not survive. The first to survive was another daughter, Elizabeth, born in 1763; she was followed by six surviving sons and three other daughters. Olivia herself was the victim of Dublin's high crime rate around 1777 when a man named John Ball, described as an officer of the revenue, was convicted of putting her "in dread and fear of her life, by presenting a pistol to her breast". He was jailed for a month and fined £10.[26]

As a businessman, Arthur was successful from the beginning. After only five years in James's Gate, he was rich enough to buy a small two-storey country mansion at Beaumont, north of the city.[27] He was clearly a joiner; as well as his leading role in the brewers' guild, he was involved in two attempts to set up a chamber of commerce and applied, unsuccessfully, for membership of the Dublin Society in 1767; he was among five applicants who were rejected by ballot while 15 others were accepted.[28] He was also involved in good works as an administrator of the Meath Hospital, founder of a Sunday school of which he was the lay superintendent, overseeing its 276 children, and churchwarden of St Catherine's parish, which included St James's Gate. His uprightness was illustrated by his proposal to the city council that it abandon the custom

20

of new aldermen buying dinner for the whole corporation and donate the money instead to a hospital. The council did not share his virtuousness; it declared that good eating and "above all, good drinking" created strong bonds and suggested that hospitality and good living were essential parts of their charter.[29]

But Arthur's civic-mindedness took second place to his own interests whenever a conflict arose. This was amply demonstrated by a protracted dispute with the city corporation over water which showed his mettle and his willingness to cut corners when it suited him. The affair dragged on for 20 years, posing a threat to the very existence of his business and also providing a sharp insight into Arthur Guinness through one of the few well-documented aspects of his business life.

Water was critical to the growing city. The River Liffey, tidal up-river beyond the medieval city, provided no drinking water or water for brewing. The smaller River Poddle, running north from the Dublin mountains into the Liffey, was the main source of fresh water. It fed a reservoir, or basin, near St James's Gate, which supplied the city and made the immediate area the main centre of industries like brewing. Surrounded by elms and grass walks, it was "much resorted to by the lower class of genteel citizens" as a local park.[30] Keeping the supply of water in touch with the rising demand of the growing city was a major problem, not made easier by widespread abuses. There were numerous illegal connections to the mains: turncocks who controlled the local supplies were occasionally found taking bribes; and, amid the endless complaints, charges and counter-charges over supplies, one brewer complained that someone had reduced his legitimate supply by putting lead in his pipe.[31]

Like all his neighbours – and contrary to another legend that his porter owed its special properties to water from a nearby holy well – Arthur Guinness got his supply from the city main. But he believed that he was exempt from having to pay the corporation for it by virtue of his lease. The corporation thought otherwise: its pipe water committee complained in October 1764 that he had rejected "all reasonable methods" of trying to induce him to become a tenant of the city for water. It got the council's approval "to take such effective measures as may be necessary to prevent his having any further supply of water, until he agrees to pay . . . and discharge the arrears."[32]

The dispute rumbled on and Arthur joined the council himself. After a series of complaints about water shortages, a sub-committee found in 1772 that Arthur had two illegal pipes, one nine inches by seven inches, the other two inches in diameter, supplying his brewery. It ordered that all "the doors opened upon the back course [by James's Gate] be immediately stopped up with lime and stone". Two weeks later, the same committee noted that Arthur was no longer paying rent for part of his ground on which the 99-year lease had expired at Michaelmas 1769. The land had originally been leased to Giles Mee, later a lord mayor of Dublin, who passed it on to his son-in-law Alderman Sir Mark Rainsford, from whose descendants Arthur had leased it. The committee recommended that the city take possession of the piece of land and collect the arrears of rent. But Arthur got in his retaliation first, claiming that the land had been swapped by Rainsford with the council for another piece of land. He sued the corporation before it sued him.

The dispute escalated when the pipe water committee decided to fill in the James's Gate section of the watercourse from which Arthur was getting his unauthorised supply of water. A sub-committee, accompanied by "a sufficient number of labourers", set off on 16 May 1775 to carry out the task. The account in the committee's report of what happened next recorded graphically how the subsequent confrontation almost got out of hand.[33]

Because the closure of the watercourse would have had a drastic effect on the Guinness brewery – and, presumably, because Arthur Guinness was by now a significant figure in Dublin's business community and a member of the corporation – the committee decided to inform him beforehand of its proposed action. His reaction was uncompromising: he said that "the water was his, and he would defend it by force of arms". The committee retorted that it would not be intimidated by threats and would carry out its task. Arthur invited them "to try how far their strength would prevail". The committee took up the challenge and decided to fill in the watercourse without further delay. First, however, they thought it prudent to get protection and called in the sheriff, Thomas Trulock, and two of his men.

The whole party of councillors, labourers and sheriff's men, excluding Arthur, set off to the watercourse and began to destroy it. One Guinness employee tried to obstruct them but desisted after Sheriff Trulock threatened to send him to Newgate prison. The labourers continued work for a little while until Arthur arrived, "violently rushed upon them, wrenching a pickaxe from one and declaring, with very much improper language, that they should not proceed". The committee, according to its own account, "expostulated on this impropriety of conduct" but Arthur remained "obstinate". He stood, pickaxe in hand, blocking the labourers when they were ordered to proceed, and declaring that "if they filled it up from end to end, he would immediately open it".

Sheriff Trulock, who had been quick to threaten the Guinness employee with jail, took a decidedly more conciliatory attitude towards Arthur. He suggested that the committee had asserted the city's right to the water and "it would be wrong to proceed further". The committee huffed and puffed a little: they said they had their instructions to fill up the watercourse and were ready to perform their duty. However, they would not act in contravention of the sheriff's opinion and "so desisted".

As the spirit of compromise replaced that of confrontation, Arthur promised, on his word of honour, that he would present his title to the water before a special meeting of the committee the following week. Instead, however, he got a court injunction to stop the corporation interfering with the watercourse and the disputed piece of land, buying more time for himself. He continued brewing with the disputed water and consolidating his public position. He became brewer to Dublin Castle, the government seat in Ireland, and was one of the council's auditors examining the corporation's accounts for 1775. The fact that he was refusing to pay it for water and suing it does not appear to have affected his standing as a member of the council.

Arthur was in no hurry to bring the dispute to an end, perhaps believing (correctly, as it turned out) that delays were in his interest. He built a stone and brick wall around the disputed land, preventing corporation engineers from even examining the watercourse. In 1782, the pipe water committee suggested that the dispute be referred to arbitration. Arthur and his landlord, Rainsford, agreed and both sides named a referee. Arthur finally put forward a settlement proposal in 1784 under which he agreed to become a tenant of the corporation for the disputed land and for a supply of water through a two-inch bore, effectively conceding that the corporation had been right all along and he wrong. He offered to pay it an annual rent of £10 for the duration of his original 9,000-year lease on the brewery and the saga was brought to a conclusion with his signature on 16 July 1784. Subsequent complaints by Arthur that he suffered losses when the corporation laid a new water main in the old watercourse were given short shrift.

Arthur had won out through a mixture of threats, delays and, at the appropriate time, conciliation. He had maintained and regularised his water supply and held on to an important piece of land at a minimal cost.

***

As well as wielding a pickaxe and using improper language, Arthur Guinness was also adept at looking after his interests in more conventional ways. His prominent role in the brewers' guild included lobbying on behalf of the brewers – appearing before the Irish parliament on several occasions as part of attempts to tilt the balance of taxation and excise advantages in favour of local producers and against English imports and local distillers. He was one of three brewers who painted a sorry picture of the state of Irish brewing before the parliament in 1773. Mr Thwaites, one of the city's major brewers, claimed that a quarter of all the breweries had failed in the previous decade because of the high price of raw materials. They couldn't raise beer prices because of competition from England, he said. The two other members of the delegation, Arthur Guinness and a Mr Andrews (presumably the prize-winning porter brewer), declared that they had considered moving their breweries to Wales because of the more favourable excise laws on the other side of the Irish Sea. Arthur went a step further and said he had even gone to Wales "in search of a brewery, and that he would this day settle there, and build a brewery, if he could be sure that the laws would stand as they are, for seven years".[34]

The brewers' special pleading did not impress everybody. A contemporary pamphlet by an anonymous "officer of the revenue" noted Arthur's threat to move to Holyhead and agreed that brewing was in decline. But he questioned the brewers' claims that this was because of increased consumption of spirits and beer imports from England. While their case sounded plausible to the uninitiated, the revenue officer set about proving that they were leading "the Publick into errors" and that, in fact, the duties on Irish beer were less than those on English beer when one compared like with like. As for spirits, official imports of rum had gone up solely because smuggling from the Isle of Man had ceased when it was purchased by the Crown in 1765, he wrote.[35]

He had no doubt about the true reason for the decline: "It was in my opinion, the very bad quality of the beer and ale brewed in this Kingdom which drove and forced the people into the use and consumption of other liquors." And he put the blame for that firmly on the frauds and abuses perpetrated by some brewers on the public, the revenue and on each other. Bribes or douceurs to publicans were regular practice, he claimed, ranging from one free barrel with every 20 to half a guinea at Christmas for every 20 barrels bought during the year. As customers complained about the quality of the beer, the shady brewers merely doubled the douceurs to the publicans. Old and established brewers withdrew from the business: others tried to reduce materials or dodge taxes by hiding part of their brew or by mixing high and low quality beer and selling it as high quality ale while paying tax on low quality beer. "By pursuing these modes, the beer and ale brewed in this Kingdom became so exceedingly bad, that it was scarcely possible to drink it; and, in consequence, the people were absolutely forced into the consumption of porter and spirits."

The author was putting forward a case and, with the eternal optimism of the taxman, trying to argue that brewers wasted more time, money and effort in trying to dodge taxes than they would have spent in paying them. But his criticism of the inferior quality of Dublin's beers was widespread and, interestingly, his equation suggests that porter was superior to other beers. Indeed, one of its attractions for brewers was that it was a much more stable commodity than beer: it kept and travelled better, actually improving with age, and lent itself to greater commercialisation.

Charges of giving douceurs to publicans were clearly widespread and persistent enough to ensure that Arthur Guinness turned up with his answer ready at another parliamentary hearing 20 years later. A Mr Brophy, a brewer turned distiller, had told MPs that he gave up brewing because he wasn't prepared to give douceurs as other brewers did. He blamed competition between brewers for depraving the quality of their drink, "in order to sell cheap and be able to give presents". Possibly in a direct reply to Mr Brophy, Arthur returned to the House of Commons to deny that established brewers engaged in such practices, although he accused "persons creeping into the brewing business and wishing to procure customers" of giving douceurs. As proof of his own rectitude, he produced a certificate signed by his customers and stating that his porter was equal if not superior to any imports and that he had not given douceurs.[36]

Otherwise, the message of the brewers remained the same in 1792 as it had been in 1773. Arthur said he had been 30 years in the brewing trade and had never known it to be in a worse state. The usual reasons were put forward: increased consumption of spirits and English imports, as well as the high price of malt, which meant, Arthur claimed, that he could make no profit at all. He suggested that the best remedy was "to imitate the sister country" by putting a heavy duty on local distilling and on imports of beer. The reality, however, was somewhat different. By then Arthur Guinness was one of the most prosperous brewers in Dublin: he valued his brewery at £10,000 in a letter in 1785 and added tellingly, "I would not take £30,000 for it."[37]

The years of lobbying eventually produced results with the help of parliamentary supporters like Henry Grattan and official concerns about increasing drunkenness – which was blamed on whiskey rather than beer. Moving a successful petition in 1795, Grattan argued that lower taxes on beer would encourage "the substitution of an wholesome and nourishing beverage for a liquid poison". Excise duty on beer was removed altogether and replaced with a higher tax on malt, while many other regulations on brewers were also eased. The malt tax had the happy effect, for the brewers, of taxing the distillers twice, once on the malt and then again with the excise duty which remained on their product. According to the authoritative history of Guinnesses during this period, this act of parliament was "the most decisive and important single event in the whole history of Irish brewing" and possibly the main reason for the emergence of Irish brewing from "local obscurity to the status of a national industry in the next thirty-five years".[38] Proving that nothing much changes in the arguments about economic policy and the state's role in business, Lynch and Vaizey added:

> The new thought favoured simple taxes and no regulations to protect consumers from producers or producers from each other. The market would solve all the problems. Economic freedom would wash away corruption and adulteration.[39]

—∞∞—

Economic freedom was not the only freedom on the agenda in the Dublin of the late eighteenth century. Political freedom was also a burning issue, spurred on by the examples of the American and French revolutions and encouraged by the majority Catholic population's increasing frustrations with the restrictions of the remaining Penal Laws. While the example of the Americans encouraged the growing mercantile class and its demands for free trade between colonies, the French revolution prompted a more radical republicanism, which was given expression by the United Irishmen. Protestants were deeply divided between conservatives, who opposed any change which would dilute their control of the city, moderates, who supported an easing of the restrictions on Catholics, and radicals, who wanted to break the link with England and the crown.

The crime and routine disorder which had exercised city councillors in earlier decades gave way to debates about political and sectarian issues, especially when the post-revolutionary period in France led to war with Britain. The council, as a body, was firmly in favour of retaining "the Protestant ascendancy in Ireland upon the principles of the glorious revolution". Frequent petitions and resolutions tried unsuccessfully to stem reforms of the Penal Laws, such as the granting of the franchise to

Catholics in 1793. But the council also contained a small minority of radicals, like James Napper Tandy, who was a prominent United Irishman, and a larger minority of moderates, which included Arthur Guinness.

Such differences in approach were apparent in a lengthy and acrimonious discussion in March 1795 over a petition to King George III rejecting any further relaxation of the Penal Laws. It declared that an application by Roman Catholics to have all restrictive laws repealed would prove highly dangerous to civil and religious liberty and the maintenance of the Protestant religion. The resolution was debated paragraph by paragraph, interspersed with procedural manoeuvres, as a minority moved a succession of amendments to support the Catholic claims and to include Catholics in the definition of his majesty's loyal subjects. They were all defeated by consistent margins of some "43 Black Beans to 18 White Beans" and the final, uncompromising, resolution was adopted by 42 votes to 18. Afterwards, 19 members of the common council, including Arthur Guinness, signed a statement saying they dissented from the day's proceedings, which they said were contrary to the king's own recommendation for "the cordial and hearty union of all classes of his subjects".

Those who voted for greater rights for Catholics were subsequently excoriated in a leaflet distributed in the city which accused them of voting against preserving the Protestant religion in Ireland and passed scathing comments on each of them. Of Arthur Guinness, it said: "an inveterate private Enemy to the Roman Catholicks, tho' their Hypocritical Friend in public Self: Interest is his predomenant [sic] Passion [?], to which his Friendship, his Conscience, and his Religion are Subservient". Others on the Black List, as it termed itself, were damned variously as republicans, insignificant, adulterers, descendant of robbers and plunderers, having the face of an assassin's mind, and being a Portuguese Jesuit.[40] It was clearly biased and searching for abusive things to say about all those involved but it was not to be the last suggestion that the Guinnesses took one position in private and another in public.

Arthur's political stance in favour of greater rights for Catholics drew the line at any radical activity. Like many other successful businessmen of the time, he had no difficulty in extending civil rights but he opposed any fundamental change in the relationship between Ireland and England, which was central to his religious and political beliefs, as well as being important for business.

The United Irishmen, an alliance between Ulster Non-Conformists and southern Catholics, attracted a cross-section of Dublin's professionals and businessmen: its city leadership covered the sectarian divide and ranged from doctors (William McNevin) to brewers (John Sweetman) and the aristocracy (Lord Edward Fitzgerald, the brother of Ireland's premier nobleman, the Duke of Leinster, and president of the Friendly Brothers of St Patrick knot, of which Arthur had been secretary). One section of society was conspicuously absent from their ranks – the new rich.[41]

Arthur Guinness was prominent among the latter and outspoken enough in his opposition to the United Irishmen to be singled out for the attentions of a broadsheet, the *Union Star*, which supported the revolutionaries and described Arthur as "an active spy" among a list of people it claimed were "detestable Traitors . . . Spies and Perjured Informers".[42] Edited by Walter "Watty" Cox, a former gunsmith who brought more than a whiff of cordite to his journalism, the paper embarrassed the United Irishmen's leadership with the bloodthirstiness of its support. Unknown to his readers, however, Cox saved himself from prosecution by being an informer.[43] It is clear also from a later publication, the satirical *Milesian Magazine*, which repeatedly attacked Cox, that Arthur was among the prime targets of his *Union Star*. The *Milesian Magazine*'s first issue, in April 1812, described the *Union Star* as the "Murder Gazette" and depicted Cox graphically as the "great murder constellation" showering the world with daggers. Among the victims of the daggers noted by name on the illustration were Arthur Guinness and the Catholic Archbishop of Dublin, John Thomas Troy. The *Milesian Magazine* added: "The Protestant had to read the name of old Arthur Guinness the brewer as a man whom it would be meritorious to slay . . ." Cox later defended himself on the grounds of youthful ardour and his desire to warn his country against the foe and "slay lest they be slain". The magazine commented: "But was Dr Troy to be slain lest he should slay? Was Arthur Guinness to be slain lest he should slay?"

The *Union Star*, however, did not intimidate Arthur or change his views. When political tensions were raised further by the United Irishmen's rebellion in 1798, the Guinnesses played their part in defending the status quo. Two of Arthur's sons, Edward and William, joined the militia formed to defend Dublin against the republicans. And Arthur junior was a key witness against three of the United Irishmen who were tried for high treason and sentenced to death, a fact that is absent from all the biographies of the family.

The three were arrested at a meeting of the Leinster directory of the United Irishmen at the Dublin home of Oliver Bond, a woollen merchant, in Bridge Street on 12 March 1798. It was a crucial moment in the planning of the rebellion: the directory was about to decide to go ahead with its revolt without the expected military aid from France. However, one of the group, 27-year-old Catholic silk merchant Thomas Reynolds, had betrayed them and they were all arrested. The authorities were disappointed not to have caught Lord Edward Fitzgerald, who was supposed to have been at the meeting, but they detained ten others and launched a city-wide round-up of the remainder of the leadership. One of the main people found in Bond's house was John McCann, the secretary of the United Irishmen in the province of Leinster. He was a clerk at the iron foundry of another United Irishman, Henry Jackson, and had worked previously as a clerk with the Guinnesses.

After the rebellion had gone ahead, primarily in Wexford, and been crushed, the Dublin detainees were put on trial in July for high treason. The main evidence against McCann was given by Thomas Reynolds but the prosecution maintained that the papers found in Bond's house showed him to be a principal agent "in the conspiracy which has laid waste this country".[44] Arthur junior gave evidence that he knew McCann and had seen him write very often.[45] He identified McCann's handwriting on several documents, including lists of numbers of United Irishmen throughout the counties of Leinster, resolutions, and notes to Lord Edward Fitzgerald. McCann was found guilty after a 15-hour trial, which continued into the early hours of the morning, and he was sentenced to death. Taken back to prison at four o'clock in the morning, he ate "hearty of mutton and drank two bottles of Porter" before he was hanged and beheaded outside the prison in Green Street later the same morning.[46]

Arthur junior was back in the special court for two subsequent trials, repeating his evidence about McCann's handwriting to help convict two others. William Michael Byrne, the 21-year-old United Irishman delegate from County Wicklow, was the addressee on one of McCann's notes about Lord Edward Fitzgerald and had been arrested in Bond's house. He was hanged and beheaded. Arthur gave his evidence as well at the trial of Oliver Bond, who was sentenced to death but reprieved at the last minute when a group of 78 prisoners awaiting trial and execution did a hasty deal with the government, revealing all their revolutionary plans in return for exile. Bond died suddenly in prison several months later.

As well as raising political passions, the rebellion also had practical effects on business, disrupting Guinness's embryonic distribution system outside Dublin. Supplies to Athy, 40 miles away by canal, were disrupted for a time. But, paradoxically, the rebellion and the war between Britain and France were generally good for business, creating an economic boom fuelled by inflation. Irish exports shot up and were further encouraged by the break in the fixed relationship between the Irish and English currencies when the gold standard was abandoned in 1797. The Irish pound dropped in value, giving Guinness a competitive advantage which helped to establish its exports to England over the next two decades. Meanwhile, the by now elderly first Arthur had expanded his business activities with the establishment of the Hibernian flour mills near James's Gate at Kilmainham, in which he had invested some £7,000.

The brewery was thriving as the new century began, concentrating on producing and improving the quality of its porter and spreading its distribution network by canal into the countryside. In spite of the political turmoil at the end of the 1790s, Arthur invested more than £6,000 into rebuilding the brewery between 1797 and 1799, a substantial sum but equivalent to the profit it made in 1797 alone; it made a further £2,000 profit from its flour mill.[47] The scale of such

31

profits can be measured by estimates that in the 1770s the richest families in Ireland earned between £2,000 and £3,000 a year and "even the richest of merchants and manufacturers, with a handful of exceptions, earned much less than £1,000".[48]

The new brewery was to concentrate exclusively on producing stout; the last brewing of ale took place in the spring of 1799 and thereafter Guinness was a one-product company. Through increased investment and continuing improvements in standards, Arthur had turned his brewery into one of the largest in Dublin and made it among the city's main employers. He had also hired John Purser, the son of a London brewer who had been brought to Dublin by another brewery as an expert in brewing stout. The Purser family's involvement with Guinness over the next 80-odd years was central to its success.

Socially, too, the family was consolidating itself. Arthur's eldest daughter, Elizabeth, married Frederick Darley, a city alderman, who was to become lord mayor of Dublin in 1809 before falling into financial difficulties. His eldest son, Hosea, graduated from Trinity College Dublin in 1788 and, the next year, became a member of the brewers' corporation. But his involvement in brewing was limited: he went on to take holy orders and became rector of St Werburgh's Church in Dublin, where Arthur's benefactor, Archbishop Arthur Price, had begun his clerical career at the start of the eighteenth century.

Two of Arthur's other daughters, Louisa and Mary Anne, were to marry clergymen, while his youngest son, John Grattan, went into the Indian army before returning to Ireland where, like his older brother Edward, he became a financial thorn in his other brothers' sides. Arthur's three other sons, Arthur, Benjamin and William, were involved with him in the brewery and the flour mills and were taking increasing responsibility for the businesses.

Arthur junior, his second son, born in 1768, was already his heir apparent and once cited by his father as among the reasons for his business success: without the second Arthur's help, he wrote, "I would not have attempted it, though prompted by a demand of providing for ten children now living."[49] Part of the brewery had already been given to him under his marriage settlement and the remainder was bequeathed to him in Arthur's will, along with the Hibernian flour mill and a silver salver presented to Arthur senior by the brewers' guild which, he directed, was subsequently "to go to the eldest Male branch of the Family then living who shall be in the Brewing Trade".

Arthur Guinness's 16-page will, dated 3 May 1802, shows an astute operator who left little to chance and set about consolidating the family's wealth by concentrating control in the hands of his main successor, the second Arthur, using both carrots and sticks to achieve his ends. His youngest brother Richard, whom he had left in charge of his first brewery in Leixlip, clearly did not share Arthur's business abilities. At the time Arthur wrote his will, Richard owed him £560 in several bonds, plus other, unspecified, amounts on a mortgage Arthur had granted him. Arthur directed that Richard's four daughters should share £800 among them and that Richard would get an annuity of £75, to be paid twice a year for life. But these bequests would take effect only if Richard retired from business and surrendered all his property in Leixlip to Arthur's family as payment for his debts. Richard appears to have accepted the deal, because the second Arthur was subsequently the owner of a considerable amount of property in Leixlip.

As well as leaving £3,000 to buy his son John Grattan a commission in the army, Arthur left his country house at Beaumont and his brewery in Leixlip to the Reverend Hosea on the grounds that his eldest son was not "in any line of life whereby he is likely by Industry to enlarge his property". His second house, in the newly built Gardiner Street, was left to his widow, Olivia, with an annual £600 to be paid to her out of the Hibernian mills. After her death the house and furnishings were to be sold and divided among his two younger daughters, Louisa and Mary Anne, provided they married with the consent of their mother or of his own executors. They also received £2,000 each on the same condition: if they married without consent, they were to get only half the amount.

His will underlined the secondary role played in the Guinness saga by the women in the family: essentially, they were looked after as long as they did what they were told. As an example of this – and of the trend Arthur established for keeping money within the family – he bequeathed a loan of £1,500 to Frederick Darley, the husband of his eldest daughter, Elizabeth. The loan was to last for Darley's lifetime but only on the basis of "good and sufficient security to be approved of by my executors". If Darley did not accept these terms, the money was to be lent elsewhere and the interest paid to him and afterwards divided up among his and Elizabeth's children.

Arthur spent his final years at Beaumont House and died on 23 January 1803 at the age of 78. He was buried in a picture-postcard graveyard with a ruined church and lopped-off round tower on the hill of Oughterard, from where there are panoramic views over the hills and pleasant farmland of his native County Kildare. His mother, Elizabeth Read, was also buried in the graveyard, which was close to her birthplace, and the original headstone erected over her grave by her husband Richard Guinness was replicated a century later by her great-great-grandson, the first Lord Iveagh. The inscription on Arthur's tombstone says that he and his wife Olivia, who died in 1814 at the age of 72, "lived universally beloved and respected by a numerous circle of friends, relations and descendants". Along with some of their children and grandchildren, Arthur's brother Richard and his wife Anne were also buried there.

Arthur's signature still adorns every bottle and can of Guinness, confirming his role in establishing the company and dynasty. But his influence was broader than simply founding a profitable business at a time of both opportunity and uncertainty. He also laid down much of the ethos which came to characterise the company and later generations, notably a determined self-interest muted by benevolence. But the solid foundations he had established were by no means guaranteed to withstand the external and internal pressures which were to come in the nineteenth century as the weaknesses, as well as the strengths, of a large and ever-richer family came into play.

CHAPTER THREE

The Second Arthur

"With contemptuous pity I dismiss the Guinnesses."

DANIEL O'CONNELL commenting on the second
Arthur Guinness's switch in political allegiance in 1837.

In 1813 the *Dublin Evening Post* opened up a can of worms which illustrated how business and politics were enmeshed in early nineteenth-century Ireland and confirmed the Guinnesses' adeptness at steering a safe course around the associated pitfalls. This ability was central to the success of the second Arthur Guinness in, as Lynch and Vaizey summed it up, inheriting a good business and leaving a thriving one.[1] Shrewd, single-minded and ruthless in his commercial dealings, Arthur made superb use of the legacy – political, commercial and financial – which he inherited from his father. Over the 40-odd years he controlled the brewery, he needed all those qualities to guide an ever-larger, and increasingly difficult, family through a series of crises which ran the gamut from high-octane political controversy through economic recessions to sexual scandal.

The new century opened with the 1800 Act of Union, which created the United Kingdom of Great Britain and Ireland, the London government's main political response to the United Irishmen's rebellion. The union was highly controversial and divided opinion, though not as clearly along the lines of Catholic and Protestant, nationalist and unionist, as later generations would have it. Many Catholics, for instance, supported the union, in the belief that they would more easily

35

achieve their freedoms under the British government than under a domestic parliament controlled by the Protestant ascendancy. Equally, many Protestant interests were uneasy at the loss of a native parliament and its power to regulate trade as well as to control political developments.

The emergence of the Orange Order (founded in 1795) as the vehicle for intransigent Protestant politics and the agitation for Catholic rights orchestrated on a popular and parliamentary level by Daniel O'Connell led to an increasing political polarisation over the following decades. Arthur Guinness's relationship with O'Connell, the dominant Irish public figure of the age, illustrated the difficulties posed for a liberal Protestant over the period. Both shared an abhorrence of violent revolution, O'Connell from his personal experiences as a schoolboy in France during the revolutionary Terror, and Guinness from his own and his family's attitude towards the United Irishmen. O'Connell's strategy to gain Catholic emancipation, the rights to political representation and to hold public offices, included regular petitions to the parliament in London. These provoked counter-petitions from Protestants, including one presented to the House of Commons by the lord mayor of Dublin, Abraham Bradley King, in 1812 which expressed alarm at "the temper and manner in which the pretensions of the Roman Catholics have recently been urged". Stability depended on the maintenance of the Protestant establishment, it declared, and any increase in the political strength of Catholics would endanger "the Protestant Establishments of Ireland and the constitution of the Empire".

The *Dublin Evening Post* subsequently acquired and published over several weeks the names of the signatories of the Protestant petition. Owned and edited by a Protestant supporter of O'Connell, John Magee, the newspaper ran the list under the sardonic headline, "The Temple of Fame", declaring: "Those Independent Citizens who petitioned the House of Commons for a perpetuity of Catholic Thraldom must come forward and cease to hope that their meritorious conduct should remain unknown."2 The first list included the name Richard Guinness of Nicholas Street.

As the names dribbled out tantalisingly, accompanied by Magee's rhetorical flourishes, a steady stream of letters flowed back from people denying that they had signed the petition. Then it became apparent that, as well as the forgeries, some of the supposed signatories were entirely fictitious: the newspaper switched from sarcasm to moral indignation, maintaining that the petition was "proof of an infamous fraud practised on the Imperial Parliament".[3] The depth of the political skulduggery at work was evident when one of the letters disavowing a signature was, in turn, shown to be a forgery.

The controversy pointed up the dilemma facing many Protestant businessmen in Dublin: proclaiming their political beliefs risked alienating the majority of their actual or potential customers, who were Catholics. Magee stressed this point, writing that some Protestants "would be happy to sell their wares for Catholic cash but . . . would disinterestedly monopolize all civil and political rights". And there were those who were happy to exploit this dilemma to further their own commercial interests, as the Guinnesses discovered.

Arthur and his two brothers who ran the brewery with him, Benjamin and William Lunnell Guinness, did not respond immediately to the inclusion of a Guinness on the *Dublin Evening Post*'s lists. It was only when the association was used in an organised and successful campaign against the sales of their porter that they reacted. Then they responded with a two-pronged attack which proved their effectiveness and their use of their father's political legacy.

On 10 May 1813 they inserted one of the first Guinness newspaper advertisements, offering a £500 reward to anyone who successfully prosecuted those who invented and circulated "this base and unfounded report" which was "in direct opposition to our sentiments and principles". They strenuously denied that either of the two Richard Guinnesses then living and related to them had signed the Protestant petition and pointed out that nobody of that name lived in Nicholas Street. Furthermore, they recalled that they had actually signed the petition to parliament seeking "the complete Emancipation of our Catholic Brethren". The advertisement went on:

We are constrained further to appeal to our long established and well known principles of brotherly love towards our Catholic fellow-subjects, which principles we derived from our late father, who was also the early and unshaken friend of the Catholics of Ireland, and who (as fully appears on public record) was amongst the few, who in the year 1795, boldly advocated their Cause in the Common Council of Dublin . . .

We now are obliged to State, that a number of Persons, evidently hired by some interested Person or Persons, have been for some weeks past going amongst the Houses of our friends and Customers in Dublin and the Country, for the purpose of propagating the above-mentioned slander, and exciting the Public by threats and persuasions against dealing in our Brewery.

The advertisement ran for more than a month in the *Evening Post* while the family reinforced its message with the help of their contacts in the Catholic Board, O'Connell's organisation for mobilising popular opinion. A meeting of the Board on 22 May passed a special resolution declaring that the Guinnesses had shown their devotion to the cause of religious liberty and "in common with our enlightened Protestant Brethren, entitled themselves to the confidence, gratitude and thanks of the Catholics of Ireland". The proposer of the motion, Nicholas O'Gorman, suggested that the forging of the Guinness name on the petition was the work of the Catholics' enemies "for the purpose of exciting the people to acts of apparent ingratitude towards their tried friends".[4]

These ringing endorsements did not find favour in all Catholic quarters, however. Watty Cox, now publishing the monthly *Irish Magazine* – which boasted the memorable subtitle: "*And Monthly Asylum for Neglected Biography*" – was driven into apoplexy and one of his periodic rants against the Guinnesses. He accused O'Gorman of "unmanly adulation" and demanded to know what the Guinnesses had done to support Catholic claims. "The Guinnesses were never distinguished for liberality or patriotism; they were not notoriously known as friends to Catholics or friends to Ireland," he thundered. "They are gentlemen but would have remained among the loyal mob from whom they recently started, if the proscribed papists had been honest enough to give a preference to popish porter."[5]

Cox proceeded to outline his complaints against the family, mainly aimed at one of his favourite targets, Richard Guinness, one of Arthur's cousins in what was to become the banking line of Guinnesses. Richard was a barrister and magistrate who had helped prosecute John Magee, the *Dublin Evening Post* editor, for sedition. He was regularly denigrated by Cox as "the lisping loyalist", primarily for having called some people who complained about police behaviour a "felonious rabble". Cox also regularly castigated the whole family for funding a "child-trap" (orphanage) in Drumcondra "for converting popish children to loyalty and imported piety". In his response to the Catholic Board's defence of the Guinnesses, he raised these issues again and added viciously: "Applicants will be received at the trap, or at the empty porter vat, James's-gate, by the widow of John McCann, a traitor, who was hanged in the year 1798." (Cox's own role as an informer against the United Irishmen was still unknown at the time.) Changing tack, Cox expressed pride at the Guinness advertisement because, he wrote, it proved "it is not safe nor prudent in any body of men, who live by trade, to insult even the very lowest classes of the Catholic population; it goes to prove that it is safer to quarrel with British Christianity than to trample on Irishmen. The Guinnesses have felt how dangerous it is to be trying experiments at the suggestions of bigots on the temper of Ireland."[6]

Such invective was not unusual in the heightened political rhetoric of the time, when abuse was unrestrained by libel laws and expectations of political change were presented in either apocalyptic or utopian terms. There was also the satire of the *Milesian Magazine* run by John Brenan, who was known as the "turpentine doctor" or the "wrestling doctor" for his medical remedy for child-bed fever and his sporting passion. He maintained that medical analysis of Guinness porter showed it to be impregnated with the "pure etherial [*sic*] essence of heresy" and had, since 1798, mashed up 136,000 "tuns" of bibles and 50,000 cart loads of hymn books and Protestant catechisms. Its drinkers were found to have "a disposition of bowels peculiarly lax, and an inclination to gravity, and to singing praises of the Lord through the nose". The same issue also added a song after his investigator-at-large, Dr Drumsnuffle, was called in to treat Archbishop Troy, O'Connell

("Counsellor Roundabout") and his henchmen who were suffering agonising spasms after drinking Guinness. It began:

> To be sure you did hear
> Of the Heresy beer
> That was made for to poison the Pope –
> To hide the brewer a sin is,
> And his name is Arthur Guinness;
> For salvation he never can hope.[7]

Such satire did not amuse the Guinnesses, who were never notable for their sense of humour. They undoubtedly feared that its finer points would be lost on semi-literate customers who might take it seriously. They were probably not amused either by the magazine's recommendation that the rival Pim's ale was the best antidote for Guinness-induced stomach spasms. Guinness and the Catholic authorities solemnly rejected the charge that they were proselytising through porter.

———⊗⊗⊗———

The second Arthur was, by now, a significant figure in public life, his standing based firmly on his commercial activities rather than on any major desire to play a political role. When his father died, he was almost 35 years old, married to Anne Lee, the daughter and co-heiress of a businessman, Benjamin Lee, and the father of three sons. Arthur's brother Benjamin married Anne's sister, resulting in many of their children carrying the middle name of Lee, which came to denote a member of the brewing branch of the Guinness family.

Arthur had been deeply involved in the business and was heir-apparent long before his father's death; he became a full partner about 1798. At the same time as he supported the campaign for Catholic emancipation, he consolidated his position within the exclusively Protestant financial establishment, epitomised by the Bank of Ireland which had a monopoly on banking in Dublin and the surrounding areas. He became a director of the bank in 1804, a year after his father's death, was re-elected in 1806, 1808 and 1810, and remained on its board continuously from then until 1847.[8] His close involvement with the bank occasionally threatened his own business, particularly between 1820 and 1822 when he was its governor (see below), but it also raised his public profile. As governor, he received King George IV at the bank during a royal visit in 1821.

He shared a public platform with O'Connell, the Duke of Leinster and Henry Grattan junior, the owner and editor of the *Freeman's Journal*, at a meeting to protest at a riot by Orangemen in December 1822. The riot took place at a performance of Oliver Goldsmith's *She Stoops to Conquer* which was attended by the Lord Lieutenant, Marquis Wellesley, the brother of the Duke of Wellington. A former governor general of India, he did not share his brother's politics and supported Catholic emancipation. He had angered the Orange Order further by preventing its annual ceremony of dressing the statue of William of Orange in College Green. The performance of the Goldsmith play descended into chaos when Orangemen in the upper gallery interrupted with shouts of "no Popish governor" and "the Boyne water" and showered Wellesley's box with placards and other missiles. The rest of the audience responded with impromptu bursts of "God Save the King", during one of which a quart bottle thrown by an Orangeman narrowly missed Wellesley's head.[9]

Arthur was one of the principal speakers at a crowded meeting several days later to protest at the Orangemen's behaviour. He described the order as a "mischievous faction" and, to prolonged applause, called for all illegal associations to be put down "by the severe but wholesome discipline of the laws". Neither religion nor the security of the state required the support of "the strange anomaly of a body of men with loyalty on their lips and treason in their hearts," he declared.[10] Arthur was a member of a 21-man delegation led by the Duke of Leinster which subsequently called on Wellesley on Christmas Eve to express their outrage at the "atrocious attack" on him. Writing to his wife about the episode, O'Connell told her that there was "the greatest unanimity and good feeling" at the protest meeting: "In short, darling, it was a great day for Ireland."[11]

However, the extended Guinness family straddled both sides of the political fence. Arthur's brother-in-law, Alderman Frederick Darley, was the chief police magistrate and was criticised for his friendly chats with the rioting Orangemen. He had caused controversy during the visit by King George IV the previous year by proposing a toast "to the glorious and immortal memory of King William the Third". O'Connell, for one, was outraged at this revival of the "obnoxious and insulting toast" and noted that it was the second time Darley had violated an understanding that had existed between all parties.[12]

Arthur carried his support for Catholic emancipation into the Bank of Ireland's court. He proposed unsuccessfully in 1825 that Catholics should be allowed become directors: the anti-Popery clause was later dropped from the oath administered to directors. He was excluded as one of two honourable exceptions among the bank's directors by *The Pilot* newspaper (founded to back O'Connell) in an attack on this "close and rotten borough" for opposing reform candidates in 1831.[13] But he also demonstrated a more conservative bent in business politics than in what, within the narrow confines of the day, might be loosely termed popular politics.

This was exemplified by his involvement in two linked business organisations, the Ouzel Galley Society and the Dublin Chamber of Commerce. The Ouzel Galley was a distinguished and influential business group called after a ship, the *Ouzel* (an old word for a blackbird) which was dispatched from Dublin in 1695 with a cargo of exports for the Levant by a company called Ferris, Twigg and Cash. It disappeared without trace and, after three years, was assumed to have been lost at sea. The company claimed compensation and was paid by its insurers. Then, in 1700, the ship turned up in Dublin again with a more valuable cargo and a tale of derring-do. It had been sized by Moorish pirates in the Bay of Biscay and subsequently taken over by Algerian pirates, who kept the crew and the ship to carry on their own trade. Eventually, the original crew saw an opportunity to escape and made off with the Algerians' cargo. Ferris, Twigg and Cash claimed this new and more valuable cargo as theirs and offered to pay back the insurance money. The insurers, however, wanted the new cargo instead. The matter was eventually decided by a committee of merchants which was deemed to be so successful at arbitration that it was decided to keep it in place as the Ouzel Galley Society. It survived from 1705 until 1888. Everyone who was anyone in Dublin business life aspired to join the society, which evolved into an exclusive business club. Membership was restricted to 40 people, the same number as the *Ouzel's* crew; officers had nautical titles and ordinary members were called hands; and all were piped to their annual dinner by a boatswain's whistle. As time went on, it became a barometer of individual power and the fluctuating alliances in Dublin's business life. Arthur and many of his banking associates were long-term members.

In many ways, the society had the role of a chamber of commerce. Several attempts had been made to set up a chamber from the mid-eighteenth century, each influenced by the dominant political movements of their time, but they all petered out. Arthur was involved in such an attempt in 1805, presiding over several of its meetings, but it also collapsed, "emphasizing how divided the Dublin business community was by what were ultimately religious and political factors."[14] It was revived again in 1820 by what were described as the liberal forces in the business community but Arthur, who was not included in their number, failed to win election to its council. The main movers behind the new venture included Quakers, Catholics and uncommitted Anglicans who tried to ensure that the organisation did not become politicised. Arthur was among their main opponents, being a leading member of a faction that wanted the body to back direct political representation for business interests. Although the liberal leaders of the chamber successfully opposed this proposal, they appear to have given up the ghost shortly afterwards when one of their number, the existing president, Leland Crosthwait, died. Arthur was unanimously elected president in the absence of the liberals and confirmed his position at a subsequent annual general meeting, which was packed with his supporters and boycotted by the liberal group. The official history of the Chamber of Commerce is unequivocal in identifying Arthur as the main strategist and force in making it "a narrow and increasingly exclusive unionist enclave" and creating a "dismal period in its history". It commented:

> The purely political nature of Guinness's interest is reflected in his poor attendance record which contrasted with that of preceding officers. After his first election in 1821 to council he was an infrequent attender at council meetings, and although he had become president in June 1826 he first took the chair at a general meeting in March 1828.[15]

Just how effectively he had taken over the chamber is evident from the fact that Arthur continued to be elected president unanimously every year from 1826 until the year of his death, 1855. Under his leadership, few Catholics and Quakers (who were amongst the most dynamic Dublin businessmen in the 1830s and 1840s) served on the chamber's council. The episode illustrated how Arthur acted before different constituencies: in the relatively private world of business he pursued a different agenda, on the surface at any rate, to the one which he adopted before the wider public of his customers.

Thus, he continued to support O'Connell and Catholic emancipation at the same time as he was orchestrating the takeover of the Chamber of Commerce. But it would be contrary to contemporary evidence to suggest that his support for the Catholic cause was entirely pragmatic and based solely on the brewery's need to keep its Catholic customers happy. A large amount of documentary evidence shows that he continued to play a prominent, if secondary, role in the emancipation campaign. He was present at a public meeting to celebrate the achievement of emancipation in 1829 and, subsequently, one of the seven men chosen by a large committee to raise a testimonial fund for O'Connell when he took his seat in the House of Commons in 1829. They raised a very substantial £30,000 for the always impecunious Liberator.[16]

Clearly, both the O'Connell leadership, which especially welcomed the support of Protestants, and the authorities were quite clear about whose side Arthur was on in the major political divisions of the day. Two years later, the attitude of the authorities towards Arthur's political beliefs was apparent when they removed him from the panel of jurors likely to try O'Connell and five of his associates under a proclamation suppressing dangerous associations in Ireland.[17] Like so many other legal attempts to curb O'Connell, the case fizzled out when the proclamation lapsed.

Arthur was even more prominent, hovering on the edge of full-scale participation, in the next major political campaign after emancipation. The Reform Bill of 1831 proposed by the Whig government, with which O'Connell allied himself and his followers at Westminster, sought to widen the franchise and get rid of the rotten boroughs, which had small and easily bribed numbers of voters. Arthur was urged by

O'Connell and his supporters to stand as one of the two reform candidates for Dublin. The *Pilot* newspaper noted on 29 April 1831 that several gentlemen had been spoken of as second candidates, along with the then lord mayor, Robert Harty, and added: "Mr Guinness has been long regarded by the citizens of Dublin as possessed of all the qualifications which render him the natural representative of this great commercial city." Arthur clearly rejected any urgings, contenting himself with seconding the two candidates selected, Harty and a lawyer, Louis Perrin, at a public meeting. They were duly elected, replacing the existing, conservative MPs, but their tenure in the Commons was short-lived. They were both disqualified by a select committee after a group of Dublin freemen and electors accused them of "great bribery and corruption" in the form of money, meals, drink and entertainment. Arthur was encouraged again to stand in the subsequent election: "A. Guinness would do very well," O'Connell wrote to an associate, "either A. Guinness or Alderman McKenny if it be impossible to stir [David] La Touche."[18]

It proved impossible to stir Arthur either. Years later, he explained his reasons for not standing in a letter to his son, Benjamin Lee.[19] He had been twice encouraged to stand for parliament, he wrote,

... backed on both occasions by offers on the part of gentlemen who were candidates themselves and who offered to resign in my favour. I then felt, and now feel, that the office of sitting in Parliament for a great city and especially such a city as Dublin where party and sectarian strife so signally abound and more especially if filled by one engaged in our line of business, is fraught with difficulty and danger.

Thereafter, relations between O'Connell and the Guinnesses began to deteriorate, primarily for political reasons but also exacerbated by commercial differences. Not the least of the latter was O'Connell's involvement in the two businesses closest to Arthur's heart, brewing and banking. In 1831 O'Connell's youngest son, also Daniel, bought one of Guinness's main rivals, Mander's porter brewery, across the road from James's Gate, with his father's financial help. He renamed it O'Connell's brewery and attempted to cash in on the family name. His porter was endorsed by the Liberator himself as "the very best Irish porter I ever tasted . . . really superlative". But it was a commercial disaster: the brewery was sold in 1840 and renamed the Phoenix brewery by its new owners.[20] O'Connell also founded his own bank, the National, to be a Catholic bank with his picture on its banknotes, and to rival the Protestant-controlled Bank of Ireland.[21] Arthur could scarcely have been pleased by such developments.

At the same time, Protestant opinion in Dublin was uneasy at several other developments, like the campaign against the Church of Ireland's tithes and promised reforms of the municipal system, which would widen the franchise and end Protestant control of Dublin city council. Municipal reform, in particular, raised fears that the Catholic masses would, as one lobbyist, Isaac Butt, put it, have power to tax Protestant property.[22] Meanwhile, O'Connell was raising the political stakes by blowing hot and cold over his next, and last, major campaign: the repeal of the Union.

Attitudes towards the Union had shifted significantly over the three intervening decades since its implementation. By now, it was commonly blamed by Catholics for the decline in Dublin's fortunes and all Ireland's ills, while it was increasingly seen by Protestants as the guarantor of their power and position. Faced with electoral reforms and outnumbered three-to-one by Catholics in the city, they feared the loss of control which would inevitably follow the return of a local parliament and a wider franchise.[23] The increasingly sectarian tenor of the political divide was underpinned by the growing confidence of the Catholic middle and professional classes, who knew they had the numbers on their side, and the resurgence of Protestant evangelicalism, which assured its co-religionists they had right on their side.

As a major businessman, a supporter of the bible societies which were one manifestation of evangelicalism, and a serious member of the established church whose position was under threat from the anti-tithes campaign, Arthur did not approve of O'Connell's more radical stances. As well as threatening the position of the Church of Ireland and facing Protestants with the prospect of minority status in Ireland, they posed a potential threat to Guinness's by now vital trade with England. The break between O'Connell and liberal Protestants began with

O'Connell's attempt to form an anti-Tory alliance after the conservatives were unexpectedly returned to power in 1834. His support for repeal of the union and his efforts to control all the anti-Tory forces in Ireland caused moderate reformers in Dublin to form a rival group which would give straightforward support to the Whigs, with whom O'Connell was in an uneasy alliance at Westminster.

In the subsequent general election in 1835 some of his Protestant supporters deserted O'Connell. The most notable was David La Touche, Arthur's co-director of the Bank of Ireland and fellow would-be O'Connellite candidate in the previous election. O'Connell publicly excoriated him for being "the most accomplished hypocrite" he had ever seen. The heat generated by politics spread directly into business, with controversy over "exclusive dealings", whereby people were encouraged to trade only with their co-religionists and those who shared their political stance. The extremes on both sides wanted details publicised of how voters had cast their ballot so that their supporters would know with whom to do business. While blaming "exclusive dealing" on Orange supporters, O'Connell claimed it was "fair and legitimate" for customers to look to a trader's politics.[24]

Arthur Guinness was the next well-known Protestant businessman to desert the O'Connell camp. The election of 1837, caused by the death of the king and the accession of Queen Victoria, was fought amid controversy over municipal reforms proposed by the Whig government and supported by O'Connell. Arthur and his sons caused a sensation when they turned up at the polling booths in Green Street courthouse on the afternoon of Wednesday, 2 August. "Public expectation was raised to the highest pitch to ascertain for whom these gentlemen would vote," the *Freeman's Journal* told its readers. "They were polled – the question was put to each of them separately, for whom would they vote? – the reply was for [J.B.] West and [George] Hamilton [the conservative opponents of O'Connell and his Presbyterian running mate, Robert Hutton]."

The Tory Dublin *Evening Mail* was euphoric, hailing Arthur as "the head of certainly the greatest establishment that is or ever was in Ireland" and praising him for his "good sense [in seeing] that what was once Whiggery is generated into revolution". On the other side of the political divide, the *Freeman's Journal* was astounded that the

Guinnesses, who were "considered staunch and true to the good cause", had "wheeled around". It noted that banking and brewing were profitable trades and O'Connell did "a little in both". The newspaper added: "it would, however, be unfair even to insinuate that Messrs La Touche were jealous of the success of the O'Connell bank, or the Messrs Guinness annoyed at the rivalry of the O'Connell brewery."

O'Connell attacked both families in his victory speech when polling ended and he and Hutton were elected the following Saturday. He declared that he was "sincerely sorry" that the Guinnesses had done what they did and went on to cheers, "I thought they had a better spirit; but, at all events, they have now the recollection of their conduct without the consolation of having inflicted any real injury." He concluded with a typical flourish, "With contemptuous pity I dismiss the Guinnesses."[25]

The shock to the O'Connell camp of Arthur's defection was evident in his most faithful media supporter, *The Pilot*, which addressed an uncharacteristically perplexed editorial to Arthur as one of "the few, the very few men of character and principle who joined the Tories". It asked Arthur – "who never committed but this one public error" – why he "who is known to be, not externally, but on principle and in his heart, a friend to civil and religious liberty, and a foe to . . . corruption and Orange domination" had voted as he did. It went on to give Arthur a strong testimonial:

> Whoever has seen Mr Guinness, as we have, contending – with no public eye upon him – in the guild of brewers against the intolerance of the [Orange] faction – when also his love of justice and known disapproval of the Orange system are recollected – when his high estimation as a trader and employer are estimated together with his personal character as a man; and when we find such a man recording a vote calculated to compromise his personal interests and contradict the tenor of his whole life – it becomes a point of public duty to ask how such a thing can be, and a matter of public regret should one act obliterate the recollection of a life of public principle and private virtue.[26]

The editorial prompted Arthur to break his public silence and take issue with the speculation about his motives. The *Evening Mail*, for instance, had declared that Arthur, if given the opportunity at the hustings, would have said the time had come "when every man should declare whether he is for the destruction of the constitution or for its preservation". In a letter to *The Pilot*, Arthur said there had been much misapprehension about his vote and regretted certain symptoms of triumph manifested by supporters of the Tory candidates. He wrote that he had no intention to identify himself with a party, had made no financial contribution to anyone, and disapproved "as much as ever of the Orange system, recollecting the evils connected with it". His sole motive was to register dissent from measures which endanger "the safety of those institutions whose abuses alone could justly be complained of, and should form the object of genuine reform". He added: "My sincere desire was to see honest men on both sides uniting for the maintenance of the constitution while promoting a sound and wholesome reform of its remaining abuses, especially those connected with the corporation system." In other words, Arthur believed that the necessary reforms – the removal of the Penal Laws against Catholics and the reform of the electoral system – had been accomplished and he would like to see everyone supporting the union with Britain in the light of these achievements.

His reply was greeted with relief by *The Pilot* but it did not save Guinness's brewery from a wave of attacks and intimidation that followed the family's votes. Immediately afterwards, the *Evening Mail* reported, several city publicans were ordered to return Guinness porter and "in some instances the mandate was complied with". Other incidents followed, reminiscent of the reaction more than 20 years earlier to the Protestant petition controversy. A haulier, Thomas Kilduff, taking a cartload of Guinness to Roscommon, was followed out of Dublin by a covered wagon from which six men emerged, broke the casks with sledges and crowbars and threatened to dash out Kilduff's brains. A Dublin publican was fined for assaulting two customers who ordered Guinness. Casks of Guinness waiting to be loaded on barges bound for Longford at the Royal Canal harbour were smashed and emptied into the canal. Another bargeman refused to take on board nine dray-loads of Guinness, also destined for Longford, which police escorted back to the brewery.

As in the earlier controversy, the family blamed some of the incidents on competitors spreading rumours. The investigation into the Kilduff incident revealed that the haulier had been told by a number of people, including a clerk from the rival Sweetman brewery, not to take porter from Guinness. Arthur's son, Benjamin Lee, produced a letter from a rural customer claiming that two emissaries from another brewery had been travelling the country, urging people to switch their business from Guinness. He told the police inquiry that various attempts had been made by "interested persons to take advantage of the recent election". He added that the working class, "who have ever been friendly to his establishment," had been urged forward, "contrary to their better feelings".

Sweetman's brewery announced that it had had 50 to 100 new applications for supplies of porter since the election but denied that it and other breweries were combining to use the situation against Guinness. In a letter to the *Freeman's Journal*, Sweetman's denied that its emissaries had gone through the country "exciting popular feeling" against anyone else. "If the conduct of Messrs Guinness has been deemed such as to induce the consumers to look to other houses . . . there is nothing in this to warrant anyone . . . in making a charge of combination against a respectable class of traders," it said.[27]

The Pilot played down the attacks on Guinnesses, assuring Arthur that "some displeasure was natural but will not be lasting". It denied claims by an anonymous correspondent from Ballinasloe in County Galway (which was emerging as a major Guinness depot in the west of Ireland) that Arthur had given £1,000 to fund an election petition against O'Connell and Hutton and ordered employees to vote against the pair.[28]

O'Connell himself was less conciliatory. He blamed Arthur's defection on "some clerical relations of his [who] got about him" and said he had been on the right side "when in the full strength of his intellect, and in the youthful vigour of his mind".[29] He criticised the attacks on the brewery's business for bringing his own political cause into dishonour but his relative lack of sympathy was demonstrated by his comment that Arthur would lose little since his property was insured and the citizens of Dublin would feel the pinch when levied for malicious damage. The depth of bitterness he felt towards Arthur, however, was demonstrated in 1839 when he successfully thwarted a parliamentary attempt by Thomas Spring Rice, the Chancellor of the Exchequer and a leading Irish Whig, to extend the Bank of Ireland's special banking privileges for a lengthy period. In letters to a close associate, O'Connell exulted at his success in beating "the very worst of the Orange confederacies in Ireland" and added gleefully: "That miserable old apostate, Arthur Guinness, was chuckling at carrying this Bill."[30]

The Pilot's prediction that the threats to the Guinness brewery would be short-lived proved to be accurate. When O'Connell's repeal campaign reached a climax during the 1841 elections, at least 15 customers stopped dealing with Guinnesses: within three months, however, all resumed their trade with the brewery.[31] But the switch in the family's political stance turned out to be more lasting. The Guinnesses moved slowly but steadily into the Tory camp after the 1837 election, although it took them another 30 years to move decisively on to the right wing of the Conservative Party, where they remained thereafter. Although Arthur had maintained that his change of heart was based on specific policies, the increasing identification of Protestants with unionism and Catholics with nationalism polarised opinion in Ireland. The manner in which Arthur's views developed is evident from the sermon given at his funeral in 1855 by the Reverend John Alcock, who blamed the "evil tendencies" of his liberal period on his associations, his circumstances and "a judgement not yet fully enlightened in divine truth". He added:

> But more marked still was the decision, the fearless and undaunted resolution, with which, when once convinced of his error, he passed over, and took his stand on the opposite side – on that side which shall ultimately be pronounced true liberality by the voice of God.[32]

Politics, however, was never Arthur's main business, although it impinged heavily upon his business interests. By the time of the repeal agitation, the main threat to the brewer's survival came not from politics but from an unexpected source: a major family scandal. By then, the political climate posed less of a threat to his business than it had during the recession of the 1820s – which almost destroyed the brewery (see below) – when the political focus was on Catholic emancipation. The Guinness brewery had become the largest in Ireland and was selling almost as much porter in England as at home. It was in a stronger position than it had ever been; and that was a result of Arthur's success in, literally, minding his own business amid the pitfalls and distractions of politics.

The second Arthur Guinness was central to two business decisions which ensured that the family brewery emerged as the dominant Irish company in the nineteenth and early twentieth centuries. The first, taken when his father was still alive and influenced by the family's partner, John Purser, was to concentrate on one product, porter, and to brew it well. The second, credited to the second Arthur alone, was to realise that success could best be achieved by getting rid of its numerous rivals in Dublin. The first was easily implemented; the second took several decades and was eventually achieved through a combination of hard work, judicious decisions and fate.

When Arthur and his two brothers, Benjamin and William, took over the brewery after their father's death, the Irish economy was booming. War between Britain and France prompted an expansion of trade in coastal areas of Ireland, and the devaluation of the Irish pound gave exports to England a competitive advantage over imports. Sales of English porter in Dublin, the main challenge to the first Arthur, virtually dried up while exports of Irish porter to England began to grow.

The building of canals also continued to open up rural Ireland to Dublin's merchants and Guinness was quick to seize the opportunities offered – and to do deals with the canal companies which tried to cut out competitors. In 1804, the Grand Canal reached the River Shannon at Shannon Harbour, which became a major distribution centre for Guinness. The commercial possibilities of the heavily populated countryside were limited, however, by the patchy and relatively underdeveloped state of the rural economy. However, Guinness later reaped a handsome reward from the rural distribution system established in this period.

Dublin itself enjoyed a particularly prosperous period between 1810 and 1815 in which the brewers participated. A three-year ban on spirits because of bad grain harvests helped them enormously and they lobbied hard to have it made permanent. On behalf of the brewers, Arthur claimed that "all the advantages derived from the sober habits acquired during the 'suspension' (of distilling)" had been lost and the brewers were threatened once again with "utter ruin".[33] No doubt he was exaggerating but the brewers lost few opportunities to do down their rivals. By 1811 Guinness was producing a quarter of the beer brewed in Dublin, St James's Gate was the city's largest brewery and second only in Ireland to Beamish and Crawford in Cork. Two-thirds of its business was in Dublin, with the remainder divided between the rest of Ireland and England.[34] Sales of Guinness had shot up from 360,936 gallons in 1800 to 2,133,504 gallons by 1815. Prices in Dublin were fixed by agreements between the brewers but that did not prevent competition between them, often leading to internal rows over people breaking the rules.

Various attempts to maximise profits by cutting raw materials rebounded on the brewers. For instance, a rise in the price of hops persuaded Guinness to halve the amount used, with negative effect on sales. The attempts by brewers generally to find cheaper raw materials prompted a fierce attack on them in Dublin city council in 1814 in which they were accused by John Giffard of using "everything that is nauseous and nasty, every deleterious drug" from Ireland and abroad instead of malt and hops.[35] Richard Guinness, Arthur's cousin and the "lisping loyalist" derided by Watty Cox's *Irish Magazine*, sprang to his defence and another brewer read out the "brewer's oath" which required them not to use ingredients like vitriol, grains of Paradise, Guines pepper or opium. Giffard retorted that they would not need such an oath if brewers were not acting suspiciously. How come, he asked, there were such people as brewers' druggists?

The controversy prompted the Guinness brothers to deny these slanders and advertise a sworn affidavit by their brewer, John Purser, that they always brewed their porter from malt and hops without any mixture of any deleterious or unwholesome ingredient or any raw or unmalted corn.[36] Their example was quickly followed by ten other porter brewers advertising similar affidavits and, incidentally, indicating the number of substantial porter brewers in Dublin at the time. The Guinness advertisement prompted a sharp retort from Cox's *Irish Magazine*. He accused the Guinnesses of denying charges that had not been made and maintained that the real issue was the ingredients that were added after brewing. He claimed that burnt treacle, made by Arthur's private secretary, Walter Myler, in his factory in Portland Street, was added to colour and sweeten the porter, and that a piece of copperas (green iron-sulphate crystals) the size of a walnut was put into each barrel before it was sent to pubs in order to produce "a delightful golden coloured froth".[37]

Such public disputes, however, were of lesser importance than the overall economic situation. The boom ended suddenly in 1815 with the defeat of Napoleon at Waterloo and recession set in for more than a decade. The output from St James's Gate dropped dramatically: by 1820 sales had been halved to just under one million gallons. Competition for a declining market became more intense, resulting partly in an increase in the number of tied houses as brewers tried to secure their individual markets or took over bankrupt pubs in lieu of debts. Guinness had a few tied houses in Dublin but, unlike other brewers, especially in England, it was always opposed to running its own pubs. That turned out to be one of the foundations of its long-term success by allowing it to concentrate on brewing rather than tying up capital in public houses.

The sharp drop in sales of porter came at a particularly bad time for Arthur and it was touch-and-go whether or not the brewery would survive. The recession coincided with Arthur's growing involvement in banking, which took up a lot of his time and energies, notably when he was governor of the Bank of Ireland from 1820 to 1822. The position involved frequent visits to London in 1821 for negotiations with the government about the bank's monopoly and discussions with the Bank of England which led to it representing the Bank of Ireland in London. The interests of Arthur the banker were also at odds with, and took precedence over, those of Arthur the brewer. He supported a policy of "sound" money which restricted credit and led to revaluations of the Irish pound which, in turn, depressed exports. In 1826, he and another director, his mother's connection William Lunnell (not to be confused with his brother of the same name), represented the Bank of Ireland at a House of Commons select committee at which they argued the bank's case for currency stabilisation. The Irish pound was subsequently assimilated with sterling, causing further deflation in Ireland.

It appears that Arthur was in two minds about continuing as a brewer. Brewing looked at the time like a declining industry and for several years his interest veered strongly towards banking, while the day-to-day running of the brewery was largely in the hands of John Purser. Arthur also had substantial amounts of money invested outside the brewery: he and his family held about £5,000 worth of Bank of Ireland stock and had significant amounts languishing in government gilts, whose value had slumped after the Napoleonic wars.[38] St James's Gate was also suffering from a lack of capital investment. Its profits dropped disproportionately with declining sales: the less that was produced, the lower the profit rate on each barrel.

Profits were also being eaten into by the demands of his extended family, which included payments bequeathed by the first Arthur to his daughters, trusts set up by Arthur and his brothers for their own children, and the costs of bailing out relations who were in financial trouble. The most costly of these was Arthur's younger brother, Edward, whose ironworks in the villages of Palmerstown and Lucan, west of Dublin, had gone bankrupt. His creditors called in Arthur's guarantees, costing him £5,900 just as the recession took hold. Edward also used up the largest individual share, a quarter, of a family fund of £9,059 distributed between 1820 and 1825.

Thus, Arthur was dangerously short of cash at a critical point for the brewery. Apart from investments in industrialisation as steam engines and other machinery were introduced (the brewery had added a Watt steam engine between 1808 and 1810), its normal running required a considerable amount of capital. There was usually a gap of at least a year between buying malt and getting cash back from the sale of the porter brewed from it. The timescale was often longer because brewers ideally stockpiled large quantities of malt from a good harvest.

The recession, with its dramatic drop in sales, plus Arthur's other interests and demands on his money, almost destroyed the brewery. There must have been some temptation for him to abandon brewing and concentrate on his banking and insurance interests. As well as his involvement with the Bank of Ireland, he was one of the founders of Hibernian Insurance, Dublin's first fire insurance company, which he had called upon when his Hibernian Mills burned down in 1806. Up to 1815 the mills were an important part of the Guinness business and linked into the brewery's accounts. In 1828 they were leased to another miller.

Arthur wisely decided to stick with brewing and appears to have limited his banking activities after his period as governor. His response to the recession proved to be far-sighted and brave: he improved the quality of his porter and set about increasing exports to England with the appointment of agents in Liverpool, Bristol and London in the mid-1820s. The decisions went against the tide as other Dublin brewers cut costs and retrenched but they turned out to be inspired moves which also made use of technological developments. Increasing industrialisation helped to standardise the quality of beer and raise output through technical refinements like the use of patent brown malt, which was cheaper and more efficient. Technology also helped exports through the introduction of the first steam ships on the Irish Sea in 1824, reducing the passage time between Dublin and Liverpool from up to a week by sailing ship to a mere 14 hours.

The increase in the beer trade from Ireland to England during the boom had been halted by the recession. Guinness was only eighth in the list of Dublin brewers sending beer to Liverpool in 1825 and its trade with Bristol, England's second port up to 1820, was negligible compared with that of the Cork brewers. But its new agents in the English cities were spectacularly successful, notably in Bristol where Arthur had several relations, including the Lunnell family. Through Bristol, they moved their sales into London with the help of an effective local agent, Sparkes Moline, who successfully targeted a rising middle class prepared to pay sevenpence a bottle for its Extra Superior Porter. Later known as Double Stout, the higher-quality porter was a third stronger than "country porter" and sold at twopence more a bottle than local

English porter. ("Country porter" was brewed with extra hops to make it keep longer for distribution to rural areas; "town porter" was brewed for quick sale locally in Dublin.)

The Extra Superior Porter, also brewed with extra hops, was one of the secrets of Guinness's success in England. Its quality was far superior to that of English provincial brewers, who were its main rivals as London brewers withdrew from porter in favour of ale. A contemporary expert, W.L. Tizard, in his book *The Theory and Practice of Brewing*, praised Irish porter and contrasted its pleasant flavour with the "black, sulky beverage" produced by many English breweries. On drinking the latter, he wrote, the stranger experienced a shake as sudden and electrical as that which seized a spaniel when quitting the water.[39] The success of Guinness in England is evident from contemporary references to it by people like the newly elected Benjamin Disraeli. In a letter to his sister describing the "tumult and excitement" of Queen Victoria's first address to parliament in 1837, he told her that afterwards he "supped at the Carlton with a large part of the flower of our side off oysters, Guinness and broiled bones".[40]

St James's Gate concentrated more and more on producing Extra Superior Porter as sales rose in England. In 1820, the product accounted for only four per cent of its output but by 1840 it represented 82 per cent. The English brewers, however, had another explanation for the success of Irish porter in their market. They put it down to tax evasion by Irish brewers, specifically the dodging of the malt tax whose collection was more haphazard in Ireland than in England. Their accusation of tax evasion was supported by the fact that revenue from the malt tax in Ireland continued to decline, while the output of Irish breweries increased.[41]

The move into England left Guinness in a particularly strong position when the recession lifted at the end of the 1820s and helped it to raise its sales back to the 1816 level by 1833. By then, there were only two Dublin brewers, Guinness and Manders, still with a significant presence in the English market. When Arthur was beginning to fall out politically with Daniel O'Connell during the 1830s, the success of Guinness's English sales had increased its output to the point where it surpassed that of Beamish and Crawford, and Guinness became the largest of the 250-odd breweries in Ireland. It never relinquished that position. In contrast with 1811, when two-thirds of Guinness sales were in Dublin, by 1840 just over half the sales by volume and 60 per cent by value were in England and Scotland. Over the next 20 years, the brewery adroitly switched its markets to maximum effect and used its strengths to develop its weak areas. This strategy eventually achieved Arthur's long-term business goal of squeezing out its rivals in Dublin.

Arthur handed over day-to-day control of the company to the next generation about 1840 when he was 72. His brother Benjamin had died at the age of 49 in 1826, while his other brother William Lunnell had also retired from the brewery and died in 1842. First, however, Arthur had to deal with a sex scandal which threatened to break up the company, just as it was poised for greater success.

"It appears . . . to be your opinion that I am extremely wealthy and my children so independent that on making my will I shall have much property to spare for others," Arthur replied to a supplicant in 1844. "Now you have formed a very mistaken estimate on both points."[42]

While he was clearly well off, the lengthy recession and other financial uncertainties had prevented Arthur's wealth from growing in a steady upward line. There were also numerous demands on Arthur's money from his extended family for which, as he once put it, he was "unavoidably obliged to act as the family banker".[43] He himself had three sons and six daughters with his first wife, Anne Lee, who died in 1817 at the age of 43, when their youngest daughter was three. Four years later, Arthur, then aged 53, married a friend of Anne's, Maria Barker, whom he also outlived. His partners in the brewery, his brothers Benjamin and William Lunnell, had families, and his two other troublesome brothers, the bankrupt Edward and John Grattan, had seventeen children between them.

After 20 years in the Indian Army, John Grattan lost all his money in the collapse of Edward's iron foundries and thereafter was a financial burden on Arthur. As well as being "born again" during his time in India, John Grattan was father to a line of evangelical and missionary

Guinnesses and married his second wife, Jane Lucretia D'Esterre, the widow of a Dublin Corporation alderman who had been shot dead by Daniel O'Connell in a celebrated duel in 1815. Arthur gave John Grattan an allowance of about £200 a year for 30 years.[44] Arthur's sister Elizabeth's husband, Frederick Darley, also went bankrupt. Elizabeth's son, Richard Lyons Darley, left Dublin in some unspecified disgrace. In all, Arthur had in the region of 40 nieces and nephews, many of whom depended on him and, directly or indirectly, on the brewery for some of or all their livelihoods.

His brother Edward was probably the main financial drag on Arthur. After his business crashed, Edward fled to the Isle of Man to escape his creditors and imprisonment. Not only did he leave Arthur to pay off his debts with £5,900 in 1815, he also continued to send back to Dublin requests for more cash while he investigated the treatment of bankrupts in Scotland and France and dithered about which country he should move to. On one occasion, he explained how he wanted to move his wife, five children and two servants to a larger house in the Isle of Man because their existing one had no yard or garden. He eventually returned to Dublin after the death in 1826 of their brother Benjamin, who left him an annuity, and he worked for a while as a clerk in the brewery.

The next generation created its own quota of problem children, many of whom also worked in the brewery. The eldest daughter of the Reverend Hosea (Arthur's elder brother) and one of Edward's sons were mentally ill. One of John Grattan's less respectable sons was fired from the brewery because he was "addicted to mixing with degraded society" and sent to Bristol where the family helped to buy him a share in a rival brewery. The deal collapsed in acrimony and later when he was destitute he unsuccessfully sued his cousin, the then head of the Dublin brewery, over his dismissal (see Chapter 4). Two of Arthur's nephews – John, a son of Hosea, and John Burke, a son of his sister Mary Anne who had married a clergyman – were alcoholics.

But it was in Arthur's own family that the most shocking development occurred. His second son, Arthur Lee, a partner in the brewery and his putative successor in practice as well as in name, was a homosexual. In the climate of the times and in such an upright religious family, that fact must have been difficult to come to terms with. And it turned into a crisis when Arthur Lee had a brief affair with one of the brewery's clerks, Dion Boucicault, who was destined to become one of the most successful playwrights and theatrical figures of the second half of the nineteenth century in Britain and the United States.

The relationship was all the more shocking to the family because Boucicault was related to them through the web of marriages between the Guinnesses and the Darleys. Furthermore, Dion's mother, Anna Maria Darley, had already embarrassed her family and relations with a scandal over Dion's paternity. She was married to Samuel Boursiquot, a wine merchant in Dublin who was 26 years her senior. But Dion was widely believed to be the son of their lodger and her lover, Dionysius Lardner, a *bon viveur*, erratic scientist and lecturer in Trinity College Dublin, who later won fame as a science lecturer in London, was satirised by Thackeray as Dr Dionysus Diddler and described by Dickens as "that prince of humbugs", before running off to Paris with the wife of a dragoon guards officer who pursued him, flogged him and successfully sued him.[45]

Lardner and Anna Maria (known as Anne) were lovers from 1820, the seventh year of her marriage and the probable year of Dion's birth. (He variously claimed to have been born in December 1820 and December 1822, though the first date is more likely: the second was probably chosen for dramatic effect to enhance his emergence as a successful playwright at the age of 19 rather than 21.) Lardner's affair with Anne was exposed publicly when he sued his own wife for divorce 12 years after they had separated, after discovering that she was living with someone else. Anne was among those called to give evidence in the sensational case in London in 1832. The tenor of the hearing is evident from the testimony of servants who told of seeing Lardner leaving Anne's holiday home by the back door early in the morning, walk around the house and knock at the front door as though he was just arriving.

There is little doubt that Lardner was Dion's father. The future playwright was christened Dionysius Lardner Boursiquot[46] and Lardner paid for his education and had him apprenticed to himself as an engineer in London after the family moved there. Dion hated engineering and Lardner in equal measure and ran away to become an actor. Using the name Leo Moreton, so that his family would not trace him, he acted in theatres in Cheltenham, Brighton and Bristol before returning to London where his first play, *Lodgings to Let*, was staged for one night in March 1839. Characteristically, he played the part of Tim Donoghue, who was described in the script as "an Irish Emigrant and a Genius of the first rate". The play was not a success and shortly afterwards Dion was back in Dublin where his mother had returned to run a boarding house after her relationship with Lardner ended in 1836. Lardner had also stopped financing Dion's education when he (Lardner) ran off to Paris with his latest lover.

Anne persuaded the Guinnesses to give Dion a job in the brewery as a clerk.[47] Arthur Lee was then in his early forties and a partner in the brewery with his younger brother, Benjamin Lee, and their father. He lived at St James's Gate and was as involved in the running of the brewery as his brother, although he appears to have been in dispute with them over his debts. But it was his homosexual relationship with Boucicault which precipitated a major crisis in the family. Boucicault later described himself physically at this period when he was in his late teens and about to become a successful playwright. In an article in the *North American Review* on "The Debut of a Dramatist", he wrote of himself in the third person as being "something older than a boy and younger than a man. His slim figure, broad in the shoulders, thin in the flank; his black hair and grey-blue eyes; his complexion, as fair as that of a girl, indicate the Irish race."[48]

The details of his affair with Arthur Lee or how it came to scandalise the family are hazy: all records concerning it were removed from St James's Gate by family members more than a century later in the 1950s, indicating the residue left generations later by the extent of the scandal. While the Guinnesses occasionally drew attention to their relationship with Dion's uncle, the minor poet George Darley, they rarely claimed their connection with Dion, a much more successful literary figure. A biography of George Darley, published in 1928, refers to Dion in a single sentence as the son of George's sister, Anne.[49]

However, the relationship between Arthur Lee and Dion did not last very long. Dion appears to have been paid off by the family: there are suggestions that he blackmailed Arthur Lee or he may have been simply given money to go away. Either way, he returned to London in May 1840 unusually flush with cash and claiming publicly to be Arthur Guinness's heir. He became a student at a dramatic academy in Dean Street, booked into a hotel in Newman Street, bought himself a horse and cab and entertained his friends lavishly. Dion maintained that Arthur was paying for his tuition but the largesse did not last long: either Arthur stopped paying him or he used up all the money he had received. He was soon penniless again and subsequently complained that Guinness had cut him off from his promised fortune.[50] Within a year, however, Boucicault had written his first successful play, *London Assurance*, and never looked back. He went on to marry twice and move to the United States, where he was a major success. The Dictionary of National Biography summed up his life sniffily (and with an interesting *non-sequitur*): "Boucicault's brilliant literary and histrionic qualities were not supported by any very rigorous moral code. He was for a time a strong advocate of Irish home rule."[51]

In Dublin, meanwhile, the crisis led to discussions about winding up the brewery. It was the period after Arthur's political falling-out with O'Connell when the brewery was under physical attack and when its sales in England were falling suddenly because of recession there. John Grattan junior had recently been fired for his "low habits" and mixing with "degraded company". (He was given an annuity of £70 for seven years on condition that he did not engage in activities in Dublin such as "teaching gymnasium or music"; he was, however, free to work for other brewers.)[52] Arthur's second wife, Maria, had died, he was in his early seventies and living in Beaumont House with his unmarried daughter. He had led a full and eventful life and, perhaps, was tired.

However, his two sons were anxious to continue the brewery and a compromise was agreed. Arthur Lee voluntarily withdrew from the partnership, leaving the brewery's capital intact but receiving a payment of £12,000 and other shares. In an apologetic note to his father, he said it was impossible to justify his conduct to him but thanked him for his forgiveness and kindness. "Believe me above all that 'for worlds' I would not hurt your mind, if I could avoid it – of all the living. Your feelings are most sacred to me, this situation, in which I have placed myself, has long caused me the acutest pain & your wishes on the subject must be *religiously* obeyed by me," he wrote.[53]

Arthur Lee moved out of the brewery to Stillorgan Park, south of Dublin and a long way at the time from the north-side areas of the city favoured by the family. He bought and rebuilt Stillorgan House, an early eighteenth-century mansion in a rural area of estates and villas overlooking the sea and revived its former reputation for lavish hospitality during the 20 years he spent there.[54] He wrote nature verses, signed his letters with drawings of young Greek gods and continued to cause financial and political embarrassments to his family. He was not cut off from them, however; he was rescued financially by them again in the late 1840s; and he was made a trustee of the properties in Leixlip which the first Arthur had accumulated in the previous century. Arthur Lee also continued his contacts with the Darleys, playing host at Stillorgan Park to Dion's uncle George, the poet, who described him as "amiable, excellent A.L.", for several months in 1844.[55] When he sold the house in 1860, he hired a harper to play funeral dirges while the contents were auctioned. After his departure, the house fell into ruin while Arthur Lee moved farther south and died at Roundwood House in County Wicklow on 11 January 1863.

Meanwhile, the agreement over Arthur Lee's departure from the brewery created another problem with John Purser junior, the fourth member of the partnership. Purser had spent his whole working life at St James's Gate, beginning as an apprentice brewer in 1799. Along with his father, he had become a partner in the brewery in 1820 and was a central figure in its day-to-day administration. With Arthur Lee's departure, he sought a larger share in the brewery, arguing that the second Arthur's imminent retirement would also increase his workload. His demands briefly soured relations between the families and was firmly refused by Arthur, who pointed out that Purser had received £28,809 from the partnership over seven years.

The crisis prompted by Arthur Lee's relationship with Dion Boucicault effectively marked the end of Arthur's close involvement in the running of the brewery. Thereafter, it was run by his third son, Benjamin Lee, and John Purser junior, although Arthur continued to take an overview and offer advice even while spending considerable periods in Torquay on the south coast of England. He went on to survive all but one of his siblings and died at home in Beaumont on 9 June 1855 at the age of 87. His family tried to carry out his wish that his funeral be private, but a large crowd turned up. His coffin was borne from his home by a hearse drawn by six horses and "attended by mutes bearing wands and mourning badges". Almost a hundred carriages carrying the lord mayor, clergy, gentry, judges, merchants and the heads of the chief manufacturing and trading firms joined the procession through Dublin city centre to Mount Jerome cemetery in the suburb of Harold's Cross. Also in the procession was a group of female orphans and their matron, paying tribute to their "best benefactor".[56]

Arthur left £180,000 in his will, although that was considerably less than the full value of his estate, since it did not include the brewery or some family trusts. As in the previous generation, his eldest son, William Smythe Guinness, was a clergyman and so was left out of the business, inheriting Beaumont House in Dublin (which had reverted to Arthur from his elder brother Hosea). William's son, Arthur William, was left a country estate in County Wexford and provided with £7,500 to develop it. The money, however, was to be controlled by two of Arthur's three executors, his son Benjamin Lee and his nephew, William Frederick Darley, the barrister son of Alderman Darley. The third executor was Sir Edmund Waller, the husband of Arthur's youngest daughter, Rebecca.

A summary of Arthur's will listed up to 50 other relatives, including nephews, nieces, grandchildren, grandnephews and grandnieces who received cash amounts of about £500 each. Mourning rings were also to be distributed to a handful of relatives and friends, including Arthur Lee and his "old friend and partner" John Purser. But the main beneficiary of his lifetime's work was his third son, Benjamin Lee Guinness, who was now positioned to become the first Guinness millionaire.

CHAPTER FOUR

The First Millionaire

"His XX labels . . . are the only famous literary works which he has left behind him; and they are read the world over with thick tongues, bloated countenances, bloodshot eyes, and staggering gait."

Temperance campaigner J.A. MOWATT on Benjamin Lee Guinness

Portraits of Benjamin Lee Guinness in later life show a well-satisfied and patrician Victorian businessman and he certainly had every reason to be satisfied. He became the sole owner of the largest porter brewery in the world and, by common consent, the richest man in Ireland; he was feted as a philanthropist; a lord mayor of Dublin; a Conservative MP for the city; and, a year before his death, a baronet. He oversaw a huge expansion in the family business and was an effective administrator but, paradoxically, he was probably a less able businessman than his father or grandfather or than the son who succeeded him. In that respect, he was an example of a common phenomenon in dynasties, whereby the generation which reaps the greatest reward is less gifted than the preceding ones which laid the groundwork. The first Arthur Guinness set up the brewery at a time of great possibilities and equally great dangers. The second Arthur Guinness consolidated its position and developed it in the face of severe financial and political challenges. By finding himself in the right place at the right time, Benjamin Lee Guinness garnered the full benefit of the financial power, political position and social status that his forebears had created.

He lived almost all his life in the shadow of his father who, even after his retirement, continued to exert a decisive influence on the running of the brewery. Benjamin Lee began working in St James's Gate when he was 16; he was over 40 when he took nominal control of the brewery and 57 when his father died. Unlike his older brothers, William Smythe and Arthur Lee, he did not go to university and found himself in sole control of the family firm by a series of accidents. As in the previous generation, William Smythe, the eldest brother, went into religion and Arthur Lee ruled himself out of his inheritance with his lifestyle. William Smythe officially took on the names Lee and Grattan in memory of two of his ancestors (his grandfather, the original Benjamin Lee, and his grandmother, Elizabeth Whitmore's niece, Mary Grattan) from whom he had inherited property. He also went one better than his brother, Benjamin Lee, in following their father's advice to keep the money in the family. William Smyth was married twice, both times to first cousins. Benjamin Lee took the same advice, marrying his first cousin Elizabeth, known as Bessie, a daughter of his bankrupt Uncle Edward.

With the exclusion of his two brothers from the brewery, Benjamin Lee became one of its three partners, along with his father and John Purser. After his father's and Purser's deaths, he became the sole owner, helped by the fact that Purser's son, John Tertius Purser, had religious scruples about profiting from the sale of alcohol. That apparently prevented him from inheriting his father's share of the partnership but John Tertius Purser nevertheless became the head brewer at James's Gate. He salved his conscience by taking a royalty off every barrel of porter produced rather than a share in the profits. That ensured a comfortable life but caused the Pursers to miss out on a major share in the explosion of Guinness wealth in the next generation. Meanwhile, his scruples meant that one Guinness, Benjamin Lee, found himself in sole control of the brewery and its growing fortune.

In spite of the undoubted strength of their religion, the Guinnesses were never troubled by scruples over making a fortune out of alcohol. Given their religious principles, they would have been prime candidates to have become involved in the growing nineteenth-century temperance movement had they been involved in any other business. Indeed, one of Benjamin Lee's first cousins, the Reverend Henry Grattan Guinness, later became a prominent evangelical preacher and critic of intemperance. He conveniently concentrated most of his efforts in England, Wales and the United States, with occasional tours of Ireland – which did not endear him to his brewing cousins – and he eventually set up training colleges for missionaries in Dublin and Harley House in London. The Reverend Henry, who was much younger than Benjamin Lee, was the son of John Grattan Guinness (the second Arthur's youngest brother) and his second wife Jane D'Esterre (the widow of Daniel O'Connell's duel victim).

The temperance movement, however, was among the challenges facing Benjamin Lee when his father retired in 1840 and continued to dog him throughout his stewardship of the company. Inspired by example from the United States, it had taken root among the Irish Protestant churches and had been steadily gaining momentum over the previous decade. Its underlying aims included political stability, economic development and proselytising. In the early 1830s particularly, the temperance movement was seen as part of the effort by Protestants to protect their socio-economic position in Ireland.[1] Whiskey, the drink of the masses, was their main target and was blamed for many of Ireland's ills, ranging from widespread poverty to the atrocities committed during the 1798 rebellion. Beer was most popular among the working and labouring class while wine remained the favoured form of alcohol in high society and among the professional and commercial classes. While it focused exclusively on distilling, the temperance movement posed no threat to Guinness or other brewers and could only, as in previous generations, help them to expand their market. However, the movement was split, partly along religious lines, between moderates who campaigned against whiskey while considering their own tipples of wine and beer to be wholesome (in moderation, of course) and the total abstainers who agitated against all alcohol. Neither side was making much headway until Father Theobald Mathew burst upon the scene in Cork in 1838.

A Capuchin friar from a landed family who struck a chord with the poor, Fr Mathew managed during four years of preaching and touring to persuade half the entire population of Ireland to pledge themselves – at least nominally – to total abstinence from all alcohol. Sales of legal whiskey plummeted, dropping from about 11 million gallons in 1839 to 5.3 million gallons in 1842, while the detection of home-distilling poteen stills dropped from 3,000 a year to a low of under 900.[2] The breweries were also hit, with total production dropping over the same period from 900,000 barrels to 500,000 barrels, the lowest level in the nineteenth century. Guinness, however, emerged practically unscathed by the enthusiasm for "the pledge". Fr Mathew's campaign was least successful in Dublin, Guinness's main Irish market, partly because of the size and importance of the drink industry in the capital. By contrast, the Cork-based Beamish and Crawford, Guinness's main Irish rival, saw its output cut by 40 per cent. Guinness's sales did fall by nearly a fifth between 1839 and 1843 but the decline was almost entirely in England and the result of an economic depression there.[3]

In the long run, Fr Mathew's crusade probably helped brewers in general by the damage it did to the distilleries and Guinness most of all by the greater impact it had on other brewers like Beamish and Crawford. After five years, the campaign itself fizzled out almost as suddenly as it had begun. Against Fr Mathew's best efforts, it became politicised and a part of the growing nationalist movement, entangled by Daniel O'Connell in his own mass movement for repeal of the union. It was also hamstrung with financial problems and rapidly lost momentum before the middle of the 1840s. Thereafter, temperance campaigners tended to concentrate their efforts on changing the law in the belief that curbing the sale of liquor would be more effective than persuading drinkers to reform themselves. One result in the following decades was the increasing identification of the Conservative Party with brewers and the Liberals with temperance. Not surprisingly, the Guinnesses involved themselves more and more with the former, leaving the Irish Temperance League appalled when Dublin's voters eventually elected Benjamin Lee as their Conservative MP.

Meanwhile, Guinness was well placed to take advantage of economic developments following the biggest catastrophe in nineteenth-century Ireland: the famine of the late 1840s in which up to one million people died of starvation and its associated diseases while a further million fled the country. The famine, following the failures of the potato crops from 1845 to 1849, had most impact in the west and south of the country. But the death rate rose all over the island, affecting the east coast by the increases in diseases associated with the famine. The elderly Arthur Guinness expressed his horror at the state of Ireland in a letter to Benjamin Lee from Torquay, where he was convalescing, asking him how they might be able to help in the relief work and declaring that "my purse is open to the call".[4] However, the Guinnesses made no substantial contribution to famine relief or, if they did, they channelled it privately through Protestant relief committees, some of which used the famine as an opportunity to proselytise. They did look after some of their own employees, giving "Gentlemen" on the brewery staff a "small gift" for several years to help them cope with the rise in prices caused by the famine. In Stillorgan Park, Arthur Lee's retainers were so grateful for his protection during that period that they erected a small obelisk of Connemara marble in the grounds "to mark the veneration of his faithfull labourers who in a period of dire distress were protected by his generous liberality from the prevailing destitution". Arthur Lee's beneficence is cited in the classic account of the famine, *The Great Hunger* by Cecil Woodham Smith, as evidence that there were "good landlords" who helped their tenants and, coincidentally, burnished the family's historical reputation for philanthropy by implying that they were prominent in famine relief, which was not merited in this instance. Unlike some other prominent and wealthy Dublin business families, there is no evidence that the Guinnesses were involved in famine relief other than in a very small way, a fact that was clear to contemporaries.

Contrary to what might have been expected, the consumption and sales of beer went up in Ireland during the famine years: neither the market for beer nor its consumers were in the areas or amongst the groups most affected by the potato blight. Indeed, the famine proved to be a boon for Guinness and one of the major reasons for its phenomenal growth during the following decade. In essence, it helped to create a crucial market for its porter by creating a cash economy to replace the barter and subsistence economy in the rural areas decimated by starvation. The famine was followed by unprecedented economic growth in rural areas. The huge drop in population caused a rise in wages, with farm labourers earning twice and three times as much as before the famine: daily wages went up from as little as 6d (2.5p) a day to 1/6d (7.5p) a day and living standards rose significantly as a cash economy took over from what had been largely a barter economy.[5]

The railways came to Ireland from the mid-1840s on, coinciding with the second phase of railway-building mania in England. They opened up the countryside to more efficient commercial communications, with a thousand miles of track within ten years. At the same time, the distilleries, already wilting from Fr Mathew's total abstinence campaign, were hit further by sharp rises in excise duties in the 1850s. The combination of circumstances allowed beer, particularly Guinness, to supplant whiskey as the popular drink in rural areas. The Guinnesses were investors in the railways which they then used to maximum effect to dominate this growing, new rural market. Experience in dealing with the canal companies helped them to negotiate tough deals with the railways. Unlike the Dublin beer market, where prices were controlled by a brewers' agreement, the rural market was open to unhindered competition and they took full advantage of it. The extent to which Guinness used its financial muscle with the railway companies was evident from the complaints by Cork brewers that Guinness was able, through preferential rail rates, to undercut their porter prices in their neighbouring county of Kerry.[6]

The concentration on the rural market paid off handsomely, both immediately and in the longer term. It led to a rapid growth of sales in rural areas to the extent that, by 1865, shortly before Benjamin Lee's death, the Irish market as a whole once again made up the bulk of Guinness sales. Some 63,000 hogsheads of porter were sold in rural areas, half of them the more expensive double stout, while 49,000 hogsheads were sold in Dublin. In England, 94,000 hogsheads were sold.[7] In total, three-quarters of the Irish beer sold in Ireland outside of Dublin came from St James's Gate, while it supplied nearly half the city's beer and half of the Irish beer exports to Britain. In the longer term, the expansion of the rural market allowed Benjamin Lee's successors to undercut other brewers in Dublin, squeeze some of them out of business and dominate the city's market as well.

Under Benjamin Lee's direction Guinness also continued its emphasis on marketing and on protecting the identity of its porter. His main, and enduring, contribution to this aspect of the brewery's activities was to adopt the harp as its trademark in 1862. The particular style of harp was modelled on the O'Neill harp – also known as the Brian Boru harp after the Irish leader who defeated the Vikings at the Battle of Clontarf in 1014 – in the library of Trinity College Dublin. The distinctive Guinness label (and close control over its use) was an important marketing tool at a time when publicans bottled and labelled the stout which they bought in barrels. As well as the huge expansion throughout the Irish countryside, Guinness benefited from falls in the price of raw materials and in the costs of cross-channel transport.

The rising tide of profits was reflected in Benjamin Lee's increasingly affluent lifestyle. He and Arthur Lee had bought 52 acres north of the city, not far from Beaumont House, in 1835. He bought out Arthur Lee two years later when he married his cousin Bessie and built a large mansion on the site, which he named St Anne's after a nearby holy well. Among the features he built there was an ornamental tower and bridge over the entrance drive to mark the birth of their first child, Anne, in 1839. He extended the estate by buying up surrounding areas, including land which had a right of way that allowed locals to walk from the village of Raheny to the sea. He tried and failed to close it but managed to keep the locals out of sight by converting the pathway into a deep trench, edged with a fence, and built tunnels for it beneath the ornamental avenues on his expanding estate.[8]

He also had a townhouse near the brewery in Thomas Street which he sold in 1856 to buy a house in the more fashionable St Stephen's Green. Number 80 there had been designed by Richard Cassels or Castle, one of the major architects of Georgian Dublin, in the early eighteenth century and had been the home of a succession of barristers, notably John Philpot Curran, who defended many of the United Irishmen and was the father of Sarah Curran, the fiancée of the executed republican Robert Emmet. It had last changed hands in 1819 for £4,500 but Benjamin Lee bought it for the bargain price of £2,500 from its debt-ridden owners through the Commissioners of Encumbered Estates.[9] Six years later, he bought the house next door and, acting as an amateur architect, merged the two behind a Portland Stone façade of his own design. While he and his family divided their time between St Anne's and St Stephen's Green, Benjamin Lee also set about acquiring a country estate in the west of Ireland. As a telling indication of his wealth at this stage, he proposed to spend what he described as "a small sum . . . (say £20,000 to £30,000)"[10] to buy land in County Mayo, eventually purchasing the Ashford estate at Cong on the border with County Galway which had been the home of the Brownes. Around the same period, the average family income of peasants in County Mayo was between £30 and £40 a year, while labourers in St James's Gate earned 13 shillings (65 pence) a week or just under £34 a year.

—⦿⦿⦿—

His rapidly growing, and increasingly visible, wealth inevitably gave Benjamin Lee a public profile which was heightened by his father's activities behind the scenes. Arthur's unease about municipal reforms, which led him to break with Daniel O'Connell in 1837, turned out to have been justified from his perspective. O'Connell and his supporters swept the board in elections to the reformed corporation in Dublin in 1841, winning 47 of the 60 seats. O'Connell became the city's first Catholic mayor since 1688 and turned the council into a surrogate Irish parliament and a platform to promote repeal of the union. As he stepped up the pressure for repeal, the political tensions overflowed once more into commerce but the effects, once again, were short-lived.

Arthur, however, was more persistent in his opposition to the new council, particularly as time went on. Sectarian tensions in nineteenth-century Dublin were focused on fierce disputes in the city council, unlike Belfast where they tended to erupt in street violence.[11] Certainly, the reform of the corporation brought all the political tensions of the time into city hall. It got to the point, particularly after O'Connell's death in 1847, where the police were in regular attendance as verbal disputes got out of hand and legal writs between councillors became almost as common as points of order. Dublin Corporation, *The Times* declared in 1850, was "the greatest political nuisance ever inflicted on a civil community". No admirer of O'Connell, it noted that

> . . . as long as O'Connell was there to control and perhaps browbeat the assembly, the semblance of decency was at least preserved, and the Assembly-house had not sunk below the level of a cockpit or bear-garden, requiring the permanent presence of a body of police to keep the members from tearing each other's eyes out.[12]

The acrimony had reached such a stage by 1850 that the corporation was paralysed by political, procedural and legal wrangles between the lord mayor, John Reynolds, who was also the Repeal MP for Dublin, and the conservative minority on the council. The city's merchants were appalled by the carry-on and the Chamber of Commerce, under Arthur's leadership, took a leading role in trying to turn it into a more workmanlike body which would also pay more attention to their interests. Part of the plan involved putting up more of their members as candidates, including Francis Codd, the Catholic secretary of the chamber and a long-time associate of Arthur.

It was in this context that Benjamin Lee contested the municipal election in November 1850. He had previously had little direct involvement in politics and was seen to be running at the behest of his aged father. The election campaign was relatively low-key, with rare shows of unanimity on issues like the maintenance of the vice-regal office in Dublin. Both repealers and those who favoured the status quo opposed the move to abolish the office, although for different reasons: every candidate, including Benjamin Lee, supported the campaign to keep it.

The only hiccup in his election campaign was caused by the Reverend Thomas Brady, the Catholic archdeacon in the diocese of Kilmore. In a letter published in the *Freeman's Journal*, he complained that Guinness, unlike other Protestant businessmen, had refused to donate any money to the building of a Catholic chapel and school in a poor parish in County Cavan. "I have not heard them refuse any of the vast sums of Catholic money they annually receive for their XX [double stout]," he wrote.

Fr Brady's letter was certainly politically motivated, as subsequent events illustrated. The Guinnesses did not react publicly but, as usual, took steps behind the scenes to limit the potential electoral damage. Two letters from Catholics appeared in the newspapers extolling the Guinnesses' generosity: a former employee at St James's Gate denied that they showed any prejudice against Catholics and said they employed 200 Catholics and donated £3,000 to £4,000 a year to charities, including Catholic schools. The Catholic curate in St James's parish, which included the brewery, wrote of receiving donations of £3 a year for his schools.

Fr Brady then revealed that an "influential gentleman" had called on him after he had sent his letter to two newspapers and asked him to suppress or delay its publication. The two newspapers, the *Freeman's Journal* and the *Dublin Evening Post* (both "Catholic" papers), had also asked him to suppress the letter, he claimed. Several days later, he had received £2 from "a respectable source" but had returned it "as I considered it would be an act of meanness on my part to accept a subscription not freely given but through fear, for no contribution whatever was offered until my letter was in type". The *Freeman's Journal* quickly denied that anybody had attempted to stop them publishing his letter and regretted that this "unpleasant controversy" had arisen. But it admitted that it had delayed publication of the letter in order to suggest to Fr Brady that it might be "misunderstood". After explaining their views to him, the newspaper published it.

(A story told about Benjamin Lee later said he was approached by someone raising funds to build a new Presbyterian Church but replied that he could not help Dissenters. However, he asked, what were they going to do with the old church? Knock it down, he was told. He said he would contribute to that.)[13]

The minor controversy did Benjamin Lee no political damage: he headed the poll in what Fr Brady had described as the "Catholic constituency" of Usher's Quay. His election and the composition of the new council was a strong testimonial to Arthur's and the Chamber of Commerce's influence and underlined the changed political climate of the post-repeal and post-famine era. The council was heavily influenced by successful businessmen of both religious and political persuasions: some 14 of the new councillors were directors of banks or railways or were members of the Chamber of Commerce. Its political tenor was also dramatically different to that of its predecessor, which had had 46 Catholics (all Repealers) and 14 Protestants (all Conservatives). Of the newly elected, according to one breakdown, 32 were Protestants (24 Conservatives and eight Whigs) and 28 Catholics (22 Repealers and six Whigs).[14]

John Reynolds, the outgoing mayor, who was among the repealers re-elected, declared his intention of standing again for the office. He was quickly outmanoeuvred by a backroom deal encompassing almost everyone else. Within days, 53 of the 60 councillors signed a public advertisement appealing to Benjamin Lee to take the office. They added that, in making the request, "we desire to associate a great public advantage with a tribute of respect and regard to your venerated Father". Benjamin Lee admitted that he had been little engaged in public life but added that he could not but yield to such an invitation. Reynolds withdrew his candidacy and Benjamin Lee was elected Lord Mayor for 1851 in a show of rare unanimity. His fellow alderman, the Whig distiller George Roe, proposed him with tributes to the family's character and to the central role Arthur played in electing the new council. He said:

> We all know the aid and assistance which [Arthur] rendered to the party who originated this corporation. We know that to him chiefly we are indebted for bringing it to completion with such evident success; and I assure you, I believe, that if Arthur Guinness were somewhat junior in years to what he is, he would have offered himself as a candidate for municipal honours.[15]

His seconder, another brewer, John D'Arcy (who was to succeed Benjamin Lee as lord mayor) thanked him for taking the office in spite of his distaste for public life. The previous mayor, John Reynolds, promised his full support and prompted laughter by noting that "after a storm comes a calm". Benjamin Lee regretted he did not have a greater knowledge of public life but added that he would endeavour to smooth political and other differences and promote harmony and goodwill.

The backroom deal under which Benjamin Lee took the chair brought a higher degree of order to the council for the following decade. Under it, most groups on the council agreed to alternate the mayoralty every year between a Catholic and a Protestant. The verbal agreement continued in force for almost three decades in spite of periodic rows over whether the holder of the office should be decided simply by his religion or by his politics. Catholics, who subsequently dominated the council, occasionally vetoed the election of Conservative Protestants in favour of Liberal Protestants.

Meanwhile, Benjamin Lee was installed in the new year with a municipal procession through the city streets, which *The Times* reported, "eclipsed anything that had been seen since the palmy days of the old 'Orange' corporation and the day, so far as business was affected, was to all intents observed as a holiday". Three weeks later, his inaugural banquet in the King's Room of the Mansion House confirmed the Guinnesses' position near the pinnacle of Irish society and evoked comparisons with King George IV's banquet in the building some 30 years earlier. The 400 guests included everybody who was anybody from the Lord Lieutenant, Lord Caradon, down. An anonymous reporter from the *Freeman's Journal* was left reaching for superlatives to describe the atmosphere and falling back on the repeated use of "gorgeous". The Mansion House had been redecorated for the event and Benjamin Lee spent his own money freely on the occasion. Guests entering the King's Room were faced with a large illuminated crown with the initials VR displayed in gas jets. The gallery, in which a military band played, was covered with evergreens and bouquets; the room's panels were festooned with wreaths of ivy and laurel and myriads of coloured lamps. Over the entrance, the lord mayor's coat of arms, surmounted by the Guinness family crest and quartered with the city arms, was also illuminated by gas jets. The tables were loaded with silver epergnes and candelabras, cut-glass centrepieces with bouquets of artificial flowers and "tasteful ornaments" in raised sugar. Many of the men were in uniform: Benjamin Lee was in his robes of office and the Lord Lieutenant, seated at his right at the raised top table, wore the Windsor uniform of blue and gold with the vice-regal star and collar of St Patrick. The waiters wore the lord mayor's liveries.

To drink, the guests had "wine of the finest quality and in greatest profusion" but, apparently, no porter. The extensive menu included fish, veal, lamb, beef, ham, chicken, turkey, pigeon, cheese, cakes, tarts, bananas, oranges and cherries. But the food seemingly was not on a par with the sumptuousness of the setting: "We are compelled to add that there was a general and very freely expressed opinion that the parties intrusted with the getting-up of the banquet did not do justice with the more than munificent expenditure which the Lord Mayor is known to have incurred on this occasion," the newspaper commented.

Among the nobles, the government officials, legal dignitaries and the two archbishops of Dublin at the banquet, there were only two other members of the Guinness family, the new lord mayor's "black sheep" brother Arthur Lee and his nephew, also Benjamin. Benjamin Lee explained his wife, Bessie's, absence on the grounds that "delicate health [precluded her] from enjoying public society". His father, he said, had not been kept away by illness alone but because he felt that he could not, at his advanced age and weak health, "sustain the kind reception which he was sure to meet".

It was all a long way from the time the new lord mayor's grandfather upset his fellow members of the council by suggesting that the annual banquet be abolished and the money saved be donated to deserving institutions.

His duties as lord mayor took Benjamin Lee regularly to London with council petitions for the House of Commons and, on one occasion, to Buckingham Palace, where he presented Queen Victoria with a petition against the plan to abolish the viceregal office in Ireland. Her reply was carefully non-committal. In the council chamber, no longer the "bear-pit" of previous years, he was workmanlike in chairing meetings and expressing opinions on routine business from the state of the city's weighbridges to the future of old corporation retainers. His fellow councillors took advantage of one of his absences in London to spare him embarrassment while raising the lord mayor's salary from £1,000 a year to £2,500. The proposers suggested that the rise was appropriate during the mayoralty of "a gentleman to whom salary was of little, if any, consideration". The proposal was adopted unanimously but raised a storm of protest among ratepayers, fanned by editorial writers: the *Freeman's Journal* loftily declared that the time had passed "when the dignity of a municipal institution can be maintained by turtle and champagne". Councillors backed off and eventually fixed the salary at a compromise of £2,000. Back from London, Benjamin Lee was distinctly unimpressed by the penny-pinching attitudes of the ratepayers and newspapers. While offering to continue on the existing salary, he argued that £2,500 was not too much and any lord mayor would find he had spent that much on the office before his inauguration "without waiting for champagne and turtle". He added that "continually talking of their poverty and cribbing about a sum of £1,500 a year" was not calculated to elevate the council in the eyes of the public.

Overall, Benjamin Lee's period in office repaid the faith pinned upon his unanimous selection. He raised the image of the lord mayoralty, campaigned for commercial causes, such as the provision of a regular steamer service from Galway to the US, and managed to calm political tensions in Dublin. He was undoubtedly helped by his wealth and by the fact that the Guinness name commanded respect across the sectarian and political divisions. It also gave him a taste for public life while encouraging others to try to capitalise on his political standing.

The city's Conservatives were eager to draft him as their candidate for the parliamentary elections in 1852. His father, however, used his influence to stop him standing. The governor of the Bank of Ireland, John Barlow, asked Arthur to persuade him to stand as a Conservative but Arthur refused, citing the delicate health of Benjamin Lee's wife and the heavy demands on his time from family pressures.[16] He also advised Benjamin Lee strongly against becoming totally identified with one party because of the dangers posed by too close a political identification for the brewery. In this, as in much else, Benjamin Lee took his advice and did not accept the invitation.

—◦◦◦◦—

The family pressures alluded to by Arthur undoubtedly included the handful of relations who continued to be a source of financial demands and social embarrassment. The main one remained Benjamin's brother, Arthur Lee, who was still drawing money to support his lifestyle in Stillorgan, although he was at odds with the family's political views. His cousin, John Grattan junior, also continued to be a thorn in the family's side after his dismissal from the brewery and his effective banishment to England. His sacking was not entirely painful as the family gave him an income of £70 a year for seven years and £100 a year for three further years. But John Grattan had become involved in what was effectively a financial scam with a brewery he had bought with a partner in Bristol.

The family supported his venture at first. His own father, John Grattan senior, gave him £800, while his Uncle Arthur offered him £400 to help him pay his half of the purchase price. Arthur, however, was justifiably outraged when he discovered that the brewery was advertising itself as Guinness & Co., Ale and Porter Brewers. He insisted that it be known by the name of the partners John Grattan Guinness and William Blake. Blake refused, Arthur withdrew his £400, and the project collapsed.

The annual payments continued for 12 years and were then stopped because of John Grattan's behaviour, which included breaking windows in his father's home. Cut off finally and more or less destitute, John Grattan took Benjamin Lee to court in 1858, claiming that his £100 a year was not a hand-out to a poor relation but a contractual result of his agreement not to proceed with the Bristol brewery.[17] He appeared in court, representing himself because he could not afford a lawyer, and cutting a sad figure as he broke down and "became abstracted" while outlining his case to the jury. But he got little sympathy from either Benjamin Lee or the judge. In evidence, Benjamin Lee denied that there had been any contract and quoted letters describing the payments as a benevolent gift while John Grattan was seeking a job. Arthur had become so angry with John Grattan after his attempt to cash in on the Guinness name that he refused to communicate directly with him. Instead, he continued to make annual payments through John Grattan senior and, after his death, through one of John Grattan's brothers. In one of his letters, Arthur wrote of John Grattan's "wretched mind" and hoped that his "weak and wretched intellect might be healed".

Presented in court with a letter of recommendation he had once given John Grattan, Benjamin Lee said he had been trying to help him and had not known at the time that his "habits were so low" and that he was "addicted to mixing with degraded company". He also complained of John Grattan's attempts to serve summonses on him: he had twice forced his way into Benjamin Lee's house in St Stephen's Green, once when he himself was seriously ill and a second time when he had company. On a third occasion, John Grattan had turned up at St Anne's during an evening party for 40 or 50 people and had "frightened the servants" before Benjamin Lee had him ejected.

The judge refused to let the case go to the jury, declaring that John Grattan had not the slightest grounds either in law or as a matter of personal honour for impeaching the high character of Benjamin Lee. He ordered John Grattan to pay the legal costs of the case and ended the hearing amidst his distraught protestations that he had no money.

———<small>∞∞∞</small>———

The temptation to become more involved in politics eventually proved irresistible to Benjamin Lee after his father died and as his wealth grew, bringing with it a desire to contribute to some major public projects and a heightened respect for his views. His public persona became closely identified with the promotion of Irish goods, evolving a sort of economic nationalism that successfully bridged political divisions and enhanced the Guinness reputation as a worthy symbol of all that was best in Dublin life. All these strands came together in the early 1860s with his involvement in two high-profile projects which led, inexorably, to his election as MP for Dublin and a title. The major one was the restoration of St Patrick's, the national cathedral of the Church of Ireland, and the second was the Dublin Exhibition Palace and Winter Garden Company, which aimed to provide a permanent exhibition of Irish arts and goods along with reading rooms and a gas-lit winter garden.

St Patrick's, built on a marsh in 1190, was in danger of collapse by the mid-nineteenth century. The heavy roof had sunk several inches as the walls crumbled and pillars cracked; piles of rubble were strewn alongside the walls and the interior was disfigured by haphazard repairs and props. The state of the building had reduced religious services to only once a week. There had been several attempts to save the cathedral from collapse, including the preparation of restoration plans by a committee in the 1840s, but an appeal for funds had raised only £3,000. Nothing other than piecemeal repairs had been attempted until 1860, when Benjamin Lee stepped in and offered to fund a complete restoration on condition that he was given "unrestricted" control over it and an assurance that there would be no interference with his plans. On the other hand, he promised "to restore them (as far as may be practicable) to their former state" without deviation from the original architectural design. His offer, expected to cost about £20,000, was immediately accepted and he threw himself wholeheartedly into the project, dispensing with architects and overseeing the work and redesign of the cathedral himself. It turned out to be a mammoth task, taking almost five years and eventually costing him the very large sum of £150,000.

It was a time when prominent businessmen liked to rebuild churches as memorials to themselves, although nobody else in Ireland had yet attempted anything on such an ambitious scale. The distiller Henry Roe subsequently followed the Guinness example by rebuilding the nearby Christ Church Cathedral, which was in an even more decrepit state than St Patrick's. Benjamin Lee's munificence meant that he was given a free hand in the restoration of St Patrick's in spite of some unease among professional architects and builders. Some predicted that the whole edifice would collapse as workmen tried to rebuild it while others questioned the historical accuracy of his work, which did not, in spite of his promise, adhere strictly to the original design.

In planning the work, Benjamin Lee's research included visits to the great English cathedrals at Westminster, Salisbury and York. As a result, he claimed to have detected the errors of previous repairs and restorations of St Patrick's and set about removing the "incongruities" and promised a restoration "as complete as ancient research and modern science can make it".[18] Modern science's main contribution to the exercise lay in the use of photography to record details of the original structure before the rebuilding took place.

The main critic of his work was J.J. McCarthy, the leading Irish Gothic revival architect of the period, who accused Lee of doing precisely the opposite of what he claimed to be doing. In a letter to the *Dublin Builder* magazine,[19] McCarthy complained that the changes of the previous three centuries had been religiously restored "in all their hideous deformity, while original works of the earlier and better period have been ruthlessly destroyed to make way for unauthorized and unnecessary features". He instanced such features as the addition of Tudor-style buttresses and the destruction of an ancient roodscreen, while he criticised some of the workmanship on details as "lifeless, coarse and clumsy". Among Benjamin Lee's other innovations was a triforium in the nave and the replacement of the windows with early English gothic-style lancets, which may or may not have been in the original.

McCarthy, who denied any element of professional jealousy, claimed that a splendid opportunity of cathedral restoration had been thrown away. He concluded:

> Thirty years ago M. de Montalembert, in his famous letter to M. Victor Hugo . . . classed those who meddled with the ancient churches of France into "Vandal destroyers" and "Vandal restorers". The present restorers of St Patrick's are earning for themselves a prominent place amongst the latter. It needs only their carrying into effect the suggestions of your contemporary [The *Freeman's Journal* which had suggested that the Lady's Chapel part of the structure be knocked down] to entitle them to the first place among the former.

Faced with the alternative, the collapse of the cathedral, and the failure of previous fundraising efforts, the cathedral authorities had little choice but to give Benjamin Lee a free hand. The attitude of Benjamin Lee and his contractors, Messrs T. Murphy & Son, to their contemporary critics was evident two months later. On St Patrick's Day 1863, the workmen on the site presented Guinness with an ode printed on white satin bordered with entwined shamrocks. One verse said of St Patrick's:

> It pleaded strongly for our aid, but willing hearts were few,
> For those who had the power to save had not the will to do,
> It was reserved, at last, for one of noble heart and mind,
> To leave to other times a name and monument behind –
> To leave a NAME inseparable from Patrick's by his gift,
> A monument by Guinness o'er the resting place of Swift!

On being presented with the ode by the foreman carpenter, John Kane, Benjamin Lee responded: "I hope this was made in Dublin, gentlemen?" Assured that it had been, he thanked God there had been no accidents on the site, praised the workers while rejecting unfair criticism that aid from other countries should have been sought for a "proper" restoration. The workers' talents were not inferior to those who originally erected the cathedral, he said, and maintained that the restored cathedral would be "a testimony that long since Ireland was not that contemptible country which some historians would present her to be".

By that stage the cost of the work had risen to some £80,000 and further problems loomed. The growing militancy among workers and the formation of "combinations" or trades unions led to strikes in the building industry which intruded on the restoration. They were dealt with swiftly and ruthlessly: a hundred stonecutters working on St Patrick's who went on strike for higher wages were immediately fired and replacements hired within hours. Bricklayers followed suit and were just as quickly replaced by others.[20]

The restoration was eventually completed early in the election year of 1865 and the cathedral's new bells – inscribed with the Guinness family motto "*Spes mea in Deo*, BLG 1864" – rang out on 24 February to mark its reopening. Tickets were issued to 3,250 people but twice that number applied to attend: there were queues outside the doors at 8.00 a.m., three hours before the ceremony conducted by the Archbishop of Dublin and six other bishops. A second ceremony was held that evening to display the interior in gas-light; it was conducted by Benjamin Lee's son-in-law, Anne's husband, the Reverend William Conyngham. Amid performances of Mendelssohn oratorios and the "Hallelujah" chorus, he claimed to speak for Benjamin Lee and declared his main motive in the restoration work to be the provision for his fellow citizens "of a great central and national temple, whither you might come and worship your God".

Mr Guinness, *The Times* reported, had done everything for the Protestants of Dublin, managing to accomplish a task that was "too great for the Knights of St Patrick, or the Ecclesiastical Commissioners, or the bench of Bishops, which the Irish Parliament refused to undertake, and which the British Parliament never entertained the thought of executing". Yet, it added with a little dramatic licence, "he took his seat among them yesterday as quietly and modestly as if he had done nothing". In fact, he and his four children occupied the front pew in the transept; his wife, Bessie, was, as usual, absent.

There was no undue modesty either in the manner in which Benjamin Lee accepted the tributes of his fellow citizens. The lord mayor led a procession of councillors and prominent citizens across St Stephen's Green to the Guinness residence to present him with a testimonial. (The only councillor notably absent was John Reynolds, who refused to take part because, he said, he worshipped at a different altar and, under attack from other Catholic councillors, declared that St Patrick's had been seized by force from Catholics in the reign of Queen Elizabeth.)[21] At a subsequent banquet in the Mansion House, Benjamin Lee attributed his generosity to "a bountiful Providence" which left him in a position to undertake the work.

One architect proposed the building of a new road from St Stephen's Green to St Patrick's to be called Guinness Street and part of the road beside the cathedral was named after him. He was given an honorary doctorate by Trinity College and a fund was established – with contributions limited to £1 to broaden its appeal – to erect a suitable testimonial. A statue of Benjamin Lee by sculptor J.H. Foley (who also sculpted the statue of Fr Mathew in Cork) was eventually erected beside the cathedral and overlooking Guinness Street in 1875. There were calls to clean up the tenements surrounding the cathedral in order to show off the restoration work to best advantage. Some of the city's worst slums were in the immediate area and the nearby Bull Lane was notorious as the haunt of 200 prostitutes and numerous pubs.[22] But it was another decade – and left to another Guinness, Benjamin Lee's son Edward – before any attempt at slum clearance began in Dublin.

Whatever about the strict accuracy of his restoration, there was no doubt that Benjamin Lee had saved the cathedral from probable ruin. As a future dean of St Patrick's, J.H. Bernard, put it: "Had it not been for the public spirit of Sir Benjamin Lee Guinness, St Patrick's Cathedral would not be standing today and the Church of Ireland owes him an abiding debt of gratitude for the preservation of one of the most splendid of her ancient temples."[23]

The other project which provided the perfect launching pad for Benjamin Lee's political career was the exhibition in Dublin opened by the Prince of Wales in May 1865. Here, too, Guinness had come to the rescue of local attempts to exploit the Victorian vogue for exhibitions and winter gardens. Efforts to establish a permanent exhibition had run into the problem of finding a suitable site, a difficulty solved by

Benjamin Lee's donation of the Coburg Gardens behind his Stephen's Green home. The Dublin Exhibition Palace and Winter Garden Company, of which he was vice-chairman, spent two years building the glass and stone centre which was to be a showpiece of Irish industry and arts, as well as providing permanent concert halls and reading rooms. Using a phrase which, 40 years later, came to have a narrower political meaning with the foundation of Sinn Féin, the *Freeman's Journal* noted the opening as "an event of which we have reason to be proud, for it illustrates the energy and self-sufficient reliance of 'ourselves alone', carried out to an extent and with a success which in our history, at least, is without parallel".[24]

His public profile meant that Benjamin Lee was assured of victory in the general election which followed in July 1865. Two years earlier, the city's Conservative Party had invited him to replace one of its retiring MPs. The Conservatives had held the two Dublin city seats since 1852 and had dominated the city's politics since the collapse of O'Connell's organisation. Benjamin Lee's selection was broadly welcomed, with the nationalist *Freeman's Journal* describing him as being "the only man against whom no citizen would like to record a vote".[25] Relations between the newspaper's owner, Sir John Gray, a Protestant nationalist and its former political writer, and the Guinnesses were exemplified shortly afterwards when Benjamin Lee was one of the organisers of a presentation to Gray to mark his knighthood, earned for his role on the city council in overseeing the provision of a controversial new water supply to Dublin from Vartry reservoir in County Wicklow.

In a near-orgy of mutual congratulation, faithfully recorded by his newspaper, Sir John described Benjamin Lee as "first among the citizens of Dublin, first in talent, first in enterprise, first in charity, first in goodwill towards his fellow-citizens, and first, I trust, to be the unanimously elected representative of the city". Benjamin Lee replied: "I love Ireland [cheers], I love its capital, my native city [applause], and I am but one of the many, many citizens who would endeavour to do what they could in their own sphere to promote the prosperity of the capital of our country [cheers]."[26]

Gray's hope that Guinness would be the first MP for Dublin to be elected unanimously did not materialise, although it was a distinct prospect almost up to the last minute. The other Tory MP, John Vance, a right-winger with Orange Order connections and a business in Leeds, ran again. But the Conservative's hopes that they would retain their two city seats without a contest were thwarted two weeks before the poll when another prominent Dublin merchant, Jonathan Pim, was persuaded to enter the contest as an independent liberal. Pim was a formidable opponent for the Tories: a Quaker, he had excellent liberal credentials and was assured of strong support among liberal Protestant and Catholic voters. He was, like Guinness, a major employer as a silk manufacturer, wholesale merchant and owner of a "monster house" (department store). In addition, he had been secretary of the Quaker relief committee, which was to the forefront in trying to help the starving during the famine and was also the author of a book, *The Condition of Ireland*, which proposed land reforms. (It was noticeable throughout the campaign that, while his supporters frequently referred to Pim's role in famine relief, none of Benjamin Lee's made any similar claims for their candidate.) Pim had also been a previous supporter of Vance, voting for him in 1852 to help him oust the then repeal MP and former lord mayor, John Reynolds. Ironically, Reynolds was now amongst those who persuaded him to run, promising him the support of his Catholic followers and guaranteeing him independence to follow his own policies. From Reynolds's point of view, the defeat of Vance was worth the price.

The main issues of the campaign were the threatened disestablishment of the Church of Ireland, land tenure and education. The contest was immediately seen as between Vance and Pim, with Guinness almost on the sidelines, assured of victory. Indeed, Benjamin Lee could scarcely have failed to win one of the seats if he had tried. Liberals and nationalists were prepared to excuse him almost anything in their desire to oust Vance and return Pim and Guinness.

Thus, the *Freeman's Journal* excused Benjamin Lee for sharing election literature, election workers and offices with Vance on the grounds that it was "a cunning device on the part of the confidential advisers of Mr Vance" to try and cling to the Guinness bandwagon.

Benjamin Lee also distanced himself from Vance by describing himself as a liberal conservative and failing to turn up at a raucous party election rally at which the trappings of the Orange Order, flags, sashes and lilies, were prominently displayed and speakers urged the crowd to "nail their colours to the mast of Protestant ascendancy". Amid the cheering and "Kentish fire" (sustained bouts of rhythmic applause usually mixed with derision about the target under attack), some insensitive members of the crowd demanded to know where Guinness was. A Dr Chatterton urged them to make allowances for him and excused his absence because he was "a modest, retiring man".[27]

The main issue for the Dublin Tories was the threat by the Liberals to disestablish the Church of Ireland, an issue on which Benjamin Lee was fireproofed because of his restoration of St Patrick's. As Dr Chatterton asked the Orange crowd, "Was that not a good test of his opinions?" Benjamin Lee declared at his nomination (where he was proposed by Colonel La Touche and his father's old Chamber of Commerce sidekick, Francis Codd) that he would preserve intact the property and rights of the established Church while also protecting the civil and religious liberties of all. Pim refused to commit himself, arguing that he would consider on its merits any proposal on disestablishment put forward by the new government.

Vance tried forlornly to hang on to Guinness's electoral coat-tails, declaring that there was "scarcely a shade of difference" between himself and Benjamin Lee.[28] The emergence of committees to elect Guinness and Pim and unsubtle posters declaring "Vote for Guinness and Pim, Out with Vance, the bigot, for he is no employer" exemplified his difficulty. His supporters tried to counter the fact that his business in Leeds gave little employment in Dublin on the grounds that he lived and spent his money in the Irish capital. But he was up against a groundswell of Catholic opinion, with declarations like that of the *Cork Examiner* which said that Irish Catholics would "as soon desire to be represented by the most ignorant and the most savage of Cromwell's drummers".[29]

However, there was one section of the electorate which Benjamin Lee had no compunction about alienating – the temperance campaigners. The Irish Temperance League tried to lobby the three candidates but Benjamin Lee refused to even meet them. James Haughton, a Quaker leader of the League and formerly a close associate of Fr Mathew, responded with a public letter to Benjamin Lee declaring him to be unfit to be an MP because of his brewing interest. Benjamin Lee retorted that he had not read more than the first page and went on: "Such has been my habit for many years with anything written by you, or reported as spoken by you. I return herewith the letter alluded to, and as I have no respect for, and take no interest whatever in, your vagaries, I beg to decline any further communication with you." The League sarcastically dismissed his attitude as typical of beer sellers everywhere in its "gentlemanly bearing, intelligent appreciation of great public questions, and a desire to thoroughly understand all the topics of the day".[30]

Such was the success of the Tories' opponents in almost taking over Benjamin Lee as their own candidate by linking the names of Guinness and Pim in a dream ticket that the Conservatives finally issued a statement denying that Benjamin Lee had broken with Vance. They attacked Pim as a "monopolist", claiming that his "monster house" had brought ruin on humble shopkeepers and forced them to emigrate. As the polling approached, they called on all electors temporarily absent from Dublin to hurry back as "one friend cannot be spared". But their efforts to bring back Protestant freemen of the city from Britain and the continent – 200 were said to have arrived from London for the poll – failed to save Vance.

The freemen duly and predictably voted heavily for Guinness and Vance but a large majority of other voters preferred Guinness and Pim. As expected, Guinness headed the poll followed by Pim, and so Vance lost his seat. The victors ascribed their success to the growth of moderation, with Benjamin Lee contrasting the conduct of the election with the "outrageous scenes" of past elections. He remembered, he said, a scene from his early youth when the "immortal Grattan [was] pelted in the streets and obliged to take shelter in a house in Henry Street". He added optimistically that such a thing would not happen nowadays because of "the improving feeling of the country".[31] Pim declared that they would both represent the moderates of all parties, while Guinness suggested that they would second each other's measures in the House of

Commons. Not everyone was so happy with the outcome, of course. Vance bitterly attacked the unnatural coalition ranged against him and maintained that the Society of Friends [Quakers] would be to blame if it led to a Roman Catholic ascendancy. The temperance movement declared that the "metropolis had been disgraced for the present by the return of Mr Benjamin Lee Guinness".[32]

The election of two prominent merchants who were well removed from the political extremes failed, however, to live up to all the hopes of the middle-of-the-road voters who supported them. Benjamin Lee was not a natural political, or parliamentary, performer and his undoubted goodwill and sentimental love of Ireland made no impact in the House of Commons: his contribution there was limited to asking a couple of parliamentary questions and he does not appear to have spoken on any subjects during his three years as an MP. He was more a symbol of what turned out to be a forlorn hope – that the deep divisions in Irish society could be submerged by wealthy pragmatists and patrons into a middle way characterised by notions of decency and a mild, benevolent economic nationalism.

Far removed from the self-congratulatory tone of middle-class and respectable politics in Dublin in July 1865, the Fenian movement of revolutionary republicans was emerging from the ruins of the abortive Young Ireland rebellion in 1848. Determined on social as well as political revolution, but heavily infiltrated by informers and spies, they eventually launched an abortive uprising in scattered parts of the country, including the outskirts of Dublin, in 1867. The Fenians caused a considerable shock to the Irish political system, especially among nationalists who had been largely directionless since the death of Daniel O'Connell. Benjamin Lee's reaction was similar to that of his father and grandfather towards the United Irishmen in 1798. They saw both movements as the work of foreign agents – revolutionary France in 1798 and disgruntled Irish-America in the 1860s – who threatened social mayhem and anarchy and the destruction of their property, as well as their social and political positions. Obviously aware of his views, some 515 of the employees in St James's Gate sent Benjamin Lee an address in December 1866 condemning "such mad and pernicious doctrines" and identifying their interests closely with those of their "valued employer". In thanking them, Benjamin Lee stressed that "the machinations of those wicked and worthless adventurers" would not only deprive Ireland of its advantages as part of the British Empire but also "reduce the industrial classes to want and misery". The Fenians' aim, he declared solemnly, was to seize property from its owners "by deception and by pillage" and "during the proposed panic to escape with their plunder to whence they came".[33]

Meanwhile, Benjamin Lee's reclusive wife, Bessie, had succumbed to her long-standing ill health and died in September 1865, within two months of her husband's election to Westminster. By then, the family had consolidated its position in society: his daughter Anne's marriage to the Reverend William Conyngham brought the first aristocrat into the family and his eldest son, Arthur Edward, was educated at Eton, the first of the family to go to an English public school rather than be educated at home by private tutors. Conyngham, the son of Lord Plunket whose title he inherited, was eventually to become the Archbishop of Dublin and also benefited from the marriage; his career was boosted by the treasurership of St Patrick's after he married Anne and while her father was restoring the cathedral. He was known for his lugubrious solemnity and ultra-evangelical views, which prompted him to support Protestantism in Spain and Italy.

Benjamin Lee won his own social recognition when he was made a baronet in April 1867 as a reward for his philanthropic work on the cathedral. His social pretensions were evidenced by his desire to have a member of the royal family visit his restoration work, an ambition that was achieved a year later, in April 1868, when the Prince of Wales came to Dublin. At an elaborate ceremony in the cathedral, the prince was installed as a Knight of St Patrick and paid full-hearted tribute to Sir Benjamin Lee at a subsequent banquet.

Benjamin Lee's own health was failing by then and, less than a month later, he became seriously ill at his London home in Norfolk Street, off Park Lane, with a severe chest infection. His eldest son, Arthur Edward, was summoned from Dublin and, after six days of decline interspersed with occasional rallies, Benjamin Lee died on the evening of 19 May 1868, at the age of 69. His body was brought back to Dublin and buried in the vault he had had built over his father's grave in Mount Jerome cemetery. The oak coffin was adorned with two scrolls, declaring: "Blessed are the dead which die in the Lord" and "Oh, death, where is thy sting? Oh grave, where is thy victory?" Warm tributes marked his passing and the Bishop of Cork, John Gregg, noted in a funeral oration that God had blessed his untiring endeavours with great prosperity. The mourners, he said, were paying respect "not to greatness derived from ancestry, not to greatness derived from learning, not to greatness derived from title, but to greatness of a higher order – greatness derived from kindness and greatness derived from universally admitted Christian worth".[34]

Among the predictable obituaries, The Irish Times declared that Benjamin Lee had proved "that merchants can be princes". The Freeman's Journal, in an obituary possibly written by Sir John Gray or, at least, by someone who knew Benjamin Lee well, gave a more measured assessment, which also indicated a degree of disillusionment with his political performance from the days when the newspaper had backed his election. It noted that he had been a staunch, unswerving Conservative in politics but had succeeded by his many amiable qualities in becoming popular even amongst those to whom his political views were most obnoxious. It added that his education had left him with "a strong religious sentiment which revealed itself from time to time in something akin to exclusiveness, and in what some persons thought a rather too zealous desire for the propagation of his own opinion".

The temperance campaigners were not people to allow their judgement to be clouded by sentiment or their certainty to be diluted by bereavement. One of them, J.A. Mowatt, wrote a ferocious summation of Benjamin Lee's career, taking issue with Bishop Gregg's oration. In an article for the Temperance Star in London, later published as a pamphlet entitled "What It Is To Die A Brewer", he attacked the bishop for being blinded by the Guinness wealth to the evils of the brewery and turning the Almighty into Guinness's "pot boy". Benjamin Lee, he claimed, had made more drunkards at home and abroad than anyone else in Britain or Ireland and he built up a horrendous picture of the brewer being confronted on judgement day by "all the suicides, murderers, forgers, wife-beaters, child-neglectors . . . the broken-hearted widows, all the perished orphans, all the waifs and strays of society" created through Guinness's double X. What useful work did he ever promote, Mowatt thundered on, except that of multiplying widows and orphans, and fatherless street roughs, and unfortunate drunken females – all who partook of his "spirit".

Mowatt's vitriol was undoubtedly strengthened by the ineffectiveness of the temperance campaign and the high-standing and popularity of the Guinness family, as well as the popularity of their porter. The aura of benevolence that hovered around them was cultivated by their well-publicised generosity. Within days of Benjamin Lee's death, reports circulated that he had left a fortnight's salary to "each employee of humble grade" in St James's Gate and his houses.[35] But his will, when it was eventually probated, showed that he had not left himself or his descendants short of cash. He left £1.1 million, the largest will probated in Ireland up to that time and confirming his millionaire status. The Guinnesses had gone from strength to strength during Benjamin Lee's lifetime and were now poised to move into high society.

CHAPTER FIVE

The Cunning Brothers

"The £5 notes were as plentiful that day in Capel-street as the autumn leaves that strewed the brooks of Vallanbrosa."

Prosecuting barrister in the trial of Sir Arthur Guinness
for bribery during the 1868 general election

On the day that Benjamin Lee Guinness was buried, his eldest son, the new baronet, Sir Arthur Edward Guinness, moved to claim one part of his inheritance. Along with their accounts of Benjamin Lee's funeral, the next day's newspapers also carried an advertisement announcing that Sir Arthur had accepted after some hesitation the suggestion of many friends that he should stand in the by-election for his father's seat in parliament.[1]

The next generation of Guinnesses, dominated by Sir Arthur and his youngest brother, Edward, was to control the family and the brewery for the next 50 years, spanning the apogee and decline of the Victorian and Edwardian eras. They made their mark on – and enjoyed to the full the delights of – that era, rising to the peerage and taking the family into the highest echelons of British society and the life of relentless leisure which epitomised the Edwardian aristocracy.

Their place in that society was bought with the wealth created by the brewery and enhanced by astute investments. And that wealth established their reputations, as well as that of the family as a whole, for philanthropy. They tend to be remembered primarily as such; indeed, the *Dictionary of National Biography* describes them both simply as philanthropists. But there was much more to "the cunning brothers", as James Joyce described them in *Ulysses*, than philanthropy alone. Both were involved in the high-stake politics of their times, particularly in trying to stem the tide towards Irish independence. Sir Arthur (who was to become Lord Ardilaun) was rarely far from political controversy, opposing all the major movements of his time, from the disestablishment of the Church of Ireland to land reform and home rule for Ireland. Edward (later to become the Earl of Iveagh and the most successful Guinness of all) played a less public and more shrewd political role, consolidated the family in high society and laid the foundations of its twentieth-century fortune.

The death of Benjamin Lee left his children with everything to look forward to. They were rich, well respected in their native city, rapidly climbing the social ladder there and in London, and in control of the largest porter brewery in the world, which now seemed to grow and grow with almost effortless ease. Benjamin Lee, like his predecessors, went to considerable lengths to try to make sure that the foundation of their fortune and of their position in the world was not dissipated after his death. His will was noteworthy for his detailed efforts to dictate the future and secure the brewery from beyond the grave. Two of his four children were left out of the serious business of the family: his eldest and only daughter, Anne, because she was a woman; and his third child, also Benjamin Lee and known as Lee, partly because he appears to have had a gambling problem. (Gambling was one of the main threats to family wealth in the nineteenth century [see Chapter Seven] and was one of three practices of the rich which were frowned upon in the Guinness family. Three unofficial rules which evolved from Victorian times dissuaded family members from gambling, becoming "Names" [underwriters] in Lloyd's insurance syndicates, and joining the Freemasons. All three practices had the possibility of involving people in unlimited financial liabilities.) Lee was left only £20,000 in his father's will, a substantial enough sum in those days but a pittance relative to his father's and his brothers' wealth. He left Ireland, joined the British Army and pursued a career in the Royal Horse Guards.

Sir Benjamin Lee's main beneficiaries were his eldest and youngest sons, Arthur and Edward, who received his main properties and, more importantly, the brewery – but with strict conditions attached. Obviously fearing that one of them might want to sell out – and probably aware of their proclivities and that the relationship between them would be uneasy – he tried to make sure that any break-up of the partnership would not destroy the brewery. While expressing the earnest hope that they would carry on brewing together, he laid down the rules under which one of them could opt out of the partnership. He directed that the business should not be broken up or divided if this were to happen. The brother who opted out should hand over his share to the other brother (and to nobody else), who would assume total control. If the retiring brother refused to do so, then Benjamin Lee revoked his bequest to him and left the brewery directly to the one who wanted to remain in the business. The retiring brother was to receive £30,000 plus the value of half the brewery's stocks, all of which was to be paid in eight equal instalments without interest. If one brother went bankrupt, the same arrangement was to apply.[2] Thus Benjamin Lee sought to ensure that one brother could not easily cash in his share or break up the brewery in order to turn his inheritance into cash or to pay his debts. The brewery, which was making considerable profits of about £100,000 a year, would not be put at risk and should easily be able to pay off one partner without putting its capital and its future on the line.

Subsequent events proved the wisdom of the thought and effort Benjamin Lee had put into drawing up his will. The two brothers were very different in character and temperament. Sir Arthur, who was 27 when his father died, had had quite a different upbringing to Edward, who was 20 at the time of his father's death. Sir Arthur had been sent to school at Eton in what was clearly a move to prepare him for his expected role in society rather than in business. Edward was educated at home, began working in the brewery at 15, and was a part-time and somewhat nominal student at Trinity College Dublin when he inherited half of St James's Gate.

It is tempting to see their different styles and attitudes in later life in terms of their educations and upbringing. Whether their education formed their characters or merely enhanced their natural inclinations, however, is a moot point. Sir Arthur adopted a patrician approach, assuming an aristocratic role as his birthright and appearing, for instance, to please himself rather than anyone else with his philanthropy and, in later life, with his political stances. Edward used his business abilities to develop his wealth and his philanthropy to buy his way into the upper echelons of society, eventually passing his brother by on the way. He was highly energetic and excitable but also paid meticulous attention to detail: on a world cruise in later years, for instance, he noted the spending of every single penny in his diary. Sir Arthur, on the other hand, appeared to have little time for details and certainly did not share his brother's aptitude for the business or Edward's interest in the minutiae of brewing.

Both had been partners in the brewery before their father's death and the transition to their control was eased by the continuing presence of John Tertius Purser, Benjamin Lee's long-time associate. At first, their relationship as joint owners worked relatively smoothly. But the strains between them would shortly emerge, exacerbated by their differing characters, their diverging ambitions and the expectations of those closest to them.

Sir Arthur's move to claim the political part of his inheritance was merely a formality and such a foregone conclusion that he was not even present to hear himself becoming a member of parliament on 2 June 1868. He was the only candidate for his father's seat, proposed by Sir Edward Grogan and seconded by John Barlow, the former Bank of Ireland governor who had unsuccessfully urged the second Arthur to persuade Benjamin Lee to stand for parliament some 16 years earlier. David Plunket, the brother-in-law of his sister Anne, and a major force in the family's future successes, accepted his election on Sir Arthur's behalf, promising that the new MP would do the utmost in his power to maintain the established church.[3]

The city's Liberals had decided not to oppose Sir Arthur but were not reassured by Plunket's comments. A decision on the disestablishment of the Church of Ireland was finally coming to a head. The Liberals, in opposition under William Ewart Gladstone, had just won a major victory in having the House of Commons pass a motion in favour of disestablishment. Their success effectively caused the collapse of the

Conservative government and set the stage for a highly acrimonious general election the following November.

Dublin's Conservatives, mostly Protestants and Orangemen, were outraged at this perceived attack, not just on the Church of Ireland but on the establishment in general. The Liberals, who spanned the sectarian divide, were equally vigorous in support of the campaign for "religious equality". The issue, of course, was not simply the status and property of the Church of Ireland but the central political and religious tensions which had divided Ireland for the previous two centuries. It did not take long for the Battle of the Boyne to surface as the common currency on both platforms. As the campaign gathered momentum and raised passions, the partisan *Freeman's Journal* declared that the election was no longer simply a question between parties but much more fundamental: "Is this country to be ruled as a conquered nation or as an integral part of the empire? Are the Catholics of Ireland to be treated as an inferior race? . . . Is the blood red flag of conquest to be ever flaunted in their faces? . . . There is now no middle course for the timid and the time-serving."[4]

The main candidates on both sides were the sitting MPs, Sir Arthur and Jonathan Pim, each of whom was backed by a more spirited and demagogic running-mate. In Pim's case, the second candidate was a Catholic doctor, Sir Dominic Corrigan, while Sir Arthur was accompanied by his sister's brother-in-law, David Plunket, a young and highly ambitious lawyer. The election campaign got underway in earnest in October 1868 and its tone was quickly set by a series of party meetings in which the candidates played to their respective galleries. One of the first was a gathering of Conservatives from their strongest centre-city wards, which packed the Molesworth Hall on 20 October 1868. To much cheering, regular rounds of "Kentish fire" and the occasional shout of "no Popery", Guinness and Plunket gave the voters what they wanted to hear.

Sir Arthur began by stressing the effect that disestablishment would have on the Church of England and the political power of England, while presenting Dublin's Protestants as the victims of a Liberal attempt to seize their property. The contest, he told them, was about the future of the Church of England and the glory and honour of everything that was to be esteemed in the future history of England. The union of church and state had been the making of England and if the church was attacked, the glory of England would be set. He declared himself happy that they had the support of Protestants of every class and Quakers, Presbyterians, Methodists and Dissenters of every creed. Even Roman Catholics, he added when a voice shouted "except Roman Catholics": many Catholics had told him they were not against the Irish church. And why should they be? he asked. It had been harmless to them, and they could not touch one penny of its money should her [the Church of Ireland's] opponents succeed in pulling her down. It was the parsons and priests, not the people, who had fallen out, he added, enunciating a common political line at the time. Roman Catholics had been influenced by their priests but he claimed that many educated and enlightened Roman Catholics saw the Church of Ireland as a safeguard against "the tyranny and oppression of the priesthood of the land".

Plunket proved himself a more effective public speaker than Sir Arthur. In a vigorous speech he presented the election as round three in a contest that began with the Reformation and continued with the Williamite victory at the Battle of the Boyne. The Protestants, Plunket asserted, had thought they could settle down to the quiet enjoyment of the freedom won for them by the Reformation and "William the Great Deliverer [loud cheers and Kentish fire]" and their forefathers. While they were simply enjoying that freedom for two centuries, their opponents had been busy and the first the Protestants heard of them was when they were again drawn up in the line of battle. Asking the audience if they were manly enough to fight again and vindicate the principles established by their forefathers, he brought his speech to a rousing climax, invoking the spirit, "the undying, unconquerable spirit that rose in the great hymn of freedom that was expressed in two words from the walls of Derry – 'no surrender'".[5]

Their speeches did not just raise the passions at the meeting but fired up their opponents as well. Commenting on reports of the meeting next day, the Liberal *Freeman's Journal* retorted that Sir Arthur and the "very warlike" Plunket had flung aside the mask and come before the electors of Dublin in their true colours. After their performances, it declared, they could neither ask nor hope for a single Catholic or

Liberal vote. "Sir Arthur spoke in the true spirit of Ascendancy. He knew no electors but 'Protestants'. He ignored the very existence of Catholics save to assail them, and rejoiced to meet the 'Protestant' electors of Dublin."[6]

The Liberal candidates replied in a similar vein, with Pim rejecting claims that the Church of Ireland was the church of Protestants: it was only the church of one Protestant sect, he said. His running-mate, Corrigan, took a more populist tack, as at one meeting near Christ Church (which predated the Reformation) where he asked his audience: "Who built it? [hear, hear] Did Sir Arthur Guinness's progenitors in blood or religion [cries of no]? And yet he and his party have not only the hardihood to retain it, but to require that you should support it for them and the further hardihood to ask you for your votes that he may continue to maintain it at your expense [hear, hear]. It is hard for flesh and blood to stand this."

Corrigan then launched into a long lament on how the Guinnesses had changed political sides, invoking a loving, and idealised, picture of Sir Arthur's grandfather, the second Arthur Guinness:

Who was foremost then amongst us, who was hailed with blessings as he passed along, side by side with O'Connell in our struggle for Emancipation? Old Arthur Guinness [cheers], the grandfather of our present opponent. I see him clearly now in my mind's eye as clearly as I often saw him when I was a child – his fine tall stately figure, and the expression in his good intellectual countenance of the conviction that he was on the right side. Alas! that we should see the change, that we meet here not to send into Parliament with one unanimous shout of respect for his name and his principles the grandson of Arthur Guinness, that we should see him sunk to the lowest depths of degradation in the Orange scum of Skinner's-alley [headquarters of the Orange Order, off Newmarket] [cheers] – that the grandson of such a man as old Arthur Guinness should so stain his name! [hear, hear].[7]

While disestablishment was the dominant factor, other issues were also played out, including denominational education, land reform and temperance. The temperance campaigners had set their sights on Sunday closing and had been making progress in the previous parliament when Guinness had helped to fund a counter-campaign by Dublin's publicans. Once the election campaign was underway, temperance campaigners lobbied the candidates, except Sir Arthur, whom they either did not bother approaching or who had, like his father, refused to see them. Temperance meetings devoted much of their time to arguing against Sir Arthur's election: speakers like J.A. Mowatt, the author of the ferocious "obituary" of Benjamin Lee, asked that the voters not send to parliament a brewer who was taking what should be "food for the people and rotting it in vats".

The election campaign came to a set-piece climax at the nomination of candidates in Green Street courthouse on 16 November. It turned into a rowdy, day-long session, during which the two Conservative candidates were howled down whenever they attempted to speak. The "popular candidates", as the Liberal press described Pim and Corrigan, appealed unsuccessfully for a hearing for their opponents. Plunket, according to the *Times* correspondent, was obliged "to deliver his speech into the ears of the reporters while an incessant howling and uproar were kept up."

Sir Arthur fared somewhat better but had to contend with questions thrown at him by, among others, Mowatt, who demanded if he would support Sunday closing for public houses. To hisses, Sir Arthur replied that he would give the proposal due consideration when the time came. After further appeals for quiet by Corrigan, Sir Arthur denied the charges that he was, as he put it, "the degenerate son of respectable ancestors". He would, he said, vote for Catholic Emancipation but it was different to grant civil and religious liberty to his fellow-countrymen and to take from his own church's members the rights they had enjoyed for 300 years.[8]

Voting took place in the courthouse two days later amid fears of violence. There was little doubt about popular sentiment: it was overwhelmingly against the Tories. Some 200,000 of Dublin's total population of 250,000 were Catholics and, thus, largely in favour of disestablishment. The total electorate, on the other hand, was a mere 12,822 voters (each of whom had two votes, one for each seat to be filled) among whom Protestants were well represented because of the property qualifications and including the 2,702 who were freemen of the city and, by definition, inheritors of their franchise and Protestants. At the climax of such an acrimonious campaign and fearing the consequences of Guinness and Plunket winning the city's two seats, extra police were on the streets and troops were standing by at strategic locations. But there was only one minor incident when a sheriff's deputy taking polling boxes from the courthouse was pursued by a mob and had to take refuge in a house in nearby Mary Street. The fears of serious violence evaporated when the result turned out to be a draw. Sir Arthur headed the poll with 5,587 votes, a single vote ahead of Jonathan Pim, and both were elected. Plunket followed with 5,452 votes and Corrigan with 5,379, revealing the near equal division of opinion among voters. The result left both sides happy to claim victory, with the Liberals pointing out that their men would both have won had the freemen been excluded from the poll. Guinness had won the votes of 2,127 freemen, compared to a mere 303 who voted for Pim, leading the *Freeman's Journal* to categorised the freeman franchise as "the curse of the city". Meanwhile, the victorious candidates made conciliatory speeches, Sir Arthur hoping that any animosities excited by the contest might be speedily healed. Pim thanked two women who were erroneously given ballot papers and allowed to vote: they balanced each other out politically, one voting Liberal, the other Conservative.[9]

The full story of the election had not yet been told, however. A petition by two Dubliners, a barrister and a stockbroker, was lodged against Sir Arthur early in the new year, charging him with bribing voters and asking that his election be declared null and void. Such petitions were common aftermaths to nineteenth-century elections and the Conservatives retaliated with Plunket bringing a similar petition against Jonathan Pim. His action was later dropped but the one against Guinness produced a sensational two-week court case which stripped away the normal secrecy covering the inner workings of Dublin's Conservatives.

The hearing began on Saturday, 23 January 1869, before the Right Honourable Justice William Keogh in Green Street, the courthouse now in its normal legal role instead of its occasional focus for elections. The building was jammed once again, with the rival camps ensconced in the raised jury boxes on either side of the bench. Guinness, Plunket and their supporters occupied, inappropriately, the left-hand box; the Pim and Corrigan camp took over the right-hand one. Sir Arthur was defended by a high-powered legal team led by Isaac Butt, a former young firebrand of Dublin Orangeism who had travelled a circuitous political road since the 1830s when he lobbied against reform of the old city council; after a brief political career, he was back at the bar and best known in recent years for his legal defence of numerous Fenians.

The evidence put before the court revealed systematic skulduggery and the existence of what would be known in a later age as a "dirty tricks" department among the Conservatives, which went to all sorts of lengths to swing the election their way. It also revealed that Sir Arthur had written brewery cheques amounting to £15,850 to secure his election, amounting, as Justice Keogh noted drily in his summing up, to a cost of almost £3 for every vote he received. It was a considerable sum at the time, compared to the £5,087 the Conservatives officially spent on the election of Benjamin Lee Guinness three years earlier and to the £9,000 that an English judge had recently ruled was excessive for a Bradford constituency which had 19,000 voters. As the Liberals had charged during the election campaign, Sir Arthur had provided the money for himself and Plunket, while his running-mate had provided most of the verbal fireworks. The cost of the election to him went some way to explaining the difference in the amounts the two brothers took out of the brewery during their first year in partnership: Sir Arthur received £42,000 while Edward (still under age, 21, for part of the year) received £2,000.[10]

Money was clearly no object to Sir Arthur's campaign, and there was no shortage of people willing to help him spend it. It was thrown, the judge noted, in a broad cast upon the waters over a period of three months and "no profession, no individual, appears to have scorned the money of Sir Arthur Guinness". He noted with severe disapproval that members of the bar figured largely among those, with one being paid £45 for drawing up street lists: "this is the first time that I have heard of a member of the bar becoming something lower than a gutter agent," he declared. Altogether, some 800 people were paid agents of the party, although it was not always clear what their tasks were. One had the sole task, it was said, of canvassing the provost of Trinity College, scarcely a demanding job when the provost was almost certainly a Conservative voter in the first place. Others, the prosecution charged, "had nothing to do but eat oysters and drink porter before dinner and eat oysters and drink punch after dinner during every working day.".

Dozens of voters, mainly freemen, openly admitted in court that they had sought and been promised or received bribes. They were equally forthright in their replies to the standard opening question on cross-examination by Sir Arthur's lawyers: yes, they had also been promised or paid money to give evidence. One told of going to an Alderman Manning to collect his bribe after the election; Manning said he would not pay him but handed two shillings to a man in his office who promptly gave it to the witness. Another complained that he was not paid his promised bribe after the election because he was told he had voted for Pim and Corrigan; questioned by the judge, he admitted that he had indeed voted for the Liberals. Yet another man testified that he was promised payment "as sure as there was a brewery in James's Street".

But the main charges against Sir Arthur centred on the activities of a man called Henry Foster, a clerk in the registry of deeds, and a member of one of the Conservatives' ward committees covering the Inns' Quay ward. The secretary of this committee was Samuel Tudor Bradburne, Sir Arthur's private secretary, but it was also noteworthy for having a second "working" committee. This was set up by Foster and included Bradburne and a handful of others: the clear implication, though it was not fully proven, was that this committee was a dirty tricks group. Foster had mysteriously (but not surprisingly) disappeared just before the court case began. He had told his employers that he was ill and was said to have left the country for health reasons. He was said to be in Torquay or France but repeated threats by the judge failed to persuade him to appear in court.

Foster was instrumental in two of the main charges of systematic bribery against Sir Arthur. One involved appeals sent by telegram to freemen from Inverness to Brighton to return to Dublin for the poll. The prosecution claimed that the telegrams, signed by the fictitious

John Wilson Johnston, were implicitly – and illegally – promising to pay the freemen's travelling expenses. "Johnston" had his own office in Dame Street (where the Conservatives' headquarters was also located) but always appeared to have just gone out when anyone called to see him. Eventually, one witness identified the person using the office and a couple of hundred letters signed "J.W. Johnston" as Davenport Crosthwaite. He, it emerged, had also been brought into the campaign by Foster and, like Foster, had disappeared from Dublin just before the trial began.

Henry Foster's second scam was an elaborate plan for paying the freemen after they had cast their votes for Sir Arthur in Green Street courthouse. The Espy printing works at number 76 Capel Street, close to the courthouse, was hired for the day and arrangements made for the payments to be handed over there by an unseen person. Espy's was the Conservatives' election printer, producing the usual posters and placards: it had also produced a poster in orange, blue and green declaring "Presbyterians, plump for Pim; Catholics plump for Corrigan", in an attempt to split the Liberals' votes. Espy's was also asked to print 25 large cards saying "Mr Marquis' Office". The night before the election a man claiming to be Mr Marquis paid Espy's manager for the use of a room in the building the following day. The room, described as a parlour, had two doors, one leading to a second room. A hole was cut in this door and a wardrobe placed in front of it, allowing space for a person to pass between it and the door. Meanwhile, Foster had hired three people from "Dr Duncan's lunatic asylum" in the village of Finglas. They were told to sit in the parlour all day, pretending to be clerks reading and writing. One was the gardener at the asylum and was paid £3 for his day's "work", nearly six times his normal weekly wage of 10/6d (52.5 pence); the other two were illiterate. Thus, the preparations were laid for election day.

At the polling booths around the corner in Green Street young men guided the freemen to the correct boxes and oversaw their voting. Once they had done what was required of them, the young men directed the freemen to William Campbell, who had been, until the day before, an inspector with the Conservative Registration Society. Campbell was waiting outside the courthouse and gave the freemen a used train ticket from the Midland and Great Western Railway and directed them to Espy printers. The train ticket gained them entry into the building and its parlour, now marked by a card as "Mr Marquis' Office". There, the lunatic asylum's gardener sent them behind the wardrobe where they handed the railway ticket through the hole in the door to an unseen figure who gave them back an envelope. They were then ushered out the back door of the building, most stopping in the yard to look in their envelopes. They all contained a £5 Bank of Ireland note.

It was assumed that Henry Foster was probably the man who handed out the envelopes, giving the prosecuting counsel the opportunity to have some sarcastic fun about the elusive "man in the iron mask". Campbell admitted in evidence that he had spent election day in Green Street but claimed he was there of his own accord to see that the freemen he had registered were brought to the proper polling booths. He denied that he sent anybody to Espy's or had handled any train tickets that day: "I never saw any Midland Railway tickets except when I was travelling on the line," he declared. He was not questioned about the evidence of some freemen, who claimed he had offered to get them payment on condition that they gave him part of the proceeds: they said they had handed over £2 of their £5 to Campbell.

The prosecution tried – but not too hard – to connect Sir Arthur directly with any of the specific cases of bribery. Suspicions abounded but they were all circumstantial, such as another extraordinary episode in which the governor of the debtors' prison went to Guinness's brewery to tell them of an imprisoned Conservative voter who could be released on payment of part of his fine. The man had been in jail for 15 months for a debt of £11 but the woman to whom he owed the money had died and her relatives were willing to accept £4 in settlement. At the brewery, the governor apparently spoke to a Mr Waller,[11] a cousin of the Guinnesses, and, possibly, to Edward. On election day, Waller was at the prison to oversee the payment of £4 by the governor and the release of the prisoner. He then took him to Green Street to vote for the Conservatives. The governor admitted that he later received the £4 back from the brewery but denied that he had ever spoken to Sir Arthur about it. However, he disclosed that the next time he met Waller was after the election – at dinner in Sir Arthur's home.

The judge concluded that the activities of the governor were scandalous and it was an insult to his intelligence to suggest that the governor's decision to pay off the prisoner's debt was benevolence. It was not bribery either, he decided, "but I say it was a transaction which trembles upon the very line that separates charity from corrupt inducement." The prosecution attempted to link Sir Arthur to Henry Foster through their membership of the Amicable Club, described by one member as "a club of loyalty and good feeling" whose 60-odd members were "of one political feeling". It turned out, however, that Foster was not a member, although the equally elusive Davenport Crosthwaite was. In his own evidence, Sir Arthur agreed that he knew Campbell and Crosthwaite and had last seen the latter at a club meeting in the Gresham Hotel but he was vague about whether or not he knew Foster.

Sir Arthur said he had given instructions to his main agent that there should be no bribery and denied that he had either known about or sanctioned any of the activities revealed in the court. His lawyers, led by Isaac Butt, claimed that there was only the merest shadow of evidence to connect Sir Arthur with Foster, Campbell or Waller. They admitted that there was bribery at Espy printers but put it down to over-zealousness by Foster, who was only one of 500 local committee members in Sir Arthur's campaign, while hinting that the whole arrangement may have been set up by the Conservative's opponents. The final submissions by both sides hinged on whether or not Foster was an agent of Sir Arthur and, if he was, whether or not Sir Arthur could be held accountable for an agent's actions which were contrary to his instructions. The prosecution argued that he was an agent and Sir Arthur was responsible for his actions; the defence denied he was an agent and insisted that Sir Arthur was not accountable for whatever Foster might have done.

On the final day of the hearing, Sir Arthur sat beneath the bench to hear his fate. Justice Keogh noted that had a hundred-odd votes been taken from Sir Arthur and given to Sir Dominic Corrigan, the result of the election would have been reversed. The city's freemen had been shown to a great extent to be corrupt voters and he had reason to believe that many more than 30 freemen had been bribed in the Espy printers or elsewhere. He declared the election void, and that Sir Arthur

Guinness through his agents had been guilty of bribery. But he made it clear that he did not think Sir Arthur was personally responsible: "As far as his personal position, or character or acts are concerned he is entitled to have from me, and he shall have from me, a certificate that his hands are clean, and that his character was unaspersed in those proceedings."[12]

In spite of the judge's certificate of his innocence and good character, the outcome was clearly a severe embarrassment to the new head of the Guinness family and a serious setback to his political ambitions. As well as tainting him with bribery, it had also shown him to be not very adept at politics. The cumulative impression left by the campaign speeches, the comment surrounding them and the evidence brought out in the court case was of a young man who was not totally in control of his own political destiny and, at best, exploited by a lot of unscrupulous backroom political types. He had lost his seat in the House of Commons and was barred from contesting elections during the life of that parliament. The consensus among his political opponents was that he had been personally duped and his wealth exploited by the Conservatives. Among the Conservatives, his political stock was undiminished, however; a meeting of the "Protestants of Dublin" a month after the petition was prefaced with prolonged cheers for Sir Arthur and his younger brother, Edward, and "growls" about Justice Keogh and Sir Dominic Corrigan. Edward was persuaded initially to stand against Corrigan in the resulting by-election but later withdrew for unknown reasons.[13]

But Sir Arthur's experience did not deter him from pursuing a political career, cause him to reconsider his political views or sour his relationship with the Conservatives. A year later his lawyer, Isaac Butt, founded the Home Government Association, the movement which was a first step in altering irrevocably the Irish political landscape and making home rule the pivotal issue for almost the next half century. The movement was initially a conservative grouping, attracting many who were disillusioned by the disestablishment of the Church of Ireland (which was passed by parliament in March 1869 and came into effect from 1 January 1871). It was grounded in the type of Protestant practical nationalism to which Sir Arthur's father and grandfather had been attracted. Butt was joined by many conservatives, like the founder and owner of *The Irish Times*, Major Laurence Knox, who were disillusioned with British party politics, and he invited the Guinness brothers and relatives like David Plunket to join him. His overtures were firmly repulsed by Sir Arthur.

In a letter to Butt on behalf of himself, his brother and Plunket, Sir Arthur firmly dismissed a rumour that they might adopt what were commonly called "National views". He added: ". . . while none can feel more strongly a truly National desire for the advancement of Ireland materially and intellectually, we do not and cannot think this is to be achieved by Repeal [of the Act of Union] or by any half measure of Repeal . . ."[14] The Guinnesses were now, and would remain, unshakeably Conservative and Unionist in their politics.

The growing success of the brewery was undoubtedly among the reasons for the family's political conservatism. In an era in which Dublin's traditional industries were in decline, brewing was one of the few exceptions. Among the brewers, Guinness was going from strength to strength, steadily increasing its dominance and using its financial muscle to squeeze out its competitors. Its market in England for high-quality porter was still of huge importance but its new strength was based on its successful exploitation of the rising market in rural Ireland, which gave it a formidable base from which to launch its conquest of the capital in the 1870s. As Ireland's largest brewery, it dominated the trade and the cartel arrangements that fixed beer prices in Dublin. Guinness used its position there to dictate prices for everybody else: by cutting them, it put huge pressure on less successful competitors, increased its market share and ensured that it won the greater proportion of the new markets opening up in the city's growing suburbs. As well as offering cheaper – and high-quality – porter, it provided inducements like free deliveries to new pubs, based on preferential deals with the suburban railways.[15]

The strategy worked perfectly. Some breweries that relied mainly on the Dublin market were forced into bankruptcy: a few, like Manders, tried to escape the Guinness squeeze by leaving the price-fixing cartel but were forced out of business anyway. Others tried mergers, while newcomers hoping to cash in on the lucrative business rarely lasted long. Sweetman's, the only other brewery which had existed since the eighteenth century, was eventually bought out and demolished to make way for the Iveagh clothes market, which was built later as part of the Guinnesses' philanthropic initiatives.[16]

The strategy cost St James's Gate a drop in its profit margins from 30 per cent to 20 per cent but led to a huge surge in output. The brewery itself was no longer large enough to cope with the growth and during the 1870s it was expanded and practically reconstructed. In 1860 the brewery covered four acres on the south of James's Street but in 1873 it added a large new site to the north, running from James's Street to the River Liffey. New machinery was introduced; a spiral, narrow-gauge railway system built to move goods between the different levels of the site; and the workforce was doubled to some 2,500 workers.

This expansionist period firmly established the Guinness reputation for high-quality porter and well-paid employment. Wages were higher than the going rates for Dublin and job security was unique; medical services were provided for staff, along with sick pay and widows' pensions. The conditions were summed up in the Dublin saying that a Guinness man meant money, dead or alive.[17] The employees were divided on social and sectarian lines: most of those on salaries were Protestant gentlemen who enjoyed a comfortable standard of living, epitomised by membership of the Kildare Street Club and the yachting clubs in Kingstown (Dun Laoghaire). Brewers, the elite of James's Gate, still came primarily from the extended Guinness and Purser families. The majority of the skilled and unskilled workers were Catholics, who also enjoyed a higher standard of living than their working-class colleagues.

Production of porter doubled between 1868, the year of Sir Benjamin Lee Guinness's death, and 1879: in one six-year stretch during that period, 1871 to 1876, Guinness turnover amounted to £7 million from the sales of porter, which was bought by drinkers at a pub price of 5.5d (less than 2.5 pence) a pint for stout and 3d (1.25 pence) for porter. In spite of its enlightened employment policies, however, only

£300,000 of its total costs went on wages and salaries, and a fifth of that was accounted for by the ration of free porter given to workers. By comparison, the two Guinness brothers kept double that amount, £600,000, for themselves out of a total profit for the period of £900,000. The balance was invested in the expansion of the brewery, whose value, estimated by John Tertius Purser at a mere £80,000 in 1869, rose to £500,000 by 1879.[18]

The main architect of this expansion was Edward, the youngest Guinness brother. In the early years after their father's death, the two brothers were equally involved in running the brewery and worked reasonably well together, possibly because of the difference in their ages and experience. As time went on, however, strains began to emerge. Sir Arthur's interest in, and aptitude for, the business waned, while Edward's increased. Edward's impatience with his brother's lack of interest also rose: he found it difficult to share control with someone who clearly did not have his own natural business ability. Collaboration became increasingly difficult between the decisive Edward and the more passive Sir Arthur, especially because Sir Arthur continued to take most of the profits while doing less of the work. In the eight years after their father's death, Sir Arthur took the enormous sum of £530,000 out of the profits of at least £1.5 million, while Edward took a not-insubstantial £350,000.[19]

The disparity in the sharing of the profits was further evidence of the divergence in the brothers' ambitions and lifestyles. Indeed, their social and personal situations contributed in no small measure to the growing tensions between the co-owners of the brewery. Their marriages in the early 1870s, Sir Arthur into the aristocracy and Edward to a cousin, were to have a significant effect on the brewery and in bringing their business relationship to an end in a relatively short time. The new Guinness wives were formidable women who appeared to have had more influence on their husbands' public lives than the women of the earlier generations.

In 1871, the 30-year-old Sir Arthur married Lady Olivia Charlotte White, the eldest daughter of William Hedges-White, the third Earl of Bantry, who was known as "Billy Hawthorne". Ten years his junior, Olive, as she was known, was a tall, handsome woman who had grown up on her family's estate at Macroom in County Cork and had a strong aristocratic aversion to trade. The marriage was arranged in advance as a *mariage blanche*, meaning that there would be no sex and implying strongly that Sir Arthur was gay. The couple never had any children and Sir Arthur's unusual arrangement may have been a factor in his leaving the brewery.

Three years later, the 26-year-old Edward took a more conventional Guinness option in marrying one of his cousins, Adelaide Guinness. She was petite, with dark hair drawn neatly back, soft-spoken but his equal in energy and vitality and three years older than he was. Dodo, as she was known in the family, was descended from Samuel Guinness, the goldbeater younger brother of the first Arthur, whose descendants became the banking Guinnesses. Her grandfather, Samuel's son, was Richard Guinness, the barrister and "lisping loyalist" derided by Watty Cox's magazine in the early years of the century. Her father was Richard Samuel Guinness who, with his brother Robert Rundell Guinness, set up the first Guinness bank in Dublin in the 1820s.

Dodo's mother was Katherine Jenkinson, a daughter of the tenth Baron of Hawkesbury, who expected to be kept by her husband Richard in the style to which she was apparently accustomed. His efforts to do so caused them to live constantly beyond their means, which was among the reasons why his brother Robert opted out of their bank. Instead, Robert Rundell joined forces with John Ross Mahon to set up a new bank, Guinness Mahon. Richard, known as "Old Pel" from a pelican-like appearance caused by his fondness for high-collar shirts which pushed up his chin, eventually fell foul of his spendthrift ways. His bank collapsed in the 1840s and he went into politics, representing Kinsale in County Cork and later Barnstable in Devon. Richard and Katherine's large family was brought up in aristocratic fashion in spite of their precarious financial circumstances. Dodo, their fourth daughter, was reared to marry into the aristocracy, spending time, for instance, at the court of the Duc de Montebello in France. Thus, her ambitious mother was underwhelmed when she decided to marry Edward; his considerable wealth seemingly was little compensation in her eyes for the fact that he was still a mere brewer.

Publicly, both brothers became notable society hosts and set about improving the conditions for their hospitality with their extensive profits from the brewery. Sir Arthur expanded his main home at St Anne's, the estate in Raheny which he had inherited from his father. He bought up surrounding land to quadruple the estate to 493 acres and landscaped it with oak and pine, an artificial lake and hollows and mounds. One of his plans for a straight tree-lined avenue to the house was thwarted, however, by a local landowner who reputedly refused to take his "beer money" for a piece of the necessary land.[20] The avenue ended up with a right-angled turn around the unavailable land. The house itself was remodelled with a view to entertaining on the grand scale. A new wing was built and linked to the existing building by an enormous entrance hall. A ballroom with marble pillars supporting a balcony and a palm court, both the height of the building, were also added. The overall effect, later described in uncomplimentary terms by a cousin and god-daughter of his wife, Katherine Everett, when St Anne's epoch had passed, was of an out-of-date luxury hotel.

It was a vast building in pseudo-Palladian style, the huge portico being flanked on either side by seven high plate-glass sash windows and surmounted by fourteen others. Externally its great size and fair proportions gave it a certain dignity, but nothing can be said in favour of the interior. The dark, enormous hall was intersected midway by a wide, cold, white marble staircase, and on the landing where the steps divided to ascend in two flights sat a female figure, also in cold white marble, hampered in her clearly expressed desire to appear modest by the lack of any rag of clothing.[21]

In the last decades of the nineteenth century, however, it was a highly fashionable society haunt, overseen by the equally fashionable host and hostess. Sir Arthur also used his money to develop the Ashford estate in County Galway, also inherited from his father, by buying more land, rebuilding a baronial-style castle, planting forests and turning the estate into a prime woodcock shoot.

Edward also extended his social base, buying another country house, Farmleigh, on the western edge of Dublin's Phoenix Park, to complement the centre-city residence he had inherited at St Stephen's Green. He subsequently had Farmleigh rebuilt into a three-storey-over-basement Victorian-Georgian mansion with 24 bedrooms, excluding those in the servants' quarters. Both brothers also maintained houses in London, Edward at Berkeley Square and Sir Arthur at 11 Carlton House Terrace, which he bought from Gladstone (then out of office) for the substantial price of £35,000 in 1875. The sale included, as Gladstone noted in his diary, "the chairs and sofa on which we sat when we resolved on the disestablishment of the Irish church in 1868".[22] Whether Sir Arthur knew of the association between his newly acquired furniture and one of the main issues in his ill-fated election campaign is not clear.

Sir Arthur's wife, Lady Olive, was unhappy with his involvement in the business and was a constant spur to his natural lack of interest in it. On the other hand, Edward's impatience with the situation in which he did most of the work while his brother and partner took more of the rewards increased after his first son, Rupert, was born in London in 1874, a year after his marriage to Dodo. Although he was to live a month short of 80 years, Edward seems to have inherited some of the ill-health of his near-permanently indisposed mother, whose favourite child he was; furthermore, he was a hypochondriac throughout his life.

The birth of his son and heir – and the childlessness of Sir Arthur and Lady Olive and, presumably, Edward's knowledge of their marriage arrangement and that that would not change – prompted thoughts of succession and of the financial consequences for his new family were he to die suddenly. It could mean, for instance, that control of the brewery would slip out of Guinness hands altogether if his brother, with no heirs of his own, were to inherit it in the near future. The degree to which Edward, in his late twenties, was really concerned about this prospect is impossible to say, although he cited it in a letter to his solicitor in May 1876.[23] It may have been, in part at least, a symptom of his frustrations with the existing partnership arrangements or it may have been a cover for concerns about his brother being gay and, in the way of the times, susceptible to blackmail or a combination of reasons. Whatever his true reasons, there is no doubt that Edward made the running on negotiating a new partnership, to the extent of threatening to stand down himself, while Sir Arthur was content simply to continue the existing arrangement when it came up for renewal at the end of May 1876.

They came to a new agreement in August 1876 which offered a retiring partner, or the successors of a deceased one, a more attractive deal than envisaged by their father ten years earlier. Half of the brewery's goodwill and plant, valued in total by John Tertius Purser at £800,000, plus half of the current year's profits (£80,000) were to be paid to the one who left the brewery. Within two months of this agreement being signed, however, Sir Arthur agreed to leave the brewery suddenly and on even more favourable terms. He was to receive £600,000 for his share of the brewery plus £80,000 as his half of the year's profits, all to be paid in six instalments over four years. The first was paid on 1 January 1877 when the dissolution of the partnership was announced publicly.

Precisely what caused Sir Arthur's sudden decision to opt out of the brewery – and Edward to agree to pay him a larger share than the latest agreement required – is not known. The apparent suddenness of Sir Arthur's change of heart and the extra financial inducement to him to go suggest more compelling reasons for the break-up of the business partnership than the ones usually put forward. The latter include the suggestion that Sir Arthur had earned a reputation as a philanthropist by 1876, was back in parliament again as Conservative MP for Dublin and was more involved with these matters than with brewing. But he had been re-elected two years earlier and his public career was not obviously any more demanding between August and October 1876, when he finally capitulated.

Lady Olive is usually credited with playing a central role in his decision to retire from the brewery; one story suggests that she and Sir Arthur were out walking in Dublin one evening when a disgruntled drinker threw a bottle of flat stout over a wall. It splattered on the pavement in front of them, providing the last straw in her mind. The next day, the story goes, Sir Arthur resigned from the partnership.[24] It is difficult to imagine Sir Arthur surrendering his lucrative birthright because of the distress caused to his wife by a broken bottle of stale Guinness.

Relations between the two brothers and between their families were undoubtedly strained by personality differences, social pretensions and

114

their unequal contribution to the brewery. But there are also strong undercurrents which suggest that the collapse of the partnership was caused by a more dramatic event or events. Whatever the full reasons behind the break-up of the partnership, the result was that Edward, at the age of 29, became the sole owner of what was now the world's largest brewery.

———— ∞ ————

The Guinnesses were now major figures in Dublin, the richest family, the most successful businessmen, arbiters of society, and influential in public affairs. Before and after he left the brewery, Sir Arthur was clearly the head of the family in the public's mind and among the extended family. Edward remained a more shadowy figure in the public's perception, eclipsed by Sir Arthur's more visible role and frequently lumped in with him in the newspapers as "the Brothers Guinness" or referred to by his middle name, Cecil, or his initials E.C. They had a reputation and a social standing to maintain which was, on one occasion, protected for them by other members of the extended family.

The destitute John Grattan Guinness, who had sued his cousin Benjamin Lee for wrongful dismissal from the brewery, died in England in 1871 in what his brother described as "the greatest misery and dirt imaginable". John's brother, Arthur Grattan Guinness, wrote back to Dublin to tell his cousins of his successful attempts to cover up the death. He had bribed the local newspaper reporters with 10 shillings (50 pence) not to publish John Grattan's connection with the rich Guinnesses, he said, since it would have been "a terrible annoyance to have the particulars stated". He also asked his cousins for his 10 shillings back but it is not clear if he got it.[25]

The "Brothers Guinness" also continued the family tradition of high-profile public benefactions, notably in the Dublin Exhibition which they funded in 1872. Two years earlier they had bought the building and grounds of the by-then bankrupt Dublin Exhibition Palace Company, with which their father had been involved. The new Exhibition of Irish Arts, Industries and Manufactures was opened in June by the Duke of Edinburgh, Queen Victoria's son, amid glowing praise for the Guinness brothers. But the whole project was quickly ensnared in controversy when the local building industry began to complain that craftsmen and designers had been brought from London to refurbish the palace. Furthermore, many of the exhibits turned out to be of English goods; one Dublin carriage-maker withdrew from it altogether when his protests that all the prime sites in his section had been given to English manufacturers were brushed aside.

The *Freeman's Journal* took an even more populist line, denouncing the pricing structure which meant, it claimed, that working men could not visit the exhibition on Saturday afternoons, their only free time. Admission was one shilling (5 pence) except on Wednesdays and Saturdays when bands played there and the price went up to 2/6d (12.5 pence). Season ticket holders had been assured, the newspaper claimed, that they would not have to associate on those more fashionable days with people who paid only a shilling. Within a week the managers of the exhibition announced that admission on Saturdays would be reduced to one shilling and that employers could buy books of discounted tickets for their workers. "The next best thing to avoiding a mistake is to mend it," the *Freeman's Journal* commented smugly.[26] Its claim of success for its campaign finally stung Sir Arthur into a public, and distinctly patrician, response. "It may not be palatable information to you, but it is nevertheless true, that your so-called efforts had nothing whatever to do with any recent changes at the Exhibition, as they had been arranged by my brother and me previous to the opening day," he wrote from Ashford Castle. "We feel as warm an interest in the poorer and working classes as you can possibly do, and I do not think they will be inclined to believe in the genuineness of, or the necessity for, the position you represent yourself as having assumed, namely – 'as remonstrating with the Brothers Guinness on their policy of excluding every working man from the palace and its enjoyments'."

Sir Arthur then received a death threat at St Anne's, coincidentally linking him to threats on the life of Justice Keogh, the judge who had barred him from his parliamentary seat. Keogh was now at the centre of fierce controversy after ruling in another election petition that the three Catholic bishops and 29 priests in County Galway had used undue influence, amounting to intimidation through "threats of

116

temporal injury and spiritual punishment" to have a Home Ruler, John Philip Nolan, elected MP.[27] The badly written threat, forwarded by Sir Arthur to the Dublin conservative newspapers, the *Evening Mail* and *The Irish Times*, called him an "orange whelp" and accused him of insulting the clergy's and people's newspaper (the *Freeman's Journal*). It demanded an apology and a contribution to the unseated MP's fund or else he and "that scoundrel" Keogh would get a bullet. "We have a person hired to shoot you and him and no mistake so take warnin [*sic*]in time," it said.[28]

The Keogh controversy was a major issue at the time and the threat to Sir Arthur was raised in the House of Commons where Gladstone, replying to a question about it, expressed regret that such letters should have the honour conferred on them of being noticed there.[29] The *Freeman's Journal* dismissed it as a sham and questioned whether Sir Arthur could have taken it seriously for a moment. But it felt obliged to add: "There are few men more respected or more universally esteemed than Sir Arthur Guinness – and deservedly so. There is not a man in Ireland who would do him harm, and few who would not willingly risk much to protect him did he need it."

There was no doubt, however, that Sir Arthur was falling out with the political temper of the times as the Home Rule movement gathered momentum. Its turning point came in the 1874 election which, in Dublin, was a curiously subdued affair in which an assortment of issues vied for dominance. They included Home Rule, denominational education and the closure of public houses on Sundays. They were not all necessarily connected but created a potent cocktail of political and sectarian issues. At first, Sir Arthur refused to stand for the Conservatives, to the dismay of the party's supporters. The Dublin *Evening Mail* urged the Conservatives to make an effort to wipe out "the reproach accompanying his previous candidature by a united and strong effort to return him at the minimum of expense to himself". Whether he was still sore over that experience or not, he changed his mind within days and agreed to stand.

The main battle in the election did not involve Sir Arthur and the Conservatives, however. It was fought primarily between the Liberals, still represented by Jonathan Pim, and the Home Rulers, represented by the city's Lord Mayor, Maurice Brooks. Pim refused to endorse Home Rule, which Brooks supported in order to "secure the integrity of the imperial interest on a juster and fairer basis".[30] While they battled it out over the main political issue, the Grocers' and Vintners' Association and various temperance groups fought an even more heated battle over Sunday closing. The vintners represented one of the most powerful lobby groups in nineteenth-century Ireland and were not averse to using their political muscle in support of their livelihoods.[31] Generally, they favoured nationalist developments, supporting Daniel O'Connell and his repeal campaign and, subsequently, Home Rule. Faced with the choice between a Conservative unionist and a defender of the drink interest on one side and Home Rulers and temperance supporters on the other side, on this occasion they opted for a Guinness.

The upshot of the election was victory for Sir Arthur and Brooks: Sir Arthur headed the poll with 5,213 votes against 4,838 for Brooks. The Home Rulers were pleased with the outcome, the *Freeman's Journal* claiming that Brooks would have headed the poll but for the licensed vintners throwing their support behind "their trade champion". But the main significance of the election in the longer term was the destruction of the liberal vote and of liberal unionism in Ireland: from then on, the political battle developed between a more unambiguously nationalist party and unionism.[32]

Back in the House of Commons again, Sir Arthur continued with his philanthropy, including the gesture for which he is best remembered, landscaping and then donating the park in St Stephen's Green to the people of Dublin in 1876. As usual in Dublin, his benefaction was not without controversy: there were several acrimonious rows in Dublin City Council about the precise terms under which it would be opened to the public. Sir Arthur initially offered to pay off a debt of £2,270 to the commissioners who controlled the Green in order to open it to the public and to spend a further £5,000 on improving it, including the provision of its centrepiece lake. The commissioners (who had taken over the Green from the Corporation some 50 years earlier) agreed but a row developed over who should pay for its maintenance and who would control it. The Board of Works agreed to take it on if Dublin Corporation would pay half the maintenance costs of £1,200 a year and forego the rent of £300 a year it had been receiving for it. At first the city council agreed to the deal, on the casting vote of the chairman, but a move was made subsequently to rescind it.

The issue became a proxy battle involving the main political tensions of the day which were, as always throughout nineteenth-century Dublin, fought out in the city hall. Led by a Councillor McSwiney, the opponents of the deal insisted that the Corporation must have control of the park if it was paying for it. Supporters of Sir Arthur argued that the Corporation should have no say because it would turn it into a parade ground for political marches, upsetting the people who lived around the square. It quickly became a straight political fight between the majority of Liberals and Catholics and the minority of Conservatives and Protestants. The rhetoric became inflamed on both sides, supported by their respective media backers. The *Freeman's Journal* complained that Sir Arthur was getting all the credit and popularity for his contribution; the Board of Works was contributing £18,000 (the annual £600 maintenance capitalised over 30 years) and getting all the control and management, while the Corporation was contributing £29,418 (in annual charges and rent foregone) and receiving nothing but sneers and abuse. It saw the issue as an attempt to destroy the only institution in the country which was based on the principle of government by the people and for the people and to replace it with government of a great city by a caste or narrow clique.

Sir Arthur warned that the commissioners who controlled the Green at that time would not hand it over to the Corporation and that he would not adhere to the promises he had made either in those circumstances. His opponents on the council bemoaned the conditions attached to his gift and repeatedly referred to the bribery of voters for which Sir Arthur had previously lost his House of Commons seat. Supporters of the deal counter-attacked by questioning the Corporation's competence, claiming it had proved itself unable to keep alive its trees in Sackville Street (the present O'Connell Street).

The original agreement was now rescinded by 27 votes to 18 and Sir Arthur's implicit threat to withdraw his offer hung in the air. Efforts then began to reach some sort of compromise. The council agreed to try to meet the wishes of the Commissioners in charge of the Green and of the residents of the square, as long as it was recognised to be the natural authority over the new public park. Eventually, however, the council gave in and control of the Green was vested in the Board of Works and its maintenance paid for by the government. A Bill to facilitate the changes was passed by parliament in 1877 and the work began on transforming the park. Severe winters in 1878 and 1879 upset the opening plans by killing off a large number of plants and shrubs but it was ready to be opened by mid-1880 – just after a general election in which Sir Arthur was defending his seat as one of the city's two MPs.

⸺⸎⸺

On the face of it, the gift of St Stephen's Green to the people of Dublin should have secured Sir Arthur's re-election but there were other, more fundamental, political forces at work in Ireland than the philanthropy of one of its richest men. After the death of Isaac Butt in 1879, a new and more forceful leader emerged to take over the Home Rule mantle: Charles Stewart Parnell. His alliance with Michael Davitt's Land League, which was campaigning for the rights of tenant farmers, galvanised politics in Ireland. Dublin for the moment remained somewhat detached from this new movement, concentrated as it was on rural issues, but it was not immune to its effects. Nevertheless, the 1880 general election in Dublin seemed set to continue on its old path, a Conservative seat and a Liberal seat, now occupied by, in the terms of the time, a moderate Home Ruler: the two sitting MPs, Sir Arthur and Maurice Brooks, looked likely to be re-elected. "Of course, there is no doubt as to Sir Arthur Guinness's re-election," the conservative Dublin *Evening Mail* declared as the campaign gathered momentum. "His claims are, party politics aside, paramount to those of all comers in the eyes of his fellow-citizens."[33]

There was no Parnellite candidate in Dublin but the growing influence of Parnell and the Land League's campaign against landlordism was clearly anathema to Sir Arthur. Parnell and he had shared a platform the previous year to mourn the death of Butt but their political interests and positions were at opposite poles. Sir Arthur clearly identified Parnell as the main antagonist in a speech during the campaign which said as much about his own views as about Parnell's.

Parnell, he declared at an election rally in the Exhibition Palace, was arousing "a false and spurious species of national feeling" in Ireland. There was a great, powerful and creditable national feeling in Ireland but it was "a feeling of nationality which has its objects and ambitions within the limits of the Empire".

The removal of the landlords would be an injustice and disastrous for Ireland, he went on. They would take their capital with them, and where would capital be found to take its place? Removing the landlords would remove the element which controlled social life. "Who is to dispense justice and who is to perform the other duties which fall to the lot of the local landed gentry? I see no machinery by which we are to supplement their loss." Parnell, he claimed, had not put up a candidate in Dublin because "the intelligence, the independence, the education and the wealth of the capital was against him".

A couple of nights later, Sir Arthur was back in the same venue to declare that he would not have contested the election if it was against a moderate Liberal. But a duty had been placed upon him to see Dublin repudiate once and for all the principles of Home Rule, that progressive Home Rule that must end in Parnellism. He went on to deny accusations from Maurice Brooks that he had opposed in parliament the removal of inequalities affecting Catholics and pointed out that he lived part of the year in the west of Ireland (in Ashford Castle) where he never had any differences with Catholics over religion or any other subject.

But the decisive factor in the outcome of the election in Dublin was not so much Parnellism as the continuing temperance campaign. Pubs had been closed on Sundays for the previous two years in an experiment that was due for renewal in 1882. Five cities in the United Kingdom, including Dublin, had been exempted from the law and the temperance campaign wanted to have the closure renewed, extended to Dublin, and to early closing on Saturdays. They claimed that a drop in the consumption of drink, of up to ten million gallons of beer, proved the effectiveness of Sunday closing and they were determined to maintain their momentum.

The temperance campaigners persuaded the Conservatives that there were a thousand temperance votes to be wooed away from the

Liberals in Dublin if the Conservatives ran a second candidate and committed themselves to Sunday closing.[34] Neither prospect found much favour with Sir Arthur but he found himself hustled along by his party and the temperance movement. At the start of the campaign, a deputation of no less than 48 people from the Society for the Suppression of Intemperance met Sir Arthur by appointment in Mr Russell's Temperance Hotel in St Stephen's Green to ask for his support. His response was tetchy but ambiguous: he declared that he had been returned to parliament "unpledged" for some years and would consider it "a great degradation" if pledges were now required of him. "If my constituents are not ready to trust to my judgement and to my perfect impartiality on such matters I would prefer not representing Dublin," he told them, as though they should accept that someone whose family wealth was based on a brewery could be impartial on the question.

However, he went on to fudge the issue, expressing his belief that the Sunday Closing Act would be continued, his pleasure at its apparent effects so far, and suggesting that his differences with the temperance campaigners was "more a difference of degree than of principle". With, presumably, the benefit of superior knowledge, he also questioned the reason for the drop in beer consumption, ascribing it to the distress and destitution of the country, rather than to Sunday closing. While he still opposed total Sunday closing in Dublin, he said he supported shorter opening hours in the city and had not opposed Sunday closing in the rest of Ireland.[35]

Sir Arthur was not enamoured of the idea of a second Conservative candidate either but was overruled by the party. Shortly before nominations closed, a strong temperance supporter, James Stirling, was chosen to contest the election alongside him. Stirling immediately declared himself in favour of "all measures to mitigate the evil of intemperance", including Sunday closing in all cities, as well as the introduction of Saturday night closing. Sir Arthur claimed, none too convincingly, that he had waived his opposition to a second candidate in the interests of defeating the existing Home Ruler, Brooks. The Conservative strategists believed they had achieved a notable political coup; the temperance campaign threw its support behind Sir Arthur and Stirling and the Conservatives expected to reap a handsome electoral reward. No doubt they were encouraged, too, by the reaction of their opponents, whose main mouthpiece, the *Freeman's Journal*, described the temperance support for Sir Arthur as "little less than a ghastly outrage upon honest politics".[36]

The election count at the Exhibition Palace in Earlsfort Terrace went on until three o'clock in the morning. The result was relatively close but it became clear well before the official declaration. Sir Arthur heard it from a jubilant opponent, John Stanislaus Joyce, the full-time secretary of the United Liberal Club and shortly to become the father of James Joyce, who was organising a tally of the count for his candidates and, by his own account, was surprised at an impending double victory for the Liberals. He later described the scene:

> Our solicitor, Stephen Sheehan, a tremendous big man, he was over at a table and says I, "By Gor, our men are in, Stephen – not one but the two of them." Who should be sitting next to me but Sir Arthur Guiness [*sic*] and his cousin the Hon. David Plunkett [*sic*], and the two were in evening dress . . . Sir Arthur asked me "Have you got the figures?" "I have, Sir Arthur," I replied, and he asked me how did it go. I then had the pleasure of telling Sir Arthur Guiness that he was no longer a member and I said that Maurice Brooks got so much and Lyons so much.[37]

Joyce thereafter liked to declare that he had won the election – "Oh dear, dear God, those were great times," he recalled later in an interview – and he received a hundred guineas (£105) from each of his successful candidates. The Spirit Grocers' Association also prided itself on having swung the election by taking 280 votes from Sir Arthur and giving them to Brooks and Lyons. The Conservatives had clearly miscalculated badly: the expected temperance vote did not swing from Liberals to Conservatives but the politically powerful publicans did swing decisively away from Guinness and to the Liberals. Sir Arthur lost his seat and Dublin was now represented by the Home Ruler Brooks and a Liberal doctor, Robert Lyons.

The Conservatives were despondent. The Dublin *Evening Mail* described Sir Arthur's defeat as "a shock and a grief to every right-minded man" and blamed it on 1,200 new voters who were mostly "semi-paupers, a proletariat class, who are as destitute of the sense of public obligation and of respect for the good name of the city as they are of pecuniary stake in its prosperity". *The Times* described the result as a surprise and a heavy blow to the Conservatives and found there was much sympathy for Sir Arthur "who has been made on two occasions the victim of mismanagement". Their opponents, however, were ecstatic. "For once and, let us hope, forever, Dublin has shaken itself from the shackles of Tory Ascendancy," the *Freeman's Journal* exulted. Its hopes were fulfilled, at least in part. The Tory ascendancy in Dublin was pretty much over and no Guinness would ever be elected to public office in Ireland again. But there was another, immediate, consolation for the family.

Within days of the 1880 general election, one of the rumours of the campaign was confirmed as fact. The outgoing Prime Minister and long-time admirer of Guinness (the drink), Benjamin Disraeli, raised Sir Arthur to the peerage in recognition of his public services and his efforts on behalf of the Conservative Party. Sir Arthur thus became the first member of the Guinness family to become a member of the aristocracy and "the first direct entry of beer into the [House of] Lords".[38] He took the title of Ardilaun, the name of one of the islands on his west of Ireland estate (from the Irish, meaning high island), since there was already a Lord Ashford.

Clearly, it was a fitting appointment for Sir Arthur at the age of 40. Although he had opted out of the brewery, he was still identified as the head of the Guinness family; within the family, he and his wife Olive were seen as the arbiters of good taste. He had cultivated the manners and attitudes of the aristocracy in his choice of life as a landed gentleman rather than as a brewer, businessman or politician. And he had used his considerable wealth to continue his disinterested funding of worthy projects. A couple of months later, St Stephen's Green was opened to the public without ceremony but to a chorus of praise from his political opponents as well as his political friends. The work there had ended up costing him an estimated £20,000 and given Dublin one of its enduring assets. "It is a boon to the wealthy classes, but it is a priceless gift to their poorer neighbours," the *Freeman's Journal* commented. It went on to suggest that a subscription be raised from the public at large to erect a monument to Lord Ardilaun in gratitude for his generosity. That drew a characteristic response from the new lord: "My efforts have sprung solely from my desire to benefit my fellow-citizens," he wrote back. "I shall esteem it my highest reward to know that they believe in the genuineness of my motives, and value anything which, with the co-operation of others, I have been able to effect." A suggestion that the park be renamed Ardilaun Park petered out. Nevertheless, a monument was raised to him in the Green some 12 years later, a statue of a moustachioed figure sitting in a slightly languid fashion in an armchair on top of a pedestal. It is at the edge of St Stephen's Green, looking westwards down York Street towards, perhaps, St James's Gate. A souvenir pamphlet about the opening, published by a sycophantic printer some months later, carried the family motto on its cover (*Spes Mea in Deo*) along with another motto, "'Tis only Noble to be Good".

With his appointment to the peerage, Ardilaun clearly had achieved the ambition to which his education, marriage and temperament had directed him. On the other hand, he was out of tune with the major movements of his times, especially but not exclusively in Ireland where the days of the landed gentry were numbered. Just as he joined it, the landed gentry were about to cease being the governing class of Ireland. Equally, the aristocracy throughout the United Kingdom was changing and, ironically, Sir Arthur's elevation was one of the turning points for the changes that were to lead to its decline. He was one of the first two representatives of what later became a flood: the ennoblement of people who had made vast fortunes out of industry and commerce – and contributed generously to political parties – rather than those who had inherited landed wealth. Disraeli's elevation of Sir Arthur to become Lord Ardilaun and of the Welsh iron industrialist Sir Ivor Guest to become Lord Wimborne in his resignation honours list in 1880 was later identified as the starting point for this trend: "in retrospect, it was clearly the thin end of the plutocratic wedge."[39]

With his social status and a seat in the House of Lords secured, Ardilaun set out to resist at every turn the changes in Irish life which he deplored, particularly the rise of nationalism, the leadership of Parnell, and the Land League's campaign against landlordism. Although a relative newcomer to the landed class, Ardilaun identified himself utterly with it through the Property Defence Association, set up to try to counter the Land League's tactics. Both ideologically and in reality, through his Ashford Castle estate, which was in one of the areas of greatest agrarian unrest, he was on the front line of the Land War of the early 1880s, during which four of his employees lost their lives.

The only landlord killed during the Land War, Lord Mountmorres, was one of his Ashford neighbours; he was shot dead while travelling home alone from Clonbur in September 1880.[40] Ardilaun was among those who attended the inquest some days later which heard that a local family would not allow the dying landlord be taken into their house from the road where he had been shot. Several locals were arrested (including, at one stage, an employee of Ardilaun's at Ashford Castle) but nobody was ever tried for the murder. The main suspect was a former tenant who had lost two court cases against Mountmorres and was then employed by him as a herdsman in lieu of rent owed to the landlord. He was arrested several times, the last time as he was leaving Queenstown in County Cork to go to America, but he was released again. It was widely believed in the area later that the killers had emigrated.

The Land League held meetings outside the gates of Ashford Castle and some of its spokesmen denounced Ardilaun's afforestation programme for replacing fields of corn with trees. A poster advertising one such meeting outside Ashford declared: "Men of Mayo and Galway, assemble in your thousands at Cong, on the 11th July [1880], and avow your resolve to prosecute the Land War, until you achieve the abolition of the Usurper of your God-given inheritance."[41] At another stage, some 200 men Ardilaun had employed on relief work were threatened to stop work unless they got an increase in pay. Ardilaun dismissed them all and left immediately for Dublin but subsequently insisted that his sudden departure was caused by the death of his wife's sister and not by anonymous threats.[42]

Ardilaun was also involved in one of the more celebrated incidents of that period – the ostracism of Captain Charles Boycott, the land agent of Lord Erne in County Mayo, which gave a new word to the language. He tried to assist Boycott, sending horses and provisions to him, protected by some of the Ashford estate workers, and taking some of Boycott's produce to Galway by the steamer service which he, Ardilaun, had introduced to Lough Corrib.[43] Rumours that he was in trouble – besieged at Ashford, with his life at risk because of his aid to Boycott and his alleged refusal to allow some tenants to cut turf on one of his hills – spread and a reporter from the *Daily Telegraph* braved a snowstorm to find out what was happening. He found that all was calm at the newly rebuilt Ashford Castle where Sir Arthur denied that he was in danger. He had been offered police protection, he said, but preferred to rely on "a little force of my own consisting of my gamekeepers, who are loyal men and true and I prefer to trust to them". He added that his tenants were on good terms with him, "even though they may be frightened by those who are about them". The *Telegraph* reporter found, to his mystification, that Sir Arthur was considered to be a good and generous landlord but was told repeatedly that he "was not liked". A local leader of the Land League told the reporter: "I consider that Lord Ardilaun would be perfectly safe if he were to walk about amongst his tenants because he is a good man and much liked here, but his agent is disliked and it is he who is unpopular."[44]

Liked or not, four of Ardilaun's employees were to lose their lives in the following two years as tensions between landlords and tenants remained and the Land Act of 1881 came into effect, cutting rents by up to a quarter and giving tenants more rights. On the other hand, two of Ardilaun's keepers were up in court after wounding two local men found cutting sticks on the Ashford estate; they were both released after one of the wounded men was paid £40 and the other £30. There was also much suspicion among nationalists about an attempt by Ardilaun to import some 20,000 Nordenfeld cartridges (the Nordenfeld was an early type of machine gun which had up to twelve barrels). Questions in the House of Commons elicited the reply that most of the 23 cases of cartridges, which normally contained 1,000 rounds each, had held only 93 rounds and none had more than 350 rounds; they were imported legally and intended for "private use" at Ashford.[45]

The implementation of the Land Act was greeted in January 1882 by protests from landlords, Ardilaun prominent among them. At a meeting of some 3,000 landlords at the Exhibition Palace in Dublin, he seconded a motion which noted with alarm that the Act was being administered in a way that was contrary to a previous pledge that it would not "diminish the value or disturb the foundations of property".[46] Ardilaun said he accepted that the Act was law, however much he might deplore the policy which had led to a 25 per cent reduction in rents throughout Ireland, depreciated the value of estates, and made them almost unsaleable. He suggested that landlords should seek compensation if the rent reductions being imposed were upheld.

About the same time, his bailiff at Ashford Castle had gone missing. The bailiff, Joe Huddy, an elderly man, and his 17-year-old grandson John had gone out to serve eviction notices on a number of Ardilaun's tenants who had failed to pay their rents in the nearby Joyce Country on the shore of Lough Mask. They did not return. Rumours circulated that they had been murdered and eventually sailors were brought from a warship at Galway to search Lough Mask. They found their bodies in bags weighted down with stones: the older man had been struck on the head with a stone and both had been shot.[47] Widespread arrests followed; one suspect turned Queen's Evidence and three local men were eventually charged with the murders, which became known as the Lough Mask Murders. They were convicted in separate trials in Dublin – Ardilaun was present on at least the opening day – during which one man, Michael Flynn's, membership of the Land League became an issue and, to the organisation's opponents, evidence of its encouragement of violence. The three men convicted of the murders were hanged in Galway jail just over a year after the event.[48]

Tensions remained high in the Connemara area around Ashford after the murder of the Huddys. Almost two months later, the wife and youngest son of the Ashford gamekeeper were ambushed by three men with rocks near the village of Clonbur on their way home. They fractured the skull of the 17-year-old youth and injured the woman; the boy died two days later. "His family was well-to-do and respectable and the only reason that can be alleged for this murder is that his father has always done his duty faithfully towards his employer," *The Times* opined. A year later, another of Ardilaun's bailiffs was attacked and beaten by two men; he died of his injuries several weeks later.[49] (The

August following the Huddy murders also saw the more famous – and unconnected to the Land War – Maamtrasna Murders in Connemara, in which three adults and two children in one family were killed. One of those executed for the murders, Myles Joyce, was widely believed to be innocent.) Among opponents of the agrarian and nationalist movements, the murder of the Huddys and the violence around Ashford were regularly mentioned in the same breath as the Phoenix Park murders five months later in Dublin in May 1882, in which the newly arrived Chief Secretary for Ireland, Lord Frederick Cavendish, and his senior civil servant, Thomas Burke, were stabbed to death by the Invincibles.

In later years, Ardilaun was in no doubt about who was to blame for all the vicissitudes, as he saw them, of Ireland, especially the agitation over land and the attempts to abolish landlordism: Parnell, he believed, was the instigator of all trouble in Ireland.[50] But his political hopes for Ireland were doomed, though he continued to fight for the rest of his life the forces ranged against the beliefs and class he had been born into and adopted. He would also be left far behind in terms of wealth, social standing and aristocratic honours by his cannier younger brother who, Ardilaun was about to discover, had acquired his share of the brewery at a knock-down price.

CHAPTER SIX

The First Guinness Scandal

"The whole thing is a very grave scandal . . . Nothing in our opinion so disheartening to the bona fide *investor as this piece of blundering jobbery in high financial circles has been perpetrated for years."*

MONEY MAGAZINE, 19 January 1887
on the flotation of Arthur Guinness Son & Co.

Edward Guinness was not, by all accounts, an easy man to get along with. Short in stature, like most of the Guinnesses, he was highly energetic and able but he was also secretive, domineering and taciturn. Known as Ned to his friends, he maintained strict control over St James's Gate while spending less and less time there, leaving the people who ran it on a day-to-day basis in a constant quandary as they tried to second-guess his wishes. He was a stickler for detail, to the point of obsession, and he was extremely ambitious. Total control of the world's biggest brewery and considerable riches while still under 30 was clearly not enough; he also wanted social recognition and the honours that accompanied it. Arguably, he was still trying to compete with his older brother, who seemed to have achieved effortless recognition as a leader of society and the head of the family. Perhaps he also wanted to prove to his mother-in-law that she had been wrong to oppose his marriage because he was not an aristocrat. Or perhaps he just wanted all the trappings that his wealth could buy. Whatever the reason, he set about making his mark on high society, which in the context of the time meant in London.

The phenomenal success of the brewery underpinned Edward's social ambitions. Investment of some £400,000 in St James's Gate during the 1870s repaid handsome rewards. Sales of stout more than doubled during the decade and then doubled again in the eight years up to 1886. Employment more than doubled from 1871, when Guinness employed 130 coopers, 900 permanent men and 90 "gentlemen" (presumed to be clerks), to 1886 when it employed a total of 2,650. Thus, sales and production quadrupled over roughly the same period as employment doubled, and that at the same time as wages tended to stand still or fall, as they did during the 1880s.[1] The brewery's land, buildings and plant were valued at £500,000 in 1879, a 25-fold increase since the start of the century, a period during which prices had generally fallen rather than risen.[2]

A quotation attributed to Edward – "you can't expect to make money out of people unless you are prepared to let them make money out of you"[3] – is illustrative of his pragmatism. But there is no comparison between the huge sums of money he began to withdraw from the brewery and the undoubtedly high wages and other benefits he paid to his workers. The normal working week in Dublin in the late 1870s was 54 hours, which was down from 60 in the 1860s and remained at 54 hours for the following 20 years.[4] Guinness workers were the aristocracy of Dublin's working class, with relative security of employment, and health and sickness benefits unmatched by any other industry in the city and few elsewhere. They had free medical care and medicines and the costs of their stays in hospitals or convalescent homes were paid while they still received up to two-thirds of their wages. Widows of labourers received pensions of up to six shillings a week, while the company made contributions to two Friendly Societies of which tradesmen were members.[5] A report by the brewery's two medical officers to John Tertius Purser in 1881, for instance, showed that they had had 19,000 visitors to their clinic and they had also made 2,260 home visits. (They also "prescribed" 764 bottles of wine, 535 bottles of whiskey and 213 bottles of brandy for their patients.)[6]

But Edward did not stint on his own drawings from the brewery. Between 1868 and 1883, he took £1,344,000 from its total profits of £3,662,000 during the period. Most of it (£925,000) was withdrawn in the three years from 1880 to 1882. Much of that seems to have gone on funding an expensive and competitive social life, the beginnings of a major art collection, philanthropy and investments. The main social issue of the day was the appalling state of poverty and atrocious housing in which most of the population of Dublin lived. By 1882, Edward was housing about a seventh of the brewery's workforce and had just built Rialto Buildings a short distance from St James's Gate. He and his brother, Lord Ardilaun, were also among the first investors in the Artisans Dwelling Company, formed in 1876, which benefited from subsidised government loans for improving working-class houses. They each invested £5,000 in the company. It eventually built more than 3,000 dwellings and had more than 13,000 tenants, mainly the better-off sections of the working class.

A larger amount of money, though, was reported to have been spent by Edward's wife Adelaide on one party in London some three years later (although one should probably allow for exaggeration). The professional socialite and travel writer Augustus Hare (whose publication of his diaries later shocked *fin-de-siècle* London), described it in the following terms:

> In the evening I was with the Prince [Royal of Sweden and Norway] at Mrs E. Guinness' ball, on which £6000 are said to have been wasted. It was a perfect fairy-land, ice pillars up to the ceiling, an avenue of palms, a veil of stephanotis [an evergreen climbing shrub] from the staircase, and you pushed your way through a brake of papyrus to the cloakroom.[7]

Competition with her sister-in-law was clearly strong. Lady Olive Guinness (later Lady Ardilaun), had just arrived in London in time for the party, although it is not known if she attended. A month later it was Olive's turn to throw a lavish ball at her Carlton Terrace house for the Duke and Duchess of Connaught and it reportedly cost between £7,000 and £8,000. "It was one of the most sumptuous revels of the London season, or rather of many London seasons," *The Irish Times* reported and noted that it caused a traffic jam of carriages of such proportions as only London or Paris could produce. "When the fete was at its height about 1 o'clock, the aspect of the palatial interior, with its five or six hundred guests, numbering among them Royalty itself, was a sight not to be soon forgotten," the report added.[8]

The wealth, the parties and the philanthropy were all means to an end, however: social recognition in the form of honours. Edward knew from the experiences of his father and his brother that the most direct route towards a title was through politics, public service and the Conservative Party. He had no apparent interest in being a politician or in politics, other than in the continuation of the association for business and social reasons. But he knew that politics and public service were the surest route to a title, and he was prepared to do whatever was necessary. Exactly how the honours system worked at the time has been described by historian David Cannadine:

They were not sold openly and in public for cash, and they were not sold indiscriminately to anyone who was prepared to pay. They were given only to party supporters; such people had to be of acceptable character and deserving in other ways; the reward usually came much later, and was rarely explicitly promised; and the money went into a party fund, not to the pocket of the party leader. Officially, Prime Ministers and opposition leaders knew nothing of the transactions between Chief Whips and donors: they did not know where the money came from, or the connection – if any – with honours nominations. But for all this decorousness, there can be no doubt that this was merely corruption in refined guise: in practice, party leaders knew what was going on; the terms of trade were clear; great philanthropy combined with great party donations did indeed have its rewards; and, as such, titles were effectively bought for cash.[9]

One of Edward's closest friends was David Plunket, his sister Anne's brother-in-law, and the fiery young Orange orator of his brother's election campaigns. Plunket was by now a well-established politician himself, representing a safe Conservative seat for Dublin University in the House of Commons since 1870 and well in with the leadership of the party. He effectively took on the task of acting as Edward's agent in the latter's political campaign for a title, following exactly the path described above.

They began planning from the late 1870s on to have Edward succeed one of the two Tory MPs for County Dublin, Colonel Thomas Taylor, who had held the seat for more than 40 years and was clearly near retirement. They believed they were successful and Edward was all set to become the Conservative candidate for the expected by-election in the constituency when Taylor fell seriously ill in 1882. However, Taylor hung on until February 1883 when he died and the party decided on another candidate, Colonel Edward King-Harman, possibly because it was aware of Edward's lack of real political enthusiasm.

The party's decision did not prevent it from touching Edward for two donations of £1,000 and £500 respectively during the by-election campaign. On the advice of Plunket, he complied promptly with the requests while expressing his disappointment that he had had to give up his own claims to the seat in the best interests of the party.[10] While King-Harman (who had inherited the family's estate at Rockingham, County Roscommon and had gone from being a supporter of Isaac Butt's Home Rule party to being a Conservative unionist) was duly elected, Plunket continued to talk to party leaders in London, emphasising Edward's selfless sacrifice and generous contributions to the party and seeking a written assurance that he would be properly rewarded in due course when the party was returned to government. The reward, though not spelled out in the correspondence, would of course be a peerage but the party leaders were as cautious about committing themselves to anything definite in writing as Plunket was imaginative in interpreting their expressions of gratitude.

Meanwhile, another opportunity arose with the planned visit of Prince Edward, the Prince of Wales, to Dublin in the spring of 1885. Edward Guinness was already recognised as one of the Prince's social circle and was an obvious choice to become involved in the organisation of the visit, all the more so because of the uncertainty of the welcome facing the Prince. The political atmosphere in Ireland was still tense with the Land War just ended, the memory of the Phoenix Park and other murders still fresh, and the Home Rule campaign, led by Parnell, going from strength to strength. The Prince's visit was the first by any member of the royal family to Ireland for 14 years and was widely seen by nationalists as a political ploy to bolster their opponents.

134

The *Freeman's Journal*, for instance, denounced the visit as an attempt by the ascendancy class to stop the last remnants of political power slipping from their hands.[11]

The city's corporation, firmly in the hands of nationalists, boycotted the Prince's visit and Edward was instrumental in forming a "citizens' committee" of loyal supporters to prepare a welcome. On the advice of the Lord Lieutenant, Lord Spencer, he persuaded the president of the Chamber of Commerce, Richard Martin, who was also the chairman of the Dublin and Wicklow Railway Company, to take over the chairmanship of the reception committee while he acted as its vice-president. They presented the Prince with an address of welcome at Westland Row railway station, which urged the royal family to establish a permanent residence in Ireland. The visit to Dublin passed off relatively peacefully, apart from one minor incident when a crowd of people waiting to see the Prince outside Dublin Castle caught sight of the nationalist lord mayor arriving at the neighbouring city hall. Some of them hissed at him and he retaliated by promising to telegraph ahead to Mallow and Cork with the news that he had been hissed at by Orangemen and Freemasons, landlords and bailiffs. (Whether it was in response to his action or not, there was a small riot at Mallow station later that day when rival crowds of royal supporters and opponents took over opposite platforms of the railway station to await the Prince's train.) Meanwhile, the Prince was "given a hearty cheer" by Guinness workers as he passed the brewery on his way to the Cork train.[12]

The royal visit was hardly a resounding success but it was not the disaster it might have been either. Prince Edward was received civilly in Dublin, with hostility in Cork where police had to guard buildings displaying welcoming decorations, and with warmth in Belfast. Dublin's "citizens' committee" prided itself on having organised the address of welcome in the city, arranged a fireworks display at Kingstown where the Prince disembarked, and also organised tours on board a steamer around the fleet in Dublin Bay for 6d a person. Two weeks after the visit, Edward and Richard Martin were made baronets by Prime Minister Gladstone "in recognition of your eminent position in Ireland and of the services which you rendered during the recent visit of the Prince of Wales". *The Irish Times* went into extravagant mode:

135

They have had this distinction conferred upon them as representatives, not only on a special occasion, of the loyalty and enterprise of our leading men, but of the energy and unselfishness shown by them at all times in promoting the interests of the community and especially of working men. Sir Edward Guinness's munificent efforts in that direction have long been the pride of Dublin, and the recollections associated with his family of this description, going back for several generations, are written deeply in the grateful memory of the public.

Sir Edward was presented at a levee in Buckingham Palace to receive the honour by Gladstone – perhaps giving them an opportunity to discuss a piece of unlikely business Edward had conducted with the Prime Minister's son, W.H. Gladstone, several years earlier. Gladstone junior was director of a company running Aston Hall Colliery near the family home at Hawarden in north Wales and in which his father also had a small stake. Sir Edward had lent the company £17,000 which was to be paid back in coal. As security, he held a mortgage on the plant and machinery of the coal mine which had been said to have a break-up value of £30,000. However, the company collapsed, with three other directors going bankrupt, and it failed to pay back the loan. Negotiations between solicitors for Gladstone junior and Edward had been going on for some years.

Less than a month before the case was due in court in April 1883, the Prime Minister's secretary, E.W. Hamilton, wrote to Edward asking that he not insist on his legal right to have the mine broken up since neither party would gain from that course of action. Edward replied that he had been owed about £15,000 for more than two and a half years and asked for a proposal before the matter came to court. The Prime Minister then became involved himself, using his secretary as a go-between, rather than communicating directly with Edward. He suggested that an independent arbitrator should be appointed and maintained that £30,000 was the mine's value as a going concern, not its break-up value. Edward disputed that claim but accepted a final offer of £10,000, either in the belief that he was unlikely to get anything further from a break-up sale or to avoid the Liberal Party leader and Prime Minister the embarrassment of taking his son to court.[13]

While Gladstone obviously owed him a favour as a result of this case, Edward was still looking for greater favours from the Conservatives as a general election approached at the end of 1885. The party's managers wanted him to contest one of the four new single-seat Dublin city constituencies which replaced the previous single city constituency which had had two seats. But he insisted that he still had a claim on Dublin County where King-Harman had proven himself to be a popular MP with the party. Indeed, he went so far as to tell the party that he did not mind standing for election in the city so long as he didn't win the seat because to represent the city would be "most distasteful" and unpleasant because he could always be found by his constituents at St James's Gate. His brother Arthur (Ardilaun) always lived in the country when he was MP for Dublin, he added.

However, Edward offered the party a carrot: if he was asked by the leaders of the party to stand he would feel bound to consider the request. That gave Plunket his cue to pressure the party leaders again about a peerage and a letter duly arrived from Sir Stafford Northcote, the Conservatives' leader in the House of Commons, asking him to stand in the city: "I know it is asking a great deal from you; but I trust you may be willing to make the sacrifice. It will be felt as a great addition to the claims you already have upon the gratitude of the Conservative Party," he wrote in June 1884. Plunket wasn't altogether happy with this (somewhat vague) commitment to claims on the party's gratitude, so he wrote to Lord Salisbury, the party leader in the Lords, who was about to take over as the sole party leader, quoting Sir Stafford and asking him to point out to Guinness that he shared the same view. He also pointed out that the St Stephen's Green constituency was the only one in Ireland outside of Ulster and Dublin University where the Conservatives had any hope of winning a seat; without Guinness standing, there was no use in even attempting to win it, he maintained. (The St Stephen's Green constituency had 10,000 voters, some 6,000 of whom were Catholics and 4,000 were Protestants.)

Salisbury wasn't fooled for a moment by all the coded correspondence. In a letter dated 16 August 1885 and marked "Very Confidential", he told Plunket: "It is fair that I should say to you that I am not in a condition to promise that 'gratitude' means a Peerage – at all events as yet." In a separate letter (marked "Private" and which he said could be shown to Guinness) he said that he earnestly hoped that Sir Edward might be induced to stand for Dublin. He added: "He has already done most valuable service to the Conservative Party, and I hope he will add yet this to his claim upon our gratitude."

Plunket didn't give up yet, however. He wrote back to Salisbury, saying that Guinness certainly did look forward to a peerage as a natural object of his ambition whenever in the future his personal position and political services would entitle him fairly to such an honour. "I have reason to know that if he stands for Dublin now, he would regard his doing so only as a further contribution towards, and not at all as a fulfilment of those conditions; and that he has no idea of asking for anything whatever at present." Salisbury replied indirectly, writing to a colleague from Dieppe that he had mislaid Plunket's address but to tell him that his letter was "quite satisfactory".

Thus there was no doubt that the leader of the Conservative Party knew of Edward's ambition and was encouraging him to pursue the path he was already following. Plunket concluded that that was the most they could get at the moment and urged Edward to dispatch a £5,000 cheque to the party treasurer and to promise a second one for the same amount if needed. Edward sent the cheque and thanked Plunket profusely: "you are certainly the best of friends and have rendered me the greatest possible service," he wrote to him from Farmleigh in September 1885. "What a splendidly plucky way you went at Lord S. and what you have succeeded in getting out of him is far more than I should have ever dared to hope."

When the election campaign began two months later, Sir Edward was ready if not entirely willing. He had suggested, and got party agreement, that he would be its only candidate in his constituency. However, the political climate had changed dramatically since his brother's election campaigns in the previous decade. Dublin's political detachment from the rest of Ireland had ended and politics had become polarised around the issue of Home Rule and become a straight fight between nationalists and unionists. The Liberal Party had been sidelined in Ireland and found itself attached to the Conservatives, where it suited the Conservatives, in a pro-union grouping which the

Conservatives used to try and garner the old Liberal vote. Another pro-union candidate, Arthur MacMurrough Kavanagh, offered himself for the St Stephen's Green constituency, leading Sir Edward to offer to stand aside if the party wished. (Plunket, observing from Ashford Castle and about to be re-elected for Dublin University without a contest, noted happily that "if they say 'stand' you are right; and if they say 'don't stand' you are 'righter'!"[14] Unfortunately for Sir Edward, the less-than-enthusiastic, would-be politician, they said "stand".

One of the sitting MPs was the Liberal Robert Lyons who had narrowly defeated Sir Arthur Guinness in 1880 and now also wanted to run in the St Stephen's Green constituency, but he was persuaded to make way for a united unionist campaign behind Sir Edward. Lyons changed his mind at the last moment as nominations were closing and made a final bid to get into the contest, causing "a flutter" among the unionists. He tried to enter his nomination but Sir Edward's solicitor, Charles Sutton, objected on a number of technical grounds – Lyons had failed to put his surname first on the form, failed to state his business or profession, and his proposer and seconder had not signed their names – so his nomination was refused. Among Sir Edward's listed supporters was Jonathan Pim junior, the son of his father's political rival more than 20 years earlier.[15]

Sir Edward's lack of enthusiasm for the election must have been evident from the start of the campaign, even to those who had no knowledge of his true motives and ambitions and of all the background negotiations that led to his candidacy. It is still evident from the daily reports: he was not visible at all in Dublin for the early weeks while his Nationalist opponent, Edmund Gray (son of Sir Benjamin Guinness's contemporary and Liberal MP Sir John Gray), went from rally to rally, night after night. The *Freeman's Journal*, which Gray had inherited from his father – he also owned the *Morning News* in Belfast and had already been an MP for Carlow and Tipperary – conceded editorially that Sir Edward was probably the strongest candidate the Tories could put forward. But it was clear that he was a largely unknown character, still in the shadow of his family and particularly of his brother, now Lord Ardilaun.

Gray and his campaigners set out to paint Sir Edward not just as "a colourless wishy-washy Liberal-Conservative landlord" (as the *Freeman's Journal* described him) but as a supporter of the Orange Order because he and Ardilaun had each contributed £100 to the building of an Orange hall in Rutland Square [now Parnell Square], close to the home of the Catholic archbishop. Its location, according to Gray, was chosen in order to insult the archbishop, William Walsh, who also intervened in the election with a letter to his clergy warning them about the Conservatives' attempts to win the old Liberal vote by subterfuge. Two gentlemen who were usually regarded as liberal in politics (one of them probably Sir Edward) had been duped "by the astute wire pullers" of the Tory party into accepting the positions of candidates for Dublin constituencies, Archbishop Walsh wrote. "The choice will not be between the national candidates and the representatives of a new coalition party of so-called 'loyalists' but between those candidates and the representatives of the old Tory Ascendancy," he declared.[16]

The Gray campaign also resurrected a four-year-old controversy which had divided political and business opinion in the city essentially along sectarian lines. Although the Guinness brewery was booming, the Irish economy generally was in a very poor state at the start of the 1880s. To try to give it a boost, a number of prominent citizens, including the Guinnesses, came up with the idea of holding another industrial exhibition. The original Exhibition Palace buildings in Earlsfort Terrace had come by now into the possession of Sir Edward. His father, Sir Benjamin Lee, had bailed out the exhibition company at one stage with a loan of £30,000 but it had gone into liquidation anyway and the buildings ended up as part of Sir Edward's inheritance. He now offered to provide the building free for the new exhibition but the plans quickly ran into political trouble. The committee behind the venture divided irreconcilably over whether or not any members of the royal family should be invited to be its patron and to open the exhibition. Nationalist members of the committee strenuously objected on the grounds that this was to be a purely Irish exhibition. A separate nationalist committee (which included Gray and another election candidate, William Murphy)[17] was formed and had gone ahead with an exhibition of its own in 1882, but Sir Edward refused to give it the use of the Exhibition Palace. Instead, he sold the main building to the government for £30,000 to house the Royal University and, more controversially, he sold its glass-and-iron Winter Palace to an English company which took it apart and re-erected it in Battersea Park in London.

At one of Gray's first election rallies, speakers revisited the controversy, with William Murphy accusing Sir Edward of "wrecking" the national exhibition. Gray suggested that Sir Edward's conduct, before seeking election, in relation to the Exhibition Palace was a fair test of whether his first object was really the promotion of the interests of the artisans and citizens of Dublin or whether it was to oppose by any means the progress of the Irish National Party. The organisers of the national exhibition had appealed to Sir Edward for the use of the Exhibition Palace, he said: they offered any rent he would name, he refused it; they offered to buy it at any reasonable price, he refused it. Instead, Gray said, Sir Edward had entered into a secret contract to sell it to one Orrell Lever for "some ridiculously low price of £8,000 or £13,000". They might have had the Exhibition Palace free if they had obeyed Sir Edward's dictation; instead, they had to build an exhibition centre in Rutland Square and pay rent to the Rotunda, all costing them £20,750.

The bribery scandal around his brother Arthur's election to the House of Commons was also resurrected, usually to delighted shouts of "the hole in the wall" from the audiences at Gray's rallies. Another campaigner who would become a major and controversial nationalist figure (as well as a persistent critic of Lord Ardilaun), T.M. Healy, told a Gray rally, to cheers: "All the odours of the flowers and all the smell of the trees in this park [St Stephen's Green] would not be sufficient to perfume and to purify the memory of the corruption with which the Guinnesses deluged the city fifteen years ago."

As the political temperature rose, Sir Edward was also accused of sectarian employment policies at the brewery, notably of not promoting any Catholics to the higher echelons of the "No. 1 Class clerks". Furthermore, furious and usually anonymous letter-writers complained that many of his domestic staff were foreigners; one who did sign his name and claimed to be a former employee accused Sir Edward of having a Welsh steward, a French cook, and an English head gardener at Farmleigh, while his wife had a French maid. His defenders were active with their pens, too: a "working man" praised Sir Edward for opening a woollen mills at Kingsbridge and employing 180 people there, mainly young girls, in very good conditions. A Catholic (who signed his name) said his religion had not prevented his promotion to an important department of the brewery for which Protestants were also competing: he had 91 Class 2 clerks under him, of whom 52 were Catholics and 39 Protestants. "It is absolutely untrue that the promotion of Catholics from 2nd class to the higher grade does not take place," he wrote. "Even within the last few years many such appointments have been made and of the gentlemen so promoted 40% are Catholics."

Sir Edward continued to be largely invisible, occasionally addressing small numbers of election workers to thank them for their efforts, and overseeing the nomination of candidates in the South County Dublin constituency in his role as High Sheriff of County Dublin. But his media supporters campaigned strongly on his behalf, attacking the Parnellite candidates for the "pledge" they had given the Irish Party to support its leader and its policies and predicting economic doom and the collapse of law and order if they and the Land League were victorious. "In this contest there is neither Whig nor Tory," *The Irish Times* declared in a typical editorial. "Those terms have ceased to possess a meaning. The question is between Mr Parnell and his organisation and the citizens of all parties, creeds and feelings who are not ready to trust their personal future and the fate of their country to the League."

Sir Edward finally appeared at a full-scale public meeting in the Antient Concert Rooms four days before the poll and delivered a well-crafted speech in which he said that the ground on which he sought electoral support was simple: "it is that we believe that in our close union with England we have the best and the only reliable guarantee for the maintenance of our liberties, the safety of our property, and the security of our homes." There was abundant proof of the kind of government that the nationalists would impose if they ever succeeded in obtaining the separate parliament they were demanding, he added. "Within the last five years we have heard these agitators preach doctrines fatal to the first principles of personal freedom, of social order, and of common honesty between man and man and we have seen these principles enforced throughout our unhappy country by a system of violence and terrorism the most cruel and oppressive."

What were the practical results of the efforts and successes in Dublin of the "Separatist Party", he asked: "Has work become more plentiful? [shouts of 'no, no'] Have wages improved? [no, no] Has business been brisk? [no, no] Has commerce flourished? [no, no]." Instead, he claimed, capital had rapidly ebbed away as a consequence of violent agitation and the insecurity it brought in its train. If Parnell got his parliament, he asked rhetorically, would it make those "men of substance", whose loss was now being felt, more likely to spend their lives and fortunes in Ireland or invest in its industries?

Sir Edward said he would not become involved in personal recriminations with Gray whom, he said, had tried to raise insinuations about his private character and his business transactions.

> I have spent all my life in this city and my actions and conduct have necessarily been to a great extent under your observation. I am fully conscious that in many respects I have failed to adequately discharge the responsibilities of the position in which I am placed. It would be difficult not to displease or disappoint some and to win the assent or approval of everyone, but I have endeavoured honestly to do my duty to the best of my humble abilities.

It was "disagreeable" to refer to the manner in which he dispensed money to public bodies and charitable institutions but he was confident there was not an honest person in the city who believed he ever allowed any sectarian considerations to influence his distribution of charity or employment of labour.

Dealing directly with the accusations about his contributions to the Orange hall, he continued:

> I have frequently subscribed to institutions and to churches to which I do not belong and, though I am not and never have been an Orangeman, I have subscribed to an Orange hall, and I am not ashamed of having done so. Though I am not a Catholic, it is equally true that I have subscribed to many Catholic institutions, and I am proud to have done so. It has always been my desire and it will always be my guiding principle to banish any sectarian consideration from the conduct of my business and the distribution of my charity.[18]

On the election day for the four Dublin city constituencies, 30 November 1885, Sir Edward was presiding over the count for South County Dublin where the nationalist candidate, Sir Thomas Esmonde, was victorious. When word of his victory reached the city centre, nationalist crowds gathered to march the streets with bands, hold impromptu meetings, and sing "God Save Ireland" continuously. As the evening wore on and the crowds, many carrying sticks and cudgels, swelled, there were clashes outside Trinity College with some students who unwisely tried to counter the marchers' song with "God Save the Queen". Windows in the college were smashed and a number of students beaten up and policemen stoned. At one stage, the marchers went up to St Stephen's Green and smashed windows in Sir Edward's house and the home of W.H.F. Cogan, a prominent Catholic supporter of Sir Edward who had taken issue publicly with Archbishop Walsh's instructions to Catholics to vote for the Parnellite candidates. Later that night, one of Sir Edward's canvassers, Joseph Callaghan, was dragged from his carriage on Leeson Street and beaten up. Two men with him were also injured but whether or not Callaghan was targeted because of his political involvement was not clear. At least 24 people were treated in hospital for cuts, bruises and concussions during the evening.

Counting of votes for the city took place the following day in the former Exhibition Palace in Earlsfort Terrace, which Sir Edward had sold to the government for the Royal University. He was at the count from early on himself, accompanied by David Plunket, while his opponent Edmund Gray was absent in Carlow, where he was also standing for election. The results of the Dublin counts were obvious immediately; the nationalist candidates had won all four city constituencies with large majorities. Sir Edward was defeated by 5,277 votes to 3,334, a majority of 1,947 for Gray. It was a decisive result but the smallest nationalist majority in Dublin, with the other Parnellite candidates, William Murphy, T.D. Sullivan and William Harrington winning even more overwhelming victories.

In a brief address after the results were announced officially, Sir Edward said it was not the time for political speeches and merely thanked those who had come to vote for him, many at great difficulty and personal inconvenience. T.D. Sullivan appealed to their supporters not to damage the victory celebrations with violence and broken window panes. They had already broken something better than windows, he said: they had broken Castle rule in Ireland. Nevertheless, the victories set off another night of torchlight marches, bands, banners, bonfires and impromptu speeches at numerous locations around the city centre. Groups cheered outside the headquarters of the National League and the home of Archbishop Walsh and broke the windows of the nearby building, which was due to become an Orange hall. A group of students from Trinity College, who had torn down a US flag from the statue of Henry Grattan, became embroiled in fist fights with nationalists outside the count and had to be escorted back to the college by the police. Two youths ended up in hospital with minor wounds from gunshots apparently fired in celebration rather than in anger.

The editorial reaction of the nationalist press was no less euphoric. The *Freeman's Journal* described it as a triumph for the nationalists that was "almost bewildering in its completeness" and described Sir Edward as "beyond doubt the very strongest candidate who could have been selected to do battle for the cause of Ascendancy". In a more conciliatory tone than it had used during the campaign, the newspaper also urged the Conservatives to throw in their lot with their fellow-countrymen, declaring that they and men of other opinions had as much to gain from the restoration of Ireland's legislative independence as any nationalist.

On the "loyal" side of the fence, the overwhelming defeat was blamed largely on the extension of the franchise to more people. The London *Times* said that the loyalists were not as organised as the nationalists and that new rules made it more difficult to challenge fictitious voters. *The Irish Times* said the fact that the great commercial city of Dublin was represented by four separatists was due to the lowered franchise, which swamped not only property in every form, but the artisan and handicraftsman as well. It hoped that people would recover from the "temporary madness" which clouded their judgement and declared that voters must be educated in the intelligent use of the franchise, instead of an ignorant use of it. But it also accepted that the old style of Dublin conservatism was dead and must be replaced by "something broader, more constitutional and generous, more comprehensive of diversified opinion, to gain the support of men of differing creeds and sentiment – one in loyalty and detestation of socialist and communist projects". It praised the loyalist candidates, singling out Sir Edward Guinness in particular, whom, it said, was known not to wish to enter Parliament, "being occupied with the charge of his great business, and with important efforts to make his workpeople comfortable, and secure continued prosperity as much on their account as his own. It conferred no distinction upon him to become a candidate in a time of turbulence. It had its perils and no reward."

Sir Edward had, as the newspaper suggested, done his duty by the mercantile men of Dublin as well as by the Conservative Party, whose views on the dangers of separatism he shared totally. He did not stand in the next election, a year later, following the defeat of the first Home Rule Bill, when the Liberal Unionist candidate in the St Stephen's Green constituency, Sir Edward O'Sullivan, was defeated by Edmund Gray by a wider margin of 2,443 votes. He still maintained a relatively high public profile, however, being appointed along with his brother, Lord Ardilaun, to the committee of the newly formed Irish Loyal and Patriotic Union, whose aim was to support election candidates outside Ulster. He was also appointed by Lord Randolph Churchill to a Royal Commission on Public Departments to examine the numbers, pay and working conditions of public servants and the efficiency of parliamentary control over them. Indeed, his profile was such as to encourage Sir John Arnott, a highly successful Cork businessman and owner of *The Irish Times*, to propose in a letter to *The Times* that he be appointed viceroy.

The opportunity of standing in the St Stephen's Green constituency arose again in 1888 when Gray died at the young age of 43. There were some attempts by leading Irish Conservatives, including the Trinity College polymath and conservative John Pentland Mahaffy, to get Sir Edward to stand again but Plunket advised strongly against it.[19] The seat was won by liberals and unionists in subsequent elections, proving that it was one of the few in Ireland, outside parts of Ulster and Trinity College, in which the nationalist tide was resistible, for another while at least. Meanwhile, Sir Edward went on contributing cash to the

146

Conservative Party, giving it at least £30,000 during the 1880s. Plunket became First Commissioner of Works in Lord Salisbury's Conservative government, which was elected with the support of the unionist wing of the Liberals in 1886, and remained an MP until he retired in 1895 and was created Lord Rathmore of Shanganagh.

With the 1885 election over, his political colours nailed firmly to the mast, his credit with the Conservative Party at a very high level, and his social ambitions clearly signalled to the relevant quarters, Sir Edward was free to pursue his other main aim – cashing in on his inheritance – which he had been keeping a close secret, known only to friends like Plunket.

⸙

By the end of 1885, Sir Edward was very rich by the standards of the time. In the 15 years after his father's death in 1868, he had received a total of £1,344,000 from the brewery, more than the £1,210,000 his brother Arthur had received in profits before his departure and in the buyout of his share.[20] He also had investments in 1885, apart from the brewery, estimated at between £2,250,000 and £2,500,000; they included property investments in New York, where he had bought a section of Fifth Avenue at one point during a depression in the late 1870s. As a point of comparison, there were only 4,000 people in England with incomes over £5,000 a year in 1875[21] and £1,000 a year was a very comfortable income in the 1880s. But Sir Edward's ambitions were social rather than commercial at this stage, as was evident from his campaign to acquire a title, and the approval of high society. Trade, especially brewing, was looked down upon in aristocratic circles but wealth also talked in those circles and the greater the wealth the louder it spoke. He had clearly been thinking for some time about maximising his wealth and stepping away from daily commercial activities as part of his plan to secure a peerage and enter into high society. Uncertainty about the political and economic future of Ireland, with the Land War and the momentum towards Home Rule, was also a probable factor in his thinking along with the advantages for inheritance and liquidity purposes of having a share-based company which could be divided up or partly sold more easily than a partnership.

Sir Edward appears at first to have been undecided as to whether to sell the brewery outright or to go for a flotation on the stock market. He was certainly thinking of one or the other from the late 1870s onwards and approached Rothschild's in London about it at the end of 1879. Nathaniel Rothschild did not offer him any encouragement, mainly because of his own (Rothschild's) excessive caution. He confirmed later that the Guinness flotation had been offered to him but he had declined it. Asked if he regretted his decision in the light of the fact that Barings Brothers subsequently made a large amount of money out of the flotation, he replied:

> I don't look at it that way. I go to the bank every morning and when I say "no" I return home at night without a worry. But when I say "yes" it's like putting your finger into a machine – the whirring wheels may drag your whole body in after the finger.[22]

Edward Baring, who had just become Lord Revelstoke, was not so nervous, or was more ambitious when Sir Edward had a discussion with him about his plans in 1885 or 1886. Sir Edward offered to sell the brewery to Barings but Revelstoke suggested instead that Barings would bring it to the stock market, even though it had minimal experience of such exercises, although Barings would not underwrite or guarantee the flotation. Revelstoke suggested that Guinness be floated for £5 million but Sir Edward argued for £6 million, backing up his figure with details of the brewery's accounts. Revelstoke agreed to the figure and they decided to divide it up into £2.5 million in ordinary shares at £10 each, £2 million in 6 per cent preference shares at £10 each and £1.5 million in £100 debentures which were redeemable at the company's option in 20 years, after 1 January 1907, at 110 per cent. Sir Edward was to retain £800,000 worth of the ordinary shares and undertake not to sell them for five years. Barings would take up £500,000 of the shares.

Sir Edward agreed to be chairman for at least three years. Revelstoke assured him he would not have to work so hard as chairman. Revelstoke also suggested that the more Guinnesses there were on the board, the better; "all Guinnesses if you can manage it", he said, according to Sir

Edward's note of the conversation. They agreed on Claude Guinness, Sir Edward's brother-in-law, who was already managing director of the brewery, and Claude's elder brother, Reginald. Sir Edward seems to have run out of suitable Guinnesses after that; he did not put forward his elder brother and former partner, Lord Ardilaun, or his other brother, Benjamin. Instead, he proposed that Barings provide a director but Revelstoke said no member of the firm could join, although his brother would be delighted to do so. In the event, however, no Baring appeared on the board initially but several others suggested by Revelstoke did, including Herman "Osman" Hoskier, a director of the Union Bank of London, described by Revelstoke as "clever and a gentleman and good at accounts". The other eventual directors were Henry R. Glyn, of the new company's bankers Glyn, Mills, Currie and Co.; Viscount Castlerosse, the son of Lord Kenmare and a friend of Sir Edward's; and James R. Stewart, a solicitor with the Dublin firm of Stewart and Kincaid. The trustees for the debentures were Revelstoke, Lord Hellingdon, a Conservative politician and partner in Glyn, Mills, Currie and Co., and David Plunket. The new company was to be registered in London and a temporary office was established there.[23] All told, Sir Edward was set to come away from the flotation with approximately £4.25 million in cash, after all the expenses had been paid, and almost a third of the ordinary shares in the company.

The first the wider world knew about the flotation was on Thursday, 21 October 1886, when advertisements were lodged with newspapers for publication the following day and the president of the stock market in Dublin was informed. The previous day, the heads of departments at St James's Gate had received a letter from Sir Edward telling them of the change. There followed, in quick succession, a public reaction of surprise at the sale, amazement at what the prospectus revealed about the scale and profits of the brewery, and anger at the way the flotation was being handled, not just in Dublin but in London as well. It became clear very quickly that the 127-year-old brewery had been priced too cheaply, and demand for shares far exceeded the supply on offer as speculation immediately pushed the still-unavailable shares into a premium on a grey market. Sir Edward could have easily earned himself considerably more.

In his letter to department heads, from his Grosvenor Place address in London, Sir Edward explained that his decision to float the company rested on the growth of the brewery and his own health.

> Owing to the constant and rapid increase of the Brewery, and its probable future developments, I have for some time felt that I should not long be able to support the evergrowing strain upon my health which the conduct of so large a business and its many anxieties of necessity entail. . . . At the same time I have felt extremely reluctant entirely to sever my connection with the Brewery and to surrender my interest in the welfare of those with whom I have been so long associated. I have accordingly arranged that I shall be Chairman of the Company, retaining a substantial interest in the undertaking. I hope and believe that the business will be conducted on the same principles in every respect as heretofore, and I trust that you and all my friends at St James Gate will continue to favour me with that assistance which you have always so ably given me in the past.[24]

The news was something of a bombshell and, as *The Irish Times* put it, an event "sufficiently large and important to arrest universal attention". Not surprisingly, the various Irish political factions immediately turned it into part of their arguments for their causes. *The Irish Times* saw it as proof that "Ireland can be made the successful site of enterprises as vast as any Great Britain has known,"[25] while the Nationalist MP Tim Healy told a meeting of the National League that the rush for shares in Guinness proved that all the talk about agitation driving capital out of the country was unfounded.[26]

The publication of the prospectus was the first time in its history that details of the Guinness business had been revealed to the public and the strength and profitability it showed caused considerable surprise. Its average annual profit over five five-year periods from 1862 to 1886 had gone from £122,119 to £452,294, with a profit in 1885 of £554,327 and the same expected for 1886. If that were achieved, the prospectus pointed out, the ordinary shares would be able to pay a dividend of 14 per cent for the year. The prospectus also used official parliamentary figures to illustrate how Guinness compared with the three other largest breweries in the United Kingdom: they showed Guinness paying nearly twice as much duty (£424,247) as the next largest brewery (£290,067) in 1885, a gap that had been widening over the previous five years. In addition, the brewery's premises and property in Dublin now covered 42 acres, all but a few freehold, and all "unburdened by mortgages" and in perfect repair. It also pointed out that Guinness brewed only porter and was not in competition with the big British ale brewers. In addition, it had no tied houses and, consequently, no loans to publicans or capital outlays beyond the mere cost of production. All sales, except to well-known and long-established customers, were for cash and there were practically no debts – only £3,000 on a turnover of £2,165,000 in 1885.

It was, in short, an extremely profitable enterprise, dominant in its market, and not in need of any development capital, and investors immediately saw it as an offer not to be refused, setting off a frenzy as they tried to get on board the bandwagon. The prospectus was released on Friday, 22 October 1886, and the subscription list was to open the following Monday morning and close on or before 4.00 p.m. the next day. Few waited until the Monday to apply. Applications began to flow into Barings' offices in Bishopgate Street in London immediately and complaints followed almost as quickly: stockbrokers in Ireland had received no copies of the prospectus or application forms and had to apply for their clients through associates in London, leaving them at a disadvantage. Nevertheless, brokers' offices in Dublin were besieged, while application forms began to change hands in London for up to £1 each and the price of the £10 shares immediately went to a premium of £5 and more, even though the subscription list had not yet opened and no shares had been allocated (except to Sir Edward).

The scene outside Barings on the Saturday morning was graphically described by the *Irish Times's* somewhat overwrought London correspondent:

Wayfarers by the great banking house of Baring Brothers were yesterday informed by their eyes that some sharp sensation had stirred the worshippers of the golden calf in that particular temple of mammon into furious fervour. Excited men rushed in and out, blocking the doors and struggling for exit or for entrance. Cab after cab drove up discharging eager fares, who dashed forthwith into the scrimmage. The scene forcibly reminded patriarchal spectators of the bank panic in Lombard Street in the year 1878. This, however, was no panic unless the term applies to the fear of losing a great chance. For the hurly-burly was all about the conversion of Guinness's brewery, and these wrestling, panting crowds, choking one another on the threshold and in the vestibule of Baring's counting-house, were candidates for the stock of the new company. I have seen the floating or the relaunching of many notable enterprises here during the past ten or twelve years, but nothing to compare with this . . . It is very doubtful whether any of the great English breweries would have inspired anything like the same confidence, and certainly the beholders of yesterday's struggle had the most impressive warrant for believing that Ireland possesses at any rate one gigantic business whose prosperity is as famous as that of any other in the world.[27]

Not everyone was convinced of the benefits of investing in the new company, however. The financial press was distinctly cool towards the flotation, with the *Financial News* declaring that the prices of the shares and debentures were "absurdly high" given that its property was located in Ireland, "where property is not more secure than elsewhere". *The Economist* thought that the recent increase in Guinness's level of profits – it calculated from the prospectus that its profit rate per hogshead had gone up by almost two-thirds over the previous decade or so – was "simply astounding", given the tough economic climate of the times. It suggested, however, that there was a "want of sobriety" on the part of investors who were putting such a high value on the company, which had no monopoly of any kind and was engaged in a business that had been declining for many years. "The bargain, as we have said, seems a very dubious one, and it would not be at all surprising to find before many years are over those who have this week been so eager to embark in it lamenting their imprudence," it said, a prediction that turned out to be very wrong. (It also noted that the prospectus proved that the public was being fooled by brewers' howls of protests against tax increases on beer and by their threats that they would have to raise the price of beer to the working class.)[28]

Their caution was certainly not shared by the investing and speculating public. The offer was closed by 10.30 on the Monday morning, shortly after opening formally, but crowds continued to arrive at Barings, pushing and shoving to try and get into the bank and, on one occasion, breaking the entrance door. Some optimists were said to have wrapped applications around stones and thrown them through Barings' window,[29] while 10,000 letters from Dublin, with many more from Belfast, Cork and Derry, were reported by the newspapers to have been delivered to the bank by the post office that morning. Sir Edward received some 300 letters that morning seeking shares but refused all appeals to him personally. In any event, those who had timed their applications for first thing on Monday morning were already too late; as The Times pointed out, the uninitiated may not have been aware that it was the practice to accept applications as soon as a prospectus was made available. Reports circulated that the offer had been over-subscribed tenfold and the price of the unallocated shares climbed to £16/10/0 (£16.50). In the event, an astounding £130 million had been offered for the £5.2 million of available shares and debentures.[30]

Many of those who applied were undoubtedly seeking to "stag" the issue – sell them on immediately for a quick profit. They could hardly fail, given that the shares were already showing more than a 50 per cent gain. Of great interest to everyone, speculators and long-term investors alike, was how applications would be treated. It was not the universal practice at the time to allocate them pro rata: proposals for such an arrangement by several letter writers to The Times were dismissed by the newspaper on the basis that the adoption of that course would merely lead in future to an enormous increase in the amount of individual applications for each new issue, as already had happened in France.[31] On the other hand, the specialist Money magazine declared unambiguously that it was the universal custom among respectable companies to allot shares as nearly as possible pro rata when they were over-subscribed. The Dublin newspapers pushed the case for Irish applicants to receive priority because Guinness was an Irish company, run by Irishmen, and most of its business was in Ireland. The Dublin

Licensed Grocers and Vintners Society urged Sir Edward to have due regard to the "immense Irish trade done by the firm" and to ensure that "an equitable proportion" of shares be allocated to Irish applicants. In spite of hints in the Dublin newspapers suggesting that Sir Edward was using his influence to make sure that Irish investors did indeed get a good allocation, there was no evidence that he played any significant role in deciding who got what. On the contrary, the suspicion was that Barings decided on it, mainly to the advantage of its friends and associates and what *Money* termed the "inner ring".[32]

Letters of regret to unsuccessful applicants were beginning to arrive by the end of the week of the launch: a reported 13,000 letters were sent out telling would-be investors they had not received any allocation. Less than half that number, 6,000 people, eventually received shares in the new company, the majority of them receiving only three or five shares.[33] The following week, successful applicants in Dublin began to receive their allocation, which amounted to between a tenth and one fifteenth of what they had sought.[34] The final shareholding revealed that Sir Edward had actually received £835,010 worth of ordinary shares, £22,000 in preference shares and £120,000 in debentures. Barings had taken up £501,050 in ordinary shares, £318,700 in preference shares and £255,990 in debentures. A further £500,000 worth was allocated to Glyn, Mills, Currie and Co., the bankers to the new company. Thus, more than £2.5 million of the £6 million flotation was taken up by an "inner ring" of those associated with bringing it to the market, all of whom stood to make very handsome profits from the demand for the shares.

Among the other people to receive shares were Lord Ardilaun, who received a relatively generous £15,000 worth; Claude Guinness, the managing director and new board member, £3,010; his brother and fellow director Reginald, £2,000; director Herman Hoskier, £6,010; director Viscount Castlerosse, £2,010; head brewer William Purser Geoghegan, £5,000; his brother and head engineer Samuel, £2,000. Sir Edward gave shares out of his own allotment equivalent to three months' pay to each of the brewers at St James's Gate. He also gave each clerk a cash payment and four weeks' extra pay to all tradesmen and labourers, all of which cost him approximately £20,000.[35]

He also offered John Tertius Purser 250 ordinary shares and 250 preference shares "as a memento of your long connection with the business".[36] Purser turned down the offer, perhaps seeing it as a meagre memento of his role as mentor and right-hand man to Sir Edward for almost 20 years, or perhaps for religious or other reasons. Purser was then 77, about to retire and apparently opposed to the flotation. Instead, he took his "centage" on each barrel of porter brewed, money which he had left on deposit with the brewery and amounted, including interest, to a substantial £217,196. The payments ended the close relationship with the brewery of the Purser family, which had been involved in St James's Gate and its successes for three generations, although the Geoghegan brothers, nephews of Purser, continued to work there as head brewer and chief engineer for a further period. Relations between them and Sir Edward were not good, however, and they were steadily sidelined and eventually left the brewery, ending the long and crucial Purser connection with Guinness. Sir Edward, rather than the new company, paid back Purser's deposit with the brewery and also paid off other employees who had used it as a savings bank with debentures to the value of £90,000 in lieu of their deposits.

Sir Edward also made a number of other gifts, in shares and cash, to friends and family. Among the main recipients were his brother Benjamin, to whom he gave a generous £150,000; his sister Anne, £52,000; and her brother-in-law and his friend David Plunket, £10,000. All the gifts and costs of the flotation came to about £750,000, leaving him with something in the region of £4,250,000 in cash and shares from the exercise.

An analysis by *Money* of the allocations when a share register finally became available (see below) divided up those who received shares into samples of 50 members of the "inner ring", 50 "favoured stockbrokers" and 50 members of the public. It identified several members of the Barings family, as well as the firm, as significant beneficiaries of the allocations and included Rothschilds, who received £350,000 worth of ordinary and preference shares, in the list. It concluded that more than half the shares had been allocated to the promoters and their friends: on the basis of a 25 per cent rise in the preference shares and a 75 per cent rise in the ordinary shares, it said that the directors had put £1,546,962 into the pockets of these 50 friends and Barings' profit alone was £355,237. "No mean profit that for a few days' work, even for millionaires," it remarked. The magazine also found that the 50 favoured stockbrokers had received shares worth £272,680 and had made profits of £108,690 on their allocation, whereas its 50 random members of the public had received £4,100 worth of shares and made a profit of £2,095.[37]

The suspicion of something shady in the handling of the flotation was given an added impetus when it emerged that Barings was providing bearer certificates to those who had been allotted shares rather than providing certificates in their names. The bearer certificates were issued to those who had not paid in full for their allotment: the prospectus had required five per cent of the amount on application and 20 per cent on allotment, with the remainder due in three monthly instalments in December, January and February. Those who paid by instalments received bearer certificates which could be then sold on and the new owners would be registered when they paid the final instalment. The arrangement was against the spirit and the letter of the law and was seen by the suspiciously minded as a way of allowing the insiders who had received shares to sell them on for large profits, without stamp duty being paid and without their identities ever being revealed on the share register. It meant, for instance, that Barings and the new company could say there was no share register to show the curious or the suspicious. *The Economist* noted that it was a novel way (it did not mean that as a compliment) of splitting up the letters of allotment "to render them readily negotiable" as well as to avoid stamp duty.[38]

The Stock Exchange refused to authorise a listing for the new shares until the bearer documents were replaced by certificates naming the owner of the shares. Barings caved in and said that owners should present their certificates to the company's bankers, Glyn, Mills, Currie, for endorsement when paying the December instalment. However, that gave more than enough time to those who wished to "stag" the shares anonymously. The bank had to hire more than 80 clerks, sometimes working until midnight, to deal with the paperwork of providing new certificates in people's names and registering them as shareholders. Guinness, the company, rather than Barings, had to pay the bank £950 for the extra work involved.[39]

The handling of the flotation by Barings left a strong stink of scandal and sharp practices over the flotation. *Money* best summed it up in an uncompromising editorial:

> We have now before us a complete train of company "dodges" in this matter, which would do credit to the sharpest and most unscrupulous promoter in the City. Beginning with that very questionable piece of sharp practice, the closing of the lists after they had been open for about an hour on the authorised day, going on through the concealment of the allottees' names, the illegal issue of scrip allotment letters "to bearer", the arbitrary rules imposed as to payment of instalments, the refusal to accept the same during the usual banking hours, and, finally, the suspicious rigging of the market until the stocks attained a wholly unjustifiable premium – all these things seem to indicate most plainly that the whole affair has been clumsily worked by a clique of wealthy speculators, in order to pocket an enormous profit at the expense of the general public.

Defenders of Barings' behaviour point out that it was the first stock market flotation it had handled and blame its mishandling of applications, allotments and the share register on inexperience rather than on any devious intent. Merchant banks had not normally brought companies to the market before then and there was no guarantee in advance that the flotation would be such a success: an attempt to launch the Manchester Ship Canal on the market some months earlier had been a failure and the market generally was in a depressed state. In any event, it has been said that it is unfair to criticise its behaviour by later standards and rules. But it is obvious from the contemporary newspaper coverage, especially in the financial press, that Barings' actions were considered to be sharp practices at the time. The bank was widely believed at the time to have made £1 million from the flotation, one way or another, which was why someone asked Lord Rothschild if he regretted not having taken it on board when Sir Edward first consulted him about it.

In spite of – or perhaps because of – the way in which the flotation was handled, it did not dampen the demand for brewing shares. Three other major brewers, Allsop, Bass and Whitbread, were floated in the following three years and there were no fewer than 87 brewers listed on the Stock Exchange by 1890. The Guinness shares climbed steadily in the months after the flotation and reached £20 the following March, doubling in value in less than six months. By then, Sir Edward was back in the market, buying the company shares himself; by February 1887 he had bought an extra 30,000 shares and he held 132,500 of the 250,000 ordinary shares a year later, giving him a majority holding in the company.

The financial scandal did not damage Sir Edward, who was in a sense seen to be a victim of Barings as well; clearly, he could have made much more money out of the sale of his firm. On the other hand, it enhanced the image of Arthur Guinness, an old family firm which had been exposed as being a very successful money-making machine as well as a good employer and efficient brewer of good quality porter. The foundation of a new image, especially in Britain, of Guinness as a source of untold wealth had been laid. Sir Edward now set about living up to it.

CHAPTER SEVEN

Finding a Home

"If the present Lord Iveagh represented the old Irish Viscount he would not have to be created a new English baron."

Anonymous letter in Dublin's *Evening Telegraph*
about Sir Edward Guinness taking the Iveagh title

B y his own estimation after he had floated the brewery on the stock market, Sir Edward Guinness expected to have an income of £367,566 in 1887, mostly from interest on his cash from the sale, dividends on his shares in Arthur Guinness Son & Company (which paid 12 per cent plus a two per cent bonus and the income tax due on the dividends in its first payments to shareholders), and from his previous investments.[1] It was a very large income by any standards but probably less than he could have had if he had retained sole ownership of the brewery, as it made a record profit of £647,622 in 1886. Assuming annual expenses of a generous £100,000, he thus expected to have a surplus of more than £250,000 a year to invest on top of the approximately £7 million he already had in investments, including his Guinness shares, and cash.[2]

Now in his fortieth year, Sir Edward was well accustomed to having considerable wealth. He already had large imposing residences in Dublin, at St Stephen's Green and in the Phoenix Park, and in central London, at Grosvenor Place, at the western perimeter of Buckingham Palace's gardens. One of the gaps in his possessions, however, was a large country estate in England; it was still an essential requirement for anyone with designs on a title and hoping to join the ranks of the aristocracy. Even though agriculture was in decline, land still had its historical cachet as the basis for power and influence, as well as providing a vehicle for a fashionable contemporary lifestyle that revolved around house-parties and hunting, shooting and fishing, all seen as the essential occupations of a gentleman. Hosting lavish parties in town residences was one thing; being able to invite friends and acquaintances to shooting parties on one's own estate was another. However, finding a suitable country seat turned out to be a complicated and time-consuming business, even for an extremely rich man.

Having looked at several other large properties, Sir Edward settled on the 22,500-acre Elveden estate in Suffolk. Known as a sporting estate – in other words, no use as agricultural land – Elveden had an odd history. It had been bought by the British government for Duleep Singh, who became Maharaja of the Punjab in 1843 at the age of five when his half-brother died. Shortly afterwards, tensions between the independent Punjab and the British East India Company erupted into two Anglo-Sikh wars which resulted in the British taking control of the region and deposing him, while also seizing from his family the famous Koh-i-Noor diamond, then the largest in the world, which became part of the British Crown Jewels. Duleep Singh's mother was imprisoned and he was kept in a form of gilded cage as he grew up, became a Christian and was brought to England in 1854. The British government rented estates and eventually bought Elveden for him in 1863 where he lived as an English country gentleman, hunting and shooting, as well as gambling and womanizing. (He never succeeded in his aim of personally shooting 1,000 birds in a day: the nearest he got to his target was 780 partridges with a thousand cartridges.) Singh oversaw the development of the run-down estate, restoring its church, cottages and school and turning the main building into a quasi oriental palace. However, he eventually tired of his version of the aristocratic lifestyle, rekindled his interest in Sikhism and tried to return to India but was prevented by the British from getting any closer than Aden. Mired in debt, he demanded the return of the Koh-i-Noor diamond or its cash value; after his request was refused, he referred to Queen Victoria as "Mrs Fagin, the receiver of stolen property".[3] Forced to remain in

Europe, he settled in Paris, where he was when the British authorities decided to sell Elveden to recoup some of the government money he had spent on it.

Sir Edward put in a bid of £125,000 for it through an intermediary at the end of 1888, upping it to £155,000 shortly afterwards. He was invited to reveal his identity, raise the bid to £165,000, and agree to a valuation of the timber on the estate, all of which he did. The trustees appointed by the British government to deal with the matter accepted his offer and signed a contract in April 1889. However, the Maharaja refused to agree; he sought £250,000 and insisted that his underage son also had to agree to the sale. As the negotiations went on, another potential buyer entered the contest and was said to be willing to offer a higher price. Sir Edward refused to increase his offer and negotiations came to an end with Duleep Singh basically challenging the British government to confiscate it if it so wished.[4]

Meanwhile, Sir Edward and his wife Adelaide spent more and more of their time engaged in the relentless pursuit of fashionable leisure. Winters and springs were generally spent in Dublin where they had already rebuilt and extended Farmleigh on the edge of the Phoenix Park at Castleknock and a comfortable carriage ride through the park to and from the brewery at St James's Gate. They also entertained regularly, and so lavishly, at their city centre home in 80 St Stephen's Green that it was often considered a grander venue than the viceroy's parties at Dublin Castle.[5] The Dublin Castle "season" was February and March and culminated at Punchestown Races to which many travelled by rail: the Viceroy's carriage was marked by an X at the station and some wag is said to have identified the Guinness carriage with an XX in honour of the brewery's extra strength porter. After Punchestown, the Guinnesses and the more established members of Irish society moved to London for the "season" there in May, June and July. There was a brief return to Ireland again for the Dublin Horse Show in early August and then it was time for the grouse season. Sir Edward leased a grouse moor for three years in Scotland from 1880 to engage in this traditional aristocratic activity. He also bought a house in Cowes and a race-winning schooner, the *Cetonia*, from Lord Gosford to indulge in the relatively more recent aristocratic pastime of sailing. It brought him an honorary lieutenancy in the Royal Naval Reserve at the suggestion of the Prince of Wales in 1885 and an excuse for a portrait of himself in uniform.

Sir Edward also indulged his interest in art, buying more than 200 paintings at a cost of more that £500,000 in a four-year period from 1887 onwards. He had been buying various pieces of art since the early 1870s, frequently on trips to Italy and Spain, but he went on a dedicated buying spree after the flotation of the brewery. Almost all were bought through a dealer in London's Bond Street, Thomas Agnew & Sons. Sir Edward went in there one day after walking out of a neighbouring art dealer's where he had been kept waiting. Ironically, Agnew's was run by William Agnew, who had been elected a Liberal MP in 1885 for the newly created constituency of Stretford in Lancashire and was a friend of Gladstone and a strong supporter of his Home Rule policies for Ireland. However, Sir Edward did not let politics get in the way of his art collection and Agnew's good fortune resulted in a huge volume of business: the firm sent Sir Edward an average of one painting a week to view and he bought almost all of them. Most of them, especially at the beginning, were portraits and they included more than 30 works by Sir Joshua Reynolds, more than 20 by George Romney, 15 by Thomas Gainsborough, eight by Sir Edwin Landseer and, most famously, two by Rembrandt, his self-portrait in old age and a portrait of a lady. The most expensive individual purchase was £27,500 which he paid in June 1887 for the two Rembrandts and a Cuyp painting of the River Maas, followed by £26,400 the following December for two Reynolds portraits of Mrs Tollemache as Miranda and of Lady Louisa Manners. Among the purchases were four other paintings by members of the Cuyp family, Vermeer's *The Guitar Player* (£1,050), and numerous other works by the likes of Van Dyck, Rubens, Canaletto and Metsu. It is clear from his collection that he had little interest in contemporary art and none in the movements of the time like Impressionism.

Sir Edward's art purchases were credited indirectly with creating one of London's most successful art dealers, Joseph Duveen, from whose family the Guinnesses were buying many pieces of antique furniture. The young Duveen noticed that they were spending much more with Agnew's, the art dealers, than with his father's business and decided to switch to art. He subsequently made a large fortune and became famous on the realisation that Europe had the paintings and Americans had the money and bringing the two together would be highly profitable. His first encounter with the Guinnesses was described thus:

One day not long after Joseph's return to London, a stocky gentleman with a marked Irish brogue, accompanied by his wife, a modest, unassuming little woman in a plumed hat, walked into his shop in Oxford Street. They looked like a country couple dressed up for a visit to the city. They asked to see some screens. Joseph Joel [his father] had recently had some made up of fine old Spanish leather, and he told Joseph to bring them out. The lady, in ecstasy, bought one screen after another. As the sales mounted, the elder Duveen whispered to his son to find out quickly who these people were. Joseph went into consultation with their coachman – an early instance of his lifelong practice of picking up useful intelligence from servants. He wrote the customer's name on a slip of paper, and handed it to his father. "You may think it strange, Mr Duveen, that I am buying so many screens," the woman was saying just then. "Not at all, Lady Guinness," replied the proprietor. "You have many fine homes, and you are quite right to supply them with screens." With the delight of anonymity welcoming recognition, Lady Guinness beamed at her husband. "You see, Edward," she said, "Mr Duveen knows who we are!" When years afterwards, Joseph Duveen told the story to one of the sons of the purchaser of the screens, Guinness said, "At last I know why we had such a lot of bloody screens in the house."[6]

While never stinting on his own lifestyle, Sir Edward continued to have an interest in philanthropy, especially in housing, which was widely recognised as one of the major social problems of the era. A very high proportion of the population lived in squalid, over-crowded and excrement-littered conditions, especially in Dublin. The state of housing and sanitary conditions had an obvious effect on health as well; the death rate in Dublin was considerably higher than in British cities and the gap widened as the nineteenth century went on and improvements took place in English cities. Even for the middle and professional classes, Dublin was a distinctly unhealthy place to live.[7] Very little was being done to provide housing for the poor; the fact that many members of the city's council were slum landlords – 17 councillors owned more than one tenement each, a report in 1914 found – may have helped to inhibit any serious action to resolve the problem.

Sir Edward had already become involved in the successful Artisans Dwelling Company but that was as much a commercial as a philanthropic enterprise, aimed at the better-off section of the working class: taking advantage of government-subsidised interest rates for housing the working class, it returned dividends of between three and five per cent as the century drew to a close. The brewery had also been involved since the early 1870s, like other companies such as Watkins' brewery and the railway companies, in providing accommodation for its workers in schemes like the Belview and Rialto Buildings but that ended with the stock market flotation and the formation of the public company.

It was in this area that Sir Edward made his largest and most effective philanthropic intervention. In late 1889 he set up the Guinness Trust with a donation of £250,000, mainly in securities, to provide accommodation for people in some of the poorest areas of London and Dublin. As trustees, he selected Lord Rowton, his old friend David Plunket and Charles Thomson Ritchie, a Conservative MP like Plunket and President of the Local Government Board, which was responsible for creating county councils. Rowton, born Montagu William Lowry-Corry, was the grandson of the Earl of Belmore who had represented County Tyrone in parliament and had had an unusual career path himself. He was a well-known socialite as a young man and had become the private secretary and friend of Benjamin Disraeli until the latter's death. He also had a social conscience and had tried to do something about housing the very poor and destitute: his solution was to set up well-run and cheap hostels which set a new standard of accommodation for the poor and became known as Rowton Houses. The model was copied throughout England and abroad and was eventually to be copied in the Iveagh Hostel in Dublin.

The £250,000 donation was divided into a London Fund of £200,000 and a Dublin Fund (which later became the Iveagh Trust) of £50,000. Sir Edward's idea was that the trusts would be self-sustaining and grow from the rents they received, modest as they were intended to be. In the deed of trust he laid down for the venture, he was also insistent that they and the accommodation provided would not be influenced by sectarianism or politics. The trust began its work in Dublin with two developments: the building of Thomas Court Buildings (subsequently sold to the Artisans Dwelling Company) and fourteen blocks of flats in Kevin Street. He subsequently expanded his donations hugely, spending some £220,000 on buying the Bull Alley area, a three-acre slum beside St Patrick's Cathedral whose notoriety as the city's worst enclave of degrading poverty, prostitution and general vice and crime had not diminished since his father had re-built the cathedral some 30 years earlier. He also spent £100,000 on providing the Iveagh Market for street traders, who had been operating in appalling conditions of filth. (The fact that the old Sweetman's brewery, once a major competitor of Guinness, was demolished to make way for the new market may have added to the satisfaction Sir Edward was entitled to feel at his generosity.) In London, the first Guinness Trust buildings went up within a year at Brandon Street, Walworth and were quickly followed by others in Draycott Avenue, Chelsea, Columbia Road, and Lever Street. All its projects were accompanied by recreational and other facilities, ranging from day-care centres to swimming baths.

The formation of the Guinness Trust received an almost universal welcome, partly because of what was perceived to be the enormous amount of money donated to the trustees. However, there were some dissenting voices, mainly from among temperance campaigners who underlined the link between the source of the Guinness money – drunkenness – and poverty. Less expected perhaps was the response of the Prime Minister and leader of the Conservative Party, Lord Salisbury, who welcomed the trust as one of the greatest, wisest and best-inspired acts of munificence ever made by a rich man. But he also warned that the problem of housing the working class could not be solved by turning the inhabitants of unsanitary dwellings onto the streets. "You have to find houses for the people turned into the streets. How do you do that? Sir Edward Guinness will only take you a little distance and you cannot afford to do it by the state," he told a meeting in Nottingham. His solution was for property and land owners to unite, not out of a spirit of altruism, but to provide commercial projects suitable for those who desired them.[8]

Salisbury's two-handed comments may have been inspired by his desire to make a political point – the belief that interfering with the property market to solve social problems would be counter-productive because nobody would then invest in providing housing – and it may also have been intended to distance himself a little from Sir Edward's ongoing campaign to become a lord. It would be excessively cynical to see the foundation of the Guinness Trust as yet another building block in Sir Edward's efforts to achieve his long-standing ambition. It undoubtedly helped his prospects of being elevated to the peerage. But he proved that his motives were primarily altruistic by his continued interest in the project for the rest of his life, becoming chairman after Rowton's death in 1903, and his continuing philanthropic largesse after he had received all the honours he had desired. The Guinness Trust (now the Guinness Partnership) in England expanded outside London in the 1960s and in 2008 provided affordable housing and other facilities for more than 100,000 people in 50,000 homes: it had an annual turnover or more than £200 million and a staff of 2,000 people.[9] The Iveagh Trust in Dublin had property valued at some €65 million in the early years of the twenty-first century and is still investing in them and in new buildings.

—————

The brewery at St James's Gate was still thriving, now as a public company. Sales of Guinness were growing, stout prices were holding up in spite of pressures to lower them, and the cost of the brewery's raw materials were low, leaving it in a position where it was heading for a profit of more than £543,000 in the nine months after the flotation. The share price was weakened somewhat by the flotation of other breweries which the successful Guinness listing had prompted: some of them, like Allsop's, were over-subscribed by an even greater ratio than the Guinness launch had been. But the share price was supported by the strong rise in profits, which, allowed the generous 12 per cent dividend, plus a three-month "bonus" of two per cent, to be paid in the first year. Even with that dividend (and the payment by the company of the shareholders' income tax on it), almost half the nine-month profit was retained for reserves.[10]

Among the changes afoot at St James's Gate as it moved towards the end of the nineteenth century was a more methodical and scientific approach to the industrial-scale brewing that had been taking place there for some time. Brewing had been traditionally more of an art than a science, partly because the scientific knowledge and instruments to make it more methodical had not been available. That had changed, however, spurred less by a desire to improve quality than by the necessity of giving technical evidence in court cases in which Guinness was accusing publicans or others of passing off inferior stout as theirs.[11] Guinness adopted a new policy in the 1890s of employing science graduates as brewers, the elite section of the staff who had previously been almost exclusively Guinnesses or Pursers (including their relations, like Wallers on the Guinness side and Geoghegans on the Purser side). Thus, the number of brewers employed increased from eight at the time the company was floated on the stock market to 14 over the next quarter century. All the new recruits after 1893 were science graduates of Oxford or Cambridge universities. It was a policy that did not go down very well in Dublin, not least among graduates of Trinity College, Sir Edward's old college, which he was subsequently to endow with significant donations and where both he and, later, his son became the long-time chancellors. Whereas Guinness had been known, rightly or wrongly, among many Catholics for employing only Protestants in senior positions, it now became known among Irish Protestants for employing only public-school educated Oxbridge graduates. It was seen by some Protestants as evidence of a bias based on class and social position rather than ability.[12] According to a later generation Guinness, though, it was a method of ensuring that the brewery was run by intelligent people who had learned the humanities at school and science at university.[13]

Sir Edward had already brought his brother-in-law Claude Guinness into the brewery as managing director and he took over John

Tertius Purser's central role after the latter's retirement at the time of the flotation. Claude's older brother, Reginald, was also a director of the company and became assistant managing director after the flotation. The third permanent Dublin director was solicitor James Stewart and these three, along with Sir Edward, formed a sub-committee which effectively ran the brewery on a daily basis while full board meetings were only held quarterly. But there was no doubt in anyone's mind that Sir Edward, now the majority shareholder, was the arbiter and ultimate authority on all issues.

Other changes were happening as well as the brewery continued its successful growth, albeit at a slower pace than in the preceding years; sales took more than another 20 years to double. Guinness's share of the Irish market rose from an already high 65 per cent to about 80 per cent between 1888 and 1914, while its share of the British market went up from 1.5 per cent to almost four per cent. This was all the more impressive since it was happening at a time when the average consumption of beer in the United Kingdom (including Ireland) was dropping from 32.53 gallons per person in 1889 to 26.11 gallons in 1909, causing smaller breweries to close or amalgamate. The importance of the British market was also evident from the fact that a smaller proportion of the brewery's steadily increasing output was being sold in Ireland (62 per cent in 1910, compared to 71 per cent in 1895).[14] This trend undoubtedly confirmed Sir Edward's unionism and the importance of the British link politically, not that it needed any further reinforcement.

Guinness also stood out as being more successful than the major British breweries, which found themselves in the late 1890s in a costly race to buy up tied houses, a policy option that Guinness had always eschewed since its earlier days. While other brewers had to use their capital to buy pubs and give loans to publicans – at a time of decreasing sales – Guinness was free to use its resources to continue expanding its plant in Dublin, doubling its capacity between 1901 and 1907. It also maintained its concentration on producing a high-quality product; letting bottlers fix their own price; and keeping discounts to distributors and publicans at a minimum. Profits topped £1 million for the first time in 1906, bringing the new company's profits between its stock market listing in 1886 and the start of the First World War to more than £25 million. The dividend reached 25 per cent in 1908, causing concern at board level that the high level of profitability would encourage the government to increase excise duty and customers to demand price reductions. This was relieved somewhat by increasing the capital of the company and issuing new shares to reduce the nominal market price. Staff shared in the largesse as well, with the introduction of a policy of giving the management an annual bonus of a month's extra salary and the labourers and tradesmen an extra week's pay.[15]

With the brewery operating very well, Sir Edward announced his intention in 1890 to retire as chairman of the company and as a director now that the three years he had promised he would remain in the position had elapsed. As usual, he explained the decision on the basis of his health, claiming in a letter to fellow directors that "it has only recently been forced upon me by my doctors". The letter also said:

I have I regret to say for some time past felt the strain of work to a serious extent and I have been urged by my Medical Advisers to lighten the burden of my business engagements and responsibilities as far as is possible. I feel that I must follow this advice and after anxious consideration I have decided that it is better without delay to take a step which I have had in contemplation for many years viz: to withdraw from active participation in the affairs of the Brewery.[16]

His stated reason was probably less than frank, although his hypochondria may have been exacerbated by the death of his sister Anne, the eldest of his siblings, the previous year at the age of 50.[17] Appearing to withdraw from "trade" was probably also an essential part of his campaign to enter the peerage and may have removed the final hurdle in achieving that ambition. First, however, he had to decide upon his successor. The obvious choice was his brother-in-law (his wife Adelaide's brother) Claude Guinness who was already managing director and recognised as an effective one. The other possibility – if, as no doubt seemed desirable, he wanted to have a Guinness at the head of the company – was Claude's older brother and fellow-director, Reginald. In what is a recurring theme in the Guinness story, the younger Claude was seen as the better businessman than the older brother Reginald.

Sir Edward made the obvious choice, picking Claude as chairman and Reginald as vice-chairman and managing director. However, Claude suggested that the positions be reversed, that Reginald be chairman and he be vice-chairman and continue as managing director. His reasons for doing so are not clear; he may have shared the general opinion that he was a more competent managing director than his brother was likely to be and that it was more important that he stay in that role. On the other hand, his own growing health problems may have been a factor. What exactly they were is not clear either but they increasingly inhibited his involvement in the brewery and came to a highly dramatic climax five years later when he had to be taken away, literally, in a straitjacket. The likelihood is that he was suffering from syphilis[18] but it was another family scandal that was more or less successfully buried. He died shortly afterwards in April 1895 at the age of 43 and his loss to the brewery was seen by many family members as a major loss to the company and even a turning point in its fortunes. Reginald succeeded him for a time, although the real power was an up-and-coming brewer and assistant managing director, Christopher La Touche, of the banking family with whom the second Arthur Guinness had been associated in the Bank of Ireland during the 1820s. Meanwhile, Sir Edward accepted Claude's proposal and Reginald Guinness became chairman, while Sir Edward's position on the board was filled by George H. Beare, who had recently retired as trade manager and secretary after fifty years in the brewery.[19]

In a farewell message to the board and the staff at St James's Gate, Sir Edward touched upon one of the growing issues of the moment, the rise of trades unions which were flexing their industrial muscles more and more. He stressed the importance of continuing the good relations that had existed between management and workers there and warned against the sympathetic strike.

> I do not wish to express any hostility to Trades Unions, between which and myself most cordial relations have always been maintained in the past, but I cannot take leave of you without referring to the efforts which I have reason to believe are being made to induce the workingmen in your employment to become members of a union which

has unfortunately been involved of late in disputes with employers. I would earnestly ask those who have joined, or who intend to join that union, that they should very fully consider the possible consequences of their action. . . . I should be apprehensive of the employees being unwillingly drawn into disputes which might arise outside the brewery with which they were not personally concerned.

He concluded his message with a promise to pay the clerks an extra month's salary and the working men a week's wages out of his own pocket in recognition "of the excellent service which has been rendered to me in the past".[20] The continuation of the policy of maintaining good industrial relations had also been emphasised by the new chairman, Reginald Guinness, at the shareholders' meeting in London a couple of weeks earlier when he said that work well done should be well paid and it was in the company's interest to aim for the contentment and well-being of the men employed by it.

Sir Edward's resignation was in many respects an illusion. As the dominant shareholder in the company and a workaholic, his detachment from the brewery was never as great as it may have appeared, or have been intended to appear, at the time. He continued to be consulted regularly about developments, even relatively minor ones,[21] but it gave him the flexibility to be as involved as his other interests and ambitions allowed. In any event, the move was the final stage in achieving his social ambitions; he was named a baron in the New Year's Honour's List for 1891, with the help of his new associate Lord Rowton, chairman of the Guinness Trust, as well as that of Plunket and their friends in the Conservative Party. All he had to do now was choose a title and find a suitable seat.

Informed officially of the ennoblement just before Christmas 1890, Sir Edward put forward two possible titles for consideration, Lord St Patrick's and Lord Iveagh, while there was some public expectation once the news emerged that he would be known as Lord Farmleigh.[22] The St Patrick's title was a reference to the cathedral his father had rebuilt and which Edward continued to fund; Iveagh was the name of the traditional home of the Magennis family in County Down from whom the Guinnesses claimed, explicitly or implicitly, to be descended; and Farmleigh, his country seat on the edge of Dublin, was not among his final choices. Even with the apostrophe "s", St Patrick's was seen to be a claim too far, leaving him open to the accusation that he was naming himself after the national saint. He was quickly dissuaded from using it by the Prime Minister, Lord Salisbury, who wrote to Lord Rowton with an impressive delicacy of touch: "Of course every one must choose their own title subject to the highest approval. My own impression (merely an impression) is that 'Iveagh' would be preferred to 'St Patrick's' but I may be wrong."[23]

The Guinness claim to be descended from the Magennis family in Iveagh was based on little more than the first Arthur's use of the Magennis and Whitmore arms on a silver cup to mark his marriage to Olivia Whitmore in 1761. His eldest son, Hosea, had sought official confirmation of the arms from the herald in the 1810s but it was not forthcoming. However, the herald, Sir William Betham, did grant him arms very similar to the Magennis ones. *Burke's Peerage* subsequently continued the fudge, claiming that there was a clear progression in the family tree from Magennis to Guinness. In fact, the Iveagh title had existed since 1623 when Sir Arthur Magennis became Viscount Magennis of Iveagh. The Magennises were Catholics and supporters of King James II against William of Orange. The fifth Viscount Iveagh, Bryan Magennis, raised two regiments for James and went into exile with some 500 of his troops after the defeat of the Jacobites at the battles of the Boyne and Aughrim in the early 1690s. They ended up in Austria, fighting against the Turks in Hungary, and Magennis was said to have died childless in 1693.[24] However, the title went on being used by his brother Phelim and his descendants in France and Spain.[25] Meanwhile, the title was officially declared extinct after William's victory and, in any event, Sir Edward was assured by Sir Bernard Burke, Ulster King of Arms,[26] that there would be no clash between the Magennis title – which was an Irish title only – and himself as Baron Iveagh – which was a United Kingdom title – if anyone still claimed to hold the Magennis one. Sir Edward was also influenced by Sir Samuel Ferguson, the poet and Deputy Keeper of the State Papers of Ireland. Sir Samuel, who was married to Mary Guinness, a distant cousin of Sir Edward's descended from the first Arthur Guinness's younger brother Samuel, confirmed the Iveagh connection to him before his death in 1886.

His elevation to the peerage did not impress those who were derisive about "beer barons" and the trend of industrialists being given honours. Sir Edward bought a tract of land in Iveagh but his rise to the peerage also set off a debate about his choice of title. "On what grounds?" a brief and pointed letter from an anonymous correspondent to *The Irish Times* asked. "The real representative of the title is General Magenis, Finvoy Lodge, Ballymoney, County Antrim." His letter went unanswered, at least publicly, but the debate took a more vigorous tone in Dublin's *Evening Telegraph*, then a fiercely pro-Parnell paper, which attracted a series of letters debating the Iveagh claim. Its correspondents basically divided between those who believed the Guinnesses were descended from the original Sir Arthur Magennis's younger son, Con – that his grandson, Ever, was the father of Richard Guinness – and those who believed that Richard was a "foundling" brought up by a nurse called Guinness and put into service with Archbishop Price. The main exponent of the first theory was John O'Hart of Kilkee, described as a genealogist and author of the book *Irish Pedigrees*, who claimed that many Ulster manufacturers had fled to the colonies, America and Dublin after William of Orange "crushed Irish manufacturers" in order to help English traders. His claim was greeted with derision by other correspondents, who pointed out that there was no evidence of this and that, if there had been, a wealthy family like the Guinnesses would have produced, as one anonymous correspondent termed it, "two reliable parents . . . for [Burke's] *Peerage*". Another correspondent, Patrick Traynor, suggested the second theory and pointed out that if Richard Guinness had been the scion of the House of Iveagh and changed his religion, he would have had an official "recantation from Popery certificate" and he and his son Arthur would have claimed the lands and castles of the banished Magennises. With an influential patron like Price, they would have succeeded in getting part of the lands if they "had the lawful blood of the Guinnesses of Iveagh in their veins", he opined. In a later letter, the same writer noted with approval, however, that "The Guinnesses of James's Gate were not Croppy-hunters in the troubles of 1798–1803 when, if they were so disposed, they could have paraded their ultra loyalty as did their fellow-trader and near neighbour, Alderman Manders."[27]

The debate was perhaps best summed up by the poet Katharine Tynan in a rare by-lined article in *The Irish Times* describing a two-hour tour of the brewery. "With the Guinness record before one, one can smile at vexed questions of descent which the College of Heralds settles with a wave of the hand, and touching which a lively controversy may rage in the columns of an evening newspaper. The Guinnesses – be they Northern Magennises or not – might write 'Noblesse Oblige' on their escutcheon, and feel they had earned the proud words."[28] Or, as another of the *Evening Telegraph*'s anonymous correspondents put it: "The ancestry of Baron Iveagh shall date from the day he parted with a quarter of a million of money for a philanthropic purpose."

The new Lord Iveagh took his seat in the House of Lords on 20 January 1891 but had not yet found himself a suitable country seat in England, a requirement that was all the more pressing now that he was a peer. One of the most interesting properties that caught his attention was an estate in Wiltshire in the south of England, which included a famous forest, 7,743 acres of pleasure grounds and parks and 44,000 acres of land, as well as a large country house and a population of some 5,000 people. Savernake Forest was famous as probably the oldest in England, dating back to at least 934 when it had been mentioned in a charter. It was also well-known for its historical connections; it was the family home of Jane Seymour, one of Henry VIII's six wives, and mother of the child king Edward VI. Furthermore, it had been in the same family since the Battle of Hastings in 1066 which, by the end of the nineteenth century, was the Brudenell-Bruces, whose titles included the earldom of Cardigan and the Marquis of Ailesbury. In the early 1890s, the current Marquis was in his late twenties and in deep financial trouble because of his gambling. The estate was in debt to the tune of some £300,000 and he himself owed £173,000 to one money-lender and apparently more to others. His grandfather had previously bailed him out when, at the age of 21 in 1884, he already had huge gambling problems and his grandfather had sold Jervaulx Abbey in the Yorkshire Dales in order to give him £175,000.

The estate had been on the market for four years to pay off the Marquis's latest round of gambling debts. It had attracted the attention of a couple of other interested parties, including an American millionaire, who had made bids but they dropped out after Iveagh offered the asking price of £700,000. The Marquis then wanted extra for the timber; Iveagh upped his offer to £750,000 and contracts were signed on 23 June 1891. The price Iveagh was prepared to pay was seen as generous and more than was considered to be the investment value of the property, whose gross income was less than £27,000 a year because rents and agricultural prices had been falling for several years.[29] That, however, was only the beginning of the saga.

The Bruce family objected strenuously to the Marquis's decision to sell the Wiltshire estate and two of his uncles took him to court, questioning his right as a "tenant for life" to sell it at all. In a succession of complicated land law cases, the courts decided at first that the Marquis did not have the right to sell but an appeal court upheld his position, which was subsequently confirmed by the House of Lords. Reporting the result, *The Times* declared that "the 5,000 people who inhabit the vast Wiltshire estate will learn the difference between a wealthy and beneficent landlord [Iveagh] and a spendthrift [Ailesbury] who has been practically a bankrupt ever since he came into possession".[30] But it wasn't over yet. Other female relations of Ailesbury challenged the effects of the sale on their incomes, which were charges on the estate, and his uncles took further legal action, accusing Iveagh of bribery by offering one of them £50,000 to drop their objections to the sale. Just back from the Royal Yacht Squadron Regatta at Cowes (where the *Cetonia* had not fared well against the German emperor's cutter), Iveagh categorically denied in court that he, or anyone authorised by him, had offered Ailesbury's uncle, Lord Henry Bruce, any money to drop his objections.[31] Iveagh also repeated his determination to go ahead with the sale; he had already appointed an agent and bought a house for him in the area. Then Ailesbury's estranged wife, Julia, threatened to sue Iveagh if he bought the property for the £3,000 a year to which she was entitled from the estate for Ailesbury's lifetime under her marriage agreement. She was already owed £15,000 which Ailesbury had failed to pay.

It all became too much for Iveagh and he finally gave up in the autumn of 1893. He got a court order that allowed him rescind the contract to buy Savernake unless Lady Ailesbury's consent to the sale was forthcoming within a fixed period. It wasn't, the contract was rescinded and the two-year episode was ended. As one door closed, however, another opened unexpectedly; within days of Iveagh giving formal notice in October 1893 that he was going to rescind the Savernake contract, Duleep Singh died suddenly in Paris after suffering an apoplectic seizure at the age of 53. His body was brought back to Elveden for burial. The British Government's trustees for Elveden contacted Iveagh again and he agreed to buy it for £160,000 (considerably less than the £271,000 it had cost the British to buy it before Duleep Singh had rebuilt the main house). Contracts were signed in April 1894. Coincidentally, some ten days later, the Marquis of Ailesbury died of heart disease at a friend's house at the age of 31. His uncle, Lord Henry Bruce, succeeded him and Savernake remained in the family.[32]

—— ∞ ——

Elveden became a key factor in the new Lord Iveagh's social success and in establishing him at the top of English society. As new honours flowed in on a regular basis – he and Ardilaun were given honorary doctorates by Trinity College Dublin on the same day – new friends included the great and the good in politics and society. He was regularly in the company of the Conservative Party leader, Lord Salisbury, and increasingly in the company of the Prince of Wales, who preferred to socialise with the plutocratic new rich rather than with the old, and increasingly less rich in relative terms, landed gentry. Their houses "were better equipped, the company was more interesting, and the moral tone was less censoriously Victorian".[33] His interest in shooting parties was said to always increase noticeably at lunchtime, when the ladies arrived.

Iveagh began reconstructing the house and lands, abandoning any pretence at farming except insofar as it would encourage and provide haunts for game. He added hugely to the somewhat exotic and vaguely Indian house that Duleep Singh had had built, more than doubling the size by adding a new wing the same size as the existing house and then connecting the two wings with an imposing domed central block. Rather than change the character of the house, he continued it to an extent by including Indian designs among the pillars and galleries of the large marble entrance hall which was used for parties. Diarist Augustus Hare – who seemed to share the Prince of Wales's interests – described it in the following terms:

> It was Duleep Singh's, and he tried to make it like an Indian palace inside. Much of his decoration still remains, and the delicate white stucco-work has a pretty effect when mingled with groups of tall palms and flowering plants. Otherwise the house (with the kindest of hosts) is almost appallingly luxurious, such masses of orchids, electric light everywhere etc. However, a set-off the other way is an electric piano, which goes on pounding away by itself with a pertinacity which is perfectly distracting. In the evenings singing men and dancing women are brought down from London, and are supposed to enliven the royal guest.[34]

A regular Irish visitor, Lady Fingall, offered another perspective:

> The new owners had added a great deal to the house. They built the vast marble hall, supposed to be a copy of the Taj at Delhi [sic]. Each pillar in it is carved with a different design and there is a gallery above, at one end of which, Casano's band used to play in the evening during those visits. It had cost a fabulous sum to put that marble hall, on the design of one made for Indian suns, down amid the cold marshes of Suffolk. If Killeen [her Irish home] was the coldest house in Ireland, the marble hall at Elveden must have been the coldest room in England! We used to assemble there for tea after a shoot and we sat there in the evening. There was only one large fireplace and during the King's visits, when etiquette and courtesy had to be observed, a good many of us froze.[35]

A new, two-storey block around a courtyard was also built apart from the main building for the servants, containing more than 30 bedrooms, as well as suites for the senior staff. The work took four years to complete and employed an average of 150 workmen full time: the total cost of the main contractor (who was not the only contractor on the project) was more than £110,000. The Iveaghs lived in the old house as the work progressed and the main purpose of the estate, the shooting, went ahead with even greater speed. To facilitate it, 15 miles of roads were built around the estate and a telephone system installed to connect all locations with the main house. A small army of 76 men were employed for the shooting under the head gamekeeper (who was on an annual salary of £80) and including 16 gamekeepers, nine underkeepers and 28 warreners. Large numbers of pheasants were reared each year to feed the huge "bags" that were shot annually. The birds that were not consumed on the estate were sold in London, helping to keep the annual costs of the shooting down to about £2,400 a year.

In the house itself, there was a permanent staff of a butler, underbutler, three footmen, a housekeeper, three cooks and their kitchen staff, six housemaids, a carpenter and a night watchman. They did not include the servants who travelled with the family, such as personal valets, ladies' maids, governesses and nursery-maids, or the servants who came with house guests and were ranked among the downstairs staff in the same order as their employers upstairs. During house parties, as Lady Fingall described it, "there were twenty or thirty housemaids . . . they seem to have been kept somewhat as novices in a convent, not being allowed to go out alone, or to visit the neighbouring cottages".[36] Outdoors, apart from those involved in the shooting, there were 20 gardeners to look after the flower gardens and another 20 to take care of the vegetable gardens. For a man with an income which had increased to some £500,000 a year at this stage, the costs of running the loss-making farm and the house – estimated at £30,000 a year[37] – were a small price to pay for the social recognition and associated influence that it brought him.

Shooting parties were treated with high seriousness and run with military-style organisation by the late Victorian and Edwardian aristocracy. Given that the birds shot were bred in captivity, effectively tame, and driven by beaters (dressed in white smocks and hats with red bands) towards the guns, it was questionable whether the shooting could be considered any kind of sport. Shooting at the time was helped by technical developments in the design and manufacture of shotguns, partly explaining the huge "bags" of birds killed on a daily basis. But there were few objectors to the fashion for shooting, leading an American ambassador to London to remark near the end of the era that "you've no idea how much time and money they spend on shooting".[38] Elveden became one of the focal points of this fashion along with other estates bought by the new rich. Not alone were the visitors guaranteed excellent, and none too strenuous, shooting but they were also sure of being accommodated in sumptuous modern luxury, well-dined and entertained, as well, no doubt, as being guaranteed a lavish serving of society gossip and intrigue while rubbing shoulders with successive Princes of Wales and, in turn, Edward VII and George V.

A shooting party at Elveden usually had up to 30 guests and ran from Monday to Friday. The number of guns was generally eight or nine but it was limited to six shooters later on days when the king was present. Hot lunches were provided with full service in heated marquees around the estate to which the ladies were brought for lunch with the men. In its first year under Iveagh's ownership, 25,000 game of all sorts were shot at Elveden, the highest daily total being 1,500. The number increased steadily – with a break during the First World War – to a peak of 145,022 in 1922. Augustus Hare described the shooting in the diary extract quoted above about the house:

> You know, probably, how this place is the most wonderful shooting in England. The soil is so bad that it is not worth cultivating, and agriculture has been abandoned as a bad business. Game is found to be far more profitable. Each day I have gone out with the luncheon party, and we have met the shooters at tents pitched at different parts of the wilderness, where boarded floors are laid down, and a luxurious banquet is prepared with plate and flowers. The quantity of game killed is almost incredible, and the Royal Duke [later George V] shot more than any one, really, I believe owing to his being a very good shot, and not, as so often is the case in royal battues, from the birds being driven his way.

On one day (15 November 1899) the duke shot 368 pheasants, 177 partridges, 28 hares, 51 rabbits and a pig, a total "bag" of 625, having fired 1,200 cartridges, an average of just over one kill per shot, as he himself calculated. The largest "bag" in a single day was 3,247 head of game shot by a party including the duke, then George V, and Edward Iveagh in November 1912.[39]

In Elveden, Iveagh had found not just an actual home – like all his station at the time, he moved regularly between his many houses and estates – but also his metaphorical home. It was the place in which he wished to be, among the higher reaches of British society. He was now more at home there than in Ireland, socially and politically: he had moved on from Irish society while, politically, Ireland was moving inexorably away from Britain, in spite of the disarray among the Home Rulers in the aftermath of the crisis over Parnell and his relationship with Katharine O'Shea. Edward was referred to frequently as an Englishman, gave his three sons English names and brought them up to be Englishmen, sending them all to Eton and following the well-worn paths of the English aristocracy. Yet, in deciding on his title, he had paid close attention to his Irish heritage in genuinely choosing one that reflected an old Irish family: in contrast, his brother Ardilaun had simply taken his title from his Ashford estate in County Galway, an example some expected Iveagh to follow by choosing Farmleigh as his title. In addition, Iveagh had the gravestones of the first Arthur's parents, Richard and Elizabeth, restored in Oughterard graveyard in County Kildare.

His choice of Iveagh left him open to controversy but was also a clear identification with Ireland at a time when his political, social, religious and business interests pushed him towards England and the empire. It was, in its way, another example of the by now traditional Guinness capacity to steer its own course through the treacherous waters of politics and identity in Ireland. The Guinnesses were now Irish and English, causing some confusion about national identity among some younger members of the family at the time. One of Iveagh's grandsons, Bryan (born 1905), thought for much of his childhood that all English people were either Irish or Scottish. He himself was Irish and Scottish (through his mother) as well as English and he was dumbfounded when he asked a nurse if she was Scottish or Irish and she said she was English: "I had never heard of anyone being just English," he wrote later.[40]

The Guinness capacity to literally mind their own business amid the political and sectarian tensions in Ireland was still required in spite of

Iveagh's new status in England. As the twentieth century began, he was widely considered to be the second richest man in Britain, after Sir John Ellerman, a reclusive shipping magnate and highly successful serial investor who eschewed political honours and high society (although he did accept a knighthood eventually). Much of Iveagh's wealth was still tied up in Ireland, primarily in the brewery and in property, in spite of diversification in England and North America. The prospect of Home Rule, which was regularly associated by its opponents with socialism and communism as well as with popery, seemed to threaten the future of the brewery and a substantial part of his income. The split in the Irish Party at Westminster and the defeat of the second Home Rule Bill by the House of Lords in 1894 slowed the momentum towards Home Rule but did not halt it. Iveagh's new position in the Lords gave him a ringside seat to observe these developments: he was, for instance, in the Lords' gallery of the House of Commons to see the disarray at first hand in a small but symbolic way one day shortly after the Irish Party split when Parnell caused consternation by taking a seat in the midst of his former colleagues and new Irish enemies, sitting there with his hat down over his eyes and a slight smile on his face and forcing a flustered Justin McCarthy – his would-be successor and, in the words of the Parnellites, the leader of the secessionists – to seek a seat elsewhere.[41]

Iveagh played no overt role in parliamentary politics; in the 36 years during which he was a member he spoke in the House of Lords on only one occasion – to support, as Chancellor of Dublin University, an amendment in 1918 preventing proportional representation being applied to the election of the university's two parliamentary seats: his contribution amounted to less than a hundred words. He was a more regular attender than that suggests, however, voting on other occasions and participating as a member of a number of parliamentary committees. However, he continued to play an active part in the struggle against Home Rule, along with his brother and sons, particularly when it came under serious threat again as the Conservative government policy of trying to kill it with kindness failed.

CHAPTER EIGHT

Threats and Fears

"Drink is doing us more damage in the war than all the German submarines put together."

DAVID LLOYD GEORGE as he considered nationalising
the drinks industry during the First World War

Relations between Lord Iveagh and his older brother Lord Ardilaun continued to be tetchy after their business relationship ended, not least when the by now well-connected Iveagh continued to receive official honours as Ardilaun found himself increasingly at odds with everyone. In 1895 Iveagh was made a Knight of St Patrick, an honour in which Ardilaun had previously expressed an interest. New knights were appointed only when a vacancy occurred through the death of an existing member of the order and the death of Lord Waterford had created such a vacancy. Iveagh was selected to receive it by Lord Salisbury, who was just back in office again as prime minister for the third time after a three-year stint in opposition. Iveagh informed his brother, somewhat gingerly, in advance of the public announcement, protesting that he had not sought this honour nor had he had any idea that he was about to receive it. Furthermore, he indicated that he had not known until after he had accepted the KP that Ardilaun had been interested in it; had he known that, he would have declined to accept.

The letter was somewhat disingenuous and it prompted a blistering riposte from Ardilaun who feigned disinterest in becoming a KP himself and added: "I have felt as far as I am concerned that my miserable

182

The first Arthur Guinness in his forties, as a successful brewer in Dublin.
(Courtesy Patrick Guinness)

The second Arthur Guinness about 1800.
(Courtesy Patrick Guinness)

Sir Benjamin Lee Guinness with a picture of
St Patrick's Cathedral.
(Courtesy National Library of Ireland)

Oughterard cemetery in County Kildare. The central headstone marks the grave of Elizabeth Read, the first Arthur Guinness's mother; he is buried in the ruin on the right; the tree between was planted by Benjamin Guinness, third Earl of Iveagh, in memory of his sister Henrietta in the 1970s.

Edward Cecil Guinness, first Earl of Iveagh, in a copy of a portrait by Arthur Cope.
(Courtesy The Irish Times)

Arthur Guinness, Lord Ardilaun.
(Courtesy Trustees of Muckross House)

Lord Ardilaun (right) with the Prince of Wales (second from right and standing on step) at Ashford Castle in the early 1900s. *(Courtesy Ashford Castle Hotel)*

Rupert and Gwendolen Guinness, second Earl and Lady Iveagh in the 1950s. *(Courtesy The Irish Times)*

Portrait of Ernest Guinness.
(Courtesy Ashford Castle Hotel)

Portrait of Walter Guinness, first Lord
Moyne, by Philip Alexius de László.
(Courtesy Honourable Rosaleen Mulji)

Walter Moyne photographed by
Vera Delves Broughton on an expedition to
Indonesian islands in 1930s.
(Courtesy Honourable Rosaleen Mulji)

Bryan Guinness and his first wife Diana Mitford with their second son
Desmond and a nurse. *(Courtesy Honourable Desmond Guinness)*

A Guinness barge on the River Liffey returning to the brewery.
(Courtesy National Library of Ireland)

Tara Browne with his wife Nicky and mother Oonagh, at the christening by the Rev John Armstrong of one of their sons. *(Courtesy The Irish Times)*

Maureen Guinness in later life.
(Courtesy The Irish Times)

Aileen Guinness signing catalogues at the sale of the contents of Luttrellstown Castle in 1983. *(Courtesy The Irish Times)*

Benjamin Guinness with his grandparents Rupert and Gwendolen Iveagh in the 1950s.
(Courtesy The Irish Times)

Benjamin Guinness and Miranda Smiley shortly before their wedding in 1963.
(Courtesy The Irish Times)

Benjamin and Miranda Guinness, third Earl and Lady Iveagh, at the christening of their youngest child, Rory, in 1975. *(Courtesy The Irish Times)*

health would prevent me (even were I inclined) from feeding the Saxon and from using other well-known ways of advertising myself, also that the large sums I have and am spending for party purposes were spent in Ireland and on more or less secret undertakings and therefore far from paying (in an honour sense) or flashy. I could not bring myself to do what some men have done to obtain this honour."[1] Iveagh could hardly fail to get the message: "feeding the Saxon" and contributing large amounts of money to the Conservative Party were among the well-known ways he had used to achieve honours. Indeed, he was already sensitive to the charge that this latest honour was in return for his contributions to party funds, which he denied. But the fact that it came several months after his friend Salisbury's return to power was bound to create suspicion.

Iveagh continued to live a life of public philanthropy and social activity while keeping a close eye on his business as Ardilaun, on the other hand, became more and more of a maverick, falling into a political limbo where he was seen in Ireland as an extreme unionist and, at the same time, developing a low opinion of the English and particularly of the Conservative and Unionist Party. Like Iveagh, he continued to be a noted philanthropist, though on a less generous scale, since he did not have his brother's level of wealth. Although they both shared fundamentally the same political views, Ardilaun demonstrated few of his brother's skills in negotiating the by-ways of public opinion. While Iveagh, by design or by instinct or both, cultivated a carefully calibrated public image, Ardilaun emerged as one of the main leaders of the Irish landlords' cause as a succession of Land Acts increased tenants' rights and undermined their traditional power and wealth. He was totally opposed to the Land League and its successors and, accordingly, a favourite target of them and of nationalist MPs. The acerbic Tim Healy referred to him derisively in the House of Commons as one of the "porter peers" and claimed he was known in Ireland as Lord Cruiskeen Lawn.[2] He was regularly accused of seeking more repressive legislation, especially after he took control of three Irish newspapers – the Dublin *Daily Express, Evening Mail,* and *Cork Constitution* – and a magazine – the *Warder* – to further his campaigns against land reforms and the spectre of Home Rule. Healy also accused him of driving from Ireland Gerald Balfour, the Chief Secretary for Ireland, who oversaw the 1896 Land Act and the 1898 Local Government Act, two significant milestones in changing the balance of power in the country: "Although he was a relative and all of the most powerful statesman of the Empire [his brother Arthur Balfour], he was thrown as a peace-offering to my Lord Ardilaun," Healy told the House of Commons. "What are we representatives of the peasants of the country to think . . . when we see a statesman who has devoted himself to the interest of our country in a small degree sacrificed with as little care for public opinion in Ireland as you would show to a dismissed policeman."[3] Ardilaun had once refused to meet Gerald Balfour, reportedly saying the he would not meet "a common thief" (a reference to his Land Acts).[4]

John Redmond, the leader of the reunited Irish Parliamentary Party, accused Ardilaun of being part of the faction that opposed every attempt to remove grievances, had always done wrong at every crisis in the history of Ireland, and been responsible for most of the blood and misery which had stained the history of relations between England and Ireland for the previous hundred years. "So far as Ireland is concerned, we know who they are – Lord Londonderry and Lord Ardilaun, two men who in the whole of their careers never contributed one useful word towards the settlement of any grievance, large or small . . . I admit his [Ardilaun's] public generosity, but I say, as a politician, he is a man who has never, either in Parliament or out of it, contributed one sensible or useful word to the settlement of any question, large or small."[5]

Ardilaun's views, however, were somewhat more nuanced than his critics liked to present them. He lived a lot of the time at Ashford Castle which had been bought by his father and which he had extended by purchasing adjoining lands; it was not land the Guinnesses had acquired through any kind of plantation or ancestral conquest; thus, he represented a narrow group of large land-owners in the struggle between tenants and absentee landlords, and one whose case was not easily articulated or heard. He was in favour of the policy of creating "a large class of peasant proprietors", as he put it in a House of Lords speech in reply to the Queen's speech opening parliament in November 1890. His own experience of selling part of his estate at Ashford to his tenants after the first Land Act in 1886 had been a success, he declared, adding: "It has, I think, been admitted by thoughtful men of all parties and classes that in such a policy alone can be found a real and final settlement of that long and disastrous struggle between the occupiers and owners of the land which has been from generation to generation the ruin and shame of our country."

Nevertheless, he opposed some of the details of the act – the compulsory acquisition of bankrupt estates, and especially the extension of the land agitation to the provision of land for the landless through the breaking up of estates. He was opposed, of course, to the lawlessness and violence that accompanied much of the agrarian unrest. Although not personally affected by it, some of his employees at Ashford Castle and elsewhere continued to be: there was an ongoing catalogue of mainly small incidents involving threats, and sometimes worse, over evictions and pressure from tenants to force him to sell, although nothing on the scale of the early 1880s when four of his employees lost their lives. In one incident, his bailiff produced a gun and threatened a man near Ballinrobe whom he was trying to evict. A local nationalist MP, Robert Ambrose, raised the incident in the House of Commons, seeking the bailiff's prosecution but was told in reply to a parliamentary question that the tenant had first stabbed one of the bailiff's assistants with a pitchfork.[6] One of his larger tenants on his estate near Athenry, County Galway had his cattle driven off and was wounded while leaving Mass with his elderly mother because he refused to hand over the land to smaller tenants.[7] As late as 1914, a speaker at a United Irish League meeting at Cong, beside Ashford, warned Ardilaun and his bailiff that they might meet the fate of Lord Mountmorres and the Huddys if they stood in the way of the Congested Districts Board taking over his estate. (However, when questioned about the incident in the House of Commons, the Chief Secretary for Ireland, Augustine Birrell, dismissed the speaker as an "irresponsible windbag".)[8]

Ardilaun blamed "agitators" and political motives rather than unjust laws or tyrannical administration for all agrarian problems and insisted that the solution was a more vigorous and even-handed use of the law. On behalf of the landlords, he took particular exception to the frequent nationalist accusation that the land purchase measures were allowing landlords to "pocket the plunder". (Parnell included Ardilaun in a list of landlords and the amounts with which, as he put it, they had absconded under the first Land Act in 1886: Ardilaun was at the bottom of the list with £38,000 for the sale of part of his Ashford lands.)[9] "I do not see why," Ardilaun told the House of Lords, "if by voluntary agreement with our tenants we sell our properties or any part of them, we shall be accused of plunder. But this I desire to say on my own behalf – and I am certain I can speak in this matter for the overwhelming majority of resident Irish landlords – it is our earnest desire to continue to live in our own country, and if we join in supporting this change in the relations which have hitherto existed between us and the people among whom our lot is cast, it is because these old relations have been rendered in many parts of the country most difficult and precarious, and we, on this account, desire to substitute for them a new state of things in which Irishmen of every class may continue to live together in Ireland, but under conditions that shall be more permanent and happy."[10]

It was not just with land campaigners and nationalists that Ardilaun was at odds. He was increasingly critical of Conservative governments and their policy of "killing Home Rule with kindness", being one of those who perceived the policy as being, as Edward Carson rephrased it, one of "killing unionism with unkindness". Ardilaun, perhaps still smarting over his brother becoming a Knight of St Patrick a few months earlier, was provoked by a Land Bill in 1896 – which turned turf-cutting rights into bog ownership rights – to write a heartfelt letter to *The Times* denouncing Salisbury and his government. He contrasted Salisbury's earlier warnings, while in Opposition, about property rights with what he termed the "highly confiscatory measure" that the government was now introducing to give away another slice of landlords' property "amidst the applause of the Dillonites, Healyites and Parnellites" whom Salisbury had previously referred to as a mob. Having trusted Salisbury to keep his word, his disillusionment was plain:

Why are owners' rights in English coal mines to be respected and owners' property in Irish bogs to be confiscated? Why are voluntary privileges of water supply and voluntary privileges of way to be forcibly legalized in Ireland and not at Chatsworth [home of the Duke of Devonshire, a member of the cabinet], Hatfield [Salisbury's home], and Bowood [home of Lord Lansdowne, also a member of the cabinet]? If such is justice in Ireland, why should it remain unrecognized in "justice-loving England"?

Some hold their estates by right of Royal signature or by some ancient act of force. Some hold theirs by purchase under the pledge and title of an Act of Parliament which, when it had served its purpose by effecting the sale of estates, was repealed and repudiated by the Parliament that had passed it without giving compensation to its dupes who had bought. As one of those I know what English honour and English justice means . . .

I believe it has been said lately by a member of the Government – "If you are not satisfied with us, why not make terms with the Home Rulers?" The answer to this high-minded suggestion is that we have been outbid by our own Government with a slice of our own estates and the transfer of our own rights.[11]

His anger with the Salisbury government also extended to Horace Plunkett, the moderate unionist MP for South Dublin and champion of the co-operative movement in Ireland who believed that Ireland needed economic development more than it needed the sectarian, political and ideological divisions that dominated public life at the turn of the twentieth century. Plunkett's main success was the formation of the Irish Agricultural Organisation Society and the creation of the Department of Agriculture and Technical Instruction, of which he was president with the status of a junior Minister. He controlled the Dublin *Daily Express* and *Evening Mail* (subsequently taken over by Ardilaun) and appointed T.P. Gill as editor with a policy of reconciling unionism and nationalism, landlords and tenants. Gill had been a Parnellite MP and was involved in the Plan of Campaign to force landlords to concede rent reductions and Plunkett controversially appointed him to be secretary of the Department of Agriculture and Technical Instruction.

Ardilaun, for one, was outraged by the appointment, although it was widely accepted that Gill was the best man for the job. He was also less than happy with Plunkett's criticism of the Royal Dublin Society, of which Ardilaun was president from 1897 to 1913, for its failure to make any marked or permanent improvements in Irish farming methods. For these and other reasons, including Plunkett's support for a Catholic university, Ardilaun led a long-running campaign with Edward Dowden, professor of English at Trinity College, to unseat Plunkett. Their opportunity came in the 1900 election when they put up a rival unionist candidate in South Dublin. Iveagh, on the other hand, contributed to Plunkett's campaign funds and broadly shared his belief that economic progress within the United Kingdom was the solution to Ireland's problems. Ardilaun told a meeting of unionists that Plunkett was lukewarm, indifferent and highly opportunistic and not the man to fight their battles with a hostile government. He also took a sideswipe at the Conservative government's attitudes towards "all independent Unionists whom they could not purchase by place or honours. They were tabooed and their views were slighted."[12]

Ardilaun and Dowden succeeded in their aim; their candidate came a poor third, but he split the unionist vote and allowed a nationalist, John Joseph Mooney, to take the seat. (There was some kind of symmetry to the result, however: Plunkett had first won the seat in 1892 when the Irish Parliamentary Party split over Parnell and the nationalist vote was divided between two rival candidates.) "I was crushed between the forces of Lord Ardilaun and those of Mr William O'Brien by arguments, or rather assertions, mutually destructive, but quite effective for the purposes of a hotly-contested election when there is no time to consider more than one side of a question," Plunkett said after his defeat in a letter to *The Times*.[13] Others were not so statesmanlike in their reactions, especially as the voting showed there had been a comfortable unionist majority in the constituency. Belfast's *Northern Whig* described Ardilaun as "a sour political fanatic" driven by the failure of his wealth to buy him the influence with the government that he thought was his due, while the *News Letter* declared that Dublin's unionists had "covered themselves with deep and indelible disgrace" with an act of insane folly and puerile spite.[14]

Having been a determined opponent of the land reformers and Home Rulers and then infuriating his fellow Unionists, Ardilaun subsequently went on to fall foul of the Irish cultural revivalists as well over the touchstone issue of Hugh Lane's proposal for a modern art gallery for Dublin. He contributed a generous £500 to the fund to provide a permanent home to the collection of modern works that Lane promised to leave the city on condition that a suitable gallery was built. His donation was the second largest made to the fund, after an anonymous contribution of £2,500, and was matched only by that of Sir William Hutcheson Poe, a member of the Mansion House Committee set up by the Lord Mayor, Lorcan Sherlock, to raise the £20,000 required.[15] However, Ardilaun also blocked what was probably the most acceptable site for the gallery, in St Stephen's Green, which met with Lane's and Dublin Corporation's approval. Lane went so far as to have Sir Edward Lutyens draw up plans for the gallery on a site behind Ardilaun's statue facing the Royal College of Surgeons. But the Board of Works, which controlled the Green, effectively gave Ardilaun a veto over whether or not the gallery should be built there. While expressing his support for the gallery, Ardilaun said no.[16] Furthermore, he refused to give any more money to the fund until he had seen more evidence that the people of Dublin actually wanted the gallery.

His decision on the Green and his attitude towards further donations infuriated Lane's supporters, led by his aunt Lady Augusta Gregory and W.B. Yeats, who sent a scathing poem entitled "The Gift" to *The Irish Times*. Its subtitle was "To a friend who promises a bigger subscription than his first to the Dublin Municipal Gallery if the amount collected proves there is a considerable 'popular demand' for the pictures" and its opening lines were

> You gave, but will not give again
> Until enough of Paudeen's pence
> By Biddy's half-pennies have lain
> To be "some sort of evidence",
> Before you'll put your guineas down,
> That things it were a pride to give
> Are what the blind and ignorant town
> Imagines best to make it thrive.[17]

The poem was published above a news item showing that the Mansion House Committee had raised only £6,180 from 320 subscribers by that stage: the latest list of donors included artist John Lavery for £10 and Oliver St John Gogarty for £25. When published the following year in Yeats's collection *Responsibilities,* the poem had some small changes and was renamed and addressed "To a Wealthy Man who promised a Second Subscription to the Dublin Municipal Gallery if it were proved the People wanted Pictures". Clearly, Yeats no longer considered Ardilaun a "friend". Yeats's intervention had Lane's approval but provoked the ire of William Martin Murphy, the leading nationalist entrepreneur and former MP who owned the *Irish Independent*, on behalf of "Paudeen" and "Biddy". He wrote, oddly, to Ardilaun's newspaper, the *Daily Express*, to complain about Dublin Corporation spending money on "fads and luxuries" when it should be replacing the foetid city slums with decent habitation. "I would rather see in the city of Dublin one block of sanitary houses at low rents replacing a reeking slum than all the pictures Corot and Degas ever painted," he declared.[18] Yeats returned to the Lane controversy later in 1913 with another poem in *The Irish Times* entitled "Romance in Ireland (On reading much of the correspondence against the Art Gallery)" which he later renamed "September 1913" and contains many of his most famous and most quoted lines.

Iveagh, too, became entangled in the Lane controversy but managed to keep his distance and avoid public involvement. He gave three pictures he had bought recently to Lane's temporary exhibition in 1908, to which Lady Ardilaun also donated two pictures. Iveagh's were Millais's *Lilacs*, G.F. Watt's *Pretty Lucy Bond* and a view of Venice by James Holland. Lane was not very impressed by the pictures themselves but thought the donation would impress Dubliners.[19] However, Iveagh refused to assist directly in the search for a site for the gallery when approached by Lady Mayo, who subsequently told Lady Gregory that his "haughty" reply effectively said, "go to the devil, I will have nothing to do with you".[20] Whether in the same approach or not, he was sounded out about providing a site for the gallery in St Stephen's Green, presumably at the rear of his house, and seemed to be susceptible to the idea until he realised that the city's Corporation would have control over it.[21]

As he aged, Ardilaun certainly did not become less irascible. He thought the Liberal Party government which replaced the Conservatives was "revolutionary and socialistic" and refused to allow a plaque to be erected on his Carlton House Terrace home in London noting that Gladstone had once lived there. The proposed plaque was more suitable to a cemetery than a suburban house, he remarked, adding his real reason in a letter to *The Times*: "I freely confess that I should rather not have on my house a memorial (whilst other places were available) of one who, notwithstanding his 'charm and genius', by his measures reduced the value of Irish property by a half and reduced vast numbers of my countrymen and women to poverty, and who disestablished and disendowed the church to which I belong."[22] (There is now a plaque on the building, home of the Foreign Press Association, recording that Gladstone lived there.)

Ardilaun died at his Dublin home, St Anne's in Raheny, on 20 January 1915 at the age of 74 and was buried in nearby All Saints' Church which he had had built. Iveagh was in Dublin at the time of his death but did not attend the funeral since he was said to be laid up with a cold in his St Stephen's Green house.[23] Among the other mourners were his 28-year-old nephew Algernon, the eldest son of his other brother Benjamin Lee (who had died in 1900), who inherited Ardilaun's baronetcy and became Sir Algernon. (Algernon had already become another black sheep of the family: he had declared himself a bankrupt almost four years earlier, owing some £185,462 to money lenders who funded his extravagant lifestyle, which revolved around motor racing, on the strength of his future inheritances.[24] His younger brother, Kenelm, also became a successful racing driver, established a profitable spark-plug company, and was later a director of Guinness. See Chapter 11.) The Ardilaun title, however, died with him. His obituaries all stressed his philanthropy, especially his gift of St Stephen's Green to the people of Dublin, his funding of the Coombe hospital, and his purchase of Killarney's Muckross estate to prevent its development. His engagement with other public affairs was generally ignored, although the *Freeman's Journal* noted that he had been "a Unionist of the most extreme type". However, the nationalist Dublin Corporation passed a resolution commending his benefactions to the city as lasting memorials of his worthiness. The Lord Mayor, Lorcan Sherlock, noted that Ardilaun tenaciously held tremendously strong views of his own but his most vigorous political opponents always regarded him as a straightforward and honourable opponent. Sinn Féin councillor W.T. Cosgrave, representing the area in which the brewery was situated, said that they regretted the loss of any member of the Guinness family.[25]

His will, probated a few months later, showed that he left between £500,000 and £600,000, a small fortune compared to his youngest brother's wealth but a fortune nonetheless. After 17 per cent estate duty, it amounted to £495,638 2s 9d, of which £332,705 15s was in England. His original will, dating from 1902, was a one-page document leaving everything to his wife, Olive, but six codicils modified it over the years. Two related to the appointment of trustees to run his four newspapers until they could be sold and the proceeds given to his widow. The most interesting was the final codicil, signed less than three weeks before his death, which left his Ashford estate in County Galway to his brother, Edward Iveagh, on the grounds that they would "impose too much care" on his wife and that his brother was "the person best fitted to deal with them". It added that this arrangement was at her wish and with her full concurrence.

Lady Olive stayed on in Dublin, selling her London house privately a year later to one of the banking Guinnesses. She was a lonely widow and was described by her cousin, god-daughter and regular companion Katherine Everett, who had moved into Sybil House on the St Anne's estate after separating from her husband, as "a very striking person of sixty; tall, dark, very upright, good-looking, with charming, expressive grey eyes, and dignified in a manner that was slightly alarming".[26] Everett's description of St Anne's, the Ardilaun home, at this time painted a bleak picture:

> Olive hated the place in winter. I can see her now in my mind, a tall, slight, black figure, flitting across that cavernous hall, and when I joined her she would say, "Listen! The wailing and crying never stops. Can't you hear it coming from a long way off?"
>
> "No," I would reply. "I hear the wind whistling in that dreadful decayed and leaking winter garden."

The house was built around this depressing failure, and rain coming through its faulty glass roof made the water seep down into the cellars, where the central heating, which never functioned well, was often put out by flooding. St Anne's may have been a good setting for very large formal parties, but for my cousin it was more like living in a mausoleum than in a home.[27]

At Everett's instigation, Lady Olive moved into 42 St Stephen's Green, where she spent the winters, and became notable for her salons and as a patron of the arts, including the Abbey Theatre, to which she regularly brought guests, and the general Irish cultural revival. She appears not to have held his critical poem about her husband against Yeats, who was a guest of honour at her salon on several occasions. She invited him along to speak to one gathering of British Army officers, Dublin Castle officials and an elderly country peer who was deaf. The poet

. . . looked past us all as if seeing some distant vision and said, "I speak of the moon". He spoke a lot about the moon in a slow, chanting voice, sometimes as if she were a siren to allure and destroy, again as a medium of strange magic, or as a cold menace, and nobody understood any of it. One officer said after he left: "Quite batty, I suppose, poor fellow", and the deaf peer rumbled: "couldn't catch it all, but there's no moon tonight." [28]

Lady Ardilaun died in December 1925, leaving St Anne's to her nephew-in-law, Benjamin John Plunket, the Bishop of Meath, who was the second son of Archbishop William Conyngham Plunket of Dublin and Anne Guinness (Ardilaun's and Iveagh's only sister) and a nephew of David Plunket (Iveagh's close friend and adviser). In her will, she told him posthumously that it was far too large for anyone to live in and advised him to dismantle it and build a smaller house or to reduce it to the original dimensions built by his grandfather, Sir Benjamin Lee Guinness, before Lord Ardilaun had extended it. Bishop Plunket sold the estate to Dublin Corporation in 1937 and part of it was used for social housing and the other part preserved as St Anne's Park. The house burned down in 1943 when being used as a store by the Local Defence Force and the remaining ruin was demolished in 1968.

Olive also used her will, valued for probate at £931,676, of which £762,310 was in England, to settle some scores, against the Black and Tans who had occupied her family home at Macroom, County Cork during the War of Independence and the republicans who burned it down during the Civil War. She left £5,000 and some paintings and items of furniture from Macroom Castle to Katherine Everett, whom, she wrote, had "rescued them from the clutches of the Black and Tans when they occupied my castle". Everett, she wrote, had also gone there again "after the brutal burning of my castle" in August 1922 by Irish republicans "on the order it is said of an Englishman, Erskine Childers by name". After the burning of the castle, a local committee was formed to turn the demesne into a golf course; they paid Lady Ardilaun £1,500 for it towards the end of 1923 or early 1924 and subsequently sold a section of it for the same amount, thereby effectively acquiring the land for nothing.[29] In October 1925, shortly before her sudden death that December, Lady Ardilaun was awarded compensation of £4,700 for the burning of the castle by a court in Macroom. Her counsel told the court that the castle would cost £17,000 to rebuild but Lady Ardilaun did not wish to live there again because four young British officers had been held hostage there in 1922 (by anti-Treaty IRA members after the Treaty and before the Civil War) and were "put to death in a most scoundrelly and atrocious fashion".[30] In her lengthy will she also left the right to nominate the rector of All Saints' church in Raheny – which had been Ardilaun's condition for helping the parish build a new rectory – to Bishop Plunket, directing "that under no circumstances is an Englishman to be appointed as rector officiating in All Saints Church and that any such rector must be Irish by birth and parentage".

Although their marriage was one of convenience, the Ardilauns were clearly kindred spirits.

While the Ardilauns went their own idiosyncratic ways, Lord Iveagh continued on his path of befriending the aristocratic and influential and steadily accumulating honours and ever greater wealth. His public profile was dominated by his philanthropy and his role as a high society host, but he was also deeply, if less visibly, immersed in politics and business, grappling with two of the main issues of his age, Home Rule in Ireland and socialism, or at least trade unionism. Both were coming to what appeared to be a head in Ireland in the second decade of the twentieth century.

By then Iveagh had taken another step upwards in the peerage, becoming a Viscount in 1905 in the birthday list of his friend and regular shooting guest King Edward VII. Two years earlier, Iveagh had been on hand to escort Edward, during a week-long royal visit to Dublin, around the new Guinness Trust buildings and the new park which he had built beside St Patrick's Cathedral: the event was notable for the fact that the king and Iveagh did, in modern political parlance, a walkabout among the onlookers, which was unusual at the time. The king was suitably impressed and was said to have personally decided to make Iveagh a Viscount because of this and his other philanthropic works. His latest major funding of a public project was the Lister Institute for Preventative Medicine, to which he gave £250,000 at the turn of the century. The story goes that he had become interested in medical research after one of his farm labourers at Elveden was bitten by a rabid dog. There was no treatment available for rabies in Britain at the time, so Iveagh had him sent to the Pasteur Institute in Paris where a successful treatment had been developed. The man was treated there and recovered. Iveagh subsequently visited the Pasteur Institute and, as a result, offered funding to the Lister Institute which was struggling because of a lack of money. Iveagh was given the authority to appoint a third of its board members, an authority that he passed on to one of his sons, Walter, in his will. He was also a generous benefactor of Trinity College Dublin, of which he became chancellor in 1907. His donations to the college in the early 1900s amounted to some £50,000 for a range of facilities including a new science building, baths for students, and a women's hostel. A special meeting of Dublin city council was held in September 1909 to present him with an address of appreciation for all his benefactions to the city and he was assured by some members that they would ease his way to election if he would agree to become the city's lord mayor.[31]

Not all Iveagh's public-spirited schemes were a success, however. In 1903, as the Wyndham Land Act went through parliament, Iveagh joined forces with William J. Pirrie, the head of Ireland's other most successful enterprise, shipbuilders Harland and Wolff in Belfast, to launch a scheme designed to promote economic development throughout poorer regions of the country by providing a distribution service to take farm and other products to markets in England and elsewhere. The idea was to use one of Iveagh's enthusiasms, motor transport, to bring products to central depots from which they could be shipped by rail and boat to the best markets. Iveagh and Pirrie were prepared to put up all the capital for the scheme, which would be a non-profit operation but expected at the same time to pay its way once it was up and running.

The idea caused quite a stir at the time. Three "commissioners" were appointed by Iveagh and Pirrie to select initial routes for the transport services in the north, south and centre of Ireland. Within a year, 17 routes had been identified, mainly but not exclusively in the west and north-west, and transport services covering some 363 miles seemed to be in the offing. Within another year, however, nothing appeared to be happening and by 1906 the project was effectively dead. The main sticking point seemed to be the state of the roads in most of the counties chosen. Four county councils – Galway, Mayo, Derry and Antrim – refused to pay for the road improvements and maintenance required. To the upset of other counties, like Wexford, which was prepared to pay, Iveagh and Pirrie decided that all 17 "experimental" routes would have to go ahead or none of them.

Exactly why the project foundered is not altogether clear. There was certainly an issue over whether central government was prepared to provide money for road repairs and maintenance. There appeared to be a "chicken-and-egg" argument over whether the roads would be repaired first or the scheme's backers would commit to specific routes beforehand.[32] There were also wider political undercurrents, with many nationalist politicians none too enthusiastic about the project, presumably for the reason, common at the time, that they believed all such economic and social issues should be put on the back-burner until Home Rule was achieved (although that did not prevent some nationalists MPs from lobbying for the service for their own constituencies). They would have been aware, of course, that people like Iveagh and Horace Plunkett had a political motive in their belief that economic development would reinforce the union and would have seen the project as another manifestation of the "killing Home Rule with kindness" ploy, a ploy that seemed to some nationalists in the early years of the twentieth century to be in danger of working. Furthermore, there appears to have been some resistance among farmers to the idea of having to pay for the service. Added to that was what *The Irish Times* referred to as the animus towards motoring as debate went on about whether or not all these new machines should be restricted to a speed limit of ten miles an hour, although they were capable of considerably greater speeds.[33]

Iveagh, meanwhile, had enough other business activities to occupy himself. He had been back on the board of Arthur Guinness Son & Company Limited since 1898 and took over from his brother-in-law Reginald who stepped down as chairman in somewhat mysterious circumstances in 1902. The brewery, as has been noted, was flourishing, unlike many of its rivals in Britain which were afflicted with a downturn in alcohol consumption, partly because of the resurgence of the temperance movement, and partly because of increased competition. The temperance movement had less success in Ireland where, for instance, the Irish Parliamentary Party vigorously opposed such measures as the extension of Sunday pub closing to Dublin, Belfast, Cork, Limerick and Waterford.[34] On this issue, at least, the Guinnesses and the nationalists were of one mind.

Capacity at the brewery more than doubled again between 1901 and 1907 as the business continued to boom. Guinness had about 80 per cent of the Irish beer market but it was also thriving in Britain with sales of Extra Stout rising three and a half fold there between 1888 and 1914.[35] The year Iveagh resumed the chairmanship, the company had a profit of £887,000: four years later it exceeded £1 million for the first time. Dividends were almost embarrassingly large – ranging from 15.4 per cent to an astonishing 35.7 per cent in the years leading up to the First World War. Indeed, Iveagh promoted the idea of increasing the share capital of the company by £2.5 million with a bonus issue of shares partly because of his continuing fears that the generosity of the dividends would encourage higher taxes as well as draw complaints from customers.[36] Other devices to deflect criticism included the annual bonus for staff of a week's pay for labourers and a month's pay for brewers and an occasional discount for publicans.

The expansion in Britain of the more profitable Extra Stout meant that the market there was increasing in importance for the company. Ireland was still the more important market for Guinness in the early years of the twentieth century but the trend was clear and it appeared to be just a matter of time before the British market overtook the Irish market and sales of porter, the main product for the Irish market, went into relative decline. What was known as the "foreign trade" was also beginning to grow, mainly in Australia, the United States and South Africa, in that order. Interestingly, the Guinness policy of not advertising – Iveagh opposed advertising in the belief that it would undermine the company's prestige – was first breached in America where the company's first representative there, A.T. Shand, a former salesman with rival brewer Allsop, strongly recommended newspaper and poster advertising in the late 1890s. He succeeded in getting £1,000 to spend on advertising for three years and proceeded to help the Guinness market there to grow steadily.[37] The ban on advertising was also lifted when Guinness tried to develop the continental European market, concentrating in the early years on Belgium.

The prospect of the British market overtaking the Irish one in size had raised the possibility within the company of building a new brewery in England to supply that market and also the foreign trade, which could be served more easily from English ports like Liverpool than from Dublin. In addition, of course, was the spectre – as Iveagh and his fellow unionists saw it – of Home Rule, which was increasingly becoming a certainty rather than a possibility after the power of the House of Lords, the unionists' hitherto immovable line of defence, to veto any Bill passed by the House of Commons was removed by the Parliament Act of 1911. The anti-Home Rule beliefs and rhetoric of unionists encouraged widespread rumours that major Irish employers like Harland and Wolff and Jacobs Biscuits would flee the country (to Liverpool and Lancashire respectively) once a native administration was formed. Unionist businessmen feared, at best, increased taxes and duties and, at worst, seizures of property and discrimination against the *ancien regime* once the nationalists took control of an Irish parliament.

After debating the question of an English brewery internally for some years, Guinness finally took the decision to go ahead in 1913. A London solicitor was used to buy an option on a 100-acre site at

Trafford Park in Manchester, with enough frontage onto the ship canal to allow three ocean-going ships to berth there. Iveagh announced the decision at the company's AGM in London in August 1913, making no reference to the Home Rule issue but saying that the growth in trade made it necessary to increase the company's brewing, storage and distribution capacity. Given the increase in business in England and Scotland and large rises in freight charges on raw materials to Dublin and finished beer from Dublin, they had decided to open "a branch of our brewery in England", he said. He declared that the company had "no intention to reduce our manufacturing operations in Dublin", adding that the Manchester brewery should result in many economies and so benefit both customers and shareholders.[38] The announcement was greeted at the meeting with cheers, and the shares of Arthur Guinness went up, as did the shares of the Manchester Ship Canal and Trafford Park Estates on the Manchester stock exchange.

Not surprisingly, the news was not greeted with equal enthusiasm in Dublin, especially not by the city's port which foresaw a serious drop in its business if Guinness traffic were no longer to flow through it. Some 200,000 tons of the 238,212 tons of porter and stout exported from Dublin came from St James's Gate, while its substantial imports of barley and hops for the brewery would also be reduced, damaging employment in the port and among those involved in the brewery in transporting stout to the docks, as well as reducing business for shipping lines. A spokesman for the port, however, opined that Guinness could not make stout as good in England as it did in Ireland: it had been tried before without success, he claimed. The water and atmosphere did not lend themselves to the production of that flavour and quality for which the Irish product had secured such a reputation, he said.[39]

Concern in Dublin would have been even greater had people been fully aware of what Guinness was planning. At first, the plan was for a huge brewery in Manchester which would have had the capacity to produce four to five times as much stout and porter as St James's Gate, which was still considered to be the largest brewery in the world. That plant, which could hardly be described as "a branch of our brewery", was scaled back as time went on and amid much dithering by the Guinness board. Eventually, it was decided to begin with a brewery with about half the capacity of St James's Gate and that any seasonal or business fluctuations would be covered by the Irish brewery. Effectively, the Manchester plant was to be an auxiliary one to the Dublin brewery but the Trafford Park site was to be Guinness's main distribution point. Brewing there was due to commence in 1917 but the First World War intervened, trade fell off, and new threats and challenges emerged, causing the Manchester plan to be shelved and never revived.[40]

The increased freight charges mentioned by Iveagh in his announcement were not the only distribution factor in the decision to build at Manchester. There was also concern about the increased disruption of shipping by recent industrial disputes and, in the autumn of 1913, the growing trial of strength between trades unions and employers came to a climax in Ireland with the Dublin lockout after a series of small-scale strikes and industrial unrest involving Jim Larkin's Irish Transport and General Workers' Union (ITGWU). Larkin had been aggressively recruiting workers involved in transport in Dublin, targeting Guinness and the Dublin United Tramway Company, owned by William Martin Murphy, in particular. By this time Guinness had almost 3,500 employees, most of whom were classed as "labourers" (a description that covered everybody except brewers and clerks and included many skilled workers) and were paid above the going rates for Dublin: the only employees not paid above the going rates were craft workers who were members of trades unions and who were paid the union-negotiated rates for the city.[41] Guinness's welfare schemes were also much more generous and far broader in scope than the recently introduced national insurance and the state old-age pensions; Guinness pensioners received 17 shillings a week for brewery labourers at the age of 60 compared to the old-age pension of five shillings a week from the age of 70. Its welfare provisions cost the company £53,000 in 1913, compared to a total wage bill of £220,000 (and an annual profit in 1912/13 of £1.25 million).

In spite of its benevolent paternalism, Guinness was acutely conscious of the threat posed by Larkin's aggressive style of leadership, especially his tactics of "blacking" the products of companies involved in disputes and the use of the sympathetic strike. Guinness had had no problems recognising and negotiating with unions but Iveagh was fiercely opposed to the Larkin tactics, especially the sympathetic strike.

More than twenty years earlier he had used his valedictory address as chairman to urge the brewery employees not to put themselves in a position where they could be dragged into other people's disputes. He was consistent in this view, applying it to other employers as well as to the workforce. Thus, at the time of his retirement as chairman, he was privately admonishing Claude Guinness for having agreed to help a small rival brewery in Dublin which was threatened with a strike. "If you make a bargain with D'Arcy [owner of the Anchor Brewery, whose customers Claude had agreed to supply if the strike went ahead] . . . are you not doing the very thing that we hoped the men at James's Gate would avoid, namely taking a side in a dispute outside James's Gate Brewery?" he wrote to him. Claude argued that the Anchor Brewery was, effectively, the first line of defence against the union concerned spreading through all breweries and, if D'Arcy was defeated, it "would have made it very much more difficult for us when our turn came". Iveagh was not persuaded but the issue was never pressed at that time because the threatened strike at the Anchor Brewery was called off.[42]

To a large extent, Guinness could afford to adopt a policy of industrial relations detachment because of its relative generosity towards its employees, its market dominance and its huge financial strength. That did not mean, however, that it did not keep a close eye on what was going on in the world around it or that it was as detached as it liked to appear. Indeed, the company hired a retired police sergeant, Michael Walsh, to keep tabs on Larkin's activities for several years and on the inroads he was making among those of their labourers involved in transport and shipping.[43] It was fully aware that up to 400 Guinness employees, less than a sixth of the labourers, had joined Larkin's union by the autumn of 1913 as the developing confrontation between Larkin's union and employers organised by William Martin Murphy came to a head. Coincidentally, the day after Iveagh announced his Manchester brewery plan in London, Murphy launched a pre-emptive move against Larkin's union at his *Irish Independent* newspaper group, firing 40 men and 20 boys who had joined the ITGWU. Matters escalated quickly from there and battle was joined in the most notorious industrial relations episode in Irish history.

Guinness, as usual, tried to mind its own business and remain aloof from a battle in which it was not involved directly and in which it had no desire to participate. It was no surprise, therefore, that Guinness steadfastly refused in 1913 to join Murphy's Dublin Employers Federation. A month or so into the lockout, Murphy called on the board members at St James's Gate to request a change of heart. He met three of the directors: Iveagh's second son, Ernest, who was now vice-chairman of the company, Charles Sutton, an assistant managing director, and the new managing director, Colonel H.W. Renny Tailyour, who had replaced the ailing Christopher La Touche. They again rejected Murphy's invitation to join the federation but they agreed to make a secret donation to the Federation of double the largest amount given by any other company. The largest amount turned out to be a mere £50 from Murphy and the secret donation cost Guinness only £100. However, Guinness made further and much more significant surreptitious donations to the Employers Federation of £5,000 as the dispute when on. Murphy also sought an assurance that Guinness would not encourage the strikers by refusing to handle "tainted" or "blacked" goods in the docks. Guinness, he claimed, was encouraging the strikers by not collecting packets of hops and empty casks lying on the docks. The directors promised that their goods would be collected if they were exactly the same goods as in normal times and left in exactly the same places they were normally left. In other words, Guinness was trying to avoid being dragged into the disputes by other companies like the British and Irish Steam Packet Company (of which Murphy was a director and which was being picketed by strikers) playing games with their cargoes. Guinness would carry on doing exactly what it normally did and so try to avoid becoming a pawn in the dispute effectively by pretending that it was detached from what was going on around it.[44]

What happened to Guinness during the lockout was seen as crucial by many people in Dublin, because of its status as the city's largest employer and in the light of its recently announced plans to build a brewery and distribution centre in Manchester. It was also of considerable interest to Larkin, who claimed to have more than a thousand members in the brewery; the company exaggerated in the other direction, claiming there were only some 120 members.[45] The company's trickiest problem was the situation in Dublin port; it needed the port to remain open in order to receive a large proportion of its raw materials and to export a large percentage of its output. The ITGWU members among the Guinness staff were carters who delivered to and from the port, as well as supplying pubs and other transport facilities, and crews on the river barges which carried export stout to the docks. The brewery's staff in general was not involved in the dispute but its transport workers were potentially at the sharp edge. The potential for conflict did not take long to be realised.

The captain of one of the Guinness river boats, Edward McCarthy, refused to collect empty casks from the docks: the company gave him 24 hours to reconsider his decision, but he did not change his mind, and was fired. Eighteen boatmen then handed in their notices and the Guinness board got tough, making it clear that anyone who failed to carry out their normal jobs would be fired and anyone thus dismissed or resigning because of an industrial dispute would not be re-hired in any circumstances. The 18 all withdrew their notices the next day. However, another boatman subsequently refused to collect "tainted" casks and four colleagues handed in their notices in sympathy with him. They were not given any second chance to change their minds: they were dismissed and the company refused to relent after the five men concerned later sought to withdraw their protests.

Larkin also tried to get tough with Guinness. He sought the reinstatement of the six who had been dismissed, reminding the company in a letter that it depended upon the goodwill of the working class, who were the principal consumers of its products. He also demanded that all the boatmen and others in the brewery should receive better wages and conditions, mentioned the "enormous profits" made by the company and threatened a boycott of its porter and stout in Ireland and Britain. He followed it up with an instruction to his members at the docks not to handle goods consigned to Guinness. Significantly, he did not tell his members to stop Guinness exports through the port (although at least one consignment of stout was left untouched on the docks) nor did he, a well-known teetotaller, make any effort to organise a boycott of its porter and stout. He may have been keeping the prospect of a boycott as a threat or the recent announcement of the Manchester brewery may have had an effect on his as well as on other people's thinking. Certainly, Larkin made no secret of his antipathy to Guinness and seemed keen to confront the company. However, his attitude towards Guinness may not have been as bellicose as his rhetoric sounded while, conversely, his deputy, James Connolly, may not have been as conciliatory towards the company as he later seemed.

During Larkin's brief imprisonment for "sedition" in the middle of the dispute, Connolly tried to close Dublin port by calling out his members, a move that Larkin had hitherto resisted. Guinness was quick to get around the problem by using workers sent from England by the British Shipping Federation to unload ships which the dockers had refused to handle. The arrival of the so-called "free labourers" (the employers' description) or "scabs" (the union's description) raised the temperature of the dispute. Among the initial tasks of the first 160 to arrive was to unload a cargo of barley for Guinness from the *SS Wearwood* which had been tied up at Alexandra Basin for some time. The barley was immediately taken by a fleet of Guinness motor lorries – which were used as a strike-breaking weapon since they were then seen as being more difficult to disrupt than the traditional horse-drawn drays – to the company's warehouse at Custom House Quay, watched by strikers, who did not try to interfere, and a large force of police.[46]

Larkin was released less than a week later and immediately attacked Guinness in a speech from his union headquarters in Liberty Hall, specifically accusing Lords Iveagh and Ardilaun by name for bringing "scabs" to Dublin from England and "the wilds of Tipperary": Guinness and the two lords would get a lesson such as they had never had before, he warned.[47] Larkin departed on a tour of Britain and Guinness continued to have its cargoes unloaded by imported labour. A week later, the ITGWU offered to end its strike at the port on condition that the shipping companies stop carrying cargoes for Guinness and Jacobs – Guinness because of its use of the "scabs", Jacobs because it had accepted flour from a miller whose workers were on strike.[48] The shipping companies refused the offer.

By mid-December, the union gave up its attempt to stop goods bound for Guinness from being unloaded by its members. In a conciliatory-sounding letter to the board, which made it clear that the union wanted to end the dispute, Connolly asked that it take back the six men it had dismissed. To do so "would help greatly to straighten out the tangle on the quays", he wrote, stressing that reinstatement of the men was not a pre-condition for the ITGWU lifting its "blacking" of Guinness imports. Connolly followed up the appeal with a telephone call before Christmas. It fell on deaf ears, as did appeals from the men concerned and a pleading letter from the wife of the captain who had first refused to pick up empty casks from the docks. Ernest Guinness told his father in a letter that it was very hard on the men concerned, but the board remained resolute. The six men would not be reinstated.[49]

Guinness had survived the lockout with little damage to its business and, unlike Murphy, none at all to its long-term reputation. (Its donations to Murphy's employers' federation remained a secret until the publication of S.R. Dennison and Oliver McDonagh's authorised history of the brewery covering the period was published in 1998, some 30 years after it had been written; its publication was blocked by Guinness for unspecified reasons which were widely believed in academic circles to be associated with the company's handling of the 1913 lockout.)

But a greater threat to its existence was approaching as the First World War began and quickly became bogged down in the attrition of trench warfare. Some 600 of the brewery's employees joined the British forces, encouraged to do so by the company, which not only guaranteed their jobs after their military service but also continued to pay half their salaries or wages while they were away. More than a hundred of them did not survive the war while other casualties included the captain and four crew members of the Guinness vessel, the *WM Barkley*, who died when it was torpedoed by a German submarine in 1917. Eight other crew members survived in a lifeboat and on a raft made of old porter barrels.

Industrially and financially, the company was faced with a series of extra excise duties and taxes and, even more importantly, official regulations which had a long-term effect on Guinness and the porter and stout it produced. The first financial impact was a trebling of excise duty in 1914 from seven shillings and ninepence on a standard barrel of Guinness stout to 23 shillings a barrel. Much worse was to follow within months when the Chancellor of the Exchequer, David Lloyd George, made it known that he was looking at methods of controlling the whole liquor industry, up to and including prohibition and the possibility of nationalising all brewing, distilling and public houses. His declared reason was the effect of drunkenness on workers in the ship-building and munitions industries where, he claimed, up to a third of the workforce were regularly absent because of drink. The war meant there was no shortage of work in those industries, pay was high, and drinking and drunkenness had risen. Lloyd George went so far as to declare: "The lure of drink is a greater danger than the power of Austria or the power of Germany." He subsequently told the House of Commons: "Drink is doing us more damage in the war than all the German submarines put together."[50] The Liberal government drew back subsequently from prohibition or nationalising the whole liquor industry, but not before Lord Iveagh had calculated that the likely compensation he could expect if Guinness was taken over by the state was an annual income from government stocks of £178,528, compared to the £315,000 he was currently receiving in Guinness dividends.[51]

Instead, the Chancellor decided on a package of measures which would give him powers to restrict pubs in certain areas, increase excise duties and limit the strength of beer being sold. Most damaging to Guinness were the proposed increases in excise duty which were tied to the gravity of beer. Lloyd George wanted to reduce the alcoholic strength of beer, determined by its gravity, in order to reduce drunkenness and also to free up land for other crops by reducing the amount of barley used by the brewers. Porter and stout were among the highest gravity beers which meant, firstly, that they faced the highest increases in duty and, secondly, their very existence was threatened by new limits imposed on the level of gravity. Reducing their gravity level meant that their taste, as well as their levels of alcohol, would be changed. Depending on how low the government pushed these limits, Guinness could, at worst, be wiped out. Even if the limits were not reduced to extreme levels, its business could be severely damaged: in reality, nobody knew how a lower gravity on stout would affect the taste of the stout, how long it would keep and what impact it would have on its transportation and storage.

In a submission to Lloyd George, Iveagh spelled out some of these concerns. Guinness porter, he explained, was brewed at a gravity of 1058 degrees with an alcohol content of about 5.5 per cent and was sold on draught in Ireland only. Its standard product, Extra Stout, had a gravity of 1074, an alcohol content of about seven per cent, and was almost exclusively bottled. Its Foreign Extra Stout also had a gravity of 1074 and an alcohol content of about 7.5 per cent and was for export only. The gravities of these porters and stouts represented the results of many years' experience and had remained unchanged for upwards of 30 years, he wrote:

> We think it necessary to emphasise the point that in the case of Stout or Porter, as brewed by us, any material reduction in gravity would have the effect of rendering it impossible to continue manufacture as heretofore, resulting in the loss if not of the whole, at least of the greater proportion of our profits. . . . Feeling strongly as we do that any material interference with brewing gravities of our Stouts and Porters would inevitably result in a reduction of our output, we feel bound to draw attention to the large number of individuals, firms and companies whose position would be seriously affected were our operations to be restricted.[52]

He also sent a copy to the Conservative Party leader, Andrew Bonar Law, with a letter saying that, whatever form Lloyd George's proposals took, the issue for the nation as well as for Guinness was of "vast importance" and seeking a private meeting with him and Austin Chamberlain, the shadow Chancellor. Guinness, he told Bonar Law, was unique in four ways: it was the largest brewery in the United Kingdom; it brewed only porter and stout; it used only malt and hops in its brewing and no added preservatives; and it neither owned nor controlled any tied house and had to rely entirely for public acceptance on the merits of its drink. The entire trade would agree that brewing stout and porter was different to brewing ale; ale brewers could adapt to a reduction in gravity which might mean that stout as brewed by Guinness would have to be discontinued altogether. Iveagh also played the Irish card, pointing out that Guinness now bought two-thirds of the malting barley produced in Ireland, and argued that the government's measures would be a "a serious set-back for Ireland's economic position". He also maintained that there was no evidence of an increase in intemperance and that the proposals might mean ruin for a large number of shareholders.

Another note to Bonar Law at the time from one of his MPs who met Lloyd George with a delegation of brewers told him that the Chancellor had said that the cabinet "seemed terrified" of the cost of nationalising the drinks industry but that he had no fear of that himself and thought nationalisation had "great possibilities of profit" if the monopoly was successfully managed or administered. The brewers told him that another of his options, of buying out the drinks industry only in areas where armaments were manufactured, was impractical.[53]

Lloyd George's eventual proposals were for an extension of the Defence of the Realm Act to give the Government powers to control pubs in areas in which ship-building and armaments were said to be affected by absenteeism caused by drink. But his main proposal, affecting all brewers, was that a new surtax would be applied depending on the gravity of the beer, starting at 12 shillings a barrel on the lightest beers: the highest rate, of 36 shillings per barrel, would apply to all Guinness's output. It meant that the tax on Extra Stout would more than double, from 31 shillings a barrel to 67 shillings a barrel, Iveagh told Bonar Law in a further note. The tax was now more than six times as high as it had been at the start of the war and nearly seven times the profit on a barrel, he added.

Lloyd George strenuously denied that his real motive in all this had more to do with the temperance movement (still a powerful influence in the Liberal Party) and Welsh Non-Conformism than with the effects of drunkenness on the war effort. But his critics were sceptical, with reason, none more so than the members of the Irish Parliamentary Party. Once again they came to the defence of the drinks industry, backed up by all-party protests in Ireland and passing a resolution describing the measures as discriminatory against Ireland on the grounds that Irish brewers and distillers would be affected more adversely than their English counterparts although there was no claim of absenteeism against any Irish workers. They also pointed out that there were no armament manufacturers in Ireland other than Belfast's ship-builders and an explosives factory in County Wicklow and neither had had any increase in absenteeism. However, the measures would have a significant impact on the country's breweries and distilleries, possibly destroying one of Ireland's few remaining major industries and undermining one of the main funding resources for the new Home Rule Irish parliament. "I am not exaggerating when I say that if the Chancellor of the Exchequer, by his surtax, succeeds in annihilating those two great manufactures in Cork [brewing and distilling], the result will be as appalling as if that city were bombarded and sacked by the Germans," local MP William O'Brien told the House of Commons. "When you have destroyed these distilleries and breweries, they are gone for ever," his fellow Corkman Tim Healy said; "When the war is over, where will all the workmen be?"[54] The nationalist leader, John Redmond, came to Guinness's defence (after being briefed indirectly by the brewery through some of its maltsters) with a warning that it could be put out of the English market if the proposals were carried.

> [Guinness's stout] only holds the market to-day because of its pure quality. . . . If Ireland is to attempt to compete with the light beers in existence in England at this moment, she must brew it not from barley at all, but from those other substitutes used in the manufacture of light beer, and the beer so manufactured will lose all the characteristics of Dublin stout and porter. . . . It would not froth like stout, or be like Irish stout at all; therefore, so far as the brewing trade in Ireland is concerned, your proposal would practically put an end to it. . . . In Ireland the surtax therefore means the ruin of the brewing trade. In England the injury, no doubt, would be great, but I do not believe it would be comparable to the injury that would be done in Ireland.[55]

Iveagh's appeals to his Tory Party friends and the pleas of his nationalist political opponents worked; the measure was dropped but it was a temporary reprieve and worse was to come. As Lloyd George went on to another cabinet position and eventually the premiership, the excise duty on beer rose inexorably year by year up to 100 shillings per barrel by 1920, more than twelve times the rate at the start of the war. Even more damaging for Guinness were the other restrictions imposed. From 1916 on, brewing output was restricted, partly to free up shipping as well as land, to 85 per cent of what it had been the previous year and further reduced to only a third of 1915 output the following year. These restrictions, with yearly fluctuations, continued until August 1919.

Meanwhile, the threatened cap on brewing gravity came into effect from 1917; its effects on Guinness were not as catastrophic as the brewery's supporters had predicted in 1915 but they were nonetheless serious and long-lasting. Maximum gravity levels were set for 1918 at 1030 degrees for Britain and, in deference to the well-voiced arguments for Irish differences, at 1045 for Ireland. To meet the average limit, Guinness had to reduce the gravity of its porter in the Irish market from 1058 to 1036 and of its extra stout from 1074 to 1049. There was no immediate fall-out from this decision, at least partly because supplies had been restricted and customers were not as fussy as they might otherwise have been about the drop in alcoholic content and change in taste. The restriction on brewing quantities was lifted in 1919 and that on gravity in 1921 but Guinness went on brewing at the restricted levels to compensate for the rise in the excise duty to 100 shillings per barrel the previous year. The effect of all these changes, however, was to lose Guinness its premium status as the top product in its markets.[56] Rivals with a wider range of products were able to keep up the gravity of their stout by dropping that of other light beers, but Guinness had no light beers to allow it to manipulate the averages: all its products were high gravity and all had to be reduced. With other stouts now of higher gravity than it, Guinness had lost its most important edge and one of the key reasons for its extraordinary success.

———⊗———

As for so many others, the First World War was a turning point for the Guinnesses. Viscount Iveagh was approaching his sixty-seventh birthday when it began and put an end to many aspects of his world and the Edwardian style of the good life. The lavish entertaining and house parties at his Elveden estate were abandoned and never resumed after the war, although shooting parties continued on a smaller, men-only, scale. A large part of the estate was taken over by the military for training purposes, including training on the British Army's secret new weapon, the tank (known by the codename, Willies), before its introduction on the western front in the autumn of 1916. On

210

16 February that year, Iveagh's wife Adelaide died at Elveden at the age of 71 after being ill for several years and was buried in the churchyard adjoining the estate. His youngest son, Walter, who was not listed among the attendance at the funeral, was a major in the British Army, serving first in Gallipoli and later on the Western Front; he was a member of parliament for the neighbouring Bury St Edmund constituency. Iveagh's eldest son, Rupert, was also an MP for Southend and a captain in the Royal Navy Volunteer Reserve, while his middle son, Ernest, was vice-chairman of Arthur Guinness & Son and based in Dublin.

From Viscount Iveagh's perspective further unwelcome changes were also visible. The worst was yet to come in relation of government interference in the brewing industry and the long-feared Home Rule for Ireland was a done deal, until the Easter Rising in 1916 raised the spectre of something even worse. The world as he knew it was changing utterly.

CHAPTER NINE

A New World Order

"To me it [the Treaty] seems to be a choice between a slippery slope and a precipice, and as between the two I prefer the slippery slope."

Walter Guinness MP in the House of Commons
debate on the Anglo-Irish Treaty.

His opposition to Home Rule took Edward Iveagh down some unusual by-ways, none more so than the arcane laneways of aristocratic politics involving the Knights of St Patrick. With the formation of an Irish parliament becoming a virtual certainty from 1910 onwards, Iveagh determined to prevent one consequence that he expected and particularly feared – that Catholics would seize St Patrick's Cathedral in Dublin from the Church of Ireland.

Iveagh was a conventionally religious man, leading morning prayers which all family members and staff were expected to attend every day at Elveden. But his religion, like most people's, was also tangled up with his political views, his lifestyle and his view of his business success. And he was especially concerned about the fate of St Patrick's under Catholic majority rule, not least because of his family's proprietorial interest in the cathedral: he had continued his father's interest in its state, contributing what were described as large sums annually and paying for repairs like the replacement of the roof of the nave in 1909. He set out to try to make sure that its status would not change, using the Order of St Patrick. How he thought this could prevent a rampant and confiscatory political Catholicism of the kind he feared from seizing St Patrick's if it so wished is not clear. Nevertheless, he did think the order could be a restraining factor, perhaps by having the authority of the British crown involved with the cathedral.

St Patrick's had been the chapel of the Knights of St Patrick from the order's foundation in 1783. Knights were installed in the cathedral, their banners were displayed over their stalls there, and the dean of St Patrick's was the registrar of the order. After the disestablishment of the Church of Ireland in 1871, the then Lord Lieutenant, Lord Spencer, moved the order to what was later renamed St Patrick's Hall in Dublin Castle and a number of Church of Ireland clerics were removed from their positions in the order: for instance, the dean of St Patrick's was replaced as registrar by the Ulster King at Arms, the chief herald. The decision to secularise the order may have been encouraged also by some criticism of St Patrick's at the last installation held there, that of the Prince of Wales, in 1868. While Iveagh's father, Sir Benjamin, basked in the praise for his restoration of the building, there were also some critical voices raised, as we have seen. The *Daily Telegraph* complained that the cathedral's recent restoration had left it with no air of antiquity and described it as "a modernised shrine" and "naked, cold and cheerless".[1] There was an attempt in 1903 to move the knights back to St Patrick's. A petition to the king, Edward VII (formerly the Prince of Wales, who had been installed in the order there), was signed by 18 of the 21 knights. He turned it down.

The order subsequently made headlines when its grand master's insignia, made of rubies, diamonds and emeralds and popularly known as the Irish crown jewels, disappeared from a safe in Dublin Castle in 1907 just before an official visit by Edward, the head of the order, to Dublin. The Ulster King at Arms and registrar of the order, Sir Arthur Vicars, was held responsible for not taking proper care of them and was dismissed: he appealed to the knights to sign a petition seeking a public inquiry into the theft before he was held accountable. Only three refused to sign it, including Iveagh, who had been told by the king's private secretary, Lord Knollys, that the petition would be "distasteful to the king" because he disliked Vicars intensely. "I am in a different position to the other knights," Iveagh told Vicars, without explanation: presumably the difference he had in mind was his social friendship and regular hospitality for the king at Elveden and his desire not to irritate him. It was probably a shrewd move on his part because the king was said to be extremely angry with the signatories.[2]

In 1910, Iveagh set in train his plan to move the order back to St Patrick's from Dublin Castle, making it clear in a letter to the dean of St Patrick's, John H. Bernard, that the reason was to try to prevent the Roman Catholics from seizing the cathedral in the event of Home Rule. The cathedral "was really rebuilt with the money of Protestants", he wrote, adding that if the Knights' move was granted, "it would make it more difficult for them [Catholics] to take it".[3] He and Bernard conspired together over several months to have the change approved by the king and especially to prevent the project being scuppered by the political authorities in Ireland, including the chief secretary, Augustine Birrell, who was also chancellor of the order by virtue of his office. Birrell strongly opposed the idea on the basis that it would provoke objections from Presbyterians and Catholics, who would not be able to attend the order's ceremonies in the cathedral because of the stricter rules now applying to them.[4] Iveagh, however, had an inside track with the king and his private secretary and he got his way: the Knights of St Patrick went back to St Patrick's.

Iveagh also held out for a time against one of the other signs of emerging Catholic power: the church's demand for its own universities. Birrell, a Liberal (both with a capital L and a lower case l), sounded out Iveagh through an intermediary to see if he would be willing to give part of his property at St Stephen's Green as a site for the new national university. He got a curt refusal, perhaps because Iveagh thought Birrell was suggesting that he give over his house to the university: Birrell's letter to his intermediary, the Conservative politician, Walter Long, was not entirely clear about what he had in mind. In any event, Iveagh later changed his mind to the extent of agreeing to give the stabling area of his garden to the university. It became one of the gestures for which he was subsequently praised widely – that he, then chancellor of Trinity College, would assist the new rival university.

Most of Iveagh's efforts to thwart the emergence of Catholic nationalism were of a more politically conventional sort than his campaign to move the Knights of St Patrick back to the cathedral. He and Lord Ardilaun were deeply involved in Irish unionism from the point that it became the politically organised antagonist of Irish nationalism in the mid-1880s. For the next 30 years, they were always in unionism's inner councils, with Ardilaun taking a more public and more independent if maverick role. Iveagh played an equally important but more private role, leveraging his great wealth into social and political connections and into becoming a political influencer and facilitator. They were notable funders of the campaign against Home Rule; indeed the Irish Unionist Alliance, the successor of the first unionist organisation, the Irish Loyal and Patriotic Union, boasted happily in a pamphlet in the 1890s "that men like Lord Iveagh and Lord Ardilaun were willing, nay anxious, to guarantee large sums" to its campaign.[5]

The Alliance was an all-Ireland body, based in Dublin, until the Ulster unionists formed their own group in 1905 and their interests began to diverge as the prospect of Home Rule increased. While they liked to claim that they represented at least a third of the population – the Protestant third – and an even higher proportion of the richest, best-educated and most successful citizens, unionist support was obviously concentrated in Ulster. In the three southern provinces, unionists represented at least ten per cent of the population (the Protestant part again) but, by 1911, there were only 15 unionist councillors out of the 700-odd council members elected to local authorities in Leinster, Munster and Connacht, only two per cent of the seats. They also had only two members of parliament, both representing Trinity College and one of whom, Edward Carson, was about to defect to the Ulster unionist cause, to the dismay of his southern colleagues.

However, southern unionists had a much greater political influence at Westminster than their electoral standing in Ireland suggested, not least because of their extensive family and social links within the Conservative Party. Some 68 members of the House of Lords had addresses in southern Ireland and more than 40 members of the House of Commons had either family, business or historical – or, like the Guinnesses, all three – connections with what became known as the 26 counties.[6] Iveagh and Ardilaun were in the Lords, while two of Iveagh's sons, Rupert and Walter, were in the Commons. Walter had been elected to the Commons in 1907 for Bury St Edmunds, near Elveden, and Rupert in 1908 for the Haggerston constituency in the East End of

London. Both were members of the Conservative Party and supported the unionist cause. Walter, a more active parliamentarian than his brother, became one of the leading parliamentary spokesmen for the southern unionists in the House of Commons as the third Home Rule Bill finally made its way towards enactment in September 1914.

Ardilaun, meanwhile, had stood in for the absent Lord Abercorn as chairman of a "monster demonstration" of southern unionist opposition to Home Rule at the Rotunda skating rink in Dublin in 1911 which attracted an estimated 6,000 people from Leinster, Connacht and Munster. "Many of us who have experienced the cruel Land League of the early eighties have only too good reason to realise the kind of men who would be rulers of this land under Home Rule," he told the crowd. "Anybody who had anything to do with that period must recollect its sad story. It was one of murder on murder, outrage upon outrage, and intimidation on intimidation." The meeting adopted a "protest and declaration" opposing Home Rule for a lengthy list of reasons, claiming that it would produce "a disastrous conflict of interests and classes, and a serious risk of civil war", "a paralysis of enterprise", imperil personal liberty, freedom of opinion and the spirit of tolerance in Ireland, and hand power to a party which had repeatedly defied the law and disregarded the elementary principles of honesty, liberty and justice. The meeting was also addressed by Carson, who promised "from the bottom of my heart to do my best for you". Ulster sought no separate parliament, he told them: "Ulster asks to remain under the Imperial Parliament and that she means if possible to do and you need fear no action of Ulster which would be in the nature of desertion of any of the southern provinces. If Ulster succeeds, Home Rule is dead. Home Rule is impossible without Belfast and the surrounding parts as a portion of the scheme."[7]

Iveagh was not present at the meeting but was host to the Conservative leader, Andrew Bonar Law, who stayed with him in St Stephen's Green when he addressed the last big unionist rally in Dublin in November 1913 in the midst of that year's lockout. From the stage of the Theatre Royal, against a backdrop of what was said to be the largest Union Jack in the world, Bonar Law described the Liberal government as a revolutionary committee which had ceased to be a constitutional government by exceeding its powers. "We never shall go back on the pledge we have given to the people of Ulster. They will not submit and we shall not allow them to be coerced," he said. Iveagh proposed a vote of thanks to Bonar Law and Carson, who also spoke, and said that Home Rule, if it came into force, would be "disastrous to the empire and fatal to the peace and the future prosperity of all classes and creeds of the Irish people."[8]

The unionists believed their last hope of stopping Home Rule rested on two possibilities. One was a general election on the issue which they and the Conservatives were demanding in the expectation that the Liberals, going on for ten years in power, would lose. The second was the belief, articulated by Carson at the Rotunda's "monster demonstration", that Home Rule without Ulster was simply unworkable, because so much of the Irish economy was tied up in the North, but also because the nationalists would not accept partition. Hence, Walter Guinness told the House of Commons early in 1914 that Ulster had every right to get out of Home Rule if it could and those who lived in the rest of Ireland would be only too glad if it did. However, that did not mean he was in favour of partition; in fact, southern unionists became one of the main opponents of partition as that emerged as the likeliest outcome of the impasse. Being part of a perhaps 25 per cent minority in an all-Ireland parliament was obviously preferable from their point of view to having some two per cent representation and being thinly scattered and isolated around the country in a partitioned Ireland. As Walter added in the same debate:

The scattered Unionists in the South of Ireland have no opportunity of making their voices ever heard if Ulster is left out, and if their allies from the North are not vocal in the Irish Parliament. Certainly civil war would be disastrous in Ireland, but only less disastrous to the real interests of the country, and its future prosperity, will be a division of Ireland. In years past the relation between all classes of the community in Ireland, all creeds, all political convictions, have been improving. The bitterness of generations has gradually been forgotten. When the first shot is fired, or when even the division of Ireland into two hostile camps, delimited by different legislatures, takes place, the exasperation of feeling will enormously increase. It will put back the cause of conciliation in Ireland for centuries.[9]

Responding to a Liberal MP who had said that unionists' real fear was of Catholic domination, Walter replied:

> There is some degree of truth in what the right honourable gentleman says. The unionists do fear religious ascendancy in Ireland. They believe that in the past a Protestant ascendancy has worked appalling injury to Irish interests, and they believe also that now that this Protestant ascendancy has at last been swept away for ever it would be disastrous to set up in its place a Roman Catholic ascendancy. But that is felt more acutely outside than inside Ulster. It affects the South of Ireland much more than it affects those coherent communities in the North, where the Protestant is really in no danger, at least in matters of local administration.

The sense that partition would be the worst of all worlds for southern unionists was also conveyed privately in a letter from the editor of *The Irish Times*, John Healy, to his counterpart, Geoffrey Robinson, at *The Times* in London. A Northern parliament unleavened by Southern conservatism would be dominated by socialism, he wrote, while a Southern parliament unleavened by the character and brains of Ulster would be another Tammany Hall.[10] In the newspaper, he wrote that the exclusion of Ulster would be permanently fatal to every Irish hope and every Irish interest: "it would condemn our country to an eternity of national weakness, industrial impotence and sectarian strife."

The tide was now running strongly against them, however. In Ireland, the new mainly Catholic middle class was poised to become the domestic ruling class. The straws were everywhere in the wind, even pervading high society as the old ruling class deserted the Irish "court" where one of their hate figures, Lord Aberdeen, the Liberal (and liberal) Lord Lieutenant, presided over society events which were now dominated by the Catholic middle class. One commentator recorded: "Social amenities were flung to the winds and the ragtag and bobtail of Dublin went to Court. Without being a snob it was no pleasure and rather embarrassing to meet the lady at dinner who had measured you for your shirts the week before. As a result of the upsetting of values, social life in Dublin, from the point of view of good breeding, rapidly declined."[11]

British politics, too, was moving on and becoming preoccupied with other issues like tariff reform. Then war broke out in August 1914. The third Home Rule Bill was passed into law as the first Home Rule Act and immediately shelved until after the war.

The Easter Rising in 1916 upset everybody's calculations. How it was viewed by southern unionists at the time was summed up by Walter Guinness, then a major in the British Army (and still an MP). He was in Egypt after the retreat from Gallipoli and on his way back to London in the aftermath of the rising and before a posting to the Western Front. His response to the rising hinged, like that of nationalists, on the British government response to it: unlike nationalists, however, it was not the subsequent executions that upset him but what he saw as a policy of appeasement towards the rebels. "After the Easter week rebellion Ireland as a whole had shown every evidence of disgust with Sinn Fein methods," he wrote later. "Asquith [then Prime Minister], however, went over and so pandered to the rebels that the country suddenly realised that the rebellion had done more for the cause of Irish independence in a fortnight than had been achieved by fifty years of constitutional agitation. Asquith on his return appointed Lloyd George to find a settlement of the Irish difficulty and with his usual adroitness Lloyd George began to offer bribes and baits all round, and to exploit the state of feeling in America for the purpose of compelling all parties in Great Britain to surrender their convictions on the union."[12]

Walter stayed on in London for two months, deeply immersed in the campaign to stymie a plan by Asquith to introduce immediately a restricted form of Home Rule which would exclude six counties of Ulster. The plan, put together with characteristic deviousness by Lloyd George in talks with Carson and Redmond, outraged almost everybody. *The Irish Times* described the scheme as a parody of self-government and added: "No unionist, no true Home Ruler, no advocate of a united Ireland can support this scheme. At the worst it means anarchy in Ireland and a serious confusion in Imperial affairs. At the best it means the permanent exclusion of the six Ulster counties from the life of Ireland."[13] Walter was instrumental in forming a unionist lobby group, the Imperial Unionist Association, with a hundred members of parliament to fight against the immediate Home Rule plan. In his "diary", he subsequently took credit that the group had managed to delay the completion of the plan long enough for nationalist opinion against it to solidify in Ireland and for Redmond to turn against it because of the partition issue.[14] The main legacy of the plan, however, remained in place: six counties of Ulster would be partitioned from the rest of Ireland. Walter went back to the war in Europe, ending it with the rank of lieutenant-colonel.

Walter's view of the situation was shared by his father, who played a behind-the-scenes role in the next initiative by Lloyd George, now Prime Minister – the establishment of the Irish Convention in 1917 to try to reach agreement between nationalists and unionists. Iveagh offered accommodation to the ten-strong southern unionist delegation, led by Lord Midleton, at his home in St Stephen's Green, as well as offering occasional hospitality to others involved in the talks. The southern unionists accepted Home Rule, with safeguards for Ulster, at the convention but the convention itself was weakened by the absence of Sinn Féin and destroyed when its narrowly agreed plan for Home Rule was linked by the British government with the extension of conscription to Ireland in the spring of 1918. By then, the main aim of people like Iveagh was to try and secure safeguards for southern unionists: partition was more or less a done deal and the only remaining unanswered question was what form the government in the south would take.

In a letter to Midleton, Iveagh argued that they should reconcile their opposition to Home Rule with "a prudent preparation for eventualities". While they should continue to present a united front to their opponents, they should not neglect any means of obtaining safeguards or modifications to mitigate the worst evils of any Home Rule Bill. In reply, Midleton denied there were any different camps in the Irish Unionist Alliance but commended the wisdom of Iveagh's stance.[15] The fact that the letters were given to *The Times* and that Iveagh was a close associate of Midleton's suggests that they were written and leaked as part of the internal politicking within the Alliance over acceptance of Home Rule at the Irish Convention and how unionists should proceed subsequently. In any event, the Alliance split the following year, 1919, with Midleton and Iveagh among a group of "moderates" who left after they failed in an attempt to exclude Ulster Unionists from voting on partition within the Alliance.

They believed that the southern unionists should decide their own fate and not have northern unionists voting on it too. These "moderates" included most of the Alliance's leadership and were depicted by their internal opponents as a group of rich peers and businessmen who, paradoxically, were effectively partitionists for wanting to exclude the Ulster unionists from decisions. The "moderates" formed the Unionist Anti-Partition League and dismissed their former colleagues in the Alliance as "nonentities" who took an "extreme" position by refusing to consider any option other than remaining in the union because the actual choice facing them was increasingly between Home Rule and a Sinn Féin-led independence.[16]

Things continued to go from bad to worse from the unionists' and Guinnesses' perspective, with Sinn Féin's electoral landslide at the end of 1918, the formation of the first Dáil, and the War of Independence in which many isolated southern unionists found themselves on the front line. As their spokesman in the House of Commons, Walter tried to amend the Government of Ireland Bill of 1920 to safeguard their future position with a number of measures. He was highly critical of the Bill for encouraging the extremes of what he described as Orange Ulster and Sinn Féin and condemned it as "outrageous" for striking "the most deadly blow at moderate opinion in Ireland which has ever been struck". Ireland was sentimentally and economically one nation and it would be disastrous if the Bill built a wall to impede intercourse between north and south, he believed. Instead of accepting the Irish Convention's majority scheme with safeguards for Ulster, Asquith's government had accepted the Ulster scheme with safeguards for no one. "The truth is that the Government has not followed the line of giving Ireland what she wants, but has merely followed the line of least parliamentary resistance. The method of least parliamentary resistance might satisfy Irish claims if all Irish parties were represented, but it cannot be regarded as an agreed settlement in the present House of Commons, where the only loud Irish voice is the voice of Orange Ulster, and where the great majority of Irish representatives take no part whatever in our proceedings," he said.[17]

He had already been instrumental in having the proportional representation system of election introduced for local elections in Ireland in the hopes of giving the unionist minority a fairer share of representation, but his efforts to amend the Act had limited success. He failed to win acceptance for a united Ireland with a parliament for Ulster; the reservation of some parliamentary seats on a religious or property basis; and the establishment of a highly conservative all-Ireland senate to act as a bulwark against what he considered to be the Bolshevik tendencies within Sinn Féin. He succeeded in having the proposed number of Irish MPs at Westminster raised to 46 by adding four university seats and by strengthening the Council of Ireland to give it control over fisheries. He also proposed making divorce a reserved matter for the London parliament rather than leaving it to the Irish ones.

Walter had no illusions that the Act would ever satisfy Sinn Féin, whose aim he rightly defined as sovereignty. His main criticism of how the situation was evolving was the fact that the middle ground was disappearing and he believed that British policies were helping to make it disappear. In one of his many criticisms of partition in the same House of Commons debate in March 1920, he declared: "The common argument of those who wish to partition Ireland is what is called the hostage theory, that if the Southern Catholics ill-treat the Southern Protestants, the Northern Protestants may take it out on the Northern Catholics. I think that that is an absolutely hateful policy. I think that it is a policy which cannot conceivably lead to anything but bitterness and strife. It is a policy at the same time which is calculated to divide Ireland into two parts mutually hating each other for centuries to come." The hostage theory was to come horribly true two years later as some southern Protestants were murdered and others run out of their homes in response to sectarian troubles in Belfast as the two new states became a reality.

While Walter was deeply involved in the debate, his oldest brother Rupert remained aloof from the public exchanges. Rupert abstained on the Government of Ireland Act, telling the local newspaper in his new constituency, Southend: "As an Irishman I could not bring myself to vote in a single division on the Irish question. I did not believe in the policy. I do not yet. I hope I am wrong. I want to see quickly – as soon as possible – a proper Government, a peaceful Government – in my native country."[18]

Meanwhile, the situation on the ground for many southern unionists, especially in Munster, was becoming impossible since they were caught between the IRA and the British Army. A group of

Unionist Anti-Partition League members travelled from Dublin to London to tell their members there, including Midleton and Walter Guinness, that they were no longer confident of a British Army victory over the IRA and that unionists were suffering terribly while the army was trying to achieve it. They suggested that dominion Home Rule might be the best option both to the Government of Ireland Bill and to Sinn Féin's demand for a republic. To Midleton's suggestion that the government might bring forward a better measure when order was restored, one of the delegations retorted: "What is to become of us while the law is being restored?"[19]

The southern unionists did play a role in the shaping of the Treaty to the extent that their support for dominion Home Rule helped to create that eventuality. In the case of the Guinnesses, their pragmatism came to the fore again, with Iveagh telling members of his family that they must work with the new Free State government and Walter describing the Treaty as a choice between a slippery slope towards independence and the precipice of civil war and personally preferring the slippery slope.[20] A meeting of the Unionist Anti-Partition League in Dublin, attended by Iveagh, passed a resolution proposed by Walter Guiness promising "to use its best efforts to secure the co-operation of all classes in establishing stable and constitutional government in Ireland" and changing its name to the Constitutional Anti-Partition League.[21]

The Civil War that followed the Treaty was not the civil war between nationalists and unionists which many had predicted and most had feared for the previous decade but a civil war within Sinn Féin. Nevertheless, there were random outbreaks of sectarian and political violence and intimidation of the kind that Walter Guinness had warned against two years earlier in his denunciation of the "hateful" hostage theory. The Guinnesses were not directly affected, other than Lady Ardilaun's loss of her family home in Macroom, and their business suffered minimal disruption. The Guinness agent in Ballinasloe, County Galway, which was at the Grand Canal's terminus and a main distribution point for the brewery, was among ten or more Protestants in the town who were threatened by the IRA and told to leave. Some had their houses burned and two former RIC men were shot in the legs; most left but the Guinness agent did not. (A Sinn Féin candidate, Francis Fahy, condemned the threats and attacks at an election meeting in the town and said pointedly that the people seizing property and persecuting Protestants there had not helped during the previous years of the War of Independence.)[22]

The troubles in Ireland impinged little on Iveagh's lifestyle, although the new political order raised numerous questions for his business interests as well as upsetting his political beliefs. He had used his involvement in the unionist cause to try and step up another rung on the peerage ladder, as was evident from a note from Lord Midleton to Andrew Bonar Law in 1914 pointing out to the Conservative leader that "a good deal of our power of resistance in Ireland, in and out of Ulster, is due to Lord Iveagh's munificence and public spirit". That Iveagh, or more likely somebody on his behalf,[23] was lobbying strongly for another honour is made more explicitly in a letter from Bonar Law to the Prime Minister, Lloyd George, in 1919 which made it clear that Iveagh had been promised promotion and that it could not be delayed any longer. "I am afraid we really must give the advancement in the peerage to Iveagh," he wrote on 28 May. "As you know this was put off last time on account of his connection with the trade but he was definitely told it would be given to him on the next list and as a matter of fact he attaches great importance to getting it on the Birthday [list]. I do not think it is possible to delay this." The letter was ticked for approval by Lloyd George.[24]

Iveagh duly headed the king's birthday list, belatedly published in August because of Lloyd George's involvement in the Versailles peace conference, and was the only earl created by it. It meant that Iveagh was now on the third rung of the five-step peerage and just short of the top two titles, a marquess and a duke. It also meant that his heir was now entitled to his father's viscountcy, requiring that his eldest son, Rupert, adopt a suitable name. After considering a variety of place names around the Elveden estate – and some Irish possibilities – they settled on Elveden itself and Rupert (and all subsequent Iveagh heirs-in-waiting) became Viscount Elveden.

Iveagh also took a precautionary move as the troubles in Ireland were at their height in 1920 and the future shape of the outcome was far from clear. He executed a deed poll in March of that year declaring "that I have for many years past wholly abandoned and relinquished my domicile of origin in Ireland, and that I have adopted, and intend to continue until my death, England as my only place of domicile."[25] The deed poll was clearly a pre-emptive measure against whatever regime might emerge in Dublin and, if his worst fears were realised, an attempt to minimise whatever confiscatory designs it might have on his wealth and property. But it also reflected the reality that he had lived in England for thirty years at that stage and all aspects of his life, including, technically, his business, were based there: Arthur Guinness Son & Company Limited was registered in London and had had its official headquarters there since its stock market flotation in 1886. Although his worst fears about the future rulers of Ireland were not borne out by events, the deed poll nevertheless turned out to be a prescient, but ultimately ineffective, precaution against the Irish taxman (see below).

Iveagh, now in his seventies, paid fewer visits to Dublin. Between the spring of 1922 and that of 1924 he did not visit at all because of illness. The deed poll said he kept two residences in Dublin but only used them for purposes connected with brewery business and, as it put it, the performance of duties which he considered his position imposed on him. He later told the Irish Revenue Commissioners that he had occupied his St Stephen's Green house for 29 days in the tax year 1924/25. From his evidence to them, he was a more frequent visitor to Farmleigh, staying there for 13 days in 1924/25, 19 days in 1925/26, and 37 days in 1926/27. He also spent six days in the last year in Ashford Castle in County Galway which he had inherited from his brother, Ardilaun. He travelled abroad quite a bit as well, staying in places like Caux, overlooking Lake Geneva in Switzerland, taking a long sea voyage to South Africa in the mid-1920s, and visiting America again. He had been there in his earlier years, after which he was reputed to have said that it was a fine country but no place for a gentleman to live as everyone worked.[26]

Meanwhile, the brewery experienced a boom after the First World War when the wartime restrictions on brewing were lifted and sales almost returned to their pre-war levels. But the boom did not last long and Britain went into a depression: by 1923/24, sales were down more than a quarter on four years earlier. Worse, from Guinness's point of view, was the fact that the new Free State kept the excise duty on beer at the wartime level of 100 shillings a barrel, while Britain offered its brewers a 20 per cent rebate on the same duty as long as the brewers passed it on to drinkers in price cuts. This caused a problem with the sales of porter in Ireland, which were already in decline: the British rebate meant that porter prices in the North had to be reduced, which raised the question of the price in the South. A price cut there would have had a dramatic effect on profitability and it was decided instead to increase the gravity of the porter and thereby improve the quality which had been diminished significantly under the wartime restrictions. The improvement, however, only brought it up to the same quality as that of their main competitor in Dublin, D'Arcy's.[27]

Guinness stout was also losing its lustre in Britain, with increasing complaints about its bitterness and acidity, a result of the reduction in its gravity enforced during the war and continued afterwards: extra hops were needed to make the stout more stable but they also had the effect of making it more bitter. British brewers did not have the same problems because they generally used chemicals to stabilise their beer and anyway were closer to their markets and could use hops only for the purposes of taste instead of as a stabiliser as well. Scientific experimentation at St James's Gate sought solutions to the problem in sterilising equipment but this approach was not encouraged because of fears that removing all organisms from the brewing equipment would have unknown consequences: the original yeast used by the first Arthur was still being used in the process and nobody knew for certain whether its qualities were or were not essential to Guinness stout. "The choice before the brewery was whether to try to cope with the new situation by ad hoc measures, such as varying hop or gyle [fermentation] rates, or to attempt to establish the lower-gravity stout firmly on a new scientific foundation," Dennison and MacDonagh wrote in their authorised history of the brewery. "The rejection of the latter was a failure of policy which was to cost the company many millions of pounds over the next twenty-five years."[28]

The failure was largely the result of the board's conservatism and its belief in the tried and trusted methods of the nineteenth century. To an extent, the significance of the problem for Guinness was masked by the fact that its profits continued to increase, mainly as a result of falls in the prices of raw materials. Even as sales declined, profits kept rising, from £1.246 million in 1914 to £3.277 million a decade later. Dividends climbed, too, from a rate of 16 per cent in 1916 to 32 per cent in 1925 and 1926: the income tax due on them was also paid by the company. Iveagh seemed more concerned until 1925 about the public relations problem created by rising profits and extremely generous dividends than about the steady decline in sales. But he did come to realise, as he put it in a letter, that "for the first time in our history, we are not progressing."[29] The board tried a price cut but it did not have the desired effect: sales of Guinness stout and porter in Britain and Ireland continued to fall, and profits finally turned downwards as well.

The falling sales were generally blamed on external factors like recessions, the general strike and other industrial disputes in Britain and high charges by middlemen. A report, by Charles J. Newbold, on the trade in Britain concluded however that Extra Stout had lost its pre-eminence as a high-gravity beer that gave good value for money. Guinness no longer sold itself on the basis of taste and value. Newbold's recommendations revolved around the fact that the company would now have to sell the stout either through a variety of inducements to retailers or by creating public demand through price or increased gravity or advertising, or by having a much stronger sales force. "Careful" advertising, he suggested, would be the quickest and cheapest means of increasing trade in England. Iveagh accepted most of his recommendations but not that for a general advertising campaign.

The question of whether Guinness would advertise or not was occasionally referred to in contemporary journals. Iveagh's objection to doing so appeared to be based on a belief that advertising was somehow vulgar and would undermine Guinness's cachet. There was also an element of snobbery involved: he did not want his house guests arriving at Thetford railway station near Elveden to be reminded by stout ads of where their host's fortune had come from. However, he did approve an advertising campaign in Scotland at what turned out to be his last board meeting on 30 August 1927: Guinness sales had more than halved in Scotland during the 1920s and dramatic measures were needed to try to revive them; they included advertising.

The board meeting coincided with Iveagh's last visit to Ireland in August 1927 when he spent some time in Farmleigh with his eldest son

Rupert and daughter-in-law Gwendolen. He also visited Ashford Castle for less than a week but his time in Ireland was not all leisure. During it, he invited the president of the Executive Council, W.T. Cosgrave (who, conveniently for Guinness, had been the Sinn Féin councillor for the St James's Gate area of Dublin), to tea at Farmleigh and was reportedly amused at the head of government's heavy police escort. The last time he had seen him, he told Cosgrave, he was also being escorted by police, but he was under arrest on that occasion.[30]

A less pleasant experience for Iveagh involved an appeal to the Irish Revenue Commissioners who had prepared an assessment claiming that he owed the Free State £2,378,814 in income tax for the previous four years on all his worldwide earnings and a further £2,048,842 in surtax for the three years up to 1926. Apart from the assessments under both tax headings for 1923/24, the rest were made up of round figures of £700,000 a year each for income tax and surtax. To put the total tax demand for £4,427,656 into context, the Free State government's estimate for all income tax in 1926/27 was for £5,150,000 out of total estimated revenue of £23,712,430. In other words, they were seeking a further 86 per cent of the year's entire income tax take from him alone.

Iveagh appealed on the grounds that he was not domiciled in Ireland and consequently owed no tax to the Free State. He was required to give evidence in person before a Revenue appeals board during his time in Dublin. The board passed the domicile issue to the High Court where the case was heard by three judges, but not until a year after Iveagh's death. In court, the Revenue Commissioners argued that Iveagh was domiciled in Ireland because he was born there, his business was there, and he had three houses there. They said his domicile was proved by the fact that he had spent some £40,000 doing up his St Stephen's Green residence (adding its impressive ballroom) and up to £18,000 on Farmleigh in the late 1890s. They saw significance in the fact that he was a Knight of St Patrick and an ordinary member, rather than a foreign member, of the Kildare Street Club. Lawyers for Iveagh's executors said he and his family had moved to England in 1890; he had five residences there worth £1,250,000 against a value of £106,000 on his Irish properties; and he had signed the deed poll in 1920 making clear his intention to remain living in England. The Revenue's counsel disparaged the deed poll as a legal device and stopped just short of claiming that it amounted to fraud when challenged by one of the judges. Iveagh's lawyers also pointed out that his Irish houses only had caretaker staffs (eight indoor staff at St Stephen's Green, five at Farmeigh, and four at Ashford, compared to 17 at his Grosvenor Place home in London) and when he visited he brought his servants with him from England; on one visit to Farmleigh in 1926 his visiting entourage from London included a butler, three parlour maids, five kitchen staff, two chauffeurs, and a valet. And they argued that the fact that his wife and subsequently he himself were buried in England proved his point.

Some 18 months after he died, the High Court in Dublin decided in his favour: he was not domiciled in Ireland and he was not a citizen of Saorstát Éireann. However, the Revenue Commissioners appealed to the Supreme Court, which upheld their position the following year, ruling that Iveagh's domicile was a matter of fact for the Revenue to decide and it had already decided that he was.[31] In the interim, of course, Iveagh had paid large amounts of tax in Britain and lengthy negotiations were then undertaken between the Free State's and the British taxmen as to how the tax should be split. The result was that the Irish Revenue Commissioners received a transfer of some £250,000 from the income tax already paid by Iveagh to the Inland Revenue in London in 1932; it was a long way short of what they had sought originally but still a welcome windfall in cash-strapped times and the largest individual sum ever paid in income tax in Ireland up until then.[32]

Iveagh's last public appearance was in Dublin at the funeral on 1 September 1927 of John H. Bernard, the former Dean of St Patrick's Cathedral with whom he had conspired over the Knights of St Patrick some 17 years earlier. He attended as chancellor of Trinity College Dublin where Bernard had become provost in 1919, stepping down as Archbishop of Dublin to take the post. Although his health had been poor for many years, Iveagh's own death came unexpectedly on Friday, 7 October 1927, a couple of weeks after he had returned to London from Dublin and just short of his eightieth birthday. His eldest and youngest sons, Rupert and Walter (still both MPs and Walter now Minister of Agriculture and Fisheries), were at the Conservative Party conference in Cardiff when they received the news. The conference chairman described his death as "the loss of a very old friend and supporter of the Conservative cause" and delegates stood for a few minutes' silence. (In true political fashion, little time was wasted in sorting out Rupert's successor as MP for Southend-on-Sea now that he was the Earl of Iveagh and a member of the House of Lords: his wife Gwendolen, the new Lady Iveagh, was quickly chosen to be the Tory candidate.)

Edward Iveagh's body was taken from his Grosvenor Place home, where he had died, to Elveden, where it lay in the mansion's Marble Hall until the funeral. He was buried alongside his wife Adelaide in the family vault in the churchyard at Elveden, the hearse drawn there by two farm horses. The funeral was private, with only members of his family and locals attending. Memorial services were held the same day in Dublin and London. The service in St Patrick's in Dublin was presided over by his nephew Bishop Plunket: among the attendance was his former unionist colleague, now Free State senator, Andrew Jameson, representing W.T. Cosgrave. At the London memorial service in St Margaret's in Westminster, King George was represented by the Earl of Lucan. There was also a memorial service at the Catholic Church of St James near St James's Gate. Flags flew at half mast on several buildings in Dublin, including Trinity College and the City Hall.

Media interest in the weeks following his death concentrated mainly on his will and the expectation that the taxman was going to get a windfall in death duties. Iveagh was perceived to be Britain's second richest man, after Sir John Ellerman, and probate on his will eventually valued his assets at £13,486,146, with death duties of some £7 million. The Free State taxman also received a share of the death duties but the amount is not known. His estate was less than some had predicted but still the largest amount officially left by an individual in Britain up to that time. Ellerman easily beat it and set a new record when he died some six years later, leaving £37 million.

However, the official figures of both their assets at death were a fraction of their real wealth during their lives. Iveagh is reliably estimated to have earned more than £40 million during his lifetime, three times as much as he left when he died.[33] He had distributed large amounts of money during his life and spent lavishly on his aristocratic lifestyle. He had contributed possibly in the region of £1 million on his philanthropic projects, created trusts for his children and their descendants, and donated generously to the Conservative Party and other political projects. (The English Sunday newspaper, *Reynolds News*, quoted a Conservative insider after his death saying that he had given the party £250,000,[34] which may well have been an underestimate of his total political spending.)

Iveagh had set up a trust for his three sons and their descendants, with £1.5 million for each of his sons as well as giving them occasional gifts. He was a cautious investor, mostly happy to watch his money compound in safe bonds and equities, but he also spread his investments abroad, especially after Lloyd George's "People's Budget" in 1909 which imposed death duties, land taxes and an income surtax and led the rich to believe the end was nigh for them in Britain. He set up the Oceanic Investing Corporation in the US with $15 million to buy property in New York and other American investments and turned it into a trust for his sons and grandchildren. Other distributions were also prompted by tax measures: when death duties were doubled from 20 per cent to 40 per cent after the First World War, he placed a large quantity of his Arthur Guinness shares in a trust for his sons on condition that they held them for at least 25 years.

As always with the Guinness legacies, there were numerous conditions imposed on all the beneficiaries. Many were "life tenants", people who could use the income and decide on investments but not actually withdraw any of the capital. The aim was, as always, to preserve the family fortune but Iveagh went further than his ancestors and, of course, had a much larger fortune upon which to decide. His aim was no less than to dictate the future livelihoods of all his descendants. His will ran to 24 typed pages, including five codicils and two lists of jewellery and pictures, and set down in one complex clause (clause 25) the rules by which all his direct descendants would benefit once they attained the age of 21 "or being female marry". In essence, trustees – who became known as the Iveagh Trustees, not to be confused with the philanthropic Iveagh Trust in Ireland – would control all the money and assets and distribute their share to everybody when they reached 21. By the 1980s it was said that every direct descendant of Iveagh received £1 million on their twenty-first birthday from the trust he established: this did not, of course, include any further inheritances or gifts or settlements they would receive then or later from their own parents, who had also benefited previously from the Iveagh Trust.

Most of Iveagh's will was taken up listing individual bequests, ranging from £20,000 down to £50 to a wide range of relatives and servants. The larger amount went to his nephews and nieces, the sons and daughters of his sister Anne and of his brother Benjamin Lee. Bishop Plunket, the main beneficiary of Lady Ardilaun's will, was one of those but Benjamin Lee's eldest son, the previously bankrupt Sir Algernon, who had inherited the title from Lord Ardilaun, was not. He was not cut off totally, however: he received an annuity of £1,000 during his lifetime which lasted for another 27 years. An annuity of £1,000 and a £6,000 bequest went to Iveagh's secretary and right-hand man, Christopher Harry Bland, to whom he also left all his private papers with discretion to deal with them as he saw fit, including destroying them. He gave a year's pay to employees on his estates who had worked for him for more than five years, six months' pay to those employed for less than five years, and two months' for anyone with less than a year in his employment. The beneficiaries included "the captain of my yacht", "my tennis marker in Dublin", clerks in the estate offices at Elveden and Ashford, bailiffs, electricians and head gardeners at Farmleigh and Elveden, some of the staff at Ashford, and all domestic servants.

Among the charitable bequests was £65,000 to St Patrick's Cathedral to provide an annual £500 payment for the organist and choir "during such time as the Cathedral shall be used for the purposes of the Protestant Church of Ireland or of the Protestant Faith". In a further explicit instruction, echoing his earlier fears about Catholics seizing the cathedral, he added: "If at any time the said Cathedral shall be used for the Ritual practice or any other purposes of the Roman Catholic Faith or for any purpose at variance with the Protestant Faith the said capital sum and securities representing the same and the subsequent income thereof shall thereupon be handed over to and vest in the Trustees or Governing Body for the time being of the Representative Church Body of the Protestant – Church of Ireland."[35] The Church of Ireland was also given £125,000 to provide funds to augment "the Livings of the poor Clergy of the Protestant Church of Ireland". In a further bequest, which illustrated his attitude towards Catholicism, he gave an annuity of £50 for life to a London nurse, Katherine E. Foucar, on condition that she did not at any time "become the inmate of any Roman Catholic Community".

He also divided up his properties, leaving Elveden (plus an endowment of £400,000 to run it) and his house at 78–81 St Stephen's Green to his trustees for the benefit of whomever succeeded to his earldom. It was a life interest for them; if they sold the properties, the proceeds would go to the overall trust for the benefit of all his descendants. His second son, Ernest, was left outright his house and other properties at Cowes on the Isle of Wight and a life interest in Ashford Castle and any other property Iveagh had inherited from his brother, Lord Ardilaun. Ernest's life interest was to pass to his male heirs and, if they did not exist – Ernest had three daughters during Iveagh's lifetime and no sons subsequently – the life interest was to go to his brother Walter and his male heirs or Rupert and his male heirs in that order. If none of them had sons, the life interest could go to Ernest's daughters. His youngest son, Walter, received Farmleigh and all Iveagh's property north of the River Liffey in Dublin (except, initially, Knockmaroon), as well as his London home at 4–5 Grosvenor Place: these were unrestricted bequests.

Much of the media interest in his will, especially in London, was in the fate of Kenwood house on Hampstead Heath, which Iveagh had bought with 74 surrounding acres in 1925 for £108,000 in one of his final philanthropic acts. The 200-acre Kenwood estate had been offered for sale to builders after the First World War by the then Earl of Mansfield in whose family it had been since it was remodelled by Robert Adam in the late eighteenth century. A protest group which opposed its development succeeded in buying 100 acres of the land and the local councils acquired a further section. Iveagh bought the rest, preventing any part of the estate falling into the hands of developers, and let it be known that he would hand it over to public ownership some time in the future. In the meantime, however, he intended to use it himself. He furnished it and moved some of his paintings there but had stayed in the house for less than a week during his remaining years. The final codicil to his will, signed in December 1926, left the house and contents to London County Council for it to be used as a public art gallery. It included a list of 40 paintings to be given to the house, many of them works he had bought during his main collecting spree in the late 1880s, along with £50,000 for its maintenance. The house and parkland are now run by English Heritage.

In spite of all the legal and other advice available to him, however, his Kenwood bequest ran into trouble immediately after his death because of a glitch in his will. The list of paintings he bequeathed to Kenwood was not witnessed and so, technically, was not part of his will and became part of his estate left to his youngest son Walter. However, Walter and the other executors agreed that it was Iveagh's wish to have the paintings in Kenwood and an act of parliament was nodded through in 1930 to give effect to this. That fact that the will was effectively rewritten by act of parliament was subsequently used by Iveagh's grandson and Walter's son, Bryan Guinness, to argue later in the House of Lords for a similar act of parliament to give effect to the similarly unwitnessed codicil of Sir Hugh Lane's will and have his paintings sent to Dublin.[36]

Iveagh's death also prompted renewed speculation about the future of the Knights of St Patrick by creating another vacancy, the twelfth, among its numbers. The newly independent Irish state had no wish to see the order continue and had been taken aback when King George made the Prince of Wales a member of the order in June 1927, the first appointment since the formation of the Free State. However, that was also the last appointment to it: neither Iveagh nor the others were ever replaced and the order was allowed to die a natural death. In spite of his fears, the Catholics never seized St Patrick's Cathedral; on the other hand, he would not have been happy to know that one of his granddaughters, Honor, and several other descendants were later to become Catholics.

"The Emperor Augustus was proud to have found Rome a city of brick and to have left it a city of marble," *The Irish Times* said on his death. "If any man ever was entitled to feel some measure of a like pride when he compared the Dublin of his youth with the Dublin of his old age, it was Edward Cecil, first Earl of Iveagh." The obituaries all concentrated on his philanthropy with little or nothing about his personal, social and political lives. In spite of his wealth and his continual appearances in court circulars and social diaries, Edward Guinness was a private person and still largely an unknown person to the general public. He left his mark most successfully through the housing and other projects he funded in the public good and through the company he steered to greater and greater success, even if it was beginning to flounder a little during his final years. He created the enormous wealth by which the Guinness name became best known in Britain, as synonymous there with its stout if not more so.

In his will, he tried to ensure that the family maintained its wealth as he was succeeded by a series of less adroit businessmen and by a new generation of spirited Guinness women, emerging at last from the family's shadows. But in failing to follow the practices of his predecessors – by not leaving control of the brewery and the bulk of his wealth in the hands of one person – he arguably sowed the seeds of its relative decline during the twentieth century.

—◦◦◦—

CHAPTER TEN

Guinness is Good for You

"The day when one of these gentlemen by raising his little finger, or when the Masonic Order by using the mailed fist, could frighten the Executive Council is gone for good."

Fianna Fáil TD MARTIN CORRY on warnings that
Guinness and Jacobs might leave Ireland in the 1930s

By the time of Lord Iveagh's death, his three sons were all middle-aged and settled into their careers. Shortly before he died, he decided that his eldest son Rupert, who had the courtesy title of Lord Elveden, would succeed him as chairman of Arthur Guinness Son & Company. The decision was something of a surprise and, on the face of it, at odds with the family's practice of handing over control of the brewery to the son best able to run it. Rupert had been a director of the company since 1899 but had never been involved in its day-to-day running. By the time his father died, he was 53 years old, a Conservative member of parliament for Southend-on-Sea, one of the safest Tory seats in England, and a farmer.

By contrast, his younger brother, Ernest (who had been christened Arthur Ernest), was aged 51, and had been vice-chairman of the brewery since 1913. He lived mainly in Dublin, at Glenmaroon in Chapelizod, which had been bought originally for his uncle Claude Guinness, the former managing director of the brewery, who had apparently gone mad. Ernest was deeply involved in the brewery's senior management and was his father's eyes and ears at St James's Gate on a daily basis. Their youngest brother, Walter (born in Dublin on

29 March 1880) was a 47-year-old full-time politician and a member of the British cabinet as Minister of Agriculture and Fisheries at the time of his father's death; he lived exclusively in England, when not cruising the world in his yacht, and had little active involvement in the day-to-day activities of the brewery, although he was also a director and, like his brothers, a substantial shareholder, in the company.

Whether he expected it himself or not – and he had every reason to – others (including his family) certainly believed that Ernest would be the one to take control of the brewery and the chairmanship of the company after the first Lord Iveagh.[1] However, his father decided otherwise for unknown reasons. Ernest was the most conventionally intelligent of the three brothers, mechanically minded and interested in engineering and machinery and the only one to emerge from university with a degree. While deeply interested and involved in the brewery's processes, he was quiet and a man of regular habits but also somewhat eccentric: his interest in things mechanical extended to having a special coal scuttle by the fire in Glenmaroon on which there was a button that produced an organ elsewhere in the room that played "Cherry Ripe", a popular folksong during the First World War. On another occasion, he had one of his yachts cut in two to insert a 12-foot section in the middle to accommodate a diesel engine: when it was pointed out to him that it would be cheaper and easier to buy a new boat with an engine, he replied that he wanted to see how it could be done. On the other hand, he was not a natural businessman and was very cautious about major decisions on the direction the company should take. But Rupert had shown little or no aptitude in that field either. Walter was dashing and daring, a natural adventurer and womaniser who seemed to prefer the uncertain spirit of politics and exploring the world to settling into a successful business enterprise. Another factor in Iveagh's decision may have been that Ernest had three daughters and no sons while Rupert had a son. (Rupert's first-born was also a son, called Richard, who died within days of his premature birth which had been brought on by his mother's involvement in a road accident.)

The Guinnesses had never practised primogeniture and Iveagh did not do so in his will to the extent that he left his shares in the brewery equally between his three sons. Having put so much of his time and energy into rising up the aristocratic ladder, it is perhaps not surprising that he felt obliged to continue some of its practices, leaving Elveden to whichever of his descendants held the earldom, for instance. The fact that he left his decision on his successor at the brewery to one of his last actions may suggest that he was undecided about what to do. In any event, the new Earl of Iveagh, Rupert Edward Cecil Lee Guinness, found himself elevated by his father's death into the House of Lords, into control of the Elveden estate and into the chairmanship of Arthur Guinness. Among his other effective inheritances was the chancellorship of Dublin University, a position his father had held for some 20 years and Rupert held for the remainder of his long life.

Rupert had been a disappointment to his parents. He had few of his father's dominant attributes: he was neither highly ambitious, determined to maintain control nor a natural businessman. Nothing in his temperament or upbringing was designed to make him an ideal chairman of a large company, certainly not in the same manner as his father had exerted close control over Guinness for more than fifty years. Rupert was born in London in his parents' then house at Berkeley Square on 29 March 1874. His mother Adelaide noted the event in her diary with the cryptic entry: "Baby born at ? to 6. Boy."[2] That set the tone accurately for his childhood relationship with his parents. His mother was certainly not maternal and his father was distant and somewhat forbidding, as well as very busy. In the manner of the time and of the class to which his parents aspired, he saw them once a day, if at all. He spent most of his childhood with nannies and in Ireland, since the family then lived mainly in Dublin, between St Stephen's Green and Farmleigh. One of his occasional childhood playmates in the Phoenix Park was the young Winston Churchill, who was staying at the Vice-Regal Lodge where his grandfather, the Duke of Marlborough, was Lord Lieutenant between 1876 and 1880. They were not happy playmates, however. In one incident, variously described as involving either a whip or a candlestick, Churchill, the younger by nine months, hit Rupert across the face when he refused to carry out Winston's commands. Rupert's eye was injured and a prominent surgeon in Dublin was brought in and applied a caustic solution around his eye which left Rupert with a lifelong scar above it.[3]

His parents' disappointment with Rupert was prompted by his apparent slowness; he found it very difficult to learn how to read or write, first at St George's preparatory school (where Churchill was also enrolled) and then at Eton. Doctors were consulted but could find nothing wrong with his eyes or other faculties; extra tuition was no help either. In fact he suffered from dyslexia, a condition that was not recognised at the time; it was only in the 1890s, after Rupert's schooldays, that it became known in England as congenital word blindness. His headmaster described him as "a model of good conduct and good temper to all" but added the damning wish that "his ability approached his character in excellence". The only subject at which he was successful was science and, from childhood on, he had some difficulty expressing himself both in speech and in writing.

He found success in sport, however, turning out to be a champion oarsman, beating the holder of the Diamond Champion Sculls, the well-known rower Guy Nickalls, by a length and a half at the Henley regatta in July 1895. Nickalls, who was "terribly distressed" by his defeat, blamed it on having won two tough races earlier while Rupert was fresh. But Rupert proved it was not a fluke result when they met again ten days later in the Wingfield Sculls, the amateur championship of the Thames, a four-mile race down the river from Putney to Mortlake, which turned out to be very dramatic with a gale-force wind behind them meeting the incoming tide ahead of them. The lead changed several times before Rupert got ahead and Nickalls' boat overturned in the heavy water just short of the finish line. However, Nickalls younger brother, Vivian, beat him in the final of the event some days later when Rupert's new scull, replacing one broken in the earlier race, failed to work properly.[4] The following year Rupert beat Vivian Nickalls in a heat and went on to win the Diamond Sculls again and then beat him again for the silver Wingfield Sculls trophy.

Rupert did not compete the following year. His rowing career was ended peremptorily by a medical diagnosis after his 1896 victories that his heart was enlarged, and therefore weak, and his father instructed him to give up rowing. Rupert went to Cambridge University where, unable to row himself, he spent his time coaching other rowers. He left at the end of his first academic year. His brother Ernest was also a good oarsman and all three brothers, particularly Walter, shared a lifelong love of boats and of the sea, using their great wealth to maintain yachts and go on lengthy cruises around the world. Unable to row, Rupert turned to sailing in his 98-ton yawl *Leander* (presumably named after the Leander Club, one of the world's oldest rowing clubs, rather than the Greek mythological hero, or perhaps both) and was a frequent competitor at Cowes, beating the Kaiser's *Meteor III* to win the King's Cup in 1901. The following year, he had a lucky escape after racing the *Leander* from Dover to Heligoland. He and some of his crew were on board a German torpedo boat when it was struck amidships by a steamer and sank within five minutes. The captain of the German vessel gave orders to put the four Englishmen in the lifeboat first and all the visitors and crew were saved. Rupert got an unexpected opportunity to show his sculling skills again, propelling the lifeboat with its single oar to a nearby ship which picked them up.

Meanwhile, the Boer War began in October 1899. Walter abandoned his plans to study biology at Oxford to enlist in the newly formed Imperial Yeomanry which was inviting members of the hunting and shooting classes to augment the regular army after a string of early Boer successes. The Yeomanry tried with limited success to counter the Boer's guerrilla tactics with similar hit-and-run raids and were involved in at least one set-piece battle. Walter received a minor wound in his cheek in an engagement near Witpoortjie in September 1900, a wound he delighted in showing off to the ladies on his return home.

Their father, Lord Iveagh, offered to fund a mobile field hospital for British troops wounded in the war and decided to recruit the staff for it in Ireland under the leadership of Sir William Thompson, a former president of the Royal College of Surgeons in Dublin. The Irish Hospital, as it was known, had more than 70 personnel, headed by a group of surgeons mainly from Dublin's Richmond Hospital, including Fred Stoker, the brother of Bram Stoker, author of *Dracula*. Members of the Royal Irish Constabulary with ambulance training were recruited by competition to be hospital orderlies – no female nurses were brought along – and dozens of mules were acquired in Ireland to haul the hospital equipment and its supply wagons. In all, the hospital provided about 96 beds and during its six months or so in southern Africa in

1900 it treated more than 2,700 wounded men and about 2,000 more as out-patients. At least two of the orderlies succumbed to typhoid and dysentery and died during the tour.[5]

While Ernest remained at home, Rupert went along as an assistant to Sir William and to help with the organisation of the expedition. Following some of Lord Kitchener's regular army units, the group ended up in Pretoria after its capture from the Boers and established a hospital in a building there. One of Rupert's tasks was to organise entertainment, including dances and a fancy dress competition, to which he went dressed as a baby. His diary recorded one "very odd evening" with an unknown woman who felt ill and he added, "we consoled her. I am glad there were no witnesses!"[6] For his troubles, he was "mentioned in despatches" along with several others of the hospital's personnel, including Dr Stoker and Lord Iveagh, who did not travel to South Africa himself. Rupert was appointed to the Companionship of the Order of St Michael and St George (CMG: for services rendered to the Commonwealth or foreign nations) on his return home.

Rupert's interest in the ladies may have been the cause of a breach of promise case taken against him in 1905 by a woman named Isabel Agnes Hales, who claimed that Rupert had bought her a house, offered her a settlement of £15,000 and agreed to marry her before announcing his engagement to someone else. She took her case to court but did not turn out to be a very persuasive witness; she had nothing in writing and no corroborative evidence and seemed confused about dates. She claimed to be 29 years old and, when presented with her birth certificate showing that she was in fact 37, she said her mother must have made a mistake. She also said she was too ill to go and look after the house Rupert had allegedly bought her in Hampton. With their well-known reputation for enormous wealth, the Guinnesses were obviously targets for all sorts of confidence tricksters, chancers and fraudsters. (Rupert was also the target of a man who claimed to be a military colleague from the South African campaign and borrowed some money from his staff before coming back once too often and being caught.) It is clear from the breach of promise court reports that Isabel Hales had received some money from the family; whether to persuade her to go away or because there was some substance to her claim is impossible to say. She complained in court that Rupert's solicitors were preventing him from making a settlement on her and had offered her only £50 after expenses. She lost her case; the judge ordered the jury to dismiss her action in the absence of any corroboration of her claims. Rupert did not give evidence.[7]

Meanwhile, he and his brothers had got married within a few months of each other in a succession of society weddings during the summer and autumn of 1903. Walter was the first to the altar, marrying Lady Evelyn Hilda Stuart Erskine, the youngest daughter of the 14th Earl of Buchan, and a member of a family of long-established Scottish aristocrats. The ceremony took place in St Mark's Church in London's North Audley Street and the reception was held in Claridges. Among the many titled attendees was Prince Frederick Duleep Singh, son of the former owner of Elveden who still lived in the same area.[8] Three weeks later, Ernest married Marie Clothilde (Cloe) Russell, daughter of the late Sir Edward Russell, at St Margaret's Church in Westminster. The list of titled attendees was not quite so long but they went to Claridges again for the wedding reception.[9] Rupert, who had been best man for both his brothers, came next in October, marrying Lady Gwendolen Onslow, the elder daughter of the 4th Earl of Onslow, a Conservative politician, former governor of New Zealand, and a member of the cabinet as president of the board of agriculture at the time of the wedding. Rupert and Gwendolen had met at a shooting party in Elveden to which she had accompanied her parents. At their first meeting, she wrote later, they had "a long and enjoyable discussion on mentally defective and crippled children" arising out of his election to London County Council for the City and his recently acquired membership of the London school board.[10] Their wedding was also held at St Margaret's and had a long list of aristocrats in attendance as well as the ambassadors from the US, France and Denmark. The reception this time was in the Onslow's London residence at Richmond Terrace in Whitehall. His father gave Rupert a wedding gift of a house, 11 St James's Square in London. The Prince of Wales (later George V) gave him a tie pin.

Rupert and Walter were pursuing parallel careers, both back from South Africa – Rupert was already mentioned in newspapers as having served there during the war, implying wrongly that he had played a military role; while Ernest was occupied fully at the brewery in Dublin.

Interestingly, in contrast to his father's efforts to play down his Irish roots, Rupert described himself as an Irishman living in Suffolk when addressing members of the local Conservative Party at Lakenheath, near Elveden, in 1902. He praised them for having among their officers a Nonconformist and the local vicar which proved, he said, that religious differences did not need to be political differences, as he knew all too well the evil effects of the reverse in his own country.[11] It was also notable that the three brothers, unlike their father, gave practically all their children what could be seen as Irish names: Honor, Arthur, Patricia and Brigid (Rupert); Aileen, Maureen and Oonagh (Ernest); and Bryan, Murtogh and Grania (Walter).

There are indications that Rupert sought Conservative nominations in a number of constituencies – there was speculation about him in Croydon, for one – but settled on Haggerston, a division of Shoreditch in the East End of London. It did not appear to be a very promising area for a Conservative, although one had been elected there some ten years earlier and its Liberal majority in the two previous elections was less than 40 votes out of about 4,500 cast. Rupert acquired a house in the area, on Kingsland Road, which was a far cry from St James's Square and, indeed, he spent little time in it. He contested the 1906 general election on an anti-free trade platform, which included slogans about free trade not being fair trade and (presumably ignoring his Irishness for the moment) "Englishmen for English work".[12] He lost to his Liberal opponent by more than 400 votes.

Walter also failed to get elected in the Stowmarket division of Suffolk, but both won seats on London County Council as Municipal Reform candidates two years later, Rupert for Haggerston and Walter in North Paddington. Walter beat him to the House of Commons, winning a by-election in August 1907 in the safe Conservative seat of Bury St Edmunds near his home, Hardwick House. The following year Rupert won a by-election caused by the death of his Liberal opponent in Haggerston, Sir Randal Cremer, with a majority of more than 1,100 votes. He was helped by the addition of a socialist candidate and by one of the issues of the campaign – opposition to plans by the temperance-supporting Liberal government for stricter licensing laws. One of the posters in the constituency this time declared: "Save the nation from

Puritan tyranny." Rupert, however, credited his victory to the Catholic vote and to Haggerston's opposition to free trade rather than to his championship of the drinks industry.[13]

He lost the seat again in the 1910 general election but found a more congenial constituency representing Southend-on-Sea in Essex, which he won in 1912. The seat (with several divisions and name changes) was to pass down through three generations of Guinnesses, from Rupert to his wife Gwendolen (after Rupert inherited his father's earldom in 1927), their son-in-law Sir Henry "Chips" Channon and grandson Paul Channon, who finally surrendered it on his retirement from politics in 1997. Its 85 years in the one unbroken family line created something of a record in twentieth-century British politics and the constituency was sometimes known in the House of Commons as Guinness-on-Sea.

Safe as it was, Rupert's large majorities fell to little more than a hundred votes during the 1920s when opponents accused him of spending little time in either the House of Commons or his constituency, where he had bought a house but didn't live. However, the constituency benefited from regular examples of Guinness benevolence, like the £97,000 Rupert contributed to build a new hospital for the town in the 1930s when Gwendolen was its MP.[14]

His real interest was in neither politics nor business but in agriculture and in the application of science to farming methods. He began his practical experiments in farming on the 700-acre estate that he and Gwendolen bought from her father's land at Clandon Park beside Guildford in Surrey. They built a house there, to Rupert's design, Pyrford Court, while he funded and carried out research into agricultural processes. Among them were work on the creation of compost and the extraction of methane from manure, piping the gas into the house as a fuel for the ovens. He and his scientific assistants also discovered a method of turning straw into animal feed with the help of bacteria and formed the Agricultural Developments Company, Adco, to exploit it commercially: it became a subsidiary of Arthur Guinness Son & Company. One of his other main areas of interest was in bovine TB and he was involved in the formation of the Tuberculin Tested Milk Producers Association in 1920, as well as funding the Research Institute for Dairying with £60,000 which allowed it purchase and equip an experimental farm near Reading. By the outbreak of the First World War he had developed a system of sterilising milk and bottling it at Pyrford.

As well as his interest in the scientific aspects of agriculture, Rupert remained deeply involved with the Lister Institute, which he had persuaded his father to fund, and was a friend of Sir Alexander Fleming, the discoverer of penicillin, and Sir Almroth Wright, the immunologist who was one of the first people to develop vaccines. He helped to fund their Institute of Microbiology at St Mary's Hospital in Paddington where most of their work was carried out.

While on visits to Canada, partly for family investment reasons and, during the First World War, in search of volunteers for the Royal Navy, Rupert became interested in the fate of emigrants from Britain who found themselves on Canadian farms with little or no training in farming. On his return, he set up an emigration training farm on a neighbouring estate, Woking Park, which taught intending emigrants the basics of farming while Gwendolen was involved with its women's section which taught girls about cooking, dairying and raising poultry. Some 200 people were trained there annually.

Rupert's interest in agriculture was deeply unfashionable in Britain, especially during his young adult years. His father-in-law, Lord Onslow, had been told in no uncertain terms while in the Cabinet with responsibility for agriculture and fisheries in the early 1900s that Britain was an industrial country, not an agricultural one. Furthermore, the prices of agricultural produce continued to go down. By the late 1920s, they were down to 38 per cent of what they had been before the First World War. By then, Rupert's brother Walter was Minister of Agriculture and trying to help farms with a system of de-rating – replacing rates on farmland with indirect taxes – which was a controversial proposal at the time.

Becoming the life tenant at Elveden after his father's death presented Rupert with a much bigger opportunity, and a greater challenge: to indulge his interest in agricultural development. Located in the area known as the Breckland, the estate was in a flat landscape (which later made it ideal for air force bases) with sandy soil that in previous decades, before the planting of trees and forests, had been noted for its sandstorms. Edward Iveagh's interest in it was primarily as a venue for shooting and the few crops sown were put there to provide cover for game; the order of importance between shooting and farming was simply illustrated by the fact that his head gamekeeper took precedence over his farm manager. The area was infested with rabbits (up to 50,000 a year were being trapped and sold) and was generally seen as an agricultural wasteland. Rupert set about transforming this situation but his plans were upset when he met King George within weeks of his father's death to return the latter's Order of St Patrick. "I hope you are going to keep up the shooting at Elveden," the king said to him. "I shall hope to come next year and I think the Queen would like to come too."[15]

Taking that as a royal diktat, he had to set about the renovation of Elveden Hall, which had been virtually abandoned for the last decade of Iveagh's life when social life there ended after the death of Lady Iveagh in 1916. The royal visit duly took place, with eight guns dispatching 3,599 game over three days, a relatively modest number compared to the previous record years. While the shooting was never abandoned – it was too valuable for that and part of the estate was let to a shooting syndicate – Rupert then set about transforming the estate into a more productive farm. He began with the introduction of TB-free dairy cattle and an ambitious project to build some thirty miles of sunken fences to control the rabbit population. With the onset of the Depression a couple of years later, even millionaires had to look to their incomes and the estate would have to do more to pay its way.

Rupert's other main task after his father's death was the chairmanship of Arthur Guinness and how to resolve the problems that had seen the brewery lose its way to an extent in the 1920s while still apparently trading successfully and profitably. One of the decisions to be taken was on whether or not to advertise, the issue that had exercised Edward Iveagh's last board meeting in Dublin in August 1927. At that time, Rupert's cousin, the racing driver Kenelm Lee Guinness, had given the directors the benefit of his experience in advertising his successful spark plugs. He employed someone to look after the advertising and deal with the advertising agency while he retained the final say on the ads and the spending. That was the pattern adopted when the board, under Rupert's chairmanship, launched its first trial ads in Scotland in April 1928 to see if they would arrest the serious drop in Guinness sales there. It appeared to work: sales went up in Scotland while they went down in the rest of Britain. As a result, the campaign was extended (and expanded significantly) to England where the first newspaper ad appeared on 7 February 1929 with the famous slogan "Guinness Is Good For You".

Like all successes, the slogan appears to have had many fathers. It has been credited to a number of people in the advertising agency, S.H. Benson, which had been hired for the campaign, and to Ernest (although he had opposed the introduction of advertising while Walter supported it: Rupert supported it, taking the advice, as he usually did, of the brewery's executives).[16] Whoever came up with the pithy phrase, the idea behind it had clearly been tossed around in February 1928 at Benson's first meeting about the project with Charles Newbold at Guinness. The minutes of the meeting said that the aim of the campaign was "to impress on the public that Guinness is good for them".[17]

While the slogan was succinct, the ad itself was anything but. It was extremely wordy, concentrating on the supposed medical benefits of Guinness, its naturalness, purity, health-giving and nourishing properties. According to it, Guinness built strong muscles, fed exhausted nerves, was a remedy for tiredness, exhaustion and insomnia, richer in carbohydrates than a glass of milk, and (doctors affirmed) a valuable restorative after influenza and other weakening illnesses. It did not mention that Guinness might make you feel good, not to mention drunk (the slogan reputedly provided by playwright Brendan Behan after he had been hired to come up with a pithy phrase much later: "Guinness Makes You Drunk" was his suggestion). The company took its health claims seriously, circularising all 28,000 doctors in Britain with a questionnaire and offering them free samples for their patients and themselves. Half of them took up the free offer while more than a thousand provided testimonials, which came in useful some years later when the pernickety US Federal Alcohol Administration challenged the Guinness health claims when it went on sale there again after the ending of prohibition.

The staid look of the ad quickly gave way to the series that made Guinness as famous for its ads as for its stout. The slogan evolved into

"Guinness for Strength", which was accompanied by perhaps the most famous of all its posters, one showing a Guinness drinker carrying a girder and another a drinker pulling a cart and horse. They were the work of John Gilroy, an illustrator with Benson's and a portrait painter, who produced a succession of iconic Guinness images, including the series involving a zoo keeper and a number of exotic animals, notably the toucan, usually with the slogan "My Goodness, My Guinness". The ditties that went with them were as smart, cheerful and amusing as the graphics and were written by other Benson employees, including Dorothy L. Sayers, who wrote the best-remembered puns on the word "toucan" and later the Lord Peter Wimsey series of novels as well as other books and plays, and Stanley Penn, who specialised in parodies of Lewis Carroll characters.[18] Within a few years, Gilroy, Sayers and their colleagues had managed to create some of the best-loved ads of the twentieth century, greatly enhancing the status and mystique of Guinness and acknowledged in their own right by the number of parodies and copycat ads that quickly followed in their wake.

The initial emphasis on Guinness as a healthy and even medicinal drink was not purely an advertising ploy. People, including many of the doctors circularised, believed it and the practice, already widespread in Ireland, of providing free stout to hospitals was extended to London by the company. When one London hospital seemed to be "prescribing" an awful lot of free Guinness, an investigation discovered that the doctors were giving it to nurses as well as to patients: the company was told, however, that it was being prescribed only for nurses who were "run down" or on night duty. Rowers at Oxford and Cambridge also developed a need for Guinness to resuscitate them after their exertions, a demand that quickly rose once it became known that free supplies could be had for this purpose too.[19]

The advertising campaign seemed to work at first; Guinness sales revived and moved ahead of its rivals in an increasingly difficult market as the Depression that followed the Wall Street crash took hold in the early 1930s. By 1930, however, Guinness sales were only about three-quarters of what they had been at the start of the First World War and that was after they had recovered from the lows of the 1920s; by 1933, they were down more than 20 per cent on the 1930 figure and at a level where they were utilising less than two-thirds of the capacity at James's Gate. For the first time, the brewery was over-staffed. Profits were £2.3 million before tax in 1933 but were lagging behind the company's earlier performance and beginning to show a weaker trend than that at some of its traditional English rivals. Among the reasons was the new cost of advertising which was in the region of £250,000 a year, a cost that had not existed during the previous Lord Iveagh's leadership of the company. A more important factor, though, was a succession of increases in excise duties in Britain in the early 1930s because of the economic situation, which were once again calculated in a way that penalised heavier beers and favoured lighter ones.

The Guinness experiment with advertising first in Scotland and then its practice in England was not repeated in Ireland at the time, mainly because the company feared that it might become a monopoly – or be seen as one – since it was already so dominant in the market. But that market declined as economic conditions worsened during the depression and sales fell throughout the 1930s to about 40 per cent of what they had been in the country before 1914.[20] The growth of Guinness in the British market tended to mask this fall, as even a slight percentage rise in Britain would compensate for a much larger percentage fall in Ireland because of the relative sizes of the markets. It was at this point, as Guinness found itself more dependent than ever on the British market, that Irish politics took a turn for the worse from the company's perspective.

In spite of its fears about Home Rule and political independence for Ireland, Guinness's relations with the Free State had been cordial and workmanlike. The first Lord Iveagh had had several meetings with W.T. Cosgrave, the first president of the Executive Council and, in reality, each needed the other. Guinness needed the benevolence of the new rulers because all its brewing was carried out in Ireland: the British market may have been its most important, accounting for 70 per cent of sales, but all its supplies of stout still came from St James's Gate. The Free State needed Guinness for its economic importance, not just in terms of excise duties and taxes on beer sales, but also for its wider economic effects in terms of direct and indirect employment and its use of raw materials. Guinness was of considerable importance to Irish agriculture, annually buying most of the barley crop and keeping maltsters in business. The company was conscious of its role, agreeing on several occasions in the 1920s and 1930s to help Irish farmers by buying more barley than it needed immediately and at higher prices than it would have had to pay on international markets.

The election of the first Fianna Fáil government under Eamon de Valera in 1932 threatened this relationship with a number of its polices which partly reflected the increased protectionism of many countries in response to the Depression and partly the old Sinn Féin policy of self-sufficiency. New government measures included state control over the amounts and prices of barley to be used for animal feeds and an import licence system, at the discretion of the Minister for Agriculture, for any imports of foreign barley and malt. Britain was also threatening its own protectionist measures, including a possible tariff on imported stout. In danger of being seriously squeezed by both sides, Guinness needed to chart a careful course. It was helped by the fact that neither government wished to damage the company: it was too important to the Irish economy and some of its Conservative Party friends were back in power in Britain in a "national" government with the Labour Party.

However, there was some hostile rhetoric coming from the new government party's backbenches. Martin Corry, a fiercely anti-British former IRA gunman, founder member of Fianna Fáil and champion of his farming constituents in Cork, lost no opportunity to lacerate Guinness for its imports of foreign barley, its treatment of farmers and stout drinkers, and its excessive profits. He welcomed what he saw as the new era: the time "when one of these gentlemen by raising his little finger, or when the Masonic Order by using the mailed first, could frighten the Executive Council is gone for good." In one of his fiercest attacks on the company he told the Dáil: "When you compare [their] profit with the price the producer gets for his barley I think that a case can be made out not alone for this Bill [Control of Prices Bill] but a case can also be made out for placing a lot of oily-faced gentlemen in jail."[21]

Guinness did not respond to such provocations and the Minister for Agriculture, James Ryan, adopted a more pragmatic approach, recognising as one opposition deputy pointed out in the Dáil, that the brewery might import some £167,000 worth of barley but it was exporting £5 million worth of stout. He also recognised that Guinness's requirement for foreign barley was not simply a matter of price or supply but also a matter of blending different types of barley, with different levels of nitrogen, which it used in the brewing process. Ryan's first meeting with Guinness in the autumn of 1932 was reassuring for the company: he made it clear that he had no intention of making it difficult for it to import the barley and malt it required or of setting minimum prices.[22]

While the controls over agricultural produce prompted most references to Guinness in the Dáil, things became more difficult with the onset of the so-called Economic War after Ireland stopped paying land annuities to Britain – the payments due on land bought out by tenant farmers under the various Land Acts of the late nineteenth and early twentieth centuries – and Britain retaliated with tariffs on selected agricultural imports from Ireland to make up for the missing payments. Beer was excluded from the list of tariffs initially but the way things were perceived was evident from the London stock market – Irish Land Annuities were not affected at all as they were guaranteed by the British government while Guinness shares immediately dropped 7 per cent from 82 shillings (£4.10) to 76 shillings (£3.80).[23] The developments prompted fears that Guinness was about to revive its pre-war plans for Manchester's Trafford Park and pull out of Dublin altogether. Guinness responded with an unnamed spokesman telling *The Irish Times*, more accurately than the media may have realised: "There is absolutely nothing I can tell you. I do not know myself."[24] At the company's annual meeting in August 1932, Rupert was philosophical, even enigmatic, when asked about the consequences of the political developments for the company. It was difficult and even impossible to say what they would be, he said, adding that one had to live from day to day and be glad when one "saw the sun rise and it looked brighter than it sometimes looked".

People like Corry derided fears that Guinness and Jacob's (which had explicitly warned that it might leave Ireland) would flee the country, pointing out repeatedly over the following months that they were both still in Dublin. However, his equanimity was misplaced: Guinness was looking at its options and dusting off once again the

Manchester plans, shelved with the onset of the First World War. They had been looked at several times in the almost 20 years since they had first been drawn up but had been shelved again each time without any definitive decisions being taken. This was, to an extent, a feature of the company's lack of decisiveness during the last years of Edward Iveagh's life; while there was no need for extra brewing capacity in England, there was always a feeling that the company needed a major distribution centre there, not least because of the labour troubles that periodically upset the docks and cross-channel transport services during the 1920s.

The company moved slowly, not wanting to upset the Irish and bring down possible retaliations upon it by deciding to open a new brewery in England. There was a financial argument against it as well: building another brewery would create a loss because there was not enough work for it. There was also a geographical argument against the Trafford Park site in Manchester as most of its English customers were around London and the south-east of England. As a result of the last factor, the company had begun looking at possible sites in London when the decision to build there was effectively made for it by the British government in the autumn of 1932. J.H. Thomas, the former trade unionist and Labour Party member who was now Secretary of State for the Dominions in the national government, sought a meeting with Rupert and told him that Britain would impose import duties on beer from Ireland unless Guinness built a brewery in England. It is not entirely clear whether Thomas's decision was another escalation of the Economic War or a strategic aspect of the domestic protectionist policy to create jobs, or both. Faced with this ultimatum, the company had no choice: in a declining market, with its sales already under pressure, and profits for the previous year down by £700,000, it could not afford a major loss of competitiveness in Britain.

The search for a suitable site in the south of England then began in earnest and in conditions of extraordinary secrecy – to keep its plans secret from its British competitors as well as from Irish opinion – while the abandonment of the Trafford Park project allowed it to continue with ritual denials that it had any plans to build a brewery in Manchester. A London solicitor, Owen Bulmer Howell, and a consulting engineer, Hugh Beaver, were charged with finding a suitable site. They needed a 40-acre site with good water supplies of half a million gallons a day and good communications for the planned six-kieve plant which would supply the London area. They eventually settled on Park Royal, a 134-acre trading estate where land was relatively cheap and which met most of the specifications. A separate company, the Park Royal Development Company, was set up to buy the entire estate and to develop it as an industrial estate, which proved to be a useful cover for the plans and a profitable enterprise in its own right. Another company with the uninformative name of Associated Agricultural Products Ltd was registered through nominees to build the brewery. In spite of all the secrecy – which involved brewery executives using false names – news leaked to the *Middlesex County Times* in May 1933 but it was deflected by a categorical and untrue denial by the London solicitor that Guinness was building a new brewery there.[25] Among the rumours circulated instead were that Associated Agricultural Products Ltd would be manufacturing industrial alcohol from potatoes or that it intended to make explosives from potatoes.

The secret remained more or less intact until the summer of 1934 when the Irish Minister for Industry and Commerce, Seán Lemass, was informed in Dublin by the managing director of Guinness, Thomas Case, of the plan shortly before the official announcement. Lemass appeared to be taken by surprise and asked if anything could be done to change the decision but it was too far advanced for that: Park Royal was expected to be brewing Guinness by the spring of 1935. Case told him that the loss of jobs in Dublin would be about 500 but assured him that Foreign Stout would continue to be brewed at St James's Gate and that the company was looking at establishing some sidelines of brewing which might create some new jobs in Dublin to replace those lost.[26]

The move was announced publicly by Rupert at the shareholders' meeting in London on 10 August. He placed the decision firmly in the context of 1913, suggesting it was now possible because of falls in building costs and increases in Guinness's trade in the south of England to go ahead with the project first outlined by his father more than 20 years earlier. He did not mention directly the Economic War or the threat of British import tariffs which had been the final factor in the decision, but the implications were there in his comments. "We have, nevertheless, only arrived at our decision after most anxious thought," he said. "We have always regarded, and we still regard, Dublin as the home of Guinness, and even though circumstances have now forced this step upon us we still hope to brew the stout for as much of our English trade as may be possible in Dublin." Rupert was also at pains to assuage one of the company's other fears: that drinkers would not consider stout brewed outside Dublin to be real Guinness. Having done nothing to dispel the myths about Liffey water and so forth, Guinness now had to explain that its stout was in no way unique to Dublin. Continuing some of the myth-making, however, Rupert told the meeting that the company had carried out investigations of all its brewing processes – including "the special processes handed down by my family for more than a century and a half" – and was satisfied that the same Guinness could be produced at Park Royal as at James's Gate. The Guinness brewed in London would be "as good for you" as that brewed by the Liffey. Finally, he also mentioned the "profitable sidelines" that the company hoped to develop to replace some of the lost jobs in Dublin.[27]

The announcement came as a shock to many people: Martin Corry was probably not the only person who did not believe Guinness would ever brew elsewhere. Its impact was blunted, as intended, by the references to Park Royal as a branch of the brewery, with only six kieves compared to Dublin's 26, and the promise of profitable new sidelines which would compensate for the loss of 25 per cent of St James's Gate's business. It was muted as well by the fact that the announcement came a couple of weeks into a ten-week newspaper strike in Ireland, which ran from late July until early October. There was no reaction in the Dáil, no parliamentary questions to Ministers, no rhetoric from the Opposition about the short-sightedness of the government's economic and political policies and their effects on the country's largest industrial employer. Guinness shares responded positively, up from about 112 shillings (£5.60) before the announcement to about 130 shillings (£6.50) in early October when the newspapers returned.

The general muted reaction and the stock market one turned out to be correct: the building of Park Royal, although forced upon it by outside agencies, turned out to be a good decision for Guinness and not disastrous for Ireland. It took until mid-1936 to get the new branch up

254

and running, delayed in part by caution and a determination to replicate the Dublin brewery as far as possible in London, even down to introducing bacteria from St James's Gate and ignoring their own scientific research in favour of sterilising all the new plant's equipment. In spite of Rupert's assurances, the company was not a hundred per cent confident that the Guinness brewed in London would be the same as that brewed in Dublin. For the first few months stout brewed in London was mixed with that brewed in Dublin until everybody was satisfied that it tasted the same. Dublin now became, as Rupert had described it, "the home of Guinness", rather than the greatest and most unique stout brewery in the world.

The advantages of the new brewery included significant cost savings on transport and on wages: its staff was generally a lot younger than those employed in Dublin, did not have to be paid long-service bonuses, and were not offered the same premium wages and social welfare benefits as their Irish colleagues. The timing of the move also proved to be fortuitous: by 1939 James's Gate was providing about 75 per cent of Guinness's total output of 1.34 million hogsheads of stout, as had been predicted, but sales then picked up during the Second World War. By 1945 overall output totalled a new record two million hogshead a year, 1.34 million brewed in Dublin – exactly the same amount as had been brewed there in 1935, before Park Royal began operations – and the rest brewed in London.

Rumours that Guinness was about to leave Ireland did not stop, however, with the completion of Park Royal but became something of a perennial myth in Irish life, circulating at regular intervals and on occasions when increased taxes on drink were threatened or imposed. The next round of rumours came within a couple of years after Park Royal's opening when Ernest Guinness, then in his early sixties and still vice-chairman of the brewery, announced his intention of vacating Ashford Castle, which he had inherited from his father. He had been a regular visitor to the estate, often arriving in the 1930s in his three-engined seaplane, which he piloted himself from Dún Laoghaire or Southampton and landed at a specially constructed jetty beside the castle on Lough Corrib. His visits became less frequent and for shorter periods from the mid-1930s on, a fact that was attributed locally to the building of the Park Royal brewery in London but which may have had a more local cause as well (see next chapter). Whatever the reason, or combination of reasons, he appeared to be spending more time in England, where he had homes at Grosvenor Place in London (later the Irish embassy there) and Holmbury House in Surrey. He offered Ashford to his nephew Bryan, Walter's eldest son. Bryan, who was a poet, was tempted, seeing it as a version of Yeats's rural home, Thoor Ballylee, but his new wife was not, and he turned it down.

In the summer of 1938 Ernest announced his decision to sell the estate (technically, of course, under his father's will it belonged to the Iveagh Trustees and was only Ernest's for life). His decision coincided with, and was possibly prompted by, industrial unrest among the hundred-odd workers on the estate, who staged a brief unofficial strike during a shoot in support of their demand for a wage increase of two shillings a week, a rise of approximately 7.5 per cent on their average pay. There were also continuing demands for the division of the estate among local farmers and "landless men", echoing the Land League troubles of earlier decades which had dogged his uncle, Lord Ardilaun, at Ashford. Minor incidents had included cattle being let loose from estate lands. On the other hand, a local meeting in Cong, beside Ashford Castle, appealed to Ernest to reconsider his decision: the estate was said to be worth a lot of money annually to the local economy, though estimates varied from £20,000 a year to £250 a month, depending on which side of the argument one was on. The local Fianna Fáil TDs for the area were as conspicuous by their absence from the meeting as the Cumann na nGaedheal TD, James Fitzgerald Kenney, was by his presence. The Fianna Fáil cumann in Clonbur, some of whose members had been campaigning for the takeover and break-up of the estate, welcomed Ernest's announcement, declaring that there were a lot more people unemployed in Rosshill (part of the estate) than the six casual workers employed on the 700 acres there by the estate. The chairman, Patrick Kyne, also claimed that many of the estate workers had done better by getting jobs elsewhere: some 2,000 acres of the estate could be divided up among 80 uneconomic holdings and 50 landless people in the area, he maintained.[28]

Those hoping for a change of heart by Ernest looked forward to his usual visit in September but he did not come to Ashford that year and he did not change his mind. The Iveagh Trustees in London put the estate on the market at the end of 1938: it was to be sold in two lots: the castle and 3,500 acres of land with timber and sporting rights; and a second lot made up of the Doon estate, which included 33 islands in Loughs Corrib and Mask. There was some speculation, unlikely as it may seem, that the Duke of Windsor, the recently abdicated King Edward VIII, was interested in buying it but that rumour was scotched by news that he and his wife, the former Wallis Simpson, had leased a mansion in Paris. Shortly before the auction was due to take place in the spring of 1939, the Irish government bought the estate for the Department of Lands. The contents were then auctioned separately.

The hopes of locals that they would at last get their hands on the land that some of them had been seeking for so many years were disappointed. The new owner, the Department of Lands, announced that it intended to keep the forests that Ardilaun had sown. The Fianna Fáil Minister for Lands, Gerald Boland, told the Dáil that the forestry section had taken it over and there would not be enough land suitable for division left to relieve congestion in the surrounding area. "There are so many employees entitled to land that there would not be one acre left to be given to people other than those employees," he said. "We propose to start a good forest centre there and give as much employment as possible and try to make it one of the best forest centres in the country." It was a very difficult position, he added: "It is a pity the place had to be closed, because it gave great employment."[29] The castle and 170 acres of land surrounding it were leased to Noel Huggard of a well-known family of Kerry hoteliers.

Hard on the heels of these developments came another decision which appeared to signal even more strongly a Guinness withdrawal from Ireland: Rupert decided to hand over the chief Iveagh residence in Ireland, the family home in St Stephen's Green, to the Irish state. The last Guinness party held in the luxurious house – soon to be named Iveagh House and to become the home of the Department of Foreign Affairs – was an afternoon affair for 700 members of the brewery's staff and their wives held on 15 July 1939. They were all welcomed by Rupert and Gwendolen (Lord and Lady Iveagh), their son and daughter-in-law, Arthur Onslow Edward and Elizabeth (Lord and Lady Elveden) and Ernest's wife, Marie

Clothilde. In a brief address to them, Rupert said the house was about to enter a new period of usefulness to the government and nation and Farmleigh was a far more convenient residence for him and his family. He urged them all to contradict the rumours that Guinness was leaving Dublin; anyone who saw the brewery would realise that departure was impossible.[30] His denial of the rumours clearly had little immediate effect as he repeated it again at the company's annual general meeting in London a few weeks later, saying that "all the rumours that have appeared in the press with regard to our leaving Éire are without foundation".

The contents of Iveagh House were sold by auction over nine days the following October: a total of 27,000 people visited the house during the auction, presumably mostly to see it and its contents rather than to buy. The final handover of the building to the state took place ten days before Christmas without much ceremony between representatives of the long-serving Guinness family solicitors, Fred Sutton, the Board of Works (which had bought many of the contents at the auction) and Battersby's Auctioneers.

As much by accident as by design, Guinness survived the economic and political turbulence of the inter-war years under Rupert's stewardship. His main interest continued to be farming; he generally took the guidance of his executives at Arthur Guinness when it came to brewery matters; and he astutely extended the family's investments in Canada, especially in Vancouver, as well as in the United States.

Rupert played less of a political role as his life went on, speaking only rarely in the House of Lords but never losing an opportunity to speak up for Guinness, the family and the stout. One of his best remembered contributions (but not, as some stories have it, his only contribution) came during a debate on a bill to control drink advertising. A Welsh Liberal peer and temperance supporter, Lord Rhayader, was inveighing against this "dangerous trade" and complaining that the public had no protection against what he considered to be its lying advertisements. He went on, becoming specific:

Lord Rhayader: I see advertisements all over the place –
    "Guinness is good for you."
Lord Iveagh: It is true.

Lord Rhayader: It is a matter of opinion, perhaps.

Lord Iveagh: My word is as good as yours.

Lord Rhayader: I am told that if I put up "Guinness is bad for
   you"...

Lord Iveagh: It would be untrue.

Lord Rhayader: Well, I have no doubt that if I did that I should
   be liable to a libel action and I should have to justify every
   word that I said. It is not quite equal treatment between us.
   I can, of course, denounce drink in general, but if I
   denounce the drink manufactured by a particular
   manufacturer then I am in danger of judgment in a libel
   action.[31]

Rupert reputedly never drank alcohol except for one bottle of
Guinness every day. He clearly believed his own advertising and his
long life did nothing to refute it.

CHAPTER ELEVEN

Adventures and Misadventures

"Fritzi of Prussia came to see me, and told me of his engagement to my sister-in-law Brigid: I am entranced, and was so moved that in a sad flash I remembered the days when we were all so happy and did not know it."

"CHIPS" CHANNON MP, diary entry for 11 December 1945[1]

By the 1930s the Guinnesses were making the headlines as often for their lifestyles as for the source of their fortunes. The next generation of eligible and extremely rich heirs and heiresses had come, or were coming, of age and gracing the society pages of the day. Their parents were not yet finished either, leading their occasionally idiosyncratic lives, none more so than Walter whose adventures in the 1930s sound like those of a real-life Indiana Jones as he cruised the world, exploring distant lands, seeking out lost tribes and bringing back exotic specimens of wild-life.

Edward Iveagh's three sons had inherited his interest in sailing and developed it into a passion which they were rich enough to indulge to whatever extent took their fancy. The three were regulars at the annual regatta in Cowes from their early adult years, each with his own yacht which were as well-known for their parties as for their racing achievements. At a party on board Walter's yacht there in 1913 a 23-year-old woman named Agnes Cuff became pregnant; she subsequently gave birth to a boy she christened Alec Guinness de Cuffe, who grew up to be famous as the actor and film star Sir Alec Guinness. Agnes, who sometimes adopted the surname de Cuffe, never revealed who the father was and

Alec Guinness once told the author John le Carré that she had slept with the entire crew of Walter's yacht and that his father was "probably the bloody cook".[2] Nevertheless, two of the Guinness brothers, Walter and Ernest, were prime suspects, in that order; Walter, 33 at the time, was known for his piercing blue eyes and, although short in stature, his perfect proportions.[3] According to family tradition, he also paid Agnes money subsequently for the upkeep of the child, not because he admitted fatherhood but in order to cover up for one of his cousins, whom he believed was the father. On the other hand, Agnes also received payments from a Scottish banker, Andrew Geddes, who thought that he was the father: he continued to pay her until his death in 1928 and left Alec a small inheritance when he reached 21 years of age.

As well as creating gossip and scandal, the three brothers' passion for sailing almost cost them all their lives: each suffered a shipwreck, in one of which a number of people died. Rupert's shipwreck happened, as we have seen, while he was on a German torpedo boat in the North Sea in 1903. Incredibly, Ernest's and Walter's both happened in the same area – Killary Harbour in the west of Ireland – and within a year of each other. Walter was sailing back to Galway from Killary Harbour with two women companions and a crew of six officers and 26 men on board his 1,447-ton motor yacht *Roussalka* on 25 August 1933 when it struck Fratlin Rock off the mouth of Killary. The vessel was in a bank of dense fog at the time and the sea was heavy with "half a gale" blowing. It was holed, listed badly and sank within an hour. All on board managed to clamber into two motor boats, a cutter and a dinghy, and make their way back up Killary harbour to the Leenane Hotel and subsequently to Castle MacGarrett, the County Mayo home of Lord Oranmore and Browne, who was later to marry Walter's niece Oonagh.

Walter was typically sang-froid about the incident, decrying the dramatic initial reports about them being up to their waists in water as the yacht sank under them in seven minutes. He praised the crew's actions and absolved the captain from any blame for the mishap, describing the area of coast as an absolute archipelago of rocks. His only regret, he told reporters as he made his way back to London by train and boat via Dublin and Holyhead, was the loss of all the mementoes of his travels which had been on board. He had crossed the Atlantic four times in the vessel, visited the South Sea Islands and the coast of Alaska and other areas. "During my travels I picked up quite a large number of priceless relics and I am sorry to say all have been lost," he said. "I have also lost a considerable number of very valuable books, which are absolutely irreplaceable, and also my sporting rifles." Among the rescued, however, were his two pet monkeys who, he said, simply clung to him as he got on board a motorboat. He declined to identify his female companion who arrived back in Euston Station in London with him, and the reporter for *The Times* was too gentlemanly to name her for his readers.[4]

The *Roussalka* had been built in 1903 as a cross-channel ferry named the *Brighton* which served the Newhaven–Dieppe route and was converted into a yacht by Walter. She was insured for £50,000 and it was expected that salvage would be possible: she was not lying in deep water, as her masts were still visible. He didn't waste much time replacing her: he bought her sister ship, the 273-foot, 1,426-ton *Dieppe*, which was also serving on the Newhaven–Dieppe route, renamed her the *Rosaura* and began converting her into a luxury motor yacht to continue his adventures.

Ernest's shipwreck had more tragic consequences. He had two ocean-going yachts, *Fantome I* and *Fantome II*, an auxiliary barque he had bought from the Duke of Westminster in which he cruised and also used for entertaining annually at Cowes during its regatta. Ernest was a veteran sailor and had gone on at least one round-the-world cruise, taking his three teenage daughters with him for most of a year, in the early 1920s. In September 1934, he and a group of friends, including his cousins, Beauchamp Kerr-Pearse, a 63-year-old retired major who had spent many years in Australia and India, and Kerr-Pearse's daughter Elizabeth, arrived at Ashford Castle. The following day they travelled to Killary Harbour where the *Fantome II* was moored. Shortly after noon that day, 26 September, Ernest decided to take his cousins and two other guests, Edward Gordon Peake, one of the Cambridge graduates who had become a brewer at James's Gate and his private secretary, Osmond Baker, for a spin on his speedboat. Ossie Baker was as enthusiastic a sailor and aviator as Ernest: both had got their pilots' licences on the same day in

1929. Two members of the *Fantome II's* crew, chief engineer Albert Foulger and able seaman Edwin White also went with them. The harbour was calm, although a storm was dying down out to sea as they raced towards the mouth of the fjord at high speed. Ernest was at the helm amidships with Kerr-Pearse and Foulger beside him; Peake, Baker and Elizabeth were on the seats behind them and White, the sailor, was in the stern.

The speedboat was travelling at full speed of up to 50 miles an hour as it came back towards the *Fantome II* along the south side of Killary. It was less than a mile away when the yacht's chief officer, Archibald Frogbrook, who was watching it through a telescope, saw it sheer suddenly to port, its bow rise up and then sink, stern first. He raised the alarm and two launches set off from the *Fantome II* to the rescue. When they arrived, they found Ernest floating in the water in his oilskins and Elizabeth clinging to a floating cushion. They were in an exhausted state and were picked up along with Baker, Ernest's secretary, who had a broken arm. Shortly afterwards, they found the chief engineer, Foulger, floating in the sea: he appeared to be still alive but efforts to resuscitate him back on the yacht failed. There was no sign of Kerr-Pearse, the brewer Peake or the sailor White. The survivors were brought back to the yacht in a state of shock and exhaustion.

The accident was believed at first to have been caused by the speedboat hitting something in the water: a log was subsequently found floating in the area but showed no signs of an impact. It was also suggested that the boat's driveshaft may have broken and ruptured the hull. At the inquest a week later, Ernest gave evidence in his cabin on board the yacht where he was still in bed. The boat had swerved suddenly to the left, he told the west Galway coroner, M.J. Allen; he had tried to correct it but it capsized to the right and they were all thrown into the water. He caught hold of a floating cushion and he and Elizabeth tried to save her father but failed to keep him afloat. By the time the launches arrived, he was in a dazed and exhausted condition, he said. He was aware of being hauled on board the launch but then lost consciousness. Ernest believed that a wave had struck the boat and driven it to the left and then another wave struck from the right and turned it over.

Peake's body was found on the day of the inquest and a local doctor gave evidence that he had been killed by a blow which had fractured his neck. The bodies of the two other victims, Kerr-Pearse and White, were recovered during the following week.[5]

Ernest arrived back in London the following month where his doctor ordered him into hospital for an operation. Neither the purpose of the operation nor the nature of his injuries is clear: reading between the lines – one newspaper report described him as a highly sensitive man who felt keenly the loss of life on his boat[6] – it seems probable that he suffered some form of nervous breakdown or post-traumatic stress disorder. His wife, Cloe, was also hospitalised for several weeks and was said to have suffered a nervous breakdown "caused by anxiety and continued attendance on her husband".[7] Ernest also appears to have injured a leg in the incident, leaving him with a slight limp thereafter. The *Fantome II* was back in Cowes the following summer as usual but it seems clear that the accident in Killary and the deaths of his friends and colleagues had a deep effect on Ernest. It may have been among the reasons he subsequently visited Ashford less frequently than in previous years and a factor in his decision to sell the estate four years later.

However, their experiences did nothing to diminish his brother Walter's interest in sailing and exploring.

———— ❧ ————

By the time of the party on his yacht at which Alec Guinness was conceived, Walter was married to Lady Evelyn Erskine, with one child and another on the way, and also had an exotic mistress, a Russian Jewish heiress, Ida Rubinstein, with whom he had a lifelong relationship. Ida was an extremely beautiful dancer, actress and, later, impresario who had caused a sensation in St Petersburg with a private production of Oscar Wilde's *Salomé* in which she had ended the Dance of the Seven Veils more or less naked. She had come to Paris as part of Sergei Diaghilev's *Ballets Russes* and created another sensation there in the title role of its *Cléopâtre*. The American artist Romaine Brooks, who painted several pictures of her and was, for a time, her lesbian lover, described her thus:

She seemed to me even more beautiful when off stage; like some heraldic bird delicately knit together by the finest of bone structures giving flexibility to curveless lines. The clothes she wore were beyond fashion, for without effort everything contributed to make her seem like an apparition. . . . I remember one cold snowy morning walking with her around the Longchamps race course. Everything was white and Ida wore an ermine coat. It was open and exposed the frail chest and slender neck which emerged from a white feathery garment. Her face was sharply cut with long golden eyes and a delicate bird-like nose; her partly veiled head with dark hair moving gracefully from the temples as though the wind were smoothing it back . . . she possessed . . . mystery. Hers was a mask whose outward glow emanated from a disturbed inner depth.[8]

Walter met her in Paris about 1910 and they fell for each other, in spite of Ida's lesbian relationships with Brooks and other women; he appears to have been the only man with whom she had a sexual relationship. Their affair lasted some twenty years and was followed by lifelong friendship; during it he helped finance some of her productions, kept a house in the rue de Poitiers in Paris to be close to her, and she accompanied him on many of his travels to Africa and elsewhere. (One of their common interests was keeping wild animals as pets: Walter was always accompanied by monkeys, while Ida, to the terror of visitors, kept a panther as a pet which occasionally clawed and drew blood from her.) Her first production in Paris was *Le Martyre de Saint Sébastien* for which Claude Debussy wrote the music and another of her close friends, the Italian poet and proto-fascist Gabriele d'Annunzio, wrote the verse. *Le Martyre* was denounced by the Catholic Church, and the Archbishop of Paris threatened excommunication to Catholics who went to it because Ida, a woman, a Jew and a lesbian, was portraying St Sebastian (who had been a gay icon since the Renaissance). She later commissioned Maurice Ravel to write what became his most famous work, *Bolero*. According to the Ida Rubinstein legend, Walter spent up to a third of his fortune on her but that is extremely unlikely, although he helped to fund many of her projects. Walter was good with money and left his descendants extremely well off and, besides, Ida was also very rich in her own right from her father's grain and other businesses in the Ukraine.

Although they met regularly in Paris, travelled together on expeditions abroad, including hunting lions in Africa, and their relationship was widely known in their own circles, their affair was conducted with discretion, not least because he was a Conservative MP and had made some powerful political enemies early in his career over the Marconi scandal in 1912/13, which involved Liberal government ministers, including Lloyd George, buying shares in a Marconi company shortly after the cabinet had decided to give Marconi a contract to provide wireless services throughout the British Empire and before the decision was announced publicly; the scandal was revealed obliquely by *Outlook*, a periodical Walter owned. The wisdom of Walter and Ida's discretion in avoiding public scandal became evident in 1917 when Ida's husband, whom she had married for convenience in Russia and never slept with in another *mariage blanche*, turned up in Paris seeking a divorce. She refused in order to avoid publicity about adultery and the damage it could do to Walter's political career. The husband hired a private detective to find evidence of their affair but he failed to unearth anything and the husband went away and left her alone thereafter.[9]

Walter's political career progressed steadily in the 1920s as he moved up the ranks of the Conservative Party in the House of Commons, becoming under-secretary at the War Office in 1922 and Financial Secretary to the Treasury in the mid-1920s. In that position, he came into direct contact with the then Chancellor of the Exchequer, Winston Churchill, who was back in the Tory Party after 20 years in the Liberal Party. They had already known each other as political opponents for many years but struck up a close political and personal friendship while working together in government; Walter was just the kind of man Churchill liked – personally brave, highly adventurous, slightly eccentric, somewhat rakish and extremely rich.[10] Churchill himself later described Walter as "a most agreeable, intelligent and unusual friend". Another description of him after his death by one of his nieces' husbands, Henry "Chips" Channon, portrayed him as

. . . an extraordinary man, colossally rich, well-meaning, intelligent, scrupulous, yet a viveur, and the only modern Guinness to play a social or political role, being far less detached than most of his family. He collected yachts, fish, monkeys and women. He had a passion for the sea, and for long expeditions to remote places. He had a curious frenzy for the very early Gothic, and all his many houses were in that style, and hideous . . . Walter with his steely-grey hair, turquoise eyes, had a distinguished appearance, and also the curious Guinness money traits. He was careful of his huge fortune, though he had probably about three millions.[11]

As Financial Secretary to the Treasury, Walter had the task of introducing the Bill to facilitate Britain's return to the gold standard in 1925, arguing that it would provide "the inestimable boon" of greater stability in the exchange value of the pound and keep prices stable.[12] Shortly afterwards, he made it into the cabinet as Minister of Agriculture and Fisheries, a post in which he tried to revive the depressed farming business by promoting sugar beet as a crop and championing a controversial policy of de-rating farmland as a method of subsidising farmers. He held the position for four years until the 1929 general election in which the Conservatives were defeated and the Labour Party came to power for the second time.

Two years later, the Labour Prime Minister Ramsay MacDonald acquiesced in the formation of a national government to try to deal with the Depression which followed the Wall Street crash: among its measures was the abandonment of the gold standard which had required a rigorously balanced budget. Churchill and his political friends, including Walter, were noticeably excluded from the cabinet. Early in 1931 Walter told his constituency organisation in Bury St Edmunds that he would not contest the next general election because he could no longer reconcile the demands of the House of Commons on his time with "the claims of his private affairs and his health".[13] The election came in October that year and he stepped down and was made a baron shortly afterwards in the New Year's honours list "for political and public services". He took the title Baron Moyne (possibly after Moyne Abbey in County Mayo), adorned his coat of arms with two Singhalese macaques, and an interesting choice of motto in the phrase, *Noli Judicare* (Judge Not).

The new Lord Moyne spent the rest of the 1930s touring the world as an adventurer, explorer and sometimes conducting official inquiries on behalf of the British government throughout the empire. The first of these was in Kenya in 1932 where he conducted an inquiry into the financial state of the region. In most of his travels, he needed to have a goal, whether it was a self-selected or an official one. After his Kenyan task, he went off to the Galápagos Islands to bring back to London Zoo four marine iguanas, or lizards which were up to three feet long, five Galápagan doves and a flightless cormorant. The search for exotic lizards, interspersed with official investigations and occasional holiday cruises, became a pattern for the decade. He took Winston and Clementine Churchill around the eastern Mediterranean in the summer of 1934 on board the *Rosaura*. They visited all the countries bordering the sea, especially Turkey, in which Walter was particularly interested. Churchill painted views of Rhodes and Jerusalem and worked on the script of a documentary film for King George V's silver jubilee the following summer for which the film producer Alexander Korda had offered him £10,000.[14] (The film was never completed because of an arcane law which required full-length documentaries to be released provisionally six months before their official release, which meant it would miss the jubilee. However, Churchill got a large segment of the money from Korda and, in the best journalistic fashion, recycled the material for a series of articles for the *Daily Mail* for which he was paid handsomely. He ended up earning more than the £10,000 originally promised for the documentary.)

A few months later, Moyne invited the Churchills to join him again on a more extensive cruise to the Pacific in search of Komodo dragons, ten-foot-long monitor lizards which weighed up to 150 pounds and had been "discovered" in the Dutch East Indies (now Indonesia) in 1907. Churchill, who found the cruises restrictive, declined but Clementine accepted and joined the *Rosaura* at Messina in Sicily for what she herself later described as "this 'Big Game' '*Boys own* annual'" adventure.[15] Also on board at that stage was Walter's cousin and fellow Guinness company director, Kenelm Lee Guinness, the motor-racing driver and former holder of the world land speed record; his wife; and Terence Philip, an urbane, forty-something Russian-born art dealer in London.

Their host Walter joined them in Rangoon in Burma, flying there with his new mistress, Lady Vera Broughton, on what was seen as a dangerously long flight from England. (His sexual relationship with Ida Rubinstein appears to have ended by this time but they remained close friends.) Vera was the wife of Sir Jock Delves Broughton, who would become notorious in 1941 as the suspect for a celebrated murder in Happy Valley in Kenya. He was tried and acquitted but was almost certainly guilty of shooting Lord Erroll, who was having an affair with Vera's successor, Delves Broughton's new young wife, the 26-year-old Diana Caldwell, whom he had married less than six months before the murder.[16]

Vera, born Vera Edyth Griffith-Boscawen, was in her early forties when she began her affair with Moyne, who was approaching his mid-fifties. Described by the Dictionary of National Biography as a cold *femme fatale* and a "hard pleasure-loving woman", she had developed an interest in big game hunting in Kenya in the early 1920s and was clearly as adventurous as Moyne. She had had two affairs before she met and left Delves Broughton for Walter, becoming his regular companion on most, if not all, his adventures for the remainder of the 1930s.

With everybody on board, the *Rosaura* set off on their dragon hunt by a very circuitous route, visiting New Zealand and Australia, Borneo, Bali, New Guinea, Celebes and Moluccas, and the Solomon Islands before arriving off Komodo island, the home of the dragons in what is now Indonesia, in March 1935. Along the way, they had explored numerous locations and Clementine had spent a lot of time with Terence Philip, who was seven years her junior, and with whom she "fell romantically in love".[17] She was also much taken with their ocean-going adventures, although she and Philip were not as keen on the long hours spent shark fishing off Australia as Walter and Vera were. "This is the genuine article," she wrote to Winston, "unchartered seas, unexplored territory, stark naked savages."[18]

Walter himself described the voyage as "an effort to get beyond the regions of semi-civilized natives dressed in cheap pyjamas or badly-fitting European clothes and to find human and animal life in primitive conditions". In an article in *The Times* in May 1935, illustrated by photographs taken by Vera Broughton, he described their visits to some of the least-visited areas of the Moluccas where, they were warned, natives were apt to shoot poisoned arrows without provocation. He also described their visit to the three crater lakes in the *caldera* of the Kelimutu volcano on Flores island – "this wonderful freak of nature" – which change their colours periodically: when Moyne and his friends were there, one of the lakes was "the deep red of clotting blood, the others of different shades of jade green and turquoise blue". At Rennell Island in the Solomon Islands, they exchanged cigarettes for some of the Polynesian inhabitants' primitive wooden axes while Vera photographed the girls. On nearby Bellona Island they received a less friendly welcome.

> As soon as we set foot ashore we were met by four fierce-looking men carrying spears. For some reason they were angry and yelled furious abuse at our guide. To prevent any suspicion of our intentions we had come unarmed, and when I went up to the leader and shook his hand his hostility melted away, though he still seemed much annoyed with our guide.
>
> About 50 yards back from the beach there was a way up the rocks to what appeared by the thatched roofs to be a considerable village. This path was guarded by sentries, and we saw a large number of natives, armed with spears and bows and arrows, lined along the low cliff wall at the top of the path. Nearby was a small house to which the natives on the beach signed me to come. As soon, however, as our little party began to approach the previous expression of fury and torrent of protest returned, and we gathered that the indignation was caused by the presence of the ladies. Hearing "Tambu" frequently repeated, we concluded that the house was one of the Tambu houses of which we had read, reserved entirely for men. We therefore judged it best to return to the ship and go to Tulagi [one of the Solomon Islands] and get information and an interpreter before attempting to explore further.[19]

The dragon hunt on Komodo island yielded numerous smaller dragons and three were kept to bring back to England on board the *Rosaura*. Walter and his friends caught them using a large wooden trap built by the zoo for the expedition before its departure. It operated on the same basis as a mousetrap but with a heavy door that slammed shut once the bait, usually a chicken, was disturbed. The trap was made to accommodate ten-foot long reptiles but the party saw some that were twelve feet long. Vera took photographs of some in their "lair" on the island which were also published in *The Times*. One of the captured dragons got out of its cage in the Red Sea on the way back, slipped overboard and swam away: the other two were presented to London Zoo.

Moyne was back in the same part of the world again in late 1935 and early 1936 with a couple of ornithologists and the keeper of London Zoo's reptile house among his guests. Vera was there too as photographer and the party also included his nephew Arthur, Lord Elveden, the son and heir of Lord Iveagh. Arthur Elveden, as he was generally known, admired his Uncle Walter and seemed to be following a similar path: he was to become a member of Suffolk County Council and was said to be keeping an eye out for a parliamentary seat before the Second World War intervened. They gathered up exotic animals, reptiles and birds – more than a hundred were presented to the zoo on their return[20] – on their cruise but the centrepiece this time was an exploration of the Ramu river in Papua New Guinea. The river had been discovered by German explorers in the late nineteenth century but was not fully mapped. Moyne and his friends, including Vera and Elveden, went some 170 miles upstream where they discovered a race of pygmies, described later in *The Times* as "not darker than a very sunburned Englishman" and up to four feet six inches in height. It was a difficult river to navigate and the *Rosaura's* two launches in which they were travelling upriver were both holed and sunk in separate incidents 70 miles and 120 miles up the river from the coast. After the second incident, the party pitched camp with enough supplies for five days on a sandbank while Elveden and a local guide set off back down the river in a dinghy to get help. It took them four days to get back to the *Rosaura* and organise help, which took a further four days to reach the stranded party. They then continued their journey upriver for another 50 miles in an open launch to the area near where the pygmies lived and some were brought by other river people to meet them.

271

Although other tribes in the area feared the pygmies and left when they appeared, Moyne found them very friendly, light-hearted, quick-witted and intelligent.[21] Artefacts including battle-axes, bows and arrows and shields were traded with the pygmies for a variety of goods ranging from curtain rings to axes: they, Vera's photographs, and other artefacts picked up along the way went on display at Moyne's house in Grosvenor Place in London before being distributed among the British Museum, the Royal Anthropological Institute and other institutions.[22]

The following year, he was off in Honduras, once again holding an exhibition at his Grosvenor Place home on his return: the exhibits this time included film, taken by himself and his younger son Murtogh. Walter published two books about his travels, with photographs by Vera Broughton: *Walkabout: A Journey in Lands between the Pacific and Indian Oceans* (1936); and *Atlantic Circle* (1938).

In the midst of all his travels he somehow found time to chair a government commission to investigate the British film industry but it was not long before he was off again. In 1938, he invited the Churchills to come with him on another cruise to the Caribbean at Christmas, this time as chairman of an official commission to investigate the social and economic conditions in the area, which was set up following serious rioting in Jamaica during the summer of 1938. Churchill, depressed by Prime Minister Neville Chamberlain's appeasement of Adolf Hitler, wrote back to him just before the "peace in our time" Munich Agreement that he was looking forward to an interlude of sunshine and peace but added: ". . . we seem to be very near the bleak choice between War and Shame. My feeling is that we shall choose Shame, and then have War thrown in a little later on even more adverse terms than at present."[23] In the event, however, Churchill did not go on the cruise but Clementine did: it turned out to be not at all like their earlier idyllic East Indies trip. The main reason was that Walter's attempt to mix business and pleasure did not work: the conditions and poverty of the local people cast an air of gloom over the *Rosaura* and its passengers. Relations between Clementine and Moyne and his mistress Vera also soured when they were in Barbados early in the new year of 1939. They were listening to a radio broadcast from London one evening in which somebody attacked Churchill, when Vera responded "hear, hear".

Clementine was upset that the remark was aimed at her and even more upset when Walter remained silent. She withdrew to her cabin, wrote a note to him and went ashore the next day and booked a passage on board the liner *Cuba* which was sailing for England the following day. Vera called on her, presumably at Walter's behest, and pleaded with her not to leave but they ended up having an argument. Clementine went back to England but Moyne's friendship with her and with Churchill does not appear to have suffered.[24]

Not long afterwards, in March 1939, Moyne had to cut short his own time in the Caribbean because of the illness of his wife Evelyn, who was diagnosed with cancer and underwent a major operation in London. Described by her one-time daughter-in-law, Diana Mitford, as very pretty, slight, fair-haired and blue-eyed, she and Walter had gone their separate ways for some time. He was absent for long periods on his travels and in parliament as an MP while she spent much of her time at their country home, Baliffscourt in Sussex where she pursued her interest in medievalism. Walter had bought a stretch of the coastline, which developers had had their eyes on, from a "Colonel" Barker.[25] The Moynes lived there mainly in wooden huts while Evelyn began the building of Baliffscourt, which she conceived as a medieval house. Stones were taken from ruins, including monasteries; gnarled trees were bought elsewhere, uprooted and replanted in the grounds; she sometimes shot up new wooden beams with a revolver to make them look old and riddled with woodworm; china or glassware were not allowed in the house, only pewter (glass wedding presents could be got rid of with a good kick, she advised Diana.)

She always spoke in what Diana described as a small hard voice, not so much a whisper, but barely audible. She kept a dog called Lady which bit men only: regular male visitors knew to arrive wearing riding boots as protection against it. She hated formal gardens and nice flowers, preferring weeds and wild flowers. When travelling by train to London, she brought bags of weeds and wild flowers to toss out of the window into the well-tended farmland of southern England. As Minister of Agriculture, Walter was not amused. She tried to carry through the medieval theme to their houses in London as well, encouraging servants to let the fires smoulder and spread smoke around the Grosvenor Place mansion to darken the wood and give it an ancient feel. She also had a playful side: when her second child Murtogh asked if he could have a slide in the house like one he had been on at a fairground, she had a huge slide installed from top to bottom on one of the house's two staircases. With Walter, when there, wandering around with a monkey on his shoulder and Lady Evelyn whispering and pursuing her medieval interests, their smoke-filled houses were unusual places to visit.[26]

Evelyn appeared to be recovering after her operation but suffered a relapse and died in their Paris apartment on 21 July at the age of 56. She was cremated at a private ceremony and a memorial service was held some days later in St Margaret's in Westminster. Vera Broughton was among those at the service, with her husband Jock Delves Broughton. She began divorce proceedings against him shortly afterwards on the grounds of his adultery. He did not contest it and she was granted a decree *nisi* and costs in April 1940; it was made absolute the following October. She may have hoped or expected that Walter would marry her but he did not.

By then, however, the *Boy's Own* adventure world they had shared throughout the 1930s was over and had been replaced by the world of war.

———

The complications created by the first Lord Iveagh's bequests began to become apparent as the sixth generation of the first Arthur's descendants came of age. It was undoubtedly equitable, but by dividing his shares in Arthur Guinness Son & Company equally among his three sons, Edward Iveagh effectively set up three equal branches of the family in relation to the brewery – the Iveagh branch (Rupert and his descendants); Ernest's branch; and the Moyne branch (Walter and his descendants). Rupert, Ernest and Walter were equal shareholders in the company and members of its board and, as their children grew up, the prospect emerged of the board accommodating another generation of Guinnesses. While Edward Iveagh had been advised when floating the company back in 1886 to have as many Guinnesses as possible on the board, family members were now in danger of swamping it. Even worse for the future, few of the new directors brought any significant business skills or even a high level of interest to it: as one of the following generation's directors admitted, the executives who ran the brewery in this era were always much smarter at business than the family directors who controlled it.[27] The balance had changed from the previous 170 years or so when there had never been any doubt that a Guinness was in charge of all aspects of the brewery's business.

Of Edward's Iveagh's ten surviving grandchildren by the 1930s, only three were male. Of those, Walter's younger son Murtogh effectively ruled himself out of the business by moving to New York and adopting a lifestyle unsuited to business; he stayed up all night and slept during the day when the curtains were kept closed and lights on so that visitors tended to lose track of whether it was day or night outside.[28] That left Walter's eldest son Bryan, who was more interested in the arts and literature than in business, although he accepted the duties imposed by his position throughout his life; and Rupert's son Arthur Elveden who was destined to inherit his earldom and his role as head of the family and brewery.

It was not considered appropriate at the time that any of Edward Iveagh's seven grand-daughters would be directors, although their husbands could be and were. That resulted in an odd collection of directors of widely varying abilities having a hand in running the company for different periods as marriages came and went. The Guinnesses, male and female, were obviously great "catches" because of their by now legendary wealth; Ernest's three daughters, Aileen, Maureen and Oonagh, in particular, were also known as the "Golden Guinness Girls" for their beauty. In the hothouse world of aristocratic coming-out parties and mating games several made hasty decisions and ended up married and divorced while still in their twenties. "The sisters are all witches, lovely ones to be sure, but witches nonetheless," film director John Huston once said of them. "They are all transparent-skinned, with pale hair and light blue eyes. You can very nearly see through them. They are quite capable of changing swinish folk into real swine before your very eyes, and turning them back again without their even knowing it."[29]

The first, and one of the briefest, of these Guinness directors-by-marriage was Philip Leyland Kindersley, a financier who married Ernest's youngest daughter, Oonagh, shortly after her 19th birthday in

1929. Kindersley and she had two children, Tessa and Gay, and he was elected to the board of Guinness at its annual meeting in 1934 but remained there for less than a year. His departure coincided with the break-up of the marriage in 1935. Kindersley sought a divorce on the basis of Oonagh's adultery with Dominick Browne, Lord Oranmore and Browne, at hotels in Folkestone and Vienna in February of that year. Lady Oranmore and Browne divorced Dominick at the same time, citing the same reasons, and Oonagh and Dominick were married six months later in April 1936.[30] Browne, who had the distinction of having been a member of the House of Lords for 72 years by the time of his death in 2001 at the age of 100 and never having spoken there, had moved back to the family's ancestral home at Castle MacGarrett, near Claremorris in County Mayo by then.[31] Oonagh already had an exotic home in Ireland, Luggala, set dramatically in the deep valley of Lough Dan in the Wicklow mountains, which her father had given her as a wedding present when she married Kindersley.

Kindersley's departure from the board of Guinness helped to make way for the two senior men among the grandchildren, Bryan and Arthur Elveden, to join the company as directors in 1935. Bryan Guinness was as different from his father Walter as Rupert had been from his father Edward. He was not a man of action like his father, uninterested in exploring the world, in sports or the shooting and hunting life. He had polio while a child at Eton and was sensitive, often vague, especially in later life, and somewhat dreamy. He was interested in writing and became part of a literary *Brideshead Revisited* set whose most famous members included the author of that novel, Evelyn Waugh. He studied law and became a barrister but gave it up when it became clear that he was not getting any briefs in his London chambers because it was believed that he did not need the money – which he did not. Thereafter, he concentrated on his writing, eventually producing a respectable body of work that extended to at least six collections of poetry, three novels, three memoirs, a play and a number of children's books.

Bryan also married young, catching his first sight of his future wife, Diana Mitford – reputedly the most beautiful of that era's most famous collection of aristocratic English sisters – about 1926 at a fancy dress ball in her family's old house near Oxford when she was about 16. The following year they became engaged unofficially: she was 17, he 23. Not surprisingly, her parents were less than delighted; more surprisingly, her mother seems to have thought Bryan was too rich, and the couple were persuaded to wait a year. In a typical Bryan sentence, he later described popping the question "somewhere out of doors, during a dance in Grosvenor Square I believe, though I have no clear recollection of where this important event occurred".[32] They were married in January 1929 in a high society wedding in St Margaret's in Westminster, the location of most major Guinness weddings.

Diana was initially happy to be taken into Bryan's high society circle of urban and rich friends, among whom they were well-known hosts: Evelyn Waugh dedicated his novel *Vile Bodies* to the young couple. But Bryan actually wanted a rural and more pastoral life and bought Biddesden House in Wiltshire in 1931. They had two sons, Jonathan (born 1930) and Desmond (born 1931), before Diana began an affair with the charismatic Oswald Mosley, the former Conservative and Labour MP who was on the point of forming the British Union of Fascists. Mosley was married but Diana left Bryan, taking her two sons with her, to live openly as his mistress in 1933. Efforts by both the Guinness and Mitford families to break up this arrangement failed. Walter Moyne and Diana's father, David Freeman-Mitford, Lord Redesdale, both called on Mosley and tried to persuade him to end the affair; he refused to be lectured by them or to give her up.[33] She was equally determined and divorced Bryan in 1934. When Mosley's wife died unexpectedly, he and Diana were married secretly at the Berlin home of the Nazi Party's propaganda genius Joseph Goebbels in October 1936. Adolf Hitler came to dinner afterwards and presented the newly-weds with a silver-framed picture of himself. Throughout her long life – she died in August 2003 at the age of 93 – Diana remained a controversial figure over her continuing defence of Mosley and her refusal to renounce her earlier admiration for Hitler. While Diana was marrying Mosley, Bryan was marrying Elisabeth Nelson, who came from a Scottish family of well-known publishers, with whom he had four more sons and five daughters.

The heir to the earldom of Iveagh, Arthur Elveden, was 23 in 1935 when he travelled with his uncle Walter's expedition to the East Indies to meet the pygmies of Papua New Guinea. Although he much admired Walter, indicating a taste for adventure, he appears to have been a steady young man, knowing that he would assume at some stage the leadership of the family and the chairmanship of the brewery, which now seemed to be accepted as an inevitable part of the Iveagh inheritance. Back in England, he married Lady Elizabeth Hare, the sister of the fifth Earl of Listowel, who was, unusually, a socialist and Labour Party member of the House of Lords, in July 1936. Among the 14 children who attended the bride, six were the offspring of Arthur's first cousins.

The next director to join the board was one of the most colourful in the assorted additions by marriage to the family. Henry "Chips" Channon was a charming American Anglophile who became famous later as a man-about-Westminster, gossip and diarist and had married the eldest of Rupert and Gwendolen Iveagh's daughters, Lady Honor, in July 1933. At the time of the wedding, Channon was 36 and claiming to be 34 (his deduction of two years from his year of birth was later exposed by a newspaper; he admitted in his diaries that telling so many lies about his age made it difficult to remember his true age). He was known by everyone as Chips, a nickname whose precise origins is now lost. The most common story suggests that he once shared rooms with a man called Fish, another that it was a corruption of the family business running a fleet of ships on the Great Lakes from Chicago. Chips was passionately interested in European aristocracy and, after a spell at Oxford, British aristocracy. He despised the industrial democracy of America and, in his diaries, described himself thus:

> I have flair, intuition, great good taste but only second rate ambition: I am far too susceptible to flattery; I hate and am uninterested in all the things most men like such as sport, business, statistics, debates, speeches, war and the weather; but I am riveted by lust, furniture, glamour and society and jewels.[34]

He had an independent income from his father and grandfather and had written three books before his marriage; a novel entitled *Joan Kennedy*; a series of sketches about the horrors of American life in Chicago, *Paradise*

City; and a history, *The Ludwigs of Bavaria,* about the kind of life he admired. He never wrote anything else, other than the diaries which show him to be a good descriptive writer, gushing about the upper-class world he loved so much but saved by a mocking sense of himself. Within two years of his marriage to Lady Honor, he had achieved one of his main aims, membership of that most exclusive of London clubs, the House of Commons, and he had done so with minimal effort. His mother-in-law, Lady Gwendolen Iveagh, effectively handed over the Southend-on-Sea constituency to him. Why the Iveaghs did so is not clear: there were indications that their own son, Arthur Elveden, was considering a political career in the footsteps of his uncle Walter Moyne: he had, for instance, become a member of Suffolk County Council. He may, perhaps, have been seen as too young at that stage or his parents may not have wanted him to follow that road: in any event, like his father, he would have had to give it up on inheriting his title and move to the House of Lords.

Chips passionately loved the House of Commons for its gossips, intrigues and rituals but he had little interest in political ideas or in the substance of its debates. He attended frequently but spoke rarely, preferring to schmooze around the Palace of Westminster, picking up gossip and enjoying the set-piece parliamentary events. In retrospect, he had an unfortunate knack of picking the wrong side on almost all the great issues of his day: predictably, he hated the idea of communism, was probably not greatly enamoured of democracy, and had a soft spot for fascism, especially if attended by royalty. He was a strong supporter of the abdicated Edward VII and Wallis Simpson; he admired Mussolini, Hitler and Franco; passionately supported Chamberlain's appeasement policy; and was a close friend of Prince Paul of Yugoslavia, who as regent sided with Nazi Germany and was overthrown in a pro-British coup in 1941. He was also friendly with Joachim von Ribbentrop, Germany's ambassador in London who spent much of his time trying to persuade the British upper classes of the benefits of an Anglo-German pact. Chips and Honor attended the Berlin Olympics in 1936 as guests of the German government. They were bored by the Games but greatly taken by the lavish hospitality of Goebbels and Herman Göring, and electrified by occasional sightings of Hitler himself. Describing Hitler's arrival in the Olympic stadium, he wrote in his diary for 6 August 1936: "I was more excited than when I met Mussolini in 1926 in Perugia, and more stimulated, I am sorry to say, than when I was blessed by the Pope in 1920."[35]

Chips and Honor had one son, Paul, who was named after his godfather, Prince Paul of Yugoslavia, with whom Chips had once shared a house in England. However, the marriage began to fall apart in 1939 when Chips had a homosexual affair with Peter Coats, a landscape designer who was nicknamed Petticoats and described by the American writer Gore Vidal as "a classic English queen".[36] That led on to numerous other homosexual affairs, becoming as Tom Driberg, the Labour MP and journalist, described him, "one of the best known homosexuals in London, and . . . rich enough to rent almost any young man he fancied".[37] His gay philandering did not seem to upset the Guinnesses unduly: neither did the break-up of the marriage. Honor subsequently walked out on him, leaving him in the style to which he had become accustomed in their home in Belgrave Square in London and their country place, Kelvedon Hall in Essex, both of which had been bought with Guinness money. Chips continued to be a director on the Guinness board, although, judging by his diaries, his main involvement was to check the stock market listings every now and then to make sure the price of his own 20,000 Guinness shares was holding up. When they finally divorced in 1945, it was on the ground that Honor had deserted him: she did not contest the divorce and Chips was given custody of their son.[38]

Honor had indeed deserted him but whether that was the real, rather than the legal, reason for the divorce was doubtful; homosexual acts were still criminal offences in Britain at the time. Gore Vidal summed up Chips in his usual pithy fashion, "Sexually, he preferred men to women and royalty to either".[39] Chips' proclivities were clearly well known in his own circles but he was relatively discreet otherwise. Honor's desertion was prompted, if not by Chips' gay affairs, by falling for a Czech fighter pilot, Frantisek Svejdar, whom she met at a village dance in Hampshire during the war. They married after the divorce and after Frankie's (as he was known in the family) discharge from the RAF, moved to Ireland where they lived on the Phibblestown estate, near her cousin Aileen's estate at Luttrellstown Castle, to the west of Dublin, for most of the year, and on the island of Mustique for the remainder.

Chips subsequently set his sights on Terence Rattigan, the successful playwright whom he met at a dinner party and subsequently showered with expensive presents, including a gold Cartier cigarette box, an Aubusson tapestry, and an Augustus John drawing. Rattigan gave in eventually, telling friends apologetically (according to the jealous Driberg) "how can one not?", and a relationship lasting several years began. Chips and Rattigan both presented similar cheerful and successful faces to the world but were also given to bouts of melancholy and self-doubt. Chips claimed to have suggested *The Winslow Boy* as the title of the play Rattigan was writing at the time and he, Rattigan, dedicated it to Chips' son Paul "in the hope he will live to see a world in which this play will point no moral". There are also said to be elements of Chips and Rattigan himself in the portrait of the central character in another of Rattigan's most famous plays, *The Browning Version*. The affair ended when Rattigan went back to a former lover in spite of Chips' jealousy and his entreaties.[40]

Meanwhile, a forerunner of things to come for the Guinness family occurred with the tragic death of another of the company directors, Kenelm Lee Guinness, the former racing driver and adviser to the board on its first advertising campaign. He had had a serious accident in the San Sebastian Grand Prix in 1924 in which his on-board mechanic was killed and he suffered head and limb injuries himself. He gave up racing and was said to have been changed by the accident, suffering from serious head pains and, in later years, delusions that he was being pursued by gangs of American blackmailers. He gassed himself in his home at Kingston-on-Thames in April 1937 at the age of 49. At the inquest, his brother Sir Algernon Lee Guinness (the inheritor of Lord Ardilaun's baronetcy) said Kenelm had told him several weeks before his death that he had been practically a madman for the previous three years. "I said I had never noticed," Sir Algernon told the inquest. The coroner was given a sealed letter Kenelm had left with his executor: after reading it, he returned a verdict of suicide while of unsound mind.[41]

By the time the Second World War began, the Guinnesses straddled the range of opinions within the Conservative Party about Nazism and the resurgence of Germany. Given his interest in farming and the temper of the times, it was perhaps not surprising that Rupert Iveagh had dallied with the then fashionable questions of eugenics during the 1930s but he was politically a supporter of Chamberlain, who was a guest at Elveden as 1939 began. (On his way there, Chamberlain predicted that it would be a more tranquil year than the previous one.)[42] With the outbreak of war, the Elveden estate was required to produce more food, which it tried to do by bringing back into production areas that had long been seen as infertile, to augment all the land that Rupert had reclaimed over the previous decade. In a classic example of one hand of the bureaucracy not knowing what the other was doing, however, the military authorities decided to use part of the estate for tank training, as it had done during the First World War. While government instructions sought more agricultural production, the tanks rolled into Elveden, destroying hundreds of acres of crops, 20 miles of fencing and a thousand acres of arable land, which was badly needed to grow food. Protests from the Iveaghs went unheeded. Rupert promptly reclaimed other areas and experimented successfully with the making of silage in open pits, a practice subsequently used widely.[43] The British Army also requisitioned Elveden Hall, which later became the headquarters of the Eighth US Air Force after America joined the war and heavy bomber bases like Lakenheath and Mildenhall were created nearby on the flat lands of East Anglia.

At the start of the war, as the brewery provided free Guinness to the British Expeditionary Force heading off to France, Walter Moyne became chairman of the Polish Relief Fund and gave it part of his Grosvenor Place home as a headquarters in London. He also had matters closer to home in mind, intervening with security officials to make sure that his former daughter-in-law, Diana Mitford, was interned. Her current husband, Oswald Mosley, was locked up in June 1940 but she was left at large and effectively took over the running of the British Union of Fascists' office and administrative matters. On 25 June 1940, Walter wrote to a Conservative Party colleague, Lord Swinton (Philip Cunliffe-Lister), who headed a security committee, describing Diana as an "extremely dangerous character"; suggesting that they might lack evidence against her, he offered them just that.[44] The evidence included comments made by Diana in the presence of the governess of one of his grandsons (he did not specify whether it was Jonathan or Desmond). Among them was a comment that the sinking of the liner *Athenia* en route from Glasgow to Montreal via Belfast within hours of Britain declaring war on Germany on 3 September 1939 was "a good beginning". Diana was also said to have been triumphant and delighted when British forces were trapped by the German *blitzkrieg* across the Low Countries and into France. The governess had also checked Diana's diary and recorded the dates of her seven visits to Germany in 1937 and eight in 1938.

Walter noted (and the security file on Diana confirms) that it was widely believed that her frequent pre-war visits to Germany were for the purpose of bringing funds from the Nazis back to England for Mosley's fascists. The governess had no dates for 1939 because she had a serious operation that year, Walter explained. His letter added: "I feel it rather embarrassing to write you this letter and am sure you will understand that it would be very hard on the governess to call on her for any evidence on the subject which would lead the Mosley family to know of the information [she] is giving. For this reason I have not mentioned the governess's name, though it will of course be readily supplied if required."

The authorities had already decided to lock Diana up but Walter's letter was passed without delay by Swinton to a Lt. Col. O.A. Harker, with a note saying the letter was "very important". Immediate arrangements for her detention were made and she was picked up by the Special Branch and incarcerated in Holloway prison four days after Walter wrote his letter. Her sister Nancy Mitford (under her married name Mrs Peter Rodd) subsequently denounced her to the security services as "the most dangerous character among them [British fascists], and should on no account be released". An intelligence assessment of Diana added: "She is a ruthless and shrewd egotist, a devoted fascist and admirer of Hitler (whom, oddly enough, Sir Oswald personally detests) and sincerely desires the downfall of England and democracy generally. For some eighteen months, or more, before the outbreak of war, she was accustomed to visit Germany not less than once a month, as can be seen from her passport. Mrs Rodd herself does not know the reason for the frequency of these journeys, which seem more than suspicious."

A year after her internment, Diana and Mosley were allowed to live together in Holloway prison. Diana was held for two and a half years altogether and the couple were then placed under house arrest after

Mosley was released because of ill-health in 1943. After the war, they settled for several years in the 1950s in a former bishop's palace at Clonfert, near Eyrecourt, in County Galway until it burned down accidentally in the early hours of 7 December 1954.[45] The fire was blamed on the central heating which Diana had had installed in the old building and which dried it out; its immediate cause was a beam in a chimney that caught fire. It was burned to the ground by the time the fire brigade arrived – there was no telephone in the house – and all the staff and family members were rescued, including a French cook who had gone back upstairs to her room to collect her clothes and been trapped. She had to be persuaded to jump from an upstairs window into blankets held by Mosley and his son Alexander. The cook survived unscathed but gave in her notice the next day, which seems to have been regarded as poor form by the family. Diana was not there at the time of the fire but lost many belongings, including sketches by the Russian surrealist Pavel Tchelitchew and Augustus John.[46] The Mosleys subsequently moved to Ileclash House on the River Blackwater, near Fermoy County Cork, close to the Irish home at Lismore of one of her sisters, Deborah, the Duchess of Devonshire. They then moved permanently to a mansion in the Paris suburb of Orsay and named (not by them) *Le Temple de la Gloire* and known by some wits with dubious taste as "the concentration of camp".[47]

When Winston Churchill took over as prime minister in May 1940, he brought Walter Moyne back into government, first as parliamentary secretary to his old post at the ministry of Agriculture and Fisheries and then, in February 1941, into the cabinet (but not the smaller war cabinet) as Secretary of State for the Colonies and Leader of the House of Lords. A month later, in Kenya's Happy Valley, a potential problem arose for Walter when Sir Jock Delves Broughton, his lover Vera's ex-husband, was accused of the murder of his second wife's lover, Lord Erroll. As Colonial Secretary, Walter would have had a role in deciding whether to execute him or not if he was convicted of the murder. In the event Delves Broughton was acquitted (although he was almost certainly guilty), came back to England, and, under investigation for insurance fraud, killed himself with a drug overdose in a Liverpool hotel in November 1942.

As Colonial Secretary, however, Walter had many more serious and less hypothetical problems to deal with, one of the thorniest being the

Middle East, where Jewish groups were seeking refuge from Nazism and pursuing their demands for their own state while the British government's main preoccupation was with keeping the Arabs, many of whom favoured Germany, on the side of the Allies. Official British policy on the future of Palestine had been set out in a White Paper before the war, which proposed an independent state of Palestine in which Jews would constitute no more than a third of the population and restricted Jewish immigration to 75,000 over five years and the right of Jews to buy land in the area. The proposals incensed Jewish groups, which saw it as rowing back on the Balfour Declaration of 1917, which had promised to support a national home for the Jews in Palestine while respecting the rights of the existing population there. Their future in the area, they believed, was of paramount practical and symbolic importance, all the more so since they were facing extermination in most of Europe. In addition, the new prime minister, Churchill, was not enthusiastic about the White Paper proposals; he was firmly pro-Zionist and favoured a Jewish homeland but the importance of maintaining Arab goodwill in the fight against Nazism was not lost on him either. The Jewish criticism of the policy was particularly acute in the US as the war progressed and Moyne and other ministers debated sending someone to counter it with the Arab view. They finally decided on the travel writer and Arabist Freya Stark, who was also a friend of the Guinness family, particularly of Gwendolen Iveagh, and she toured the US in 1943 to counter the Zionist view.[48]

As well as the overall balancing act the British government was trying to maintain in relation to Palestine, Walter had to contend with two highly contentious issues during his year in the Colonial Office. One was continuing pressure from Zionists to allow Jews to join the Allied forces and fight under their own flags or insignia. The number of Jews in Palestine allowed into the armed forces was limited to the number of Arabs volunteering in the same area: many more Jews were prepared to sign up to fight Nazism than Arabs but many of those who were allowed into the British forces were restricted to non-combatant pioneer units. This policy was not just an attempt by the British to be even-handed; they were also reluctant to arm too many Palestinian Jews who might then use their training and their weapons against them and the Arabs. The restrictions did not just apply to Palestine and there was pressure from Zionist groups worldwide to form a Jewish brigade among the Allied forces. After all, as their spokesmen repeatedly pointed out, they would form a highly motivated and effective force against Nazism. Moyne's predecessor as Colonial Secretary had agreed to form a Jewish unit but Moyne, in office, kept postponing its establishment.

The second, more contentious and highly emotional issue was the fate of 769 desperate Jewish refuges who were allowed by the pro-Nazi and anti-semitic Romanian government to leave Constanta in October 1941 on board a 70-year-old 240-ton steamer *Struma* – a fraction of the size of Moyne's own *Rosaura*. Officially described as "a mere hulk and badly overcrowded",[49] the unseaworthy *Struma* limped across the Black Sea to Istanbul where its engines broke down altogether. Nobody was allowed ashore because they did not have visas for Turkey or for Palestine, their ultimate destination. The Turkish authorities refused to let them into a refugee camp on shore, which Jewish agencies abroad offered to fund, while the British government refused them visas to go on to Palestine. Negotiations between the neutral Turks and the British continued for more than two months, with the Turks wanting to send the ship back into the Black Sea whence it came. Some on the British side agreed, while Moyne was adamant against allowing the ship to continue to Palestine. Arguing that allowing the passengers into Palestine would encourage an influx of Jewish refugees, he urged that the Turks be asked to send the ship back to the Black Sea as they originally proposed. Among the reasons he put forward against allowing the refugees into Palestine was the fear that Nazi agents and infiltrators might be among them, planning to foment trouble in Palestine: "We have good reason to believe that this traffic is favoured by the Gestapo, and the Security Services attach the very greatest importance to preventing the influx of Nazi agents under the cloak of refugees," he wrote to the Foreign Office.[50]

As the refugees waited on board the ship in appalling conditions, the British eventually offered at the last minute to allow children aged between 11 and 16 into Palestine. But the offer was hardly practical or humane, expecting that age-group to abandon their families in the circumstances in which they found themselves. Domestic critics in

England blamed the government for making the offer too late while the government blamed the Turks for blocking it by refusing to allow the group to cross its territory to get to Palestine. On 23 February 1942 the Turkish authorities broke the impasse by towing the *Struma* back out to sea where it was blown up the following day. One man survived. The only other survivor of the *Struma* was a woman who had been allowed ashore to give birth before it was sent back to sea. No one knew for certain at the time how the ship was destroyed. Many feared that the refugees, in despair at being sent back to face their fascist persecutors, had blown it up themselves; another group of Jewish refugees refused permission to land in Palestine had done that at Haifa harbour the previous year. Long afterwards, it transpired that the *Struma* was sunk by a Soviet submarine which was hunting shipping in the area.

Walter Moyne had had overall ministerial responsibility for Palestine and thus for the fate of the *Struma*. However, he did not have to deal directly with the groundswell of public and political opinion in Britain which the sinking prompted. A couple of days before the sinking, he was removed from office in a cabinet reshuffle in response to dissatisfaction with Churchill's government following the fall of Singapore to the Japanese on 15 February. As Colonial Secretary, Moyne could be seen as having some responsibility in that region too and he was replaced both as secretary of state and Leader of the House of Lords by Lord Cranborne, who was in a better position to deal with the *Struma* controversy, from the government's point of view, since he had not been involved directly in it.

That Moyne's demotion had little if anything to do with his handling of the Palestine situation is suggested by the fact that Churchill brought him back into the cabinet as deputy Minister of State for the Middle East six months later. He was to be based in Cairo and assist the Minister, Richard Casey, an Australian politician and diplomat, to cover an area that ranged from Persia to South Africa. Walter's fate was now strongly tied up with the Middle East, as was evident from a tough debate in the House of Lords in June 1942 during the few months when he was out of office. Lord Wedgwood – Josiah Wedgwood, a former Labour MP and strongly pro-Zionist descendant of the original pottery maker of the same name, and a contemporary of the first Arthur

Guinness – went into the House to defend a controversial broadcast he had made to America calling for the Jews in Palestine to be armed and allowed to fight the Nazis. He made no bones of the fact that he believed they should also use those arms against the Arabs and the British to create the homeland they wanted, declaring: "We want the Jews of Palestine armed in the sure and certain conviction that, once armed, they will never surrender those arms, save with their lives, either to Hitler's Germans or the British Administration in Palestine. First arms, then land, then freedom!" Claiming there were enough anti-semites and crypto-fascists in Britain to back the Hitler policy and spirit, he added: "I hope yet to live to see those who sent the *Struma*'s cargo back to the Nazis hanged as high as Haman, cheek by jowl with their prototype and Führer, Adolf Hitler."[51]

In response, Moyne accused him of treason and directly inciting the Jews of Palestine to take up arms against Britain, to seize political control of the area and take the land from its original inhabitants. In a defence of the current policy, he argued that neither the Balfour Declaration nor the British Mandate (the post First World War sphere-of-influence agreement which divided up the former Ottoman Empire between Britain and France) intended Palestine to be converted into a Jewish state against the will of the Arab population. "The tragedy of the Palestinian question is, as was said by the Royal Commission, that it is a conflict between two rights," he said. "We cannot wash our hands of Palestine and let the Jews and Arabs wage a civil war, as suggested by Lord Wedgwood."

He expressed the problem in Palestine as one of overcrowding and maintained that Zionist hopes of moving three million Jews into the area were unrealistic – not just trying to put a quart into a pint bottle but three pints, as he put it. He urged the Zionists to abandon their appeal to force and seek a settlement with the Arabs by consent and suggested that they look as well at other areas in the Middle East which were not so crowded rather than concentrate on the pre-Christian Jewish home in Palestine. "Palestine itself is but a small fraction of the ancient land of Syria. I do not believe that the problem of overcrowding applies to Syria and the Lebanon and Transjordan as it does to Palestine. It would be physically possible for these states to absorb large numbers of Jews to mutual advantage. If the fear of Jewish domination could be removed they might well be glad to welcome Jewish capital and industry."

More controversially, however, Moyne gave voice to a not-uncommon view in London at the time that central European Jews were not "real" Jews.[52] In a passage noting that the Zionist movement had its roots among the Jews of eastern and central Europe, and which was subsequently cited as proof of anti-semitism, he said: "It is very often loosely said that Jews are Semites, but anthropologists tell us that, pure as they have kept their culture, the Jewish race has been much mixed with Gentiles since the beginning of the Diaspora. During the Babylonian captivity they acquired a strong Hittite admixture, and it is obvious that the Armenoid features which are still found among the Sephardim have been bred out of the Ashkenazim by an admixture of Slav blood."[53]

Moyne replaced Casey as the Minister Resident in the Middle East in January 1944. Shortly afterwards, one of the most extraordinary episodes in the Second World War occurred with the arrival of a Hungarian Jew, Joel Brand, in Turkey with a message for the Allies from Adolf Eichmann, the logistics manager of the Holocaust. Eichmann was offering to release a million Jews in return for 10,000 trucks and large quantities of consumer goods like tea and coffee, an offer that became known as "blood-for-trucks" or "blood-for-goods" (from the German *Blut für Ware*). Brand was detained by the British and taken to Cairo where he was questioned repeatedly while the British tried to figure out if the offer was real and, if so, what motivated it, and what to do about it.

At one point, on a largely social occasion in the garden of an Anglo-Egyptian club, Brand was introduced to a tall, thin Englishman who took part in a conversation about the Nazi offer. The Englishman replied, "What can I do with a million Jews? Where can I put them?" Brand said at Eichmann's trial in Jerusalem in 1961 that he was told afterwards that the Englishman was Lord Moyne.[54] Whether it was or not is not absolutely certain; Brand himself changed his story on several occasions, saying sometimes that he was not sure who the Englishman was. His description of him as "tall and thin" does not accord with the usual descriptions of Walter: like most of the Guinnesses, he was not tall in the conventional western sense. However, the authorship of the remark about the million Jews was widely attributed to him and clearly was consistent with the view he had expressed in the House of Lords two years earlier about the overcrowding of Palestine. It could also be interpreted as a bureaucratic question, in the sense of the problems there would be in dealing with an influx of that magnitude. However, when allied with the *Struma* tragedy, his resistance to arming the Jews, his declared concerns for Arab rights and the Zionist plans for Palestine, it was not difficult to portray him as anti-Zionist, anti-Jewish and even anti-semitic.

On 6 November 1944, Walter Moyne left his office in Cairo to go back to his official residence on Gezira Island in the middle of the River Nile for lunch. He was driven in his official car by Lance Corporal Arthur Fuller, accompanied by his aide-de-camp, Captain Andrew Hughes-Onslow, and his personal assistant, Dorothy Osmond. When they drew up outside his residence, Hughes-Onslow got out of the car to go and open the door of the residence. Two gunmen appeared, one on the steps of the house, the other beside the open window of the back seat of the car where Moyne was sitting. "Don't move," he said, before reaching into the car through the window and shooting Moyne slowly and deliberately three times. "Lord Moyne put his hand to his throat and said, 'Oh, they've shot us'," Osmond told the official investigators afterwards. "He leaned forward and I saw that blood was coming from his neck as he did so. I got out of the car on the left-hand side. As I did so I saw Corporal Fuller lying on the ground behind the car and heard him groaning."[55] The two gunmen took off on bicycles and Hughes-Onslow pursued them briefly before turning back to raise the alarm and get help. Moyne, shot in the neck, chest and stomach, was taken to a Scottish hospital nearby, operated on and given blood transfusions. He died there some seven hours later. Corporal Fuller was also brought to the hospital but was dead on arrival.

The two gunmen didn't get far. They were spotted cycling back across the bridge to the mainland by an Egyptian policeman on a motorbike who gave chase and caught up with them easily. They fired shots in his direction but clamed later not to have shot directly at him because they did not want to injure an Arab. They were detained and hid their identities for more than 24 hours to allow other members of their group to get away. It was assumed almost immediately that the assassination was the work of the Irgun, the main militant Zionist group in the Middle East and then under the command of Menachem Begin. However, they were eventually identified as Eliahu Bet-Zuri and Eliahu Hakim of the Lehi group, generally known in Britain as the Stern Group or Stern Gang after its founder Abraham Stern, who had broken with the Irgun over its earlier decision to suspend attacks on the British while they were fighting the Nazis. Lehi's three-man leadership included Yitzhak Shamir, who was to succeed Begin as prime minister of Israel in 1983.

The assassination was condemned almost universally, including by Chaim Weizmann, the head of the World Zionist Organisation, who was said to be as shocked by it as he was by the death of his own son, an RAF pilot who had been shot down over the Bay of Biscay in 1942. He later wrote that the harm done by the assassination, "apart from the profound moral deterioration involved – was not in changing the intentions of the British Government, but rather in providing our enemies with a convenient excuse and in helping to justify their course before the bar of public opinion".[56] In an initial response, Churchill told the House of Commons that Moyne had dealt over the previous year with the most difficult, tangled, anxious and urgent problems, often having to take decisions at the shortest notice and without reference home. "These affairs affected not only matters in the Middle East, but the relations with Allied Governments and enemy Governments seeking to surrender, and were of a most complex character," he added in a veiled reference to the "blood-for-trucks" affair, which some in Britain interpreted as a roundabout attempt by Eichmann's boss Heinrich Himmler to open negotiations with the western Allies. "In particular, Lord Moyne devoted himself this year to the solution of the Zionist problem, and I can assure the House that the Jews in Palestine have rarely lost a better or more well-informed friend."[57]

Churchill returned to the assassination ten days later. "This shameful crime has shocked the world," he said in the Commons. "It has affected none more strongly than those, like myself, who, in the past, have been consistent friends of the Jews and constant architects of their future. If our dreams for Zionism are to end in the smoke of assassins' pistols and our labours for its future to produce only a new

291

set of gangsters worthy of Nazi Germany, many like myself will have to reconsider the position we have maintained so consistently and so long in the past."

Such strong words from a long-time champion of the Zionist cause underlined part of the reason for the widespread condemnation of the attack among Jews. As well as opposing attacks on the controllers of Palestine – who were also engaged in a war against the Nazis – many Jews also feared major retaliation by Britain, which had responded very aggressively two decades earlier when its governor in Sudan was assassinated and in 1937 when its commissioner in Galilee was killed by Arabs. Churchill did indeed consider halting all Jewish immigration to Palestine and trying to disarm all the Jewish paramilitary groups there, including the 36,000-strong Haganah, but he desisted. However, a proposal to set up a Jewish state, which was before the cabinet at the time of Moyne's assassination, was postponed indefinitely and never resurrected by the British.[58] Most of the pressure Churchill exerted behind the scenes was applied to Egypt rather than to the Zionists, to ensure that the assassins were executed. They were duly hanged in Cairo on 22 March 1945 after a trial during which they and their Egyptian lawyers presented them, with considerable success, as freedom fighters trying to make common cause with anti-colonial Arabs against British imperialists.

Shamir, the hard man among the leaders who ordered the attack, continued to justify the assassination on the grounds of Moyne's views and policies as well as his symbolic role as the senior British government representative in the Middle East. In a book published in 1993, he wrote: "He was not only a personification of British power. He was also a man who, in all his capacities – Colonial Secretary, member of the House of Lords, finally minister in Cairo – had played a prominent role in the enforcement of British policy in Palestine, making no secret of his extreme opposition to Zionism or of his negative feelings towards the Jews."[59]

It may be difficult to sustain Churchill's depiction of Moyne as a great friend of the Jews of Palestine but it is even more difficult to sustain a charge of anti-semitism against him, a charge that has been dismissed generally by historians. As one concluded: "It was the symbolic status of his office, and a not-entirely-deserved notoriety that earned Lord Moyne his unhappy end by the assassin's bullet."[60] He was not the author of the Palestine policy which had been set down in the late 1930s when he was out of government; neither was he as clearly anti-Jewish as he was portrayed by his killers. He was obviously not personally anti-semitic, as his long friendship with Ida Rubinstein proved. Although their affair was long over, he was instrumental in persuading her to leave Paris after the fall of France and he helped her make her way from Casablanca to London via Lisbon.[61] As a result of the circumstances of her departure, Ida had no access to her own money and Walter put her up in the Ritz Hotel in Piccadilly for the duration of the war. He also funded a hospital in Camberley in Surrey for the Free French which she ran. After the war, she found that her Paris flat had been ransacked by the Nazis and her large literary collections, including original manuscripts of her many commissions, destroyed or stolen. She moved to Vence, near Nice, shortly afterwards and died there in 1960 just short of her seventy-fifth birthday.

It is clear from events that Lehi had planned to assassinate the British minister in Cairo for several years before it was actually carried out. As a very small group, Lehi's tactic was to make a big impact by attacking high-profile and selective targets. Among them was the British High Commissioner for Palestine, Sir Harold MacMichael, who was seen by many Jews as being too assiduous in implementing official policy and limiting emigration to Palestine. Lehi tried and failed on five occasions to kill him and, on the sixth occasion, succeeded in wounding him in an ambush on a convoy in which he was travelling in August 1944. MacMichael was quickly withdrawn from the Middle East and replaced by Lord Gort. According to historian J. Bowyer Bell, Lehi's plan had been to kill MacMichael and then follow it up with an attack on Moyne some time later. After MacMichael's departure, they immediately turned their attention to Moyne. "More than Moyne's personal failings or his responsibility for policy, his position as Minister of State in Cairo, his value as a responsible symbol of British policy, determined his selection by Lehi. His death would not be a tactical vengeance, but a deed which would change the history of the Middle East," Bowyer Bell wrote.[62]

Bowyer Bell concluded that the assassination did not change British policy but did succeed in bringing the Palestine issue to world attention even in the midst of a world war. While arguments about the reasons and rights and wrongs of his assassination continued for a long time afterwards, and to break down along predictable lines, the bodies of Bet-Zuri and Hakim were returned to Israel by Egypt in 1975 in exchange for 20 Arab prisoners from Gaza and the Sinai. They lay in state for five hours in the Hall of Heroes before they were reburied with full military honours in a section of Mount Hertzl in Jerusalem, Israel's national cemetery reserved for heroes and martyrs. The Israeli prime minister Yitzhak Rabin was among those who filed past their coffins and the funeral was attended by many members of the Israeli political and military establishment, while a pamphlet about them was issued to all schools and they were included in a series of Israeli stamps commemorating its heroes. That the assassination still caused controversy 30 years later was evident from the fact that the British ambassador to Israel expressed official "regrets" at the ceremonies and some leaders of the Jewish community in Britain again condemned it.[63]

Back in 1944, Walter's eldest son Bryan was a British Army liaison officer with the Free French forces in Africa and the Middle East and, at the time of his father's death, was based in Damascus. The British consul there told him of the shooting on the day it happened and he set off for Jerusalem, where he was told his father had died, and from there by air to Cairo. At the funeral he and Captain Hughes-Onslow marched behind the gun-carriage carrying his father's coffin.

> We went at a slow march. I put all my energy into standing up straight and marching correctly. This somehow made things easier. I didn't take my eyes off the back of my father's coffin just in front of me. Now and again I would realize that his head was there just a few feet away and tears would run down my cheeks. Having to stand up stiffly made it all easier. The tears just ran down and that was that.[64]

Bryan flew with Walter's body on a Dakota military transport to Benghazi, across the Mediterranean to Malta, on to Marseille and across the south of France to England for cremation at Golders Green in Middlesex on 17 November. Lance Corporal Fuller was buried in the Heliopolis military cemetery in Cairo. (Walter's other companions in the car when he was shot, Captain Hughes-Onslow and Dorothy Osmond, were employed by the Guinness brewery and family, respectively, after the war.)

A preliminary estimate of Walter's estate a month after his death valued it at £2 million and estate duty of £1.3 million was levied on it. He left his houses at Grosvenor Place in London and Knockmaroon, County Dublin, to Bryan and the Baliffscourt estate in Sussex to his daughter Grania. The rest was divided two-fifths each to Bryan and Grania and one fifth to his second son, Murtogh. His will also said that he was leaving no charitable bequests as the rates of income taxes, surtaxes and death duties were making an adequate contribution to services of public assistance which had been left previously to private philanthropy.[65]

In 1950, David Hacohen, a former member of Haganagh, the main Zionist paramilitary group in Palestine during the war, and subsequently an Israeli politician, visited Bryan, the new Lord Moyne, in Dublin. Bryan told him his father had supported the idea of partitioning Palestine (which was on the British cabinet agenda at the time of his assassination) and this had subsequently been accepted by the Zionist organisations. "Why then did your people murder my father?" Bryan asked. "In the end Palestine was partitioned and you are now consolidating your state on the basis of that partition, yet none of you has been assassinated for accepting this solution." Hacohen, describing the encounter in the *Jerusalem Post* at the time of the return of the assassins' bodies in 1975, wrote: "I had no simple, unequivocal answer to give. I did not know how to explain the reason for the assassination."[66]

Walter Moyne was the only member of the British cabinet to be killed during the Second World War. He also had the unwanted distinction of being the only serving British minister to be assassinated in the twentieth century.

———∞———

Three months after Walter's death, the Guinness family suffered another grievous blow. Arthur Elveden, son of Rupert and heir to the earldom of Iveagh and thus to the leadership of the family, was killed on active service in Holland. Like his uncle Walter, he had joined the Suffolk Yeomanry and become a major in an anti-tank regiment. He was killed on 2 February 1945 by a stray V2 rocket, presumably aimed at the south of England, which hit a farmhouse at Nijmegen where Arthur's unit was billeted. Its inhabitants were asleep at the time and the casualties included his batman, John Stiles. Arthur was 33 and he left three children, his son Benjamin, aged seven, who became the heir to the earldom, and two daughters, Elizabeth and Henrietta, aged five and two respectively. (The same edition of *The Times*, noting a memorial service for him and "his servant", Stiles, at Elveden church, carried an ad for Guinness with a smiling face in the creamy head and declaring "Life is brighter after Guinness".)[67] He is buried at the Jonkerbos war cemetery near Nijmegen.

The third branch of the family, Ernest's branch, did not escape from the war unscathed either: one daughter's husband and another's former husband were killed, while his third daughter suffered the loss of two children, although not as a result of the war. Ernest's second daughter, Maureen, had married a cousin, Basil Sheridan Hamilton-Temple-Blackwood, who became the Marquess of Dufferin and Ava shortly after their wedding in 1930. His family owned the 3,000-acre Clandeboye estate in County Down which was in a rundown condition but revived by the injection of Guinness money. Maureen was known for her love of practical jokes, like pretending to be a foul-mouthed maid and insulting house guests. Once described in the 1930s by society photographer and diarist Cecil Beaton as "the biggest bitch in London", she was the model for Osbert Lancaster's *Daily Express* cartoon character, Maudie Littlehampton, and was said to be the model in later life, in appearance but not in character, for Australian comedian Barry Humphries' Dame Edna Everage.[68] Dufferin was active in politics and held a number of junior posts in the British government, including as under-secretary for the colonies in the late 1930s, before turning down an invitation to join Churchill's government in 1940 in favour of enlisting in the British Army. After a spell involved with propaganda, he went back to being a staff officer with the rank of captain in the Royal Horse Guards in Mandalay in Burma. During an undercover operation there in March 1945 he was killed when his unit was ambushed by Japanese soldiers.

Ernest's eldest daughter Aileen had married another cousin, Brinsley Sheridan Plunket, a grandson of Edward Iveagh's sister Anne, in 1927.

They had moved to the 570-acre Luttrellstown estate beside the Phoenix Park in Dublin, which Ernest bought for her on their wedding and where she became a hostess noted for her lavish parties, with guests like the "King of Hollywood", Douglas Fairbanks Jnr, and other international celebrities and jet-setters.[69] Plunket was a well-known sportsman, keeping racehorses and running shoots on the estate. The marriage broke up, however, and they were formally divorced in 1940. During the war he was a flight lieutenant in the RAF Volunteer Reserve and was killed in Sudan in November 1941. (His death was noted in *The Irish Times* but Irish wartime censorship prevented any mention of his military status, or the circumstances of his death: an appreciation of him noted, however, that his older brother had died in an air crash in California in 1938 and both had now "passed on, early in life, as a result of the aeroplane".)[70]

The youngest of Ernest's daughters, Oonagh, had divorced her first husband, Philip Kindersley, in the 1930s and moved with her new husband, Dominick Browne, Lord Oranmore and Browne, to his Mayo home with her two Kindersley children, Gay and Tessa. As part of the divorce proceedings, the children were made wards of court and it was specified that Gay would be sent to a preparatory school in Yorkshire and from there to Eton. However, Oonagh refused to let Gay go back to England while the war was on because of the danger of air raids, and Kindersley got an English court order against her in 1940. Kindersley was subsequently captured in North Africa in December 1942 where he was a captain in the British Army and was incarcerated in a prisoner-of-war camp in Italy.

Apparently on their own initiative, Kindersley's father, Lord Kindersley, and his business secretary, Grace Charker, who had power of attorney for the prisoner-of-war, got a court order in Dublin to have the English court order enforced and the boy sent to Eton in September 1943. The fate of the Kindersley boy became something of a *cause célèbre* in Dublin as the court proceedings stretched on over seven months and the initial deadline was missed. Oonagh, who was pregnant with her second child by Browne, told the High Court that she had agreed to have the children made wards of court because Kindersley had promised on oath not to take her children from her. She said he had agreed that they should stay with her in Ireland until the war ended but he had changed his mind in 1939 and told her to send Gay to the preparatory school in England. She wanted him to stay in Ireland because it was safer and they had subsequently agreed to send him to Castle Park school in Dalkey, County Dublin. She was willing to send him to Eton if the war ended and conditions returned to normal in England but, meanwhile, she had applied and received Irish citizenship for him and he wanted to stay with her. Kindersley had visited her and the children three times in Ireland between 1940 and 1942 and had not indicated to her that he wanted Gay taken to England, she claimed.

The High Court decided that the wishes of the father must be ascertained directly and the case was adjourned for several months while attempts were made to contact Kindersley in his prisoner-of-war camp. Meanwhile, Gay was enrolled in St Columba's in Rathfarnham, County Dublin as the legal arguments went back and forth before the High Court over the autumn of 1943. Lord Kindersley produced a message received through the British legation in Berne saying that his son knew and approved of the application to have Gay sent to Eton. In a letter to him as well, Philip Kindersley wrote: "I am more pleased and grateful than I can possibly describe. It is really wonderful for you to have done this for me, as I had visions of Gay being educated as a Sinn Feiner."[71]

The court ruled that the order of the English court should be upheld and Gay should go to Eton.[72] Oonagh appealed to the Supreme Court and lost just before her pregnancy came to an end. On 28 December she gave birth to another son in Dublin, who died two days later. Another last-ditch legal attempt to have general custody of Gay granted to her also failed and he was handed over to his grandparents at the Four Courts in Dublin in January 1944 by his stepfather, Lord Oranmore and Browne, in time for the new term at Eton. Oonagh was not in the court for the final act.[73]

Worse was to follow for her. In August 1946, the Brownes were at Castle MacGarret in Mayo when their eldest son, Garech, was threatened with a mild form of diphtheria. A local doctor, C.B. Heneghan, recommended that all members of the family, including Oonagh, be inoculated against the disease as a precaution. He vaccinated seven members of the household and the last to receive the injection was Oonagh's daughter Tessa Kindersley, then aged 14. About 15 minutes later she told her mother she had an attack of asthma and the doctor gave her an injection of adrenaline. However, she showed signs of cardiac failure and he gave her other stimulants which seemed to work temporarily but she died two and a half hours after receiving the diphtheria injection. An inquest the following week decided she had died of severe heart failure caused by anaphylactic shock.[74] She was buried in the private cemetery on Oonagh's estate at Luggala in County Wicklow.

Less than three years later, Ernest himself died suddenly at Glenmaroon in Dublin on 22 March 1949 at the age of 72. The funeral was held at St Patrick's Cathedral with most of his family members present, except his widow Cloe, who was seriously ill. The President, Seán T. O'Kelly, and Taoiseach, John A. Costello, were represented and the Minister for External Affairs, Seán MacBride, was among the attendance.

Ernest's sudden death gave the inter-party government in Dublin an unexpected windfall as his will was probated at £3,182,427 in Ireland; he also left £156,726 in England and a further £229,719 was ascribed to "foreign assets". The Irish taxman alone took a substantial £1,325,775 while the British revenue probably did even better, as the rate of estate duty there was 75 per cent compared to the 41.6 per cent rate in Ireland. Ernest did not pass on his wealth to the next generation as cleverly as the Guinnesses usually did: in a rare financial mistake by any of the main family members, he left the making of his will too late to avoid substantial taxes. Less than five years before his unexpected death, he had divided £2,746,203 in shares and other property between his three daughters and given various other gifts to relatives, including the freehold interest in his Glenmaroon estate plus £200,000 to his grandson, Gay Kindersley, when he reached 25. As a result, most of these gifts became liable for death duties because he had not lived the requisite period after making them – three years in Ireland and five years in England – which would have exempted them from tax.

As his trustees he had selected his wife Cloe, his private secretary Ossie Baker (who had survived the Killary Harbour sinking, and many other sailing and flying adventures, with him), Bernard Norfolk of the Iveagh Trustees in London, and Henry Bliss (one of Edward Iveagh's secretaries who was "inherited" by Ernest). Ernest's will instructed them to pay his widow £5,000 a month after his death, an annuity of £20,000, and allow her the use of his properties in England and Glenmaroon for her lifetime. Afterwards, Glenmaroon was to go to his youngest daughter, Oonagh, for her lifetime and then to her children. His other two daughters, Aileen and Maureen, were to receive cash sums equal to the value of the furniture and general effects at Glenmaroon at the time of his death. To his employees at Glenmaroon and his other properties, a total of 105 people, including the captain and crew of his yacht, he left up to a year's pay if they had been with him for more than ten years and lesser amounts depending on their years in his employment. These amounted to about £20,000.

His will specified that any taxes due on these gifts should be paid out of his estate. He had also set up a pension fund for his employees and his will specified that any taxes imposed on it should have priority from his estate. The upshot of his belated financial planning was that there was not enough money left in his estate to pay all the amounts he had willed, including the taxes, and his executors had to go to court for guidance on how to cut down his bequests.

Of the £3.5 million in his estate in Ireland, England and abroad, the trustees were left with approximately £2,036,959 after death duties. When taxes were paid on his earlier gifts, this was between £300,000 and £400,000 short of what was needed to carry out his liabilities and wishes and his trustees asked the High Court in Dublin how to deal with this problem. The case was a field day for lawyers, with 18 barristers taking part, representing all the interests involved. Inherently complex, it was further complicated by the different rules on death duties and tax rates between Ireland and England and which jurisdiction covered which part of the legacies. (As a useful yardstick of the value of the amounts of money involved in Ernest's gifts and will, *The Irish Times* estimated at the end of the week-long court hearing that the legal costs of all the lawyers involved could amount to about £5,000.)

In 1946 and 1948 Ernest had transferred 150,000 Guinness shares, in which he had received a life interest from his father in 1907, to his three daughters. The shares were worth just over £1 million but, because they were registered in England and were given within five years of his death, the death duty on them was about £750,000. He had also given them gifts worth £500,000 on which tax in England and Ireland amounted to about £378,000. In 1948, as well, he had given 34,288 Guinness shares to trustees to provide pensions for his former employees; because these shares had been registered in Ireland, they were subject to the lower tax rate and £97,000 was due on them. The court eventually ruled that all taxes on prior gifts must be paid from Ernest's estate. They amounted to about £2,290,000, leaving a deficit of some £300,000 in his bequests. It was met by cutting all legacies down by a sixth, except for the employees' pension fund, which was untouched.

There was also an indication during the hearing that relations between the three sisters were not altogether harmonious. Ernest's widow, Cloe, had not taken up her £20,000 annuity and had surrendered her life interest in Glenmaroon, which meant that the furniture and effects in it went to Oonagh. After Ernest's death, auctioneers Adam & Sons had been called in to do a valuation of the furniture for probate. They had come up with an estimate of £10,948. In accordance with the terms of the will, Oonagh's sisters Aileen and Maureen had been given the same amount each in cash. However, Oonagh sold the furniture a year later at auction for £22,846, double what her sisters had received. The court asked Adam & Sons to look again at their valuation after representations from her sisters' lawyers.[75]

Ernest's failure to follow the usual adroit Guinness handling of wealth down through the generations was to have further repercussions in the following years. His branch of the family ran into more financial problems than the other two branches. Some time after their father's death in 1927, Walter had taken his share of the trusts set up by Edward Iveagh's will and managed it himself through a company registered in Switzerland. Among his highly successful investments was the purchase of a large tract of land in West Vancouver and the formation of British Pacific Properties to develop it as an exclusive suburb with minimum lot sizes. It was an extraordinarily good deal for the Guinnesses, who received control of some 4,700 acres of development land in return for promising to spend one million Canadian dollars on public works, which would be handed over to the municipality, and paying a mere Can$75,000 in cash directly to the city. The city, which was suffering the effects of the Depression, got cash and the guarantee of work for its citizens; the Guinnesses received an extremely lucrative deal, effectively getting the land in return for public works which, in their turn, increased the value of the land. It turned into an even more lucrative investment when they received permission to build the Lion's Gate toll bridge, popularly known as the Guinness Bridge, linking the area to the city centre. The 1,823-metre suspension bridge cost Can$6 million in the late 1930s and spans Burrard Inlet, a fjord which separates the North Shore mountains from the flat city centre. Cars were charged 25 cents to cross the bridge until the Guinnesses sold it to British Columbia in 1955 for about the same price as it had cost to build it. Meanwhile, however, West Vancouver developed into one of the most affluent suburbs in Canada, vying for the top of the list with Montreal's Westmount, Toronto's Rosedale and Ottawa's Rockcliffe.

Rupert Iveagh had lost his two brothers and his son and heir within the space of five years when he addressed the annual meeting of Arthur Guinness & Son in London in December 1949. "Now they have gone and I am getting old," he said. "It is time that the next generation begin to take up their burden."[76] He announced that his nephew, Walter's son Bryan Moyne, would become vice-chairman to replace Ernest, and Maureen, Ernest's middle daughter, would become the first woman to join the board of directors. Though not known to anyone for his business acumen, Bryan was effectively the only Guinness male available in the brewing branch of the family, while Maureen was there to represent Ernest's strand of the family. (There were no suitable husbands available at the time: Aileen's had been divorced and killed in the war; Maureen's had also been killed and she had recently remarried an army officer 13 years younger than her; Oonagh's second marriage, to Lord Oranmore and Browne, was heading for divorce the following year as he continued his philandering.) There were still two sons-in-law on the board, Chips Channon (now an ex-son-in-law but still there) and Alan Lennox-Boyd, husband of Rupert's second daughter, Patricia, and a politician who was later to play a major role in the company.

With the new heir to the Iveagh title, his grandson Benjamin, st
only 12 years old, Rupert had little choice but to continue as chairma
of the company himself at the age of 75. The family was running out of
options.

———∞∞∞———

CHAPTER TWELVE

The Seventh Generation

"The only problem the Guinnesses don't have is money."

MAUREEN GUINNESS, Marchioness of Dufferin and Ava

Unlike the Guinness family, which had a tragic war, the Guinness company had had a relatively good war. Halting a long slow decline, the consumption of all beers increased in Britain, in spite of tax increases and restrictions on supplies of raw materials similar to those imposed during the First World War. Reductions in gravities were ordered again, affecting Guinness stout more than lighter beers. Nevertheless, Guinness output had increased to two million hogshead by 1945, surpassing the 1921 high.[1] The benefit of having the two breweries worked to the company's advantage; while Park Royal was damaged in a German bombing raid in October 1940 which killed four employees, St James's Gate was unhindered in its activities, although significant numbers of staff joined the British forces and were once again guaranteed to have their jobs after the war. The three Guinness ships that plied the Irish Sea did so without incident throughout the war, keeping supplies of stout steady in spite of breaks in Park Royal's output. On the other hand, having Park Royal servicing the London area solved the communications problems caused by German bomb damage to roads and rail lines throughout Britain. By 1945, James's Gate was producing as much stout as it had in the year before Park Royal opened, while the new London brewery was producing half as much again and supplying almost two-thirds of the demand in Britain.

With the end of the war, Rupert Iveagh tried to secure the management of the company by offering a top position to Hugh Beaver, the engineer who had overseen the purchase and construction of Park Royal. On the surface, it appeared an odd choice; Beaver was an engineer, not a brewer, scientist or businessman, but he was highly organised and exceptionally energetic, even restless. He, too, had had a good war, as director-general of the Ministry of Works, in charge of all construction and building supplies in Britain and had been knighted in 1943 in recognition of his success at that task. He had been offered a seat on the Guinness board previously and turned it down but he accepted Rupert's invitation to become assistant managing director in 1945 at the age of 55. It was clearly understood that he was to succeed the managing director Charles Newbold, a succession that came sooner than expected when Newbold (who once swam 12 miles across Dublin Bay to win a bet)[2] died suddenly in 1946 at the age of 65.

Beaver had a major effect on the company, revitalising and energising it in numerous ways. Among them was the adoption of the results of scientific experiments conducted by the company itself, such as the introduction of sterile brewing, which it had been dithering over since the 1920s. The reluctance to change century-old (and longer) practices had created problems with the short "life" of the stout but there had been a fear of changing anything in case the change would upset what Beaver once referred to as the "medieval magic" of brewing. One of the main results of these changes was the blending of a new stout for the foreign market, which had been badly affected by problems of high acidity in the previous product. The company also took control of the distribution and marketing of its stout abroad, instead of simply handing it over to local bottlers. The result was a huge increase in foreign sales, particularly and not altogether coincidentally (see below) in areas of Africa and Asia that had been part of the by-now collapsing British Empire. By 1961, what was called the "foreign trade" accounted for the sale of 286,000 barrels, twelve times the pre-war total and about 12 per cent of the output of St James's Gate.

Another technical development that emerged was the introduction in the 1960s of the Easy Serve cask – a barrel with a container of carbon dioxide and nitrogen in it – which made the task of serving draught

Guinness much simpler by replacing a system which had required two barrels with a single barrel. Invented by one of company's brewers, Michael Ash, it was seen as a significant development, not least because draught Guinness was less bitter than the bottled variety and thus more attractive to new stout drinkers.[3] It helped to increase consumption in Britain where the vast majority of Guinness sold was the bottled variety. However, the profit margin on draught was less than that on bottled stout.

The success of the foreign sales, scientific developments, and technical improvements in brewing and distribution allied to low costs tended, however, to mask a growing problem for Guinness. The long-term steady decline in beer sales in Britain resumed after the war for a further decade and a half and then began to pick up again. But the increases, when they came, were in a significantly different segment of the beer market to the one in which Guinness had for so long traded comfortably and profitably. Lifestyle changes between the 1950s and 1970s included developments as disparate as the spread of television (which offered a new form of entertainment in areas where the pub had been hitherto the only regular leisure outlet), an increase in spirits and wine drinking (as a result of more foreign travel) and, most importantly in the beer market itself, the emergence of lager as the most popular beer, replacing traditional ales and stout. Alcohol consumption was going up but not in the product in which Guinness was expert: beer sales in Britain rose by 15 per cent between 1968 and 1987 but spending on spirits doubled and on wine and cider trebled in the same period. Within the beer market, lager went from less than four per cent in 1967 to more than 45 per cent twenty years later and 52 per cent by 1993.[4]

The shape of things to come was evident long before then to at least one of the Guinnesses. Jonathan Guinness, the eldest son of the company's vice-chairman, Bryan Moyne, got a stark preview of the future when working as a reporter for Reuters news agency in Bonn in the mid-1950s. Researching an article on German beer drinking, he found that it had broken down 85 per cent to 15 per cent in favour of dark beers over light beers in the early twentieth century; halfway through the century, the proportion was almost exactly reversed, 85:15, in favour of light beers over dark ones.[5]

The answer for Guinness was the obvious one: it needed to abandon its highly successful policy of some 150 years – concentrating on one product and doing it very well – in favour of diversification. There were two forms of diversification to be considered: within the drinks trade and outside of it altogether. One of Guinness's great advantages over the previous century had been the absence of its own tied houses, which left it free to plough its profits into brewing rather than into property. But this turned into a disadvantage now in relation to diversification within the trade. In the absence of its own tied houses, Guinness relied on other brewers in the crucial British market to sell its stout in their pubs. If it tried to introduce more mainstream beers which competed with the other brewers' own products, these brewers were unlikely to sell them and might even retaliate by curbing the sales of Guinness stout.

This problem did not exist in Ireland, where there were no tied houses, giving the company the opportunity to buy breweries like Smithwicks in Kilkenny, the country's oldest brewery, which it did in 1965, and to sell its ale. It also began brewing its own lager, Harp, under the guidance of a German master brewer, Herman Muender, who was brought from Hamburg to brew it in Dundalk in 1960. The Harp name and the marketing were clever plays on the Guinness logo, Brian Boru's harp, and on its Irishness, making connections to the main brand while creating a new identity at the same time. Harp was successful, particularly in Northern Ireland, and Guinness managed to extend it to Britain by coming to joint brewing arrangements with regional brewers there. Thus, it produced Harp in association with the likes of Courage and Bass Charrington in the south of England and with Scottish and Newcastle in the north. These arrangements worked well for a number of years until some of its partners decided they needed to have their own lager products as that market grew explosively.

The pressure on beer sales led inevitably to more competition between existing brewers and to increased advertising. Guinness began advertising in Ireland in the early 1950s, not (as Beaver maintained at the time) to attract the natives but to catch the attention of tourists. "After all, if you went to Mecca, you'd expect to see some quotations from the Koran," he told *Time* magazine.[6] (His explanation may have been a little disingenuous; Guinness, as usual, was wary of being seen as a monopolist in the Irish market and Beaver may have wanted to deflect any criticism that it was trying to use its financial muscle to take over the small section of the stout market it did not already control.) More advertising meant more costs, which was not welcome news to the Guinness directors, as Bryan Moyne had made clear in a speech to the House of Lords in which he opposed the bill to set up ITV in 1954. He argued that the new commercial channel would simply involve manufacturers in more advertising costs, bring down their profits, and thereby reduce taxes to the exchequer and dividends to shareholders while doing nothing to increase any manufacturer's output. As to the arguments that the new channels would provide an advertising opportunity, he said it was no more than the right to take part in a race which ought never to be run.[7]

Bryan's fears were well-founded. The proportion of beer advertising on television in Britain went from 5 per cent in 1955 to 75 per cent of television advertising 20 years later while the total spent on it rose from £2.2 million to more than £30 million.[8] Guinness advertising changed too during the period as it tried to angle its old messages towards new markets. Its first scientific surveys of Guinness drinkers in the 1950s confirmed what was already known and apparent from its classic ads: they were older men and manual workers, the people who needed the strength to lift girders and pull a horse and cart. The message was changed in the 1960s to replace that – and the broader feel-good message of the ads that mixed wit and whimsy – with a more direct hard sell. The emphasis was turned to the pint of stout itself and young people, especially young women, replaced the older, working men of the initial campaigns. But it could only go part of the way towards a hard sell; as Jonathan Guinness has noted, by then the public was attuned to Guinness ads as free entertainment and it would have been dangerous to the brand to disabuse them of that.

It was perhaps appropriate that one advertising project turned out to be Guinness's most successful non-brewing diversification. *The Guinness Book of Records* had its origins in the Wexford slobs where Beaver was out shooting with friends in the winter of 1951. A discussion developed with his fellow-shooters and hosts in the village of Castlebridge about which game bird flew the fastest. Unable to resolve it with the help of any available reference book, he came up with the idea of a collection of facts that would settle the sort of debate that arose regularly in pubs. He discussed the idea with Chris Chataway, a long-distance runner who worked for Guinness in London, who suggested a couple of sports journalists, twins Norris and Ross McWhirter, with whom he had been at Oxford. They operated a small agency in London providing odd facts and figures to Fleet Street newspapers. Their first production was given away free by Guinness as a marketing tool for stout. It was subsequently published as a book – its first cover was adorned with the Guinness harp logo – and went on to immediate success. Its publishers, a separate company within the Guinness group until the early twenty-first century, later claimed it was the bestselling copyrighted book of all time.

As the company moved towards its bicentenary in 1959, it seemed to be in a strong position but it was actually feeling its age behind the healthy-looking façade and the infusion of Sir Hugh Beaver's energy. It was rigidly stratified, with up to seven different dining rooms and canteens at St James's Gate, reflecting the status of the different categories of employees. The categories of employees went, in descending order, from directors to brewers, chemists, engineers, No. 1 staff, No. 2 staff, lady clerks, technical assistants, supervisors, foremen, coopers, tradesmen, labourers, lads and boys (who came in as messengers straight from primary school).[9] Those at the top had a very comfortable existence; many were people who had served the British Empire and saw a position at Guinness as little more than a congenial form of retirement reward, coming into their offices at 10 a.m. and leaving by 4.00 p.m. "Some of them did little more than sit in front of the fire and read the paper, rarely getting involved in any serious problems involving the company . . . one manager had his slippers laid out for him every morning," according to Finbarr Flood, a future managing director, who joined the company as a messenger boy at 14.[10] On the other hand, work at the bottom was hard manual labour and not very well paid at the basic level, although it was topped up substantially by overtime and regular annual bonuses of an extra month's pay, as well as the medical and social benefits for which Guinness was well known.

The company's diversifications also had an air of amateurism about them, albeit sometimes inspired amateurism like *The Guinness Book of*

Records. Projects were taken on in a random fashion, often because somebody came to the company with an idea or somebody knew somebody. Back in the 1930s, Beaver had suggested that Guinness buy a much larger site than it required at Park Royal and develop the surrounding land itself. That led to the formation of a property development subsidiary, which had the unusual and limiting distinction of not being allowed by its parent to borrow money, thereby virtually undermining the whole basis of property development. However, it did develop an industrial estate around its Park Royal brewery and its occupants in the 1950s included William Nuttall, a group of confectionery companies that made well-known sweets like Callard & Bowser butterscotch and mintoes. Guinness bought the company after an approached from William Nuttall's chairman, who continued to run it on their behalf. Another venture was into pharmaceuticals, a common diversification by breweries on the basis that they already had chemistry departments which carried out research into brewing. A plastics division arose initially out of a project to provide work for redundant coopers.

Thus, the company grew by adding bits and pieces but they were all minor contributors to its overall strength. The family remained in control, although none of the Iveagh descendants were seriously engaged in the company. The only Guinnesses employed by the company were Edward and Peter Guinness, two members of the banking Guinness family, who were thus doubly related to the Iveagh Guinnesses through the first Lady Iveagh as well as through the brother of the first Arthur Guinness. Other members of the family who considered a career in the brewery were dissuaded from pursuing it because they were not science graduates.

The board of the company was an entirely different matter, however. There was a large number of Guinnesses on it at any one time in the 1950s and 1960s. Rupert Iveagh remained chairman and Bryan Moyne vice-chairman, representing two of the three sons of Edward Iveagh. Rupert's branch of the family was also represented by his daughter Honor or her ex-husband Chips Channon (and, later, their son Paul Channon) and his daughter Patricia or her husband, Alan Lennox-Boyd (and later their son Simon, Viscount Boyd). Ernest's branch was represented by his daughter Maureen, the Marchioness of Dufferin and Ava (and later, her son Sheridan, the Marquess of Dufferin and Ava).

Walter's branch was represented by the vice-chairman, Bryan, and subsequently by his son, Jonathan Guinness.

In the 1950s and later, the family still owned a very sizeable share of Arthur Guinness Son & Company, probably a little under half, but it was declining slowly and steadily. All family members were under instructions not to sell their shares or, if they had to, to sell them to other members of the family. This arrangement was policed closely by Rupert and Bryan in relation to their own immediate families but the arrangement was less rigid among the three daughters of Ernest. They were the family members most often in need of cash, not least because of their father's mistake in leaving his will and the dispersal of his shares too late but also because of their expensive lifestyles. For instance, they sold off 25 of Ernest's inherited paintings, including five portraits by Romney, a landscape by Gainsborough and six works by seventeenth-century masters, for £42,874 in 1953.[11]

The Iveagh Trustees in London managed the funds on behalf of the Iveagh branch and Ernest's branch of the family, while the Moyne branch managed its own funds. As the number of descendants grew, disputes arose occasionally among the beneficiaries of the funds managed by the Iveagh Trustees, sometimes over complex legal issues of interpretation of the original Edward Iveagh's will and sometimes over issues like tax domiciles; the latter issue especially affected those descendants who lived in Ireland but were considered to be domiciled in England for reasons of birth or parentage or the trusts' location. The Moyne trusts, on the other hand, were set up on a more flexible legal basis and generally avoided disputes requiring court actions.

The money pressures facing Ernest's daughters were relative to the great wealth of the family as a whole, of course. Neither was the family wealth all concentrated on Guinness shares. For instance, the Guinness investments in Canada by Rupert and Walter were doing very well and spreading across the country: they built one of the first shopping centres in the country, the Park Royal Centre in Vancouver in 1950; the first skyscraper on the prairies, the Elveden Centre in Calgary, in 1959; and developed more office buildings, as well as the British Pacific Properties affluent suburb in West Vancouver and a ranch in Alberta. By the late 1970s, the third Lord Iveagh was to say that the family investments in

Canada had grown a thousand-fold in the 40 years since their beginnings in the 1930s.[12] British Pacific Properties in Vancouver is still the cornerstone of the Moyne trusts.

The family was also doing well in society terms, even if it was increasingly likely to appear in the more irreverent tabloid gossip columns as frequently as in the traditionally deferential broadsheet society columns. In terms of the latter, Rupert finally surpassed his father in the British honours system in 1955 when he was invested into the Knights of the Order of the Garter, the oldest and highest honour in England. Restricted to 24 members at any one time (excluding members of the royal family), membership after 1948 was in the gift of the king or queen alone and not at the behest of the government. At a ceremony conducted by Queen Elizabeth in St George's Chapel in Windsor Castle, he became the 916th knight of the order since it was created in the mid-fourteenth century; Sir Anthony Eden, the new British Prime Minister, was also invested at the same ceremony and the Queen had them to lunch afterwards.[13] At a rehearsal of the ceremony beforehand, Rupert found himself sitting beside the recently retired Prime Minister, Winston Churchill, who had become a knight of the order the previous year. "Do you remember that fight we had in Dublin?" Churchill asked him, referring to their scrap in the Phoenix Park more than 75 years earlier.[14] Rupert's reply is not recorded.

Coincidentally, on the same day, 15 June 1955, there was another event in Germany which also confirmed the status of the Guinnesses in high society: Rupert's latest grandchildren, a twin boy and girl, were christened in the chapel at Burg Hohenzollern in Germany. They were the children of his youngest daughter, Brigid, and her husband Fritzi, officially Prince Friedrich von Preussen, the grandson of Kaiser Wilhelm II and a great-great-grandson of Queen Victoria. Rupert was one of the godfathers of the boy, along with the King of Denmark, Prince Louis Ferdinand of Prussia and Rupert's other grandson, Benjamin Elveden. The boy was christened Rupert Alexander Frederich and the girl Antonia Elizabeth Brigid Luise.[15] Prince Friedrich had studied at Cambridge during the 1930s, become an Anglophile, and had been introduced to Brigid by her brother-in-law Chips Channon. He remained in England at the outbreak of the Second World War and was detained in an internment camp in Canada for two years before being released and returning to England, where he joined the

Pioneers Corps and worked on a farm under the alias George Mansfield. He and Brigid were married in 1945 and he became a British citizen two years later but he subsequently decided to resume his German nationality and to try to recover some of his family's German estates. The marriage began to disintegrate in the 1950s; they subsequently agreed to divorce in Frankfurt, where the law prohibited publicity about such cases. Shortly before the divorce hearing, scheduled for April 1966, Fritzi disappeared from Schloss Rheinhartshausen, the family seat near Wiesbaden which had been converted into a country hotel. His body was found in the Rhine near Bingen twelve days later; his brother said he had been suffering from depression and it was presumed that he had killed himself.[16] Brigid subsequently married her neighbour at Little Hadham in England, Major Patrick Ness.

As Rupert was preparing to leave the stage, the first members of the seventh generation of Arthur Guinness's descendants were preparing to step to the forefront. The main one was, of course, Benjamin (christened Arthur Francis Benjamin), who already had his late father's title of Lord Elveden and was in line to become the third Earl of Iveagh in succession to his grandfather Rupert. The title was deemed to carry with it the chairmanship of Arthur Guinness & Company and the leadership of the family, with major roles in a variety of inherited duties like the Iveagh Trustees, running estates in England and Ireland, and a number of philanthropic organisations. Benjamin was, perhaps, one of the members of the seventh generation least fitted for the role but it was imposed on him by birth, or at least by the perceptions and decisions of the family that the heir to the Iveagh title had to be the head of the company and family. The old Guinness practice of giving control to the one most able to exercise it, which had served the family and business very well in the past, had been dropped. There was, in any event, a shortage of possible contenders: Benjamin was not Rupert's sole grandson but he was the only one who was a Guinness; the others were Paul Channon (son of his daughter Honor), Simon, Christopher and Mark Lennox-Boyd (sons of Patricia), and the newly christened Rupert von Preussen and his older brothers Nicholas and Andrew (sons of Brigid). None of them had been involved closely in the brewing business. The idea that the head might be female was clearly unthinkable at the time.

Benjamin had had a somewhat isolated upbringing, mainly in his grandfather's shadow, in Elveden and had inherited his interest in farming. His mother, Elizabeth, who also lived there, had married again, to Rory More O'Ferrall, of an Irish bloodstock family. Benjamin was sent to Eton and went from there to Trinity College, Cambridge, where he studied history, rather than the science that was seen as a prerequisite for working in the brewery. His twenty-first birthday in 1958 was marked by a party for 1,500 at Elveden, including practically all the inhabitants of the four villages on the estate. "I may stay at Cambridge after this year but I intend to come and live here and learn to be a real East Anglian farmer," he told the local correspondent of *The Times*.[17] On his twenty-first, he inherited the Elveden estate and intended to run it as a partnership with his grandfather Rupert. He was also appointed to the boards of Arthur Guinness & Co. the same year. (The company had now been broken into four separate corporate entities: a holding company; a Dublin company running St James's Gate; a London company running Park Royal; and a Belfast company running operations in Northern Ireland). Two years later Benjamin became assistant managing director of the parent company, with responsibility for a time for metal containers at Park Royal. Two years after that, in 1962, he became chairman of the company when Rupert finally stepped down after 34 years in the job and at the age of 88.

Benjamin was chairman and Bryan Moyne vice-chairman of all the Guinness companies but only executives were on the boards of the three operating companies, while the board of the holding company was made up mainly of family members and other non-executives. Two of Benjamin's cousins and contemporaries joined the board of the holding company in 1961: his second cousin Jonathan Guinness, the eldest son of Bryan Moyne and Diana Mitford; and his first cousin Paul Channon, the only son of Chips Channon and Honor Guinness. Chips had died in 1957, aged 61, a year after he had been knighted as Sir Henry Channon; he never made it into the peerage. Paul, born in 1935, had been evacuated during the Second World War to the US, where he stayed with the Astors and, as a five-year-old, sang "God Save the King" for President Franklin Roosevelt and wished him luck in his 1940 re-election campaign against Wendell Wilkie.[18] From an early age

314

he was also involved in his father's electoral campaigns, so there was little doubt that he would stand in the Southend constituency in the by-election after Chips' death, although he was still a 23-year-old student at Oxford. The Conservative Party's central office, egged on by the *Daily Express* amid accusations of nepotism, thought otherwise and tried hard to have another candidate selected. But Chips, and the Guinnesses, had clearly taken good care of the constituency. The local party resisted all outside pressures and selected Paul as the candidate from an initial field of 130 and a shortlist of three. In what was described as a brief and forceful speech afterwards, Lady Gwendolen Iveagh – Paul's grandmother, who had held the parliamentary seat herself before she handed it on to Chips – told the selection convention: "I think you have done right by backing a colt when you know the stable he was trained in."[19] Paul went on to win the by-election and hold the seat for 38 consecutive years.

Shortly after the two cousins had joined the Guinness board, Jonathan's wife Ingrid Wyndham and Paul fell in love. With the insouciance which those brought up as aristocrats manage so well, she and Jonathan, who had three children together, agreed to divorce so that she and Paul could marry. "I was offended, I suppose," Jonathan wrote later, "but not intolerably so; over the previous ten years my wife and I had slipped into a mode of resigned incompatibility."[20] It was before the tabloids got into their full stride, all concerned kept their nerve and the switch was accomplished with remarkably little trouble, he concluded. They continued to share the Guinness board and family relationships amicably as well as the Conservative Party, where they were on opposite wings – Paul on the more liberal wing, who became known as "wets" under Margaret Thatcher's leadership, and Jonathan dallying with the wilder fringes of the right-wing Monday Club. Paul and Ingrid went on to have three children and Jonathan married Suzanne Lisney the following year. The situation prompted Woodrow Wyatt, the acerbic columnist, diarist and sometimes politician, to describe Ingrid as "the girl who thought that more than one Guinness was good for you".[21]

A year after becoming Guinness chairman Benjamin also married. His bride was Miranda Smiley, whose parents, Major Michael Smiley and Lavinia Pearson, owned the imposing Castle Fraser in Aberdeenshire, an elaborate "z-plan" castle made up of a central rectangular block surrounded by smaller circular towers and dating from the sixteenth century; they later donated it to the National Trust of Scotland. The wedding took place in March 1963 at the priory church of St Bartholomew the Great in Smithfield in London, with a reception afterwards at Claridges.[22]

As the 1960s progressed, the company was ticking over, continuing to expand its ancillary activities in a somewhat erratic way, and making unexciting after-tax profits of about £4.5 million a year. Edward Guinness, one of the relations from the banking Guinnesses who worked in the brewery, headed one of its most successful projects, the development of Harp lager, and later was its influential voice in the Brewers' Society in Britain. But most of the Guinnesses were busy with other activities.

It was the decade in which the traditional aristocracy was supplanted to an extent as leaders of society by a new aristocracy of youthful rock musicians and other people in the arts who preoccupied the media, especially the tabloids. While young rock stars, many of them working class, bought stately homes with their sudden riches and prompted outrage with their hedonistic behaviour and spending, many scions of such homes and of previously outrageous families tried to pretend they were now part of the working class. How they fed off each other in this bizarre role-playing was partly exemplified in the Guinness case by the short life and tragic death of Tara Browne, the youngest son of Oonagh Guinness and her second husband, Dominic Browne, Lord Oranmore and Browne.

The 21-year-old Browne was married to a 24-year-old woman from County Down, Noreen "Nicky" MacSherry, and they had two sons, aged three and one and a half, who were made wards of court in England in 1966 in a case that had echoes of the wartime legal battle between Oonagh and her first husband, Philip Kindersley, over their son, Gay's, schooling in England. On 14 October 1966, Nicky asked the High Court in London to order her husband and his mother Oonagh to send the two boys back to England from Ireland. Her lawyer told the court that the boys had gone to Ireland for a ten-day holiday with their grandmother: "When my client went there last Saturday to see the children and bring them back, the grandmother had taken up the position that she was in *loco parentis* and that she had taken the children under her wing and was not going to allow them to return to their mother," he said. Matrimonial difficulties had arisen between husband and wife and it was necessary that the children be brought back to England where they had recently been made wards of court, he added. The court refused an order in the absence of the husband and on the basis that the children were not in any danger while they remained with their grandmother.[23]

It was the start of a lengthy court case which was heard in private over the following weeks and had not concluded when Tara Browne was killed in a car crash in London in the early hours of Sunday, 18 December 1966. An agent for Lotus cars, he was driving his Lotus Elan sports car in South Kensington when it struck a parked van at the corner of Redcliffe Square and Redcliffe Gardens. He died in hospital shortly afterwards; his passenger, 20-year-old model Suki Potier, was shocked but not otherwise injured. Tara had been staying in the Ritz for the previous three weeks and Suki's family said he was driving her home after dinner when the accident occurred.[24] She later told the inquest that a "long low car" had appeared from nowhere, going fairly fast, and Tara swerved to avoid it: "I remember we hit something and I sort of blacked out," she said. Another witness said she saw the blue Lotus Elan travelling very fast before the crash. Police failed to trace any other car. A pathologist said Tara had drunk between half a pint and a pint of beer before the accident and died from brain injuries. The coroner's jury returned a verdict of accidental death.[25]

Less than two weeks after the inquest into Tara's death, the High Court case over his sons came to a conclusion with the judge directing that they remain wards of court until further notice under the care and control of their grandmother Oonagh and that every effort should be made to enable their mother to play an increasing part in their lives. Both women were present at the private hearing in which the judge gave his decision, which was revealed afterwards by a joint statement to the press on behalf of all the parties.[26] (Oonagh still used the title Lady Oranmore and Browne, although she and Browne had been divorced since 1950. She had married Miguel Ferreras, a Cuban-born dress designer based in New York, in 1957 and divorced him in 1965. Thereafter, she called herself Lady Oranmore and Browne again.)

After his death, Tara's body was brought back to Ireland for a funeral service at Christ Church in Dún Laoghaire and burial at Oonagh's estate in Luggala, County Wicklow, where her daughter Tessa had been buried as well. Tara Browne is rarely mentioned without being described as the inspiration for part of The Beatles' classic song "A Day in the Life" which closed their 1967 album, *Sgt Pepper's Lonely Hearts Club Band*. It was recorded towards the end of January 1967 and partly based on news reports about his death in a copy of the *Daily Mail* which John Lennon was reading. Lennon did not use the details of the accident but said he had it in mind when he wrote about someone blowing their mind out in a car after failing to notice that traffic lights had changed.[27] Tara and Lennon did not know each other well, if at all, although they are now inextricably linked and sometimes referred to as friends. Tara's first musical love was opera but he was friendly with some other rock musicians at the time, including Paul McCartney's brother Mike, who used the stage name Mike McGear. He was not a public figure at the time of his death, as the song implies.

The Irish composer Sean Ó Riada also put a poem by Hans Arp to music which he entitled "In Memoriam Tara Browne": Ó Riada knew Tara through his elder brother Garech, who was deeply involved in the Irish music scene and was the founder of Claddagh Records and an instigator of The Chieftains, one of the most successful Irish music groups.

Contemporary newspaper reports of the accident and the inquest all mentioned that Browne was in line to inherit about £1 million from a family trust when he reached 25. His death led inadvertently to another court case over those trusts in 1989 when his sons, Dorian and Julian Browne, were in their twenties. The Iveagh Trust went to the High Court in London to have it determine complex questions over whether or not the two were entitled to inherit directly from the trust founded by their great-great-grandfather, Edward Iveagh, in the 1920s for the benefit of his children and grandchildren, through a trust their grandmother Oonagh had set up in 1959. She had passed on one of the Iveagh funds she had inherited to a trust for her three surviving sons, Tara, Garech (who had adopted the Irish version of his surname, de Brún) and Gay Kindersley, and their children. One of the questions to be decided was whether she was entitled to pass it on to her grandchildren directly under the terms of the original Iveagh trust or could leave it only to her children. It involved a legal wrangle over the definition of "issue" in the first Lord Iveagh's will. There were also questions about domicile to be decided, which would affect the taxes paid on the trusts.

Dorian and Julian's Uncle Garech arrived at the court to give evidence "looking like a cross between an eastern guru and a cheerful friar" in a three-quarter-length wool cloak with a newspaper stuffed down its front, "a frothing grey beard" and "his wiry, receding hair in a pigtail", according to *The Independent*. He argued that his mother was not entitled to stipulate that funds she inherited from Lord Iveagh should be transferred to his children, if he had any. However, the judge ruled against Garech's "narrow construction" of a clause about "issue" in Iveagh's 1920 will and in favour of a wider construction which would allow Oonagh to include her grandchildren in the division of the trust fund. As a result of the ruling, Dorian and Julian were said to be entitled to a sum "in the low millions". Although the decision was not to his benefit, Garech said afterwards that the ruling was "highly satisfactory because we have been trying to get this problem sorted out for a very long time". His nephews had been frozen out of their money for five years because of doubts about the meaning of the clause in the Iveagh will, he said. He denied that the dispute had created a split in the Guinness family: "I am deeply fond of my nephews and I am delighted that they will now receive their money after considerable delay," he told reporters.[28]

The death of Tara Browne was only one of a series of accidental and other tragedies that affected the descendants of the first Lord Iveagh over the following decades, prompting tabloid newspapers to create a Guinness "curse" to explain the apparent bad luck of the family. Among them was the death of Benjamin's younger sister, Henrietta, who apparently killed herself in 1978 by jumping off the Ponte delle Torri aqueduct in the town of Spoleto in central Italy. Fondly remembered by her contemporary cousins as being great fun, she had never recovered fully from a car crash in France in 1963 in which her boyfriend, Michael Beeby, once described as "Britain's best known beatnik", was killed. She suffered neck injuries in the crash which left her with psychological problems and occasional episodes of disorientation. The medical advice suggested that these would fade with time but she suffered a nervous breakdown shortly before her death at the age of 35. Being a Guinness and an heiress, she had inevitably caught the interest of the tabloids when she planned to marry an Italian waiter in London, had become a Catholic, and bought him a house before the wedding was called off. She finally married another Italian, Luigi Marinori, and they and their baby daughter lived with his parents in Spoleto. On the day of her death, she was seen walking across the aqueduct, climbing onto its parapet and disappearing; the Italian police treated her death as suicide. The Press Council in Britain subsequently upheld complaints against the *Daily Mail* and *Daily Express* for publishing photographs of her body lying in the stream where she died and her mother, Lady Elizabeth More O'Ferrall, complained about journalists adding to the suffering by pursuing the family.[29] The day on which she died, coincidentally or otherwise, her trust funds were released to her. Her brother Benjamin subsequently planted a tree in her memory in Oughterard cemetery in County Kildare, between the graves of the first Arthur Guinness and his parents.

The family also suffered its share of the fall-out from the waves of drug-taking that washed through the young and rich of British society during and after the 1960s. It was such a common phenomenon at the time that detectives in London knew them as the "sugar people", an ironic amalgam of "sugar daddy" from their rich parents and the drugs they were taking.[30] The same year as Henrietta Guinness died, one of Maureen's granddaughters, 17-year-old Natalia Citkovitz, died in the bath in her Chelsea flat while trying to inject herself with heroin after attending a literary party. The inquest heard that she had passed out and returned an open verdict of death by asphyxiation due to alcoholic intoxication.[31] A not-dissimilar tragedy was the death in 1986 of Olivia Channon, the 22-year-old daughter of Paul and Ingrid Channon, from drink and drugs at a party following her final history exam at Oxford. She was, as the coroner put it later, no stranger to drugs and her best friend had gone to London to collect heroin for the party. Her friends met Olivia outside the examination hall with glasses of champagne and they all went on to the college buttery for more drinks, including "black velvets" (Guinness and champagne), and ending up in the rooms of Count Gottfried von Bismarck, the 22-year-old great-great-grandson of

Germany's "Iron Chancellor". She was seen taking the heroin by her second cousin, Sebastian Guinness, the son of Jonathan and Suzanne Guinness, who had travelled to Oxford for the party. Later, she had lain down on a bed and gone to sleep. She was found dead there in the morning. A pathologist said she died from breathing failure as a result of a toxic cocktail of heroin and alcohol and the inquest returned a verdict of death by misadventure. In the aftermath, her best friend was sentenced to nine months in jail for possessing and supplying the heroin, her cousin Sebastian to four months for possessing drugs, and a man described by the judge as an "out and out pusher" in London to four years.[32] Olivia was posthumously awarded a third-class degree in modern history and left an estate with a gross value of £686,000; her will, made the previous Christmas, left it to her brother and sister.[33]

———

As the new chairman of Arthur Guinness Son & Company, Benjamin presided over his first annual general meeting in January 1963, an event that was to cause him an enormous amount of anguish over most of the following 25 years. He was painfully shy and public speaking was an excruciating ordeal for him, even with pre-scripted remarks, the support of fellow-directors and executives, and, usually, an audience of benign shareholders. He was known on occasions to have thrown up before such ordeals and the pressure cannot have been helpful to his increasingly bad health as the years went on.

It was recognised within the family that he would need help with the running of Guinness. Sir Hugh Beaver had suffered a heart attack in the late 1950s and a successor as managing director was required: Alan Lennox-Boyd, Benjamin's uncle by marriage, was chosen for the job. Lennox-Boyd was a successful Conservative politician, representing Mid-Bedfordshire in the House of Commons since 1931, and a director of Guinness on and off since 1942. He stepped down from the company during periods when he was in government as a minister in the Colonial Office and the ministry of Transport and Civil Aviation. From 1954 on he was Secretary of State for the Colonies, a position in which he laid the groundwork for decolonisation, although he was a high Tory with a romantic notion of the British Empire and its positive effects.[34] An imposing six feet five inches tall, Lennox-Boyd was highly personable, warm and charming to the extent that he was well-liked by many political opponents who did not share his right-wing politics. By the late 1950s he had gone as far in politics as he was likely to go and was also at odds with some of his cabinet colleagues about the faster pace of decolonisation that they wanted. Thus, he decided not to contest the next general election and was about to announce his intentions in March 1959 when it emerged that 11 detainees had been beaten to death by their guards in a detention camp at Hola in Kenya at the end of what was popularly known in England as the Mau-Mau rebellion. As the Conservative government came under intense political pressure, Lennox-Boyd withheld his announcement to avoid appearing to step down in response to the massacre and the usual attempted official cover-up (the detainees were first said to have died from drinking contaminated water). He fought and won the election in October 1959 and was replaced as Colonial Secretary afterwards. The following summer he was given a peerage as Viscount Boyd of Merton and moved to the House of Lords and, effectively, to Guinness as its managing director.

Within a few months of his takeover – and presumably not entirely coincidentally – Guinness announced that it was going to build its third brewery, in the newly independent Nigeria. The foundation stone for the £2 million plant was laid at Ikeja, near Lagos, by Benjamin before he became chairman of the company, and it opened the same month as his marriage. Nigeria was already Guinness's largest foreign market and its Ikeja brewery, with a capacity of 100,000 barrels a year, was a joint operation with Unilever and some local investors. It was followed a couple of years later by a brewery in Malaysia (in whose independence Lennox-Boyd had played a key role) and then by a succession of new breweries or contract arrangements with brewers in a variety of countries from Canada to Japan. The foreign breweries used concentrate for Foreign Extra stout produced in Dublin, a stronger and sweeter stout than the traditional brew that went down better in hotter countries and resolved the recurring problems of high acidity, which had affected foreign sales in earlier decades. Later, most of the Foreign Stout was brewed abroad although St James's Gate continued to provide a portion of it as well as being involved in research and marketing. Some of the foreign breweries gave rise to occasional problems about repatriating profits but they were generally successful in contributing to the overall group's profits.[35] Sales in Europe and America also increased but jointly accounted for only about 10 per cent of the total export trade of more than 500,000 barrels by 1970, compared to almost 50 per cent in Nigeria, 20 per cent in Singapore and Malaysia and eight per cent in the Caribbean.[36]

Benjamin became the third Earl of Iveagh five years after becoming Guinness chairman when Rupert died after suffering a heart attack at his Pyrford home in September 1967 at the age of 93. (His wife of 63 years, Gwendolen, had died at Pyrford some 18 months earlier and they are both buried at Elveden churchyard.) Agricultural development had remained his prime interest and he had succeeded by the 1950s in turning Elveden into one of the largest, if not the largest, farming enterprise in England.[37] Rupert had not made the same mistakes as his brother Ernest when it came to passing on his wealth: he had already tied up most of it in trusts and investment vehicles in the US and Canada long before he died. As a result, he left a gross estate in England of a mere £262,149, on which estate duty of £38,050 was paid. His will was written less than two weeks before his wife died in February 1966 and appointed two of his daughters, Lady Honor Svejdar and Lady Patricia Boyd as his executors, along with Bernard Norfolk of the Iveagh Trustees. His three daughters, including Lady Brigid von Preussen, were given £50,000 to be divided equally between them "for the purposes which I have made known to them". They were also to receive equal shares of his residuary estate after several bequests had been made, including £1,000 each to his three sons-in-law and his daughter–in-law, Lady Elizabeth More O'Ferrall.[38] Rupert was domiciled in Ireland and his will specified that it was to be interpreted under Irish law.

Rupert's success in farming, his widely acknowledged role in medical research, his continuation of the Iveagh philanthropic ventures, and his long experience as head of the company had given him an authority in the family and the company that it was virtually impossible for Benjamin to replicate. Benjamin's ambition may have been to be an East Anglian farmer but there was no prospect of him being left to be that alone. Not surprisingly, as chairman he relied heavily on the company's executives, a strategy that did not win the approval of his cousin and fellow director, Jonathan, who, unflatteringly christened him King Log after the Aesop fable about the frogs who wanted a king and were given a log as their king by the gods. Unhappy with the inert log as their king, the frogs sought a new one and were given a stork, which gobbled them all up. As Jonathan admitted, the analogy turned out to be more prescient than he could have realised.[39] Benjamin does not appear to have sought the advice of family members on the board, taken them into his confidence, or used them as a united front. As tradition required, the family directors continued to meet for tea with the company managers the day before the annual general meeting, but it was just an old habit, not a forum for decision-making or planning collective action. In any event, most of the family directors were remote from the business and had little expertise in its activities.

Nevertheless, the company seemed to be progressing satisfactorily. Annual profits were going up again in the late 1960s – to an after-tax £7.25 million by 1969 – after a period of stagnation which had been marked, if not created, by a policy stance along the lines outlined by Rupert at one AGM in the late 1950s that now was not the time to over-commit themselves in any direction.[40] Alan Lennox-Boyd remained as managing director until 1967, when he stood down and became joint vice-chairman with Bryan Moyne.

By this stage, several family members were living full-time or most of the time in Ireland. They included Rupert's daughter Honor (Phibblestown House); Ernest's daughters Aileen (Luttrellstown Castle), Oonagh (Luggala) and Maureen (Clandeboye) and grandson Garech de Brún (Luggala); and Walter's son Bryan (some of the time at Knockmaroon) and grandson Desmond (Leixlip Castle). Benjamin took out Irish citizenship and joined them in the 1970s to take up residence full-time at Farmleigh because of the high wealth and other taxes imposed by the Labour government in Britain; they included a 98 per cent tax on any investment income over £20,000 a year and counted all assets, including art works, as wealth for taxation purposes. In a letter to company shareholders, he said he was "confronted by unusual personal and family taxation problems" and recent and proposed taxes in the United Kingdom could make his financial position "intolerable" if he were to remain there.[41]

Changing his tax residency required that he not enter the UK for three years, which also had the benefit from his point of view of not having to chair the Guinness AGM in London for those years; instead, the retiring managing director, Robert McNeile, who had succeeded Alan Lennox-Boyd, was appointed joint chairman to carry out such functions.

However, Benjamin was given another public role in Ireland which he probably did not want but felt he had little choice but to accept graciously. The newly elected Taoiseach, Liam Cosgrave, named him as one of his eleven nominees to the Seanad in 1973, giving him the distinction of being both a member of the Oireachtas and the House of Lords, although he never exercised the latter right that came with his earldom. Cosgrave's decision to appoint him was entirely his own: he did not consult anyone else but chose Benjamin "mainly because I thought the country owed something to the Guinness family".[42] He also knew Benjamin slightly from their mutual interest in horse racing and the bloodstock industry and through his friendship with Roderic More O'Ferrall of Kildangan Stud whose brother, Rory, was Benjamin's stepfather. Benjamin never spoke in the Seanad but he attended and voted regularly with the Fine Gael-Labour coalition government during his four years as a member and also attended Fine Gael parliamentary party meetings. Apart from his public shyness, Benjamin's period as a senator was also upset by a series of operations he underwent for diverticulitis, a painful condition of the digestive tract which can be very debilitating. Over the years, he had no less than thirteen operations for the condition.[43]

He gave the use of Farmleigh to the government for an informal meeting of EEC foreign ministers in 1975 during Ireland's first presidency of the community, foreshadowing the house's later role in the twenty-first century. The hospitality was later reciprocated when the Minister for Foreign Affairs, Garret FitzGerald, allowed him to use Iveagh House as the venue for a dinner of European brewers, a rare occasion on which the building was used for a private event since it had been donated to the state by Rupert Iveagh. Apart from these obligations, he spent most of his time farming, leasing an extra thousand acres of land near Mulhuddart in County Meath and being among the first to import and develop a herd of Charollais cattle in Ireland. His main hobby was as a bibliophile, collecting first editions of Irish authors – he built up a near-complete library of the first editions of all the main writers from Edmund Spenser and Jonathan Swift to W.B. Yeats and James Joyce – and becoming an authority on book-bindings. He also had an extensive collection of books, pamphlets and manuscripts on Irish history. Unlike some bibliophiles, he was said to enjoy reading the books he collected.[44]

His departure to Ireland did not make him popular among the residents of Elveden and the other villages around his Suffolk estate who depended on the estate for their livelihoods. They feared that he would sell up altogether, a fear that was not relieved by his decision in the mid-1980s to sell off the contents of Elveden Hall on the grounds that he could not foresee living in the house again because he now lived in Ireland. The four-day sale in May 1984 provided a rare opportunity for the curious to view the mansion and its contents, helped by Christies' advance publicity, which described the house as "one of the strangest stately homes in Britain".[45] The hype was effective and the sale attracted many rich locals, as well as antique dealers and some with specific historical interests. The last included a group of Sikhs from Birmingham who were interested in a large portrait of Duleep Singh, which went to an American collector for £15,120, three times its upper estimate; the Sikhs had to content themselves with a lithograph copy, which went for £918, compared to the auctioneer's estimate of £60 to £100. The Hall's paintings made a total of £972,872, instead of the £540,000 pre-auction estimate. Dozens of what were described as ordinary coal scuttles went under the hammer, some making up to £1,000. By the end of the sale, some £6 million had been raised, more than double the expected £2.5 million.[46]

By the early 1980s, Benjamin's marriage had broken down. While he still lived in Dublin, but was now free to visit England, his wife Miranda spent more and more time in London. She was granted a divorce at the end of 1984 on the grounds that they had not lived together for two years.[47] His health was also under pressure and he was drinking and smoking heavily.

Meanwhile, the Guinness company had been going through a transformation. During his absence from board meetings in London, the other seven family directors had united to block a proposed rights issue to raise £19 million, mainly on the grounds that it would dilute their shareholding in the company.[48] The proposal came from the management and was a recognition that the company was on the slide – not a precipitous one but nonetheless a steady downhill slope. It was unable to fund needed re-equipment at St James's Gate and further diversification without borrowing more and more money. Benjamin was allowed back into the UK for brief visits from 1978 onwards, in time to preside over a series of less-than-impressive annual results which confirmed the company's problems. Everything was not going wrong but significant elements were and attempts at resolving the problems were not working.

One attempt to address stout's perceived weakness as an old man's drink was Guinness Light, a lighter stout designed to appeal to new drinkers and women. Launched with considerable fanfare by the Guinness PR machine as the first major new product from St James's Gate in almost two centuries, it went on sale in selected pubs only in Dublin and Belfast in the summer of 1979 and was extended to Limerick some months later. Preceded by extensive market research, it was backed by an extensive advertising campaign with the slogan "They said it couldn't be done". That proved to be a double-edged tag line because it quickly became apparent that it could not be done, at least not on this occasion. In spite of all the hype, Guinness Light did not catch on, although nobody could put their finger on exactly why. Traditional stout drinkers derided it, of course, but people claimed to like it and then did not buy it. At the end of the day, a spokesman for St James's Gate concluded: "People saw it as something that looked like Guinness without being Guinness. They thought of it as being neither one thing nor the other."[49] Guinness Light was withdrawn officially in February 1981, but it had failed long before then.

The Guinness Light disaster, although limited to only three cities in Ireland, could not have come at a worse time, coinciding with a string of bad financial results and tending to confirm a belief that Guinness had lost its way. On the surface, the results might not look particularly bad but they were, and were seen to be, bad both in comparison with other brewers and when the details were analysed. For instance, the results for the year to September 1980 showed that Guinness was doing well in Ireland – which accounted for more than half its profit for the first time since the company had become a major force in the British market in the nineteenth century –

but its efforts at diversification had gone seriously awry. Whereas the non-brewing parts of the company had contributed £15.2 million to pre-tax profits in 1979, their contribution had collapsed to £5.4 million in 1980; overall, profits were down from £53 million to £43 million, with half of that coming from Ireland where it had about 92 per cent of the beer market.[50] (The results were affected by the break in parity between the Irish pound and sterling, which also prevented Irish employees from receiving share bonuses because of exchange controls.) The decline continued: its half-year results in June 1981 showed profits down another 13 per cent and came with a warning from Benjamin that the final dividend might not be maintained. The prospect of Guinness skipping a dividend was unheard of – and it did not actually happen – but the warning had an immediate effect on its share price. It had stood at about 90p in London a year earlier but it closed down more than ten per cent to 66p after the announcement and continued to drift in the following months; by the end of September 1981, the end of the company's year, it was down to 53p.

Something needed to be done and done with increasing urgency, although that was not immediately obvious to the family: "decline looked likely, but catastrophe did not seem imminent", as Jonathan Guinness put it later.[51] The managing director, Tony Purssell, was more perceptive about the seriousness of the problem and the side of the business that needed to be addressed if it was to be rectified – marketing. A major improvement in marketing was obviously critical if there was no new product available to reverse the slide in sales of stout. A head-hunting agency was employed and it found Ernest Saunders, a marketing executive with Nestlé, based in Vevey in Switzerland.

Aesop's fable of King Log was about to come true.

CHAPTER THIRTEEN

Success and Scandal

"We could have been the British Rockefellers or Rothschilds . . . but we lost our way."

Attributed to BENJAMIN GUINNESS, the third Earl of Iveagh, by Ernest Saunders

Ernest Saunders was born Ernest Schleyer in Vienna in 1935, the son of parents of Jewish origin who fled to England from Nazism in 1938. They subsequently changed their name to Saunders, chosen from a phone book, and he was brought up as an English boy, baptised in the Church of England, educated at St Paul's in London and studied law at Cambridge.[1] His lack of interest in law led him on to business and a job in 3M where he discovered marketing and his niche. He moved on to the marketing department of the advertising agency J. Walter Thompson, and from there to the Beecham group, Great Universal Stores and on to Nestlé, where his tasks included trying to combat boycotts and criticisms of the company's efforts to persuade new mothers in developing countries to use its baby milk preparations in environments with inadequate hygiene and in preference to breastfeeding their newborn babies.

Saunders agreed to take on a position with Arthur Guinness & Co. but only if he was managing director rather than marketing manager. That led to a brief standoff with the existing managing director, Tony Purssell, who had seen the newcomer as being on a lower level. However, Benjamin Iveagh agreed with Saunders' request and a deal was reached with Purssell, who became a joint deputy vice-chairman of the company, while Saunders took up office as managing director on 1 October 1981. Other board changes around the same time saw Simon Lennox-Boyd replace his father Alan, who was killed in a road accident in London in March 1983 at the age of 78. He and Bryan Moyne had had dinner together in Chelsea and were crossing the Fulham Road to look in the window of an antique shop when he was struck by a car and was dead on arrival in hospital. Bryan Moyne had finally retired as vice-chairman in 1979 after being a director since 1934 and Maureen, the Marchioness of Dufferin and Ava, stepped down in favour of her son, Sheridan, the Marquis of Dufferin and Ava. Two of Bryan's sons, Jonathan and Finn Guinness, were also on the board, along with Edward and Peter Guinness, the two company executives who came from the banking branch of the Guinness family. It was still very much operating as a family firm at board level in an era when family firms were being gobbled up by professionally managed conglomerates.

Saunders' arrival in the company was generally welcomed by the family directors. He himself found Benjamin "charming and diffident" but looking much older than his 44 years when he met him for the first time, for dinner at Farmleigh (Benjamin was just out of hospital at the time). Saunders' description of Farmleigh was less than flattering and somewhat exaggerated: an "enormous entrance hall" lined with dozens of Wellington boots; a table for two "in a huge, draughty dining room" that could have seated 50; a cat walking through the butter on the table; and the "tremendous impact" of Benjamin's dog farting in the study. "Despite the provocation I kept my nose tightly closed and my mouth shut," he said later.[2]

Saunders made a good impression on the family (with the exception of Benjamin's then wife Miranda, who never warmed to him).[3] He was not brash and aggressive or in any way a caricature of the gung-ho financial wheeler-dealer who came to epitomise the Thatcherite 1980s. On the contrary, he was very tall and slightly stooped, giving him a mildly academic air which appeared to fit in perfectly with the culture and traditions of the Guinness company and its Oxbridge recruits. He was also charming and a good listener. Almost everybody was pleased, other perhaps than his predecessor, Tony Purssell, who, in rightly seeking to strengthen management, had not sought to replace himself.

Saunders quickly discovered that Guinness was going to be a challenge. It was his first position as a managing director, not just in charge of marketing but of all aspects of the company, and there were huge gaps in its administration. He found that the company lacked adequate financial information and back-up services, such as legal services, and there were the problems of all the non-brewing companies, of which Guinness now had an astonishing 150. They had been acquired in a largely haphazard manner and many of their previous managers or owners remained in charge of them; some were even said to be competing with each other without realising it.[4] Rather than a solution to the declining demand for stout, they had become part of the problem and central to the belief among financial commentators and analysts that Guinness had lost its way.

To fill the management gap and get a grip of Guinness's disparate activities, Saunders hired an American multinational business consultancy, Bain & Co., which had recently opened an office in London. Among its consultants seconded to Guinness was a very talented Frenchman in his early thirties, Olivier Roux, who effectively became Guinness's financial director and a member of the company's board while still working for Bain. The "Bainies", as they quickly became known within Guinness, spread out through the group and were greeted with the normal suspicion accorded to outside consultants. They came up with a five-year plan, which involved cutting costs and getting rid of extraneous companies in the first two years and then moving to an expansionist mode. In his first year, Saunders, who became known as "Deadly Ernest" to some executives, especially in Ireland, managed to divest the group of a range of interests, including Callard and Bowser sweets, river cruisers, holiday villages, horticultural services, veterinary products, plastic containers and an expensive film finance division which nobody seemed to understand, but which was losing money and eventually wound up at an astronomical cost of £49 million.[5] The sale raised some £40 million for the company over a couple of years and allowed it reduce borrowings, which had been running at around £100 million at the start of the decade.[6]

The clearing-out of subsidiary companies and the reorganisation of the management saw pre-tax profits rise by some 18 per cent from £42 million to £51 million in a year. New advertising campaigns – one playing on its oldest theme with the slogan "Guinless isn't good for you"; another on the similarity between the words Guinness and genius – received a lot of ancillary, and positive, publicity. The share-price rose steadily again, more than doubling to 134p by the beginning of 1984 when the re-organisation part of the plan was completed. Little time was wasted before turning to expansion: Guinness took over the quoted newsagents' group Martin, which had some 500 shops in Britain, in June 1984. It followed that by acquiring Neighbourhood Stores plc, which held the franchise for "7-Eleven" stores in England; Lewis Meeson Ltd; and RS McColl Ltd. These acquisitions gave it some 1,100 shops, making it the largest CTN (confectionery, tobacco and newsagent) chain in Britain. But its expansionist phase was only really beginning.

Guinness took a quantum step forward in 1985 with its next targeted acquisition – an ambitious and aggressive £347 million hostile bid for control of Arthur Bell, the most successful Scottish distiller, with up to 25 per cent of the Scotch whisky market. Guinness began by offering Bell shareholders nine Guinness shares for every ten they held in Bell or a cash alternative of 225p per Bell share, almost twice the pre-bid price of Bell's shares. The Guinness share price at the launch of the bid was 270p a share and its continuing value was obviously important and relevant to the progress of the bid. As a measure of the change in Guinness's corporate attitude, Benjamin Iveagh sent a circular to Bell's shareholders telling them that their company had lost its way, had no credible strategy for future growth and was making inadequate returns from its subsidiaries and acquisitions[7] – criticisms that had been levelled at his own company less than five years earlier. On the other hand, Bell's ran a newspaper ad asking pointed questions, such as: "If Guinness' management is so good, why does it appear to depend so extensively on American consultants Bain & Co, and at what cost?" The answer, though it was not known publicly at the time, was £8.7 million in 1985 for up to 100 "Bainies" working on Guinness business at any one time.[8] Asking the headline question of Guinness, "What's Under the Froth?" Bell's answer was "Not Much".[9] But it was enough to persuade Bell's shareholders to throw in their lot with Guinness after the latter had raised its bid to £370 million.

The bid was far and away the most ambitious move by Guinness since it had become a public company; its largest acquisition previously was the takeover of Martin newsagents at a fraction of the cost, £47 million. Its own market value at the launch of its bid was about £500 million and it had taken over a company about three-quarters of its own size. Bell's was also a drinks company, albeit in the new field for Guinness of spirits, a fact that did not please all the Guinness family; Bryan Moyne, for one, disapproved of any involvement with spirits, in the time-honoured belief that spirits were harmful, while beer, especially stout, was wholesome. The takeovers were funded by new shares in Guinness which diluted the family's holdings. They had been reduced by about ten per cent by the takeover of Martin's newsagents and after the Bell's takeover it was reckoned that the family held approximately 12.5 per cent of the newly enlarged Guinness group.[10] But, of course, it was 12.5 per cent of a much bigger company: on the basis of the share price, the reduced family holding was worth perhaps four times what its larger holding had been worth in 1981. Some thought Guinness had paid too much for Bell's but the company was now seen by the market as having turned the corner and gone from being a fading family business to being a successful predator in a market fuelled by takeovers. By the end of 1985, the Guinness share price was up to 320p, six times what it had been four years earlier, in the trough of 1981 when Saunders arrived on the scene.

Takeover battles were high-octane events, especially when two or more rivals wanted the same company and when based on share prices. The tactics in such battles included measures to keep up one's own share price; buying the shares of the target company; and trying to undermine the share price of the rival bidder. The rules governing takeovers restricted the amounts of the target's shares a company could hold and the price it could pay for them, and required the disclosure of various interests. In the heat of often intense, high-stakes takeover battles, however, the rules were not always easy to police. Guinness and Saunders had been exposed to some of these tactics in its takeover of Arthur Bell, but its next venture brought it into a higher league in many senses.

The Distillers Company was the main supplier of Scotch whisky, with well-known brands like Johnnie Walker, Haig, White Horse and Dewars, as well as the likes of Gordon's gin and other spirits. It had been created by an amalgamation of family-owned distilleries in the 1920s, had drifted along on the strength of its brands, a bit like Guinness itself, and tried its hand at diversification. Unfortunately, like many other brewers and distillers, the diversification included pharmaceuticals and Distillers had distributed a new tranquilliser called Thalidomide, invented in Germany in the 1950s. It was prescribed to pregnant women for morning sickness in the 1960s in the belief that it had no side-effects; as it turned out, it caused serious birth defects, notably stunted arms and legs, and Distillers had fought a highly damaging rearguard action over it for years. By the early 1980s, the company was seen as a likely takeover target.

Shortly after the Guinness takeover of Bell's, another company primarily involved in retailing but with a small distilling arm, Argyll plc, made a bid to take over Distillers in a share deal that would value Distillers at £1.9 billion. The timing was bad for Guinness. It was still absorbing Bell's but, on the other hand, a revitalised Distillers would threaten its move into distilling; a significant factor in Bell's success had been Distillers' doziness. An analysis by Bain & Co. for Guinness put a value on Distillers of £2.7 billion.[11]

While Guinness was debating what to do about this threat, Distillers approached it, asking it to be a "white knight" and save it from Argyll by merging the two companies. Although it was to be a "merger", Distillers was conscious of being seen to be swallowed up by a company, Guinness, that was half its size and afraid of losing its Scottish identity to a company known for an Irish brand and based in London. There was no doubt in anyone's mind, however, that Saunders and Guinness would run the merged group if the merger went ahead. Guinness offered that both companies would retain their own boards of directors but there would be a new holding company to manage the group as a whole. Both Benjamin Iveagh and the chairman of Distillers, John Connell, had to be persuaded that neither of them could be the new board's chairman and they, along with Saunders, were to be vice-chairmen. To assuage Scottish fears about Distillers' loss of identity, they chose a pillar of the Scottish establishment, Sir Thomas Risk, the governor of the Bank of Scotland, as chairman of the new entity – "a Scottish Lord Iveagh", in Saunders' description. They also made a commitment to site the headquarters of the new company in Scotland and that Distillers would pay Guinness's costs if the latter's bid failed and Argyll won.

Saunders claimed later to be a reluctant convert to the idea of taking over Distillers because of the speed at which it followed the Bell acquisition and other factors. But he was carried along by the momentum of fast-moving events and convinced by the opportunity to create one of the world's major drinks companies with a portfolio of brands with worldwide reputations. He found Benjamin to be an enthusiastic supporter of the idea.

> Iveagh was extraordinary. He was completely positive and said he would support any move I wanted to make. He said the family could have been the British Rockefellers or Rothschilds, with the Guinness Mahon bank as well, but they had lost their way. So anything that could put the Guinness family back in the big time he was in favour of.[12]

The agreement was approved by a Sunday meeting of the Distillers board followed by a separate late-night meeting of the Guinness directors the same day. For most of the Guinness directors, it was the first confirmation (there had been rumours and speculation about a Guinness bid) they had received of the high-risk move on which they were about to embark and they approved it. The next day, 20 January 1986, Guinness launched its bid for Distillers with the latter's support, offering eight Guinness shares and £7 cash for every five Distillers shares or a cash alternative of 584.8p per share. The offer significantly upped the ante on the Argyll £1.9 billion offer, valuing Distillers at £2.27 billion – more than twice Guinness's own market value. Argyll replied with a £2.3 billion offer. Much hinged initially on whether or not the Guinness bid would be referred to the Mergers and Monopolies Commission (which had already cleared the Argyll bid) on the grounds that Guinness's success would give it an unfair dominance of the whisky industry in the UK through Bell's and its new brands. An inquiry could take months and effectively hand victory to Argyll.

The conventional wisdom at the time, as expressed by newspapers, was that it would have to be investigated and fate intervened to seem to confirm that prospect. Paul Channon was suddenly appointed to the British cabinet as Secretary of State for Trade and Industry – the ministerial position which had to decide on a referral – by Prime Minister Margaret Thatcher to replace Leon Brittan, who had resigned over a scandal about the fate of the Westland helicopter company. Channon had been a junior Minister in Conservative governments on and off since the early 1970s, when he served a stint in Northern Ireland – not least because of his Guinness connections

– during which the then Northern Ireland Secretary William Whitelaw had flown republican leaders, including the IRA chief of staff, Seán MacStiofain, and Gerry Adams, to London for talks at Channon's home in Cheyne Walk in Chelsea. Although seen as an able administrator, Channon was not above indulging some of his eccentricities as a Minister; in the Department of the Environment, he had his office furnished with black wallpaper interspersed with shiny, abstract blobs, a tiger-skin sofa, and kidney-shaped chairs. According to the Labour politician Gerald Kaufman, the effect "evoked the same terrified awe customarily aroused by the wilder extravagances of Mad King Ludwig [of Bavaria]".[13] Thatcher and Channon were never mutual fans: he was one of a group of "wets" who, over a famous dinner, identified her as one of the least likely people to become party leader shortly before she became just that; she once confided in a colleague that there would be no room in her government for "that millionaire".[14] However, she did appoint him to a succession of junior ministries, notably as Arts Minister in the early 1980s, but they were all seen as reluctant appointments – that is, when others had turned down the jobs. It was in such circumstances that she finally appointed him to the cabinet, as Secretary of State for Trade and Industry; he was suddenly seen as a safe pair of hands to steer the government out of the Westland mess.

His cabinet appointment came within days of the Guinness bid for Distillers and initially seemed to scupper it. Saunders, for one, thought that Channon would want to demonstrate his impartiality "by stabbing us in the front as well as in the back".[15] As a millionaire whose wealth depended on Guinness, a senior member of the family, and a former director of the company, Channon could not adjudicate on whether or not to refer the bid to the commission. He did the only thing he could do – excused himself and handed the decision to a junior minister, Geoffrey Pattie, who proceeded to refer the bid to the MMC. That set off an intense round of lobbying on behalf of Guinness with Sir Jack Lyons, a highly successful financier, retailer and arts patron (who was also Bain's landlord in London), appealing to Thatcher herself while others tried to devise a way around the problem. The solution was a promise that Guinness would divest itself of enough of its whisky interests to keep its remaining ones below 25 per cent of the British whisky market if it succeeded in taking control of Distillers. On that basis, a new bid could be made. Argyll went to court but failed to change the decision.

A final round of rival offers pushed up the value of Distillers to £2.45 billion from Guinness and £2.5 billion from Argyll. However, the value of the offers now depended on the Guinness and Argyll share prices and Guinness claimed it was offering more because its share price was rising. On 18 April, Guinness declared victory with more than 50 per cent of the Distillers' shareholders accepting its offer. The move that seemed to decide the outcome was the declaration of support for Guinness by a Swiss bank, Bank Leu, which had just spent £70 million buying three per cent of Distillers shares. It had been a fierce and exhausting battle for everyone involved – but the aftermath proved to be even more controversial.

Ernest Saunders wasted little time after the battle in gathering control of the new drinks company into his own hands. The chairman of Distillers, John Connell, was pushed upstairs to become president of that company to make way for Saunders himself as a new director and chairman of the distilling company. The move was contrary to what Guinness had said it would do during the bid and he followed it up with an even more controversial decision – to drop the idea of a two-tier board structure altogether. Sir Thomas Risk, the "Scottish Lord Iveagh" who was to have been chairman of a new overall holding company, was abandoned and Saunders himself became chairman of the Guinness board – which would run the new group – while Benjamin Iveagh was also moved upstairs to become president of Guinness. (Saunders had already tried to kick Benjamin upstairs as president the previous year after the Bell's takeover.)[16]

What became known as the Risk Affair caused outrage over the way Guinness went back on the promises it had made in its bid documents for Distillers. Saunders claimed that Risk was now demanding a greater role for himself than had been agreed, but few people were impressed by his claim. It was seen as arrogant and high-handed, and feelings were particularly strong in Scotland, which was also told now that the new company headquarters would not be in Edinburgh after all but would remain in London. But it was not just what Saunders dubbed the "Scottish mafia" who were angered by the repudiation of the earlier promises. The powers-that-be were unimpressed too; Michael Howard, Paul Channon's junior minister, warned that a Department of Trade and Industry inquiry would be launched if Guinness did not implement the commitments in its bid documents. Agreement was quickly reached again on a compromise formula involving independent directors, some Scottish, with power to select or remove the chairman. Crucially – although people did not necessarily appreciate how crucial it was at the time – the Guinness share price began to slump, partly as a result of the controversy, partly as a result of the market in the shares calming down after the heightened atmosphere of the takeover battle.

Four new non-executive directors were selected by Saunders and appointed to satisfy the DTI: Ian McLaurin, chairman of Tesco; Anthony Greener, chairman of Dunhill; Sir Norman Macfarlane, chairman and chief executive of the Macfarlane Group; and Sir David Plastow, managing director and chairman of Vickers. On the same day, Finn Guinness and Sheridan Dufferin stepped down from the board. (Sheridan died of AIDS the following year: married without children, he was well into his thirties before he was said to have realised he was gay when he noticed the attractions of a male – and gay – ballet dancer.) Some others of the Guinness family were also disillusioned. Simon Boyd had already resigned from the board several weeks after the victory, feeling that the family was being ignored. Neither he nor Jonathan Guinness was invited to a victory party at Saunders' home in Buckinghamshire. Boyd reminded Benjamin of their grandfather Rupert's dictum that "others run the brewery, we say who will run it". Benjamin reportedly replied: "I will continue to run the brewery."[17] The only family directors left at this stage were Benjamin and Jonathan (as well as Edward Guinness from the wider Guinness family).

However, Guinness shareholders were more than happy with their saviour, Ernest Saunders. His appointment as chairman and continuation as chief executive of the expanded group was endorsed by a crushing ten to one majority at a special meeting chaired by Benjamin in September 1986. As *The Irish Times* reported: "What had been billed in advance as the trial of the board's sincerity turned out to be Mr Saunders' belated coronation, as shareholder plaudits rained down on his head amidst congratulations for pushing through the £2.5 billion takeover of Distillers and thanks for lifting the Guinness share price sixfold since his arrival in 1981." In his last outing as chairman, Benjamin gave the performance of his life, according to his cousin Jonathan, who had christened him King Log: according to the newspaper report, Benjamin and Saunders skilfully side-stepped criticisms of past actions by blaming faulty communications and concentrating on the future of the new group and the challenges ahead.[18] Saunders' victory appeared to be complete.

However, things were about to fall apart and the cover lifted on what had gone on beneath the surface of the battle for Distillers. Across the Atlantic, the stock market speculator Ivan Boesky was arrested by the FBI for insider trading and did a deal which would see him spend two years in an open prison and pay a $100 million fine. His arrest was one of the defining events that ended several years of a bull market on Wall Street and in London's City that was fuelled by aggressive takeovers and financial engineering. Both in the US and Britain the "greed is good" ethos identified by the film *Wall Street* was causing increased outrage among the public and politicians; in Britain, as a result, Department of Trade and Industry inspectors were given additional powers to compel people to answer questions under oath.

As part of Boesky's deal with prosecutors, he told the authorities all he knew; part of what he knew involved his role in the Guinness bid. He had bought up to four per cent of Guinness's shares at a cost of almost £42 million in the last week of the bid, as well as buying Distillers' shares, and he was left facing losses of £14.3 million at the end of the battle as the Guinness share price dropped. Guinness had given him an indemnity against loss and a promise of a fee of five per cent per month on the Distillers shares. The company now had a problem accounting for these losses and the sale of these shares. It agreed to make a $100 million investment in Boesky's own partnership, which allowed him take 40 per cent of all profits and be liable for only ten per cent of losses. The investment was agreed by the Guinness board, which was told that it was part of a plan to prepare the ground for further American activities, but was not told that its primary purpose was actually to recompense Boesky for his help during the takeover.[19] The American authorities informed the British authorities about Boesky's information and the long-threatened Department of Trade and Industry inquiry was formally launched on 28 November 1986.

Things spiralled rapidly out of control for Saunders. As 1987 began, Olivier Roux, his chief adviser from Bain and effective financial controller of Guinness, made a full statement to the board and agreed with the Serious Fraud Squad to give evidence in return for immunity from prosecution. Saunders claimed this was the first he heard about these alleged activities and, under pressure from the company's executive directors, he agreed to step aside on full pay while the allegations were investigated. But he was quickly cut adrift without pay and without any financial support to help him fight the subsequent charges against him by the Guinness board, under its new chairman, Sir Norman Macfarlane. Asked about the sacking of Saunders at a board meeting, Benjamin said he himself had been kept in the dark about what had been going on and added enigmatically: "Once a friend, always a friend." Saunders later claimed in court that Benjamin had promised him that the family would look after him even if the company "ratted" on him.[20] Two of Saunders' closest associates on the board, Dr Arthur Fürer, of the Swiss Bank Leu, and Tom Ward, an American lawyer, and both former colleagues since his Nestlé days, were also asked to resign and stood down as Guinness directors.

As things unravelled, Saunders suggested to Benjamin that Guinness might be moved back to Ireland to remove it from British jurisdiction. Benjamin told him the idea was "ludicrous".[21] Some months later, the new chairman, Sir Norman Macfarlane, increased Jonathan's director's fees from £4,000 to the £10,000 the new non-executive directors were receiving. Shortly afterwards he invited him to tea and suggested that he had been a director of the company for long enough, 27 years. Jonathan agreed and stepped down at the 1988 annual general meeting.[22]

It took ten years before the DTI report was published,[23] uncovering a systematic and extensive share support scheme whereby people were paid to buy Guinness and Distillers shares (and encouraged to sell Argyll shares) and promised that they would be indemnified if they lost any money on the Guinness shares. It was no surprise to experienced investors that some dubious things had been going on during the battle; *The Scotsman* newspaper, for instance, had opined during the bid that "the share price of both bidders are now no more the result of pure market forces than the . . . outcome of your average wrestling match on TV".[24] But the DTI inspectors, barrister David Donaldson and accountant Ian Watt, declared that they were not prepared for the enormity of the share support operation revealed by their detailed analysis of the transactions. A quarter of all Guinness shares were bought by Guinness supporters during the three-month battle, most of them during the last two weeks, at a total cost of £257,559,961.[25] (Not all those purchasers were paid to do so or indemnified against losses if the share price went down.) The share support scheme had involved a wide cast of characters in the US, Switzerland and Austria as well as in Britain. The Guinness pension funds – at that stage there were four, one for Dublin, one for Park Royal, a senior executives fund, and one for the Martin newsagents – were pressured to buy Guinness shares. The Irish fund bought a million shares, raising its stake in the company to more than 1.4 million shares, on instructions from London from Victor Steel, the managing director of Guinness brewing worldwide, at the behest of Saunders, the DTI report said. One of the English pension funds broke its own rules against self-investment and all the pension fund purchases should have been publicly revealed under takeover rules but were not.[26]

In the final two weeks of the bidding – when the share prices of the respective bidders were most important – the main supporters of the Guinness shares were Boesky and Bank Leu. The bank also played a crucial role in the final, dramatic days of the bid. The day before it closed, Warburg Investment Managers decided to sell 10.6 million Distillers shares, approximately three per cent of the company. The market price of the shares was 680p, which was generally considered to be too high, but whoever bought these shares could have a decisive influence on the outcome of the battle. Their fate was obviously of keen interest to both Guinness and Argyll. However, there was a problem for Guinness in particular. It and people acting in concert with it had already bought 14.99 per cent of Distillers shares and the rules said that if they bought any more they would have to raise the price of their bid – which equated to 630p in cash – to match the highest price they paid for the shares – which was already 731p. (In reality, they had already secretly exceeded the 15 per cent limit but that was not known at the time.) Effectively, they could not buy the Warburg shares within the rules. Argyll and its supporters were in a stronger position to buy them; they had not quite reached the 14.99 per cent limit and had not yet exceeded their cash offer price for Distillers shares of 660p: they were in a position under the rules to go up to 703p for about two million of the shares.

Guinness used Bank Leu to buy the shares through a subsidiary called Pipetec for 705p each for immediate cash settlement of approximately £75.6 million. With fears that the money from Switzerland would not arrive in time on the day, Guinness scrambled to raise the £76 million and had to pay an annual interest rate of 22 per cent on some of it. However, the money arrived in time from Switzerland and was followed by a note setting out the terms on which the shares were bought – that Guinness would buy them back at the original price within 60 days plus fees and interest. Argyll complained about the purchase to the Takeover Panel and one of the panel's officials contacted Bank Leu and Pipetec and was given the impression there was no connection between it and Guinness, Argyll or Distillers. According to the DTI report, the denials were "at the extreme boundary of literal truth with consequent risk of misunderstanding". Guinness also denied, in a carefully worded letter to the Panel, that it had made any financial arrangement with the purchasers of the shares.[27]

The inspectors also decided that £3 million of a £5.2 million fee paid to the American lawyer Tom Ward for his services during the takeover had actually been paid to Saunders himself. The £5.2 million was paid to a Jersey company called Marketing and Acquisition Consultants Ltd. and, after further movements, £3,029,421.21 (£3 million plus interest) of it was transferred into a numbered account in the Union Bank of Switzerland, which had been opened by Saunders back in 1973 and been effectively dormant since his return to England in 1981. Ward and Saunders claimed that the former had "borrowed" the UBS account while deciding what to do with the money and that it was set aside to cover American tax. However, the inspectors concluded that the natural inference to be drawn from the £3 million transfer was also the correct one: that the payment was intended for Saunders' benefit. "It would have required almost superhuman powers of self-denial for Mr Saunders to agree payments of huge sums to Sir Jack Lyons, Mr [Anthony] Parnes, and Mr Ward while he, the architect and dynamo of the successful bid, received nothing but his regular salary," they suggested.[28]

After the battle, Guinness was suddenly faced with large payments to supporters holding its shares which had gone down in value and to whom they had promised indemnities against losses. There were up to 50 million Guinness shares involved; they could not simply be sold on the market without further depressing the share price – and increasing the indemnity payments – or raising eyebrows, if not questions, about where all these shares were coming from. Bank Leu ended up buying most of them, on the basis of Guinness agreeing to buy them back at an unspecified date at the original price plus charges and fees. Meanwhile, they attempted to place them on the international market. Awkward questions were also likely to be asked by auditors and others about large payments to disparate individuals and organisations. The inspectors suggested that this problem was the real reason why Saunders controversially dropped Sir Thomas Risk and made himself chairman instead: "one way or another, Mr Saunders could reckon that these matters were unlikely to remain concealed for ever from a new chairman, who could not be relied upon to be quiescent," they wrote. "The problem disappeared if Mr Saunders himself became chairman in addition to chief executive."[29]

In the months after the scandal broke, seven people were charged with criminal offences, including Saunders. Guinness was sued by Argyll and settled by paying it £54 million plus interest; it also paid some £65 million compensation to Distillers shareholders because of the Bank Leu purchase of Distillers shares, which the Takeover Panel ruled was done in concert with Guinness. For its part, Guinness set about recovering funds improperly paid to some people as well. But the merger/takeover could not be undone and Guinness went from strength to strength under a new chief executive, Anthony Tennant, who came to it from Grand Metropolitan, where he had been deputy chief executive. In 1989 it was the best performing share in the FTSE 100, had made another leap forward with a cross-shareholding and marketing deal with the French luxury goods company LVMH – owners of Moët champagne, Hennessy brandy and Louis Vuitton, among other brands – and was reporting pre-tax profits up by a third to £691 million, most of it from spirits.[30]

It took three years for the first criminal cases to come to court in London in what was widely depicted by British newspapers as the "City trial of the century". Saunders, Sir Jack Lyons, stockbroker Anthony

Parnes, and businessman Gerald Ronson were convicted by a jury of a variety of conspiracy, theft and false accounting charges after a 112-day trial. Saunders was sentenced to five years in prison, Parnes to two and a half years, Ronson to one year and fined £5 million. Lyons was fined £3 million and escaped prison because he was 74 and suffering from cancer. He was later stripped of his knighthood.[31]

The charges, trial and convictions took an enormous toll on them, particularly Saunders and Parnes, who both suffered breakdowns; Parnes collapsed in court as the sentences were being handed down. Saunders was ruined financially as well as having his reputation shredded; he became obsessed with clearing his name and the belief that he was being made a scapegoat and, like many in his position before and after him, insisted that he had done nothing that others had not done regularly as well. Some observers thought that his decision to give evidence, spending seven days giving direct evidence and several more in cross-examination, was a mistake because of his angry and emotional outbursts.[32] He was not alone in thinking, with some justification, that it was a "show trial" for the stock market excesses of the late 1980s; there was certainly a political mood at the time to make an example of someone. His supporters and others also found it noteworthy that all those on trial were Jewish, most the sons or descendants of immigrants, and that nobody of blue blood was charged.

The Guinnesses who had been on the board of the company were exonerated because they had been kept in the dark about what was going on during the takeover battle. Benjamin had to endure the ordeal of two days in the witness box for the prosecution and being cross-examined by Saunders' counsel, Richard Ferguson, who accused him of being "utterly confused" and asked if he had had "drink-related problems" in 1986/87. "I had no drink problems in 1986/87," he replied.[33]

The aftermath of the Saunders trials tended to support the belief that the treatment of the four accused was influenced by the public mood of the time. Ronson was released after serving six months of his one-year sentence. Saunders appealed in 1991, mainly on the grounds that the trial judge had erred in his summing-up to the jury. His lawyers also introduced evidence from a leading neurologist, backed by other observers, including the governor of the open prison in which he was held, that he was suffering from pre-senile dementia. All but one of his convictions were upheld by the appeal court but his sentence was cut in half on the grounds that five years was too long. In a lengthy ruling, the judges said they were satisfied on the balance of probabilities that he was suffering from pre-senile dementia and that, notwithstanding the illness, the original sentence was too high. They decided that the gravity of the offences was such that they should not reduce the sentence so much that he was released immediately.[34] However, his revised sentence allowed his released from Ford Open Prison in Sussex the following month, June 1991.

The reference to his state of health at the time of the trial gave rise to the widespread belief that he was released because he was suffering from Alzheimer's disease, leading on to cynical observations afterwards that he was the only person ever known to recover from the condition; however, there were no suggestions that he ever actually suffered from the disease. He was clearly affected badly by the trauma of the whole affair and some who saw him in court during the appeal were shocked by his appearance, compared to his previous appearance when he was running Guinness five years earlier. The others also had their sentences reduced; the appeal court decided that allowance should be made for the fact that Parnes spent six months in jail in the US awaiting extradition and reduced his sentence to 21 months while it cut the £440,000 in costs that Ronson and Lyons had been ordered to pay to £300,000 each.

A second trial of two men involved in the Guinness takeover was stopped in 1992 when one of the accused, Roger Seelig, formerly the corporate finance director of Morgan Grenfell, who was defending himself, suffered a nervous breakdown and the judge decided the trial should not continue. His co-accused, Lord Patrick Spens, former finance director with Ansbacher, was formally acquitted of the charges in November 1992. In a third trial, Tom Ward, the American lawyer, was acquitted by a jury of stealing £5.2 million from Guinness, money that the prosecution claimed he and Saunders planned to divide between them. His defence was that the money was a legitimate success fee for his services during the takeover.[35]

A further appeal by the four who had been convicted at the first trial on the basis that their compulsory interviews with the DTI inspectors should not have been used in evidence against them was rejected by the Court of Appeal in 1995. However, the European Court of Human Rights subsequently upheld Saunders' complaint that his trial was unfair because the prosecution used the interview transcripts, thereby denying him the right to silence and protection against self-incrimination. Aspects of the case were "a remarkable departure from one of the basic principles of fair procedure," the European Court ruled. However, it refused to clear his name and rejected his claim for £4.6 million in damages.[36] The human rights court later gave the same judgement on the trials of his three co-accused. Back in London, the appeal court and the House of Lords subsequently refused to quash the convictions on the basis of the European judgement on the grounds that the procedures ruled to be unfair had been expressly permitted by parliament.[37]

Meanwhile, Guinness went from strength to strength. In the five years after the Distillers takeover, its pre-tax profits doubled from £408 million to £956 million, turnover went up to £4 billion, dividends were up 135 per cent, and the share price more than trebled. In ten years the Guinness company had been reconstructed as a major international drinks company, with a reach, value and basket of brands that would have been beyond its wildest dreams a decade earlier, when it went looking for a marketing manager to save it. It was not altogether a happy story for the Guinness family, however. The family's share of the company was down from a controlling 25 per cent or so to a tiny three per cent but the value of its holding was greatly increased. On the other hand, their influence on the company which still bore their name was nil.

In May 1992, Benjamin Iveagh stepped down from the company's board, the last Guinness to sit on it and have a say in the running of the brewery founded by his great-great-great-great-grandfather in 1759. His departure was announced at the annual general meeting where the outgoing chairman, Sir Anthony Tennant, told the shareholders that the company expected to make over £1 billion in profit that year. Benjamin was seriously ill, dying of throat cancer at the time and being cared for by his former wife Miranda in her Cottlesmore Gardens home in London. He died there three weeks later, on 18 June, at the age of 55.

EPILOGUE

A third memorial service following those at St Margaret's in Westminster and St Patrick's Cathedral in Dublin, was held for Benjamin Guinness at St James's Catholic church on James's Street, near the brewery. His family were there again, the Guinness Choir sang selections from Bruckner, Mozart and Bach, and the lesson was read by Finbarr Flood, the managing director of the Dublin brewery. It was a less elaborate service than the preceding ones and there were few, if any, people with titles present other than members of his own family. Afterwards, his sons and daughters walked the short distance back to the brewery for lunch.

Benjamin's wills in Ireland and in England valued his personal estate at some £50 million, IR£37 million in Ireland and £14 million in England. His executors in both cases were his sister Elizabeth, cousin Henry Channon and Ian Ferris of the Iveagh Trustees. They were also the trustees of two new trusts he set up for his children and grandchildren, an Irish Trust Fund for the assets in Ireland and an Overseas Trust Fund for the rest. The sons were each to receive three parts and the daughters one part each. His Irish will detailed a long list of trusts from which he had benefited, including money left over from Edward Iveagh's pension funds for his employees in 1927, and movements of funds between trusts, settlements and debentures. Shares in Guinness, held in various vehicles and places, amounted to £22.7 million; investments in Canada (where he had been a director of the Bank of Nova Scotia) came to Can$14 million; in the US$3 million; and there were numerous other shares and deposits like 5,237,844 Swiss francs, US$444,208 and 635,514 German marks in the Union Bank of Switzerland (which collectively translated into IR£2,848,053 at the current rates of exchange).

His home at Farmleigh was valued by Hamilton Osborne King and Megran at a modest IR£800,000 and described as well maintained and generally in good decorative order but the valuation excluded a structural survey. When it was put on the market by the Iveagh Trustees some seven year later, it had a tired Edwardian air to it. It was bought by the Office of Public Works for IR£23 million for use as a government guest house for visiting dignitaries and a venue for international meetings. The OPW subsequently spent a further IR£18 million renovating and redecorating it and adding facilities like a basement swimming pool and gym before it was opened to the public in July 2001.

Meanwhile, Bryan Guinness, Lord Moyne, had died within three weeks of Benjamin's death, on 6 July 1992 at his Wiltshire home, Biddensden, at the age of 86. His last collection of poems, *On a Ledge*, was published after his death. In one of his last meetings with his former wife, Diana Mitford, he was as vague as ever. In the House of Lords for lunch with Lord Longford in 1983, she saw "a very very old man totter in dressed in corduroys" and hang "a filthy mac and a plastic bag on a hook". When she said his name tentatively, he came over and said "Which of you is it?"; he later told a friend it was the first time he had seen her in 50 years that he had not wept afterwards.[1] Diana died in Paris in August 2003 at the age of 93, still refusing to condemn Hitler and the Nazis in the terms others demanded of her. Their eldest son, Jonathan, inherited Bryan's baronetcy and became the third Lord Moyne in 1992.

Bryan's contemporaries and first cousins, the "Golden Guinness Girls" of the pre-Second World War era, all lived long and eventful lives, replete with endless dramas and tinged with occasional tragedies. Maureen held on to her first title, the Marchioness of Dufferin and Ava, through two subsequent marriages to Major Desmond "Kelpy" Buchanan and Judge John Maude. She went on being outrageous into old age: in the mid-1990s her two surviving daughters, Caroline and Perdita, and her daughter-in-law, Lindy Guinness (whose husband Sheridan, the last Marquess of Dufferin and Ava, had died in 1988) took her to court over her attempt to cut them out of a trust from which they had been receiving income. She wanted to leave the £15 million trust, and the current income from it, to her two grand-daughters Evgenia and Ivana, the surviving daughters of Caroline Blackwood, and her second husband Israel Citkowitz (although Ivana was actually, according to a death-bed confession, the daughter of the Anglo-American scriptwriter Ivan Moffat).[2] Caroline's son with Robert Lowell, also called Sheridan, was left out of his grandmother's plan, apparently because he was born before his parents' marriage.

The Iveagh Trust had tried but failed to dissuade the family members from going to court over Maureen's reorganisation of the trust fund she had set up in 1948 to divide her inheritance from her father Ernest equally among her three children. Her daughters and daughter-in-law argued that she did not have power to change that arrangement in favour of her grandchildren. Maureen's lawyers argued that she did have power and that she had already given each of her children a substantial fortune over the years. The judge agreed with her that she could change the will. Maureen was not in court for the hearing but said in a statement afterwards that she was saddened that her daughters and daughter-in-law had caused the family "such distress and expense" and hoped they could all put this behind them and "be a happy and united family".[3] (Caroline Blackwood, a talented, relentlessly dark novelist, died of cancer in New York a year after the court case, leaving an estate estimated at $3 million.) Maureen died two years later, in 1998, at the age of 91. Her younger sister Oonagh had suffered a heart attack at Luggala in County Wicklow while phoning their eldest sister Aileen and died in 1995. Aileen, who complained frequently of poverty, spent her last years in England after selling Luttrellstown House in County Dublin and died in 1999 at the age of 94.

Paul Channon went on to become Secretary of State for Transport after the 1987 British general election, with responsibility for roads and rail among other things, leading him to remark once that it was the only job in which he had to apologise to people who arrived late for meetings with him because of transport delays, instead of the other way round.[4] He was unlucky in that his term in office coincided with a succession of transport disasters from the *Herald of Free Enterprise* (a ferry that capsized off Zeebrugge, killing 187 people), to the Kings Cross underground fire in London (which killed 31), the Clapham Junction rail crash (which killed 35), and the bombing of the PanAm jet over Lockerbie in Scotland (which killed 270 people on board and on the ground) just before Christmas 1988. His departure for Christmas two days after the last incident to one of the homes he had inherited from his mother Honor on the private island of Mustique in the West Indies left him open to opposition outrage. He was dropped from the cabinet in a reshuffle in 1989, some two years after his appointment. He was made a life peer in 1997, taking the name Lord Kelvedon, after his country home he had inherited from his father, Chips, who had once fantasised in his diary 60 years earlier about waking up there as Lord Kelvedon.[5] His departure from the House of Commons ended the Guinness hold on the Southend parliamentary seat they had occupied since Rupert first won it in 1912, passed it on to his wife Gwendolen in 1927, to their son-in-law Chips in 1935, and to Paul in 1959. Paul suffered from Alzheimer's disease during his final years and died at Kelvedon in January 2007 at the age of 71.

The Guinness company, meanwhile, went from strength to strength, increasing its cross-shareholding in LVMH to 24 per cent. In the early 1990s, the two companies operated some 17 joint ventures around the world, providing wholesalers and retailers with packages of top drinks brands, including Johnny Walker whisky, Gordon's gin and Guinness (from Guinness) and Moët champagne and Hennessy brandy (from LVMH). The relationship was not always plain sailing, especially after the controversial French financier Bernard Arnault took control of LVMH and indicated his intention to move it into other areas. It changed over the years to Guinness taking a 34 per cent share in Moët Hennessy, the drinks arm of LVMH, and LVMH becoming Guinness's largest shareholder, with 14 per cent of the company. It almost broke down in 1997 when Guinness indicated its intention to merge with another distilling giant, Grand Metropolitan, which had begun its life in the 1930s as a hotels and holiday resort company until it acquired a collection of distilleries. Arnault firmly opposed the move – although the possibility of a three-way merger was floated briefly – and threatened legal action to try to prevent it. Agreement was reached, however, with Guinness paying LVMH £250 million and Arnault accepting the £20 billion-plus merger between Guinness and Grand Metropolitan.

The new group – named Diageo, a combination of the Latin for day, *dia*, and the Greek for world, *geo* – continued to own 34 per cent of

Moët Hennessy while its own brands included top-selling drinks worldwide like Smirnoff vodka (Diageo's biggest seller), Johnny Walker and J&B Scotch whiskies, Captain Morgan rum, Cuervo tequila, Tanqueray gin (the main ingredient of the classic American martini), Guinness stout (its third biggest seller)[6] and Bailey's Irish Cream (one of the world's top liqueurs and the main success of the Irish drinks industry in recent decades). Diageo subsequently divested itself of many of Grand Met's food businesses, including the Burger King chain, and went on to take over more drinks businesses, including Bushmills Irish whiskey and parts of the giant Canadian Seagrams group. It is now the world's largest drinks company, employing 22,000 people internationally. The sale of Guinness stout accounted for about 13 per cent of its £7.3 billion (€10.8 billion at the time) turnover in 2006.[7]

Guinness continued to decline steadily in its home market, hit by changing fashions towards lagers, wine and spirits, as well as factors like the ban on smoking in public places, which spread throughout many countries, and tougher implementation of drink-driving laws. On the other hand, the spread of Irish pubs abroad helped to increase its sales, but its main growth has been in Nigeria which overtook the Irish market in 2007 as the second biggest consumer of its stout after Britain.[8] Diageo denied annual rumours in the mid-2000s that it planned to sell Guinness, rumours that were given support by its closure of the Park Royal brewery in London in 2005 and its sale to an industrial property group for £47 million. Production of Park Royal's four million kegs of stout a year was moved back to St James's Gate, which was producing eight million kegs a year and had the capacity to absorb the extra demand. Ironically, part of Diageo's public relations spin on the move was to suggest that Londoners would now be able to sample "real" Guinness; the company had insisted since the 1930s that there was no difference in the stout brewed in Dublin and London.

Further uncertainty about Diageo's plans for Guinness was created by its announcement in 2007 that it was looking at the future of St James's Gate as part of a review of its brewing activities in Ireland. It began a search for a site for a new brewery, specifying that it had to be in Dublin because of the long-time connections between the city and Guinness. It finally fixed on a site in Leixlip, fortuitously the village in which Arthur Guinness had opened his first brewery and on land owned by Desmond Guinness, the son of Bryan Moyne and one of Arthur's direct descendants. Less fortuitously, it was on the wrong side of the River Liffey, which is the boundary between counties Dublin and Kildare in the area. Some Diageo marketing people asked if the river might be diverted to shift the site from County Kildare into County Dublin; whether or not they were serious is not clear. In any event, the plan to move the brewery was shelved with the collapse of the Irish property market in 2008; the move and investment in a new brewery had been dependent on selling most of the 58-acre brewery site around St James's Gate in the centre city. It had been valued at more than €750 million at the height of the property boom, enough to fund the new brewery and leave some profit. The property crash halved that valuation, at least, and removed any prospect in the foreseeable future of demand for such a major city redevelopment.

The Guinness family had no involvement in any of the company developments since the death of Benjamin in 1992. A considerable proportion of their wealth, about 30 per cent or some £200 million according to the *Sunday Times* Rich List for 2009, remains tied up in the shareholdings in Diageo, although they own a relatively small slice – less than two per cent – of the company, which had a market capitalisation of some £15 billion. The newspaper ranked them the fifty-second richest family in Britain (on a par with composer Lord Lloyd-Weber) and, unlike many people on the list, higher than the ninety-second position they occupied on the 2008 list. It estimated the family's wealth at £750 million, down from £830 million the previous year; more than half, some £400 million, was accounted for by British Pacific Properties in Vancouver, double the value of its Diageo holdings. Other property-based wealth listed included the £20 million sale of Farmleigh to the Irish government in 1997 and its £29 million in net assets in Elveden Farms and Burhill Estates (a land development company involved in golf courses in southern England). In spite of its rise up the rankings again in 2009, it has been in a steep decline from the twelfth position it occupied in the newspaper's listings in 1993 shortly after the death of Benjamin Iveagh.

The Sunday Times calculation of the family's wealth may well be an underestimate, however. The tangle of family trusts which have grown out of the first Lord Iveagh's legacies in 1927 have always been complex and opaque, even to members of the family. All the direct descendants of Edward Iveagh benefit from the initial trust he established but most benefit as well from trusts set up by their own Guinness parent, grandparent or great-grandparent. (Many of Iveagh's direct descendants do not bear the name Guinness and include Lennox-Boyds, von Preussens, Brownes, and Blackwoods, along with more recent married names.) The British Pacific Properties holdings in Canada belong to the Moyne branch of the family and are the largest but not the only elements in their trusts, which are held through a company registered in Switzerland. To suggest that the other two branches of the family, the Iveagh branch and the descendants of Ernest Guinness, are worth only about £300 million between them is probably an underestimate. Paul Channon alone, for instance, was reputed to be worth £184 million at one stage when he was in parliament and his will was probated at £78 million.

Family members have had different interests at different times, some requiring an income while others wanted capital growth. The demands upon the Iveagh Trustees often ranged from straightforward wealth management to providing a concierge service for family members. As with other rich families, the interests of the trust's beneficiaries diverged over time as more and more descendants became entitled to a share in it. The occasional public court cases over the years were the tip of the iceberg and were usually over some complex issue of interpretation. Such trusts are known in financial circles as family offices and the experiences of the Guinness family have been replicated by that of other similar families; as well as differing demands upon the trust, it is also difficult for family offices to keep the services of good fund managers, who are usually ambitious for a share of the financial action themselves.

The 75 or so family members entitled to the Iveagh trust funds finally split up in 2005, wound up the trust and went in two separate directions. "Some members of the family had begun agitating for change in a way that became difficult to manage," the fourth Lord Iveagh, Ned Guinness, told the *Financial Times*.[9] Some members of the family moved their share of the fund to the investment manager and accountancy firm Smith & Williamson, while Ned, his younger brother Rory and their cousins, Henry Channon and Henry's sister Georgia Fanshawe, took their money – described as several hundred million dollars or about a third of the family's wealth – along a path trodden previously by members of other rich families. They invested their money with a fund of hedge funds, Arundel, and were given a 25 per cent share in the company in return. The company was subsequently renamed Iveagh Ltd. and Ned, Henry and Georgia became non-executive directors. Following the example of other similar family offices, the aim was to attract other rich families to the fund, as well as opening it to rich individuals; in 2008, Iveagh Ltd. opened its investment fund to anybody with more than £50,000 to invest. One of the main models for these arrangements is that of the Rothschilds, whose investment fund, RIT Capital, is open to anyone with a minimum of £1,000, or monthly contributions as little as £20, to invest. It is quoted on the London stock exchange, while the Iveagh fund is listed on the less-visible funds section of the Dublin stock market as the Iveagh Wealth Fund. It had a total of $800 million under management, most of it presumed to be Guinness money, when it opened its services to the less wealthy in September 2008.[10] The fund said its losses in 2008 were minus 2.1 per cent, compared to a fall of almost a third in its benchmark FTSE index. In March 2009 more than half its funds were invested in government bonds and 14 per cent was in cash.[11]

Ned Iveagh has followed in what is now the family tradition of farming. Born in August 1969, he studied agriculture and took over the running of the Elveden estate, where he lives. He has developed it into a multi-faceted agricultural enterprise, which ranges from providing Christmas trees to a shop and restaurant serving farm produce in the old farmyard. The familiar portrait of the first Arthur Guinness hangs on the restaurant wall and Guinness merchandise is on sale in its shop. Game birds are no longer bred in captivity and released for shooters, but shoots of wild fowl are still organised for paying visitors. Elveden Hall remains closed apart from occasional events like an annual Christmas party for local children, which requires industrial-sized fan heaters to warm its central marble hall sufficiently for the event. The marble hall, in which Edward Iveagh once led morning prayers for the family and staff, has also been used occasionally as a film set, notably for the "orgy" scene in Stanley Kubrick's last film, *Eyes Wide Shut*, and a few brief scenes in *Lara Croft: Tomb Raider*.

Epilogue

Ned Iveagh served as a cross-bench member (not taking any party whip) of the House of Lords from 1996 to 1999, making his maiden speech in 1997 on what turned out to be his main parliamentary contribution, the right to full British nationality of the islanders of St Helena, the South Atlantic island most famous as the final and involuntary home of Napoleon. He led a campaign for their citizenship rights which succeeded eventually in 2002 and he was a member of a syndicate which unsuccessfully sought British government aid to build an airport on the island and develop it for low-volume tourism.[12] Among the other business ventures he has tried was the launch, with the scion of another famous family, Auberon Waugh, of a plan to make short stories available through vending machines on London's underground and railway stations,[13] and brewing at Elveden. He lost his seat in the House of Lords in 1999 in the first election among hereditary peers, whose numbers had been severely culled under the Labour government's reforms. He tried again without success to be returned at subsequent by-elections in 2003 and 2007. He is married and his first son and heir, the current Lord Elveden, was born in January 2003 and named Arthur Benjamin Jeffrey Guinness.

The Guinnesses are no longer near the top of the super-rich league, where Ned's great-great-grandfather and namesake, Edward, put them at the turn of the twentieth century, but they are still well-off by any standards. They have disproved an old Chinese saying that "wealth never survives three generations" or the western variation of it – from clogs to clogs in three generations. In their first hundred years, three generations of the family built their brewery up to dominate the Irish market, make major inroads into the British market and make their name as synonymous with stout as it is with Ireland. The next generation, of Lords Iveagh and Ardilaun, took them into the heights of British society through their business and political successes. While their fame and fortune rested on stout, the brewery Guinnesses have always been involved as well in other areas of life, from farming to finance, motor-racing to modelling, politics to the arts. It was the misfortune of Benjamin, the head of the seventh generation, that all the weight of the family's history, along with the more difficult business climate for brewers of stout in the second half of the twentieth century, fell on his shoulders.

Although the latest generation of Arthur Guinness's direct descendants are no longer involved in the brewery which made their fortune, their forebears have left Ireland and the world a great brand name and numerous monuments to their success.

ENDNOTES

Chapter One: The End of an Era

1 Patrick Lynch and John Vaizey, *Guinness's Brewery in the Irish Economy 1759–1876*, Cambridge University Press 1960, p. 7.

2 Lynch and Vaizey, op. cit., p. 72.

3 Lynch and Vaizey, op.cit., p. 125.

Chapter Two: The First Arthur

1 Lynch and Vaizey, op.cit., p. 39.

2 Lynch and Vaizey, op. cit., p. 44. The Dublin Society became the Royal Dublin Society in 1820.

3 Henry Seymour Guinness and Brian Guinness, *The Guinness Family*, 1953. In fact, Dublin Corporation records show that William was a blacksmith: he had a son named Richard, which may indicate a link with the other Richard.

4 Patrick Guinness, *Arthur's Round*, Peter Owen, London, 2008, p. 21. He cites a privately printed book by Henry Seymour Guinness and a land lease for George as evidence of the connection.

5 Frederic Mullally, *The Silver Salver*, Granada Publishing, 1981, page 14.

6 Mullally, op.cit, pp. 230–1.

7 Patrick Guinness, p. 24.

8 F.E. Ball, *Swift Correspondence Vol III*, Bell, 1914, p. 57.

9 Oakley Park is now run by the St John of God Brothers as a centre for children and young adults with mental disabilities.

10 Most of the information about Richard Guinness in Celbridge is based on a series of articles in a local magazine, *Celbridge Charter*, January to April 1974 issues, and an interview with their author, Lena Boylan.

11 Thrift Presentations, a series of summaries of legal and other documents, in the Irish National Archive.

12 Guinness Genealogical Notes.

13 Cox's *Irish Magazine*, February 1815.

14 John Bush in *Hibernia Curiosa*, quoted in *County Kildare: A Geographical Background for Planning*.

15 Lynch and Vaizey, p. 69.

16 Maurice Craig, *Dublin 1660–1860*, The Cresset Press, London, 1952, p. 149.

17 Mary E. Daly, *Dublin, The Deposed Capital: A Social and Economic History 1860–1914*, Cork University Press, 1984, p. 3.

18 Craig, p. 158.

19 Walker's *Hibernian Magazine*, May 1775, p. 619.

20 Craig, p. 211.

21 Lynch and Vaizey, p. 70.

22 H.S. Corran, *A History of Brewing*, David & Charles, London, 1975, p. 144.

23 A ballad about the 1767 ceremony took a neutral attitude to the brewers – "The Brewers next well mounted doth appear / These are the men brew humming ale and beer" – unlike other groups such as the apothecaries, "Whose monstrous bills immoderate wealth procure / For drugs that kill as many as they cure." The anonymous balladeer also took a jaundiced view of the whole ceremony: "Then homeward steer their course without delay / And fall to drink, the business of the day".

24 F.G. Hall, *The Bank of Ireland 1783–1946*, Hodges Figgis, Dublin, 1949, pp. 499–500. Lunnell became a common middle name among subsequent generations of Guinnesses. The family name died out in Dublin in 1907 with the death of the last, unmarried, member of the Lunnell family.

25 Lynch and Vaizey, op. cit., p. 58. The view that beer was a wholesome drink compared to spirits was common and allowed the brewers to benefit from the periodic temperance campaigns of the late eighteenth and early nineteenth centuries.

26 Walker's *Hibernian Journal*, March 1777.

27 Now a nursing home.

28 *Proceedings of the Dublin Society*, Vol IV.

29 Lynch and Vaizey, op.cit., p. 72.

30 Walkers' *Hibernian Magazine*, p. 618.

31 Gilbert ed., *Calendar of Ancient Records of Dublin*, Vol XII, Dublin, 1905, pp. 433.

32 Ibid, vol. XI, p. 238.

33 Ibid, vol. XI, pp. 372–4.

34 *Journals of the Irish House of Commons*, Vol. XVI, p. 188–90.

35 *Observations on the Brewing Trade of Ireland, Submitted to the Publick*, by an Officer of the Revenue. Dublin, c.1775 Presumably, this was not the same "officer of the revenue" who put Olivia Guinness in fear and dread of her life with a pistol in 1777.

36 *History of the Proceedings and Debates of the House of Commons of Ireland*, 1793, p. 258.

37 Corran, p. 151.

38 Lynch and Vaizey, op. cit., p. 68.

39 Lynch and Vaizey, idem.

40 Rebellion Papers, Irish National Archive.

41 Thomas Pakenham, *The Year of Liberty*, Granada Publishing, 1972, p. 45.

42 Patrick Guinness, p. 192.

43 Pakenham, p. 48.

44 *High Treason: Trial of John McCann*, a broadsheet published in 1798: NLI.

45 *A Report of the Trial of John McCann*, J. Connor, Cork, 1798.

46 *Freeman's Journal*, 21 July 1798.

47 Patrick Guinness, p. 195.

48 L.M. Cullen, *Princes and Pirates: The Dublin Chamber of Commerce 1783–1983*, Dublin Chamber of Commerce, 1983, p. 19.

49 Quoted by Lynch and Vaizey, p. 72.

Chapter Three: The Second Arthur

1 Lynch and Vaizey, p. 242.

2 *Dublin Evening Post*, 1 April 1813.

3 Ibid, 17 April 1813.

4 Ibid, 25 May 1813.

5 *Irish Magazine*, June 1813, vol. VI, p. 214.

6 Ibid, p. 264.

7 *Milesian Magazine*, October 1813.

8 Hall, *The Bank of Ireland 1783–1946*.

9 *Dublin Evening Post*, 15 December 1835.

10 Ibid, 21 December 1835.

11 Maurice O'Connell, *The Correspondence of Daniel O'Connell*, Vol. II, Irish University Press, 1973, p. 412.

12 Ibid, p. 328.

13 *The Pilot*, 25 May 1831.

14 Cullen, p. 58.

15 Ibid, pp. 62–63.

16 Oliver MacDonagh, *O'Connell: The Life of Daniel O'Connell 1775–1847*, Weidenfeld and Nicolson, London, 1991, p. 275.

17 O'Connell correspondence, Vol. IV, pp. 273–4.

18 Ibid, Vol. IV, p. 350.

19 Quoted in Lynch and Vaizey, p. 178.

20 MacDonagh, pp. 396 and 498.

21 The Bank of Ireland eventually took over the National Bank in 1965.

22 R.B. McDowell, *Public Opinion and Government Policy in Ireland, 1801-1846*, Faber & Faber, London, 1952, p. 184.

23 Protestants made up about 27 per cent of the population in Dublin in the 1830s (cf Daly p. 112).

24 *Dublin Evening Post*, 18 February 1835.

25 *The Pilot*, 7 August 1837.

26 Ibid, 14 August 1837.

27 *Freeman's Journal* and *Evening Mail*, 22 August to 12 September 1837.

28 *The Pilot*, 25 August 1837.

29 Quoted by Lynch and Vaizey, p. 107.

30 *O'Connell Correspondence*, Vol. VI, pp. 271–6.

31 Lynch and Vaizey, p. 145.

32 Quoted by Lynch and Vaizey, p. 108.

33 Letter to John Foster, Chancellor of the Irish Exchequer, on 25 February 1811, quoted by Lynch and Vaizey, p. 86.

34 Lynch and Vaizey, op. cit., p. 123.

35 *Freeman's Journal*, 15 October 1814.

36 *Dublin Evening Post*, 5 November 1814.

37 *Irish Magazine*, December 1814.

38 Lynch and Vaizey, p. 126.

39 Quoted by Lynch and Vaizey, p. 81.

40 Quoted by Mullally, p. 18.

41 Lynch and Vaizey, p. 83.

42 Quoted by Lynch and Vaizey, p. 112.

43 Lynch and Vaizey, p. 125.

44 *Saunders News Letter*, 26 June 1858.

45 Richard Fawkes, *Dion Boucicault*, Quartet Books, 1979.

46 Dion later amended his surname to Boucicault.

47 Fawkes, p. 29.

48 *North American Review*, April 1889, quoted by Fawkes.

49 Claude Colleer Abbot, *The Life and Letters of George Darley, Poet and Critic*, Oxford University Press, 1928.

50 Fawkes, p. 31.

51 DNB, Volume XXII Supplement, p. 238.

52 *Saunders News Letter*, 26 June 1858.

53 Lynch and Vaizey, pp. 113–116. The book deals elliptically with this episode, referring to debts that Arthur Lee had run up, but it makes no mention of his relationship with Boucicault, whom it refers to in a later chapter as one of the most interesting of the brewery's clerks.

54 Francis Elrington Ball, *Stillorgan Park and Its History*, lecture delivered on 28 September 1897.

55 Colleer Abbot, p. 250.

56 Dublin *Evening Mail*, 13 June 1855.

Chapter Four: The First Millionaire

1 Elizabeth Malcolm, *Ireland Sober, Ireland Free: Drink and Temperance in Nineteenth-Century Ireland*, Gill & Macmillan, Dublin, 1986, p. 86.

2 Ibid, p. 144. Malcolm notes that other economic factors, like a rise in excise duty and poor harvests, also contributed to the decline.

Endnotes

3 Lynch and Vaizey, p. 141.

4 Ibid, p. 167.

5 L.M. Cullen, *An Economic History of Ireland since 1660*, B.T. Batsford, London, 1972, p. 137.

6 Daly, p. 13.

7 Lynch and Vaizey, p. 200.

8 Arthur Garrett, *Through Countless Ages: The Story of the Church and Parish of All Saints', Raheny*, p. 151.

9 Nicholas Sheaff, *Iveagh House*, Department of Foreign Affairs, Dublin, 1978, pp. 17–18.

10 Lynch and Vaizey, p. 178.

11 Daly, p. 17.

12 *The Times*, 5 September 1850.

13 *The Irish Times*, 7 March 1891.

14 Dublin *Evening Mail*, 27 November 1850. It credited the Chamber of Commerce and the death of O'Connell with the transformation.

15 *Evening Post*, 3 December 1850.

16 Lynch and Vaizey, p. 178.

17 *Saunders News Letter*, 26 June 1858.

18 *The Times*, 19 September 1861, quoting the (Dublin) *Daily Express*.

19 *The Dublin Builder*, Vol. V, 15 January 1863.

20 *The Irish Times*, 13 December 1864.

21 *Freeman's Journal*, 7 February 1865.

22 Daly, p. 291.

23 *A History of St Patrick's Cathedral, Dublin*, p. 19.

24 *Freeman's Journal*, 9 May 1865.

25 Ibid, 10 February 1863.

26 Ibid, 29 July 1863.

27 *Freeman's Journal*, 12 July 1865.

28 *The Times*, 15 July 1865.

29 Quoted by the *Freeman's Journal*, 11 July 1865.

30 Malcolm, pp. 194–5.

31 *The Irish Times*, 18 July 1865.

32 Malcolm, p. 194.

33 Lynch and Vaizey, pp. 179–180. They add that the image of a small band of revolutionaries grabbing the biggest porter brewery in the world as part of their loot was an engaging flourish of the pen.

34 *The Irish Times*, 28 May 1868.

35 *Freeman's Journal*, 30 May 1868.

Chapter Five: The Cunning Brothers

1 *Freeman's Journal*, 28 May 1868.

2 Lynch and Vaizey, p. 184.

3 *The Times*, 3 June 1868.

4 *Freeman's Journal*, 27 October 1868.

5 *The Irish Times* and *Evening Mail*, 21 October 1868.

6 *Freeman's Journal*, 22 October 1868.

7 Ibid, 5 November 1868.

8 Ibid, 17 November 1868.

9 *The Times*, 21 November 1868.

10 Lynch and Vaizey, p. 186.

11 George and Edmund Waller, brothers and cousins of the Guinnesses, were working as brewers in St James's Gate at the time but the reports of the court hearing do not make clear which one was involved in this episode.

12 Ibid, 6 February 1869.

13 The by-election was eventually postponed after 98 freemen were disenfranchised until August 1870 when Sir Dominic Corrigan was elected.

14 Quoted by Lynch and Vaizey, p. 188.

15 Lynch and Vaizey, p. 215.

16 Daly, p. 24.

17 Finbarr Flood, *In Full Flood*, Liberties Press, Dublin, 2006, pp. 66–7.

18 Lynch and Vaizey, pp. 240–1.

19 Ibid, p. 194.

20 Garrett, op. cit. p. 154.

21 Katherine Everett, *Bricks and Flowers, Memoirs of Katherine Everett*, Reprint Society, London, 1951, p. 162.

22 Quoted in Roy Jenkins, *Gladstone*, Papermac, 1995, p. 388.

23 cf Lynch and Vaizey, pp. 191–4.

24 Michele Guinness, p. 105.

25 Letter quoted in Michele Guinness, p. 106.

26 *Freeman's Journal*, 25 June 1872.

27 Ibid, 4 June 1872.

28 *Irish Times*, 10 July 1872.

29 Ibid, 13 July 1872.

30 *Freeman's Journal*, 30 January 1874.

31 K. Theodore Hoppen, *Elections, Politics and Society in Ireland 1832–1885*, Oxford University Press, 1984, p. 52.

32 David Thornley, *Isaac Butt and Home Rule*, MacGibbon and Kee, London, 1964, p. 179.

Endnotes

33 Dublin *Evening Mail*, 20 March 1880.

34 *The Times*, 7 April 1880.

35 *Freeman's Journal*, 22 March 1880. Sir Arthur's claim that he had not opposed Sunday closing in the rest of Ireland was disputed by one temperance campaigner, who said he had voted against it in parliament in 1876.

36 *Freeman's Journal*, 27 March 1880.

37 John Wyse Jackson and Peter Costello, *John Stanislaus Joyce*, Fourth Estate, London, 1998, p. 87. John Stanislaus Joyce married May Murray a month after the election and their second son, James, was born two years later (their first child died eight days after his birth). The same month, Parnell, to whom Joyce was to give his full allegiance, was elected leader of the Irish Parliamentary Party.

38 Malcolm, p. 250.

39 David Cannadine, *The Decline and Fall of the British Aristocracy*, Yale University Press, 1990, pp. 179 and 199.

40 Mark Bence-Jones, *Twilight of the Ascendancy*, Constable, London, 1987, p. 30.

41 The text was read to the House of Commons during a debate on a bill to provide compensation for "disturbances" in Ireland: 29 June 1880, Vol. 253, col 1134, House of Commons debates.

42 *The Irish Times*, 11 October 1880.

43 Derek Wilson, *Dark and Light: The Story of the Guinness Family*, Weidenfeld & Nicolson, 1998, p. 99.

44 Quoted in Bence-Jones, pp. 33–35.

45 House of Commons, 24 June 1886.

46 *The Times*, 4 January 1882.

47 Ibid, 31 January 1882.

48 The other two were Pat Higgins, aged about 65, who was executed on 15 January 1883, and Tom Higgins, aged about 30, executed with Michael Flynn, aged 44, on 17 January 1883.

49 *The Irish Times*, 6 March 1883.

50 Michele Guinness, *The Guinness Legend*, Hodder and Stoughton, London, 1989, p. 134.

Chapter Six: The First Guinness Scandal

1 Daly, pp. 25 and 70.

2 Lynch and Vaizey, pp. 240–1.

3 Ibid, p. 177.

4 Daly, p. 72.

5 Lynch and Vaizey, p. 238.

6 Michelle Guinness, p. 184.

7 Augustus J.C. Hare, *Story of My Life*, Vol. 5, George Allen, London, 1900, p. 204. Entry for 18 June 1879.

8 *The Irish Times*, 18 July 1879.

9 Cannadine, p. 312.

10 George Martelli, *Man of His Time: A Life of the First Earl of Iveagh*, Geoffrey Bles, London, 1957, p. 115.

11 *Freeman's Journal*, 8 April 1885.

12 Ibid, 14 April 1885.

13 Martelli, pp. 104–9.

14 Ibid, pp. 327–35.

15 *Freeman's Journal*, 26 November 1885.

16 Ibid, 24 November 1885.

17 Better known in later life as William Martin Murphy, the most successful Irish nationalist businessman of his time, owner of the *Irish Independent* and the Dublin Tramway Company, and instigator of the 1913 lockout in an attempt to break trade unionism. He was elected the Nationalist MP for the neighbouring St Patrick's constituency in 1885.

18 *The Irish Times*, 27 November 1885.

19 Martelli, pp. 126–7.

20 Ibid, p. 82.

21 Mark Bence-Jones and Hugh Montgomery-Massingberd, *The British Aristocracy*, Constable, London, 1979, p. 62.

22 Virginia Cowles, *The Rothschilds, A Family of Fortune*, Futura, 1975, pp. 151–2.

23 S.R. Dennison and Oliver MacDonagh, *Guinness 1886–1939: From Incorporation to the Second World War*, Cork University Press, 1998, pp. 16–17.

24 Dennison and MacDonagh, p. 24.

25 *The Irish Times*, 22 October 1886.

26 *The Times*, 27 October 1886.

27 *The Irish Times*, 25 October 1886.

28 *The Economist*, 23 and 30 October 1886.

29 Jonathan Guinness, *Requiem for a Family Business*, Macmillan, London, 1997, p. 26.

30 Ibid.

31 *The Times*, 27 October 1886.

32 *Money: A Journal for Investors and Speculators, and Review of the Money Market*, 19 January 1887.

33 Dennison and MacDonagh, pp. 20–21.

34 *The Irish Times*, 9 November 1886.

35 Dennison and MacDonagh, p. 24.

36 Ibid, p. 24.

37 *Money*, op. cit.

38 *The Economist*, 4 December 1886.

39 Dennison and MacDonagh, p. 23.

Endnotes

Chapter Seven: Finding a Home

1 The company made it a practice to pay the income tax payable by shareholders on dividends until 1929. In 1887, the tax amounted to eightpence in the pound (3.3%) but ranged up to six shillings in the pound (30 per cent) during the four years following the First World War. cf Dennison and MacDonagh, p. 28.

2 Martelli, pp. 136–8.

3 Mullally, p. 40.

4 Martelli, pp. 199–204.

5 Bence-Jones, p. 52.

6 S.N. Behrman, *Duveen*, Hamish Hamilton, London, 1972, p. 58.

7 Daly, p. 270.

8 *The Irish Times*, 27 November 1889.

9 The Guinness Partnership annual report for 2007.

10 Dennison and MacDonagh, pp. 27–8.

11 Cf Jonathan Guinness, *Requiem for a Family Business*, Macmillan, London, 1997, p. 30.

12 Jack White, *Minority Report: The Anatomy of the Southern Irish Protestant*, Gill and Macmillan, Dublin, 1975, pp. 159–160.

13 Jonathan Guinness, p. 29.

14 Dennison and MacDonagh, pp. 37–9.

15 Ibid. pp. 40–45.

16 Martelli, p. 147.

17 There is a memorial window to Anne in St Stephen's Chapel in St Patrick's Cathedral with the inscription "I was thirsty and ye gave me drink".

18 Jonathan Guinness, p. 35.

19 *The Irish Times*, 1 August 1890.

20 Ibid, 23 August 1890.

21 Dennison and MacDonagh, p. 29n.

22 *Weekly Irish Times*, 10 January 1891.

23 Martelli, p. 191.

24 *The Irish Times*, 20 January 1891.

25 Mullally, pp. 230–1.

26 Sir Bernard Burke was a son of John Burke, the founder of *Burke's Peerage*, which he took over after his father's death. He was also Keeper of the State Papers in Ireland.

27 *Evening Telegraph*, April–May 1891.

28 *Weekly Irish Times*, 18 July 1891. Interestingly, the tour taken by Tynan was already popular with visitors to Dublin and included a trip on the brewery's internal railway. There was also a guide book to the brewery.

29 *The Times*, 8 August 1891.

30 Quoted in *The Irish Times*, 11 August 1892.

31 *The Times*, 13 and 20 August 1892.

32 The forest now covers 4,500 acres and has been in the same family for 31 generations, never being bought or sold but handed down by inheritances. It is the only privately owned forest in England.

33 Cannadine, p. 360.

34 Hare, 14 November 1895.

35 Countess of Fingall, *Seventy Years Young, Memories of Elizabeth,* The Lilliput Press, Dublin, 1991, p. 296. Others have pointed out that Elveden was centrally heated and the fireplaces largely for show.

36 Ibid, p. 303.

37 Martelli, p. 207.

38 Cannadine, p. 365.

39 George Martelli, *The Elveden Enterprise*, Faber & Faber, London, 1952, pp. 50–1. How the pig came to be in the "bag" is not explained.

40 Bryan Guinness, *Dairy Not Kept*, Compton Press, 1975, p. 11.

41 *The Irish Times*, 21 February 1891.

Chapter Eight: Threats and Fears

1 Martelli, pp. 225–7.

2 House of Commons, 8 May 1885.

3 House of Commons, 22 February 1901.

4 Lady Fingall, p. 232.

5 House of Commons, 13 March 1902.

6 House of Commons, 4 September 1893.

7 *The Times*, 19 November 1907.

8 *The Irish Times,* 6 March 1914.

9 House of Commons, 21 April 1890.

10 *The Irish Times*, 26 November 1890.

11 *The Times*, 27 July 1896.

12 *The Times*, 25 August 1900.

13 Ibid, 17 October 1900.

14 Quoted in *The Irish Times*, 12 October 1900.

15 Robert O'Byrne, *Hugh Lane 1875–1915*, The Lilliput Press, Dublin, 2000, pp. 174–5.

16 *The Irish Times*, 17 March 1913.

17 *The Irish Times*, 11 January 1913.

18 *Daily Express*, 18 January 1913, quoted by O'Byrne, p. 176.

19 Ibid, p. 111.

20 Ibid, p. 174.

21 Lady Fingall, p. 266.

22 *The Times*, 7 January 1909.

23 *The Irish Times*, 28 January 1915.

24 *The Times*, 30 June 1911.

25 Ibid, 24 January 1915.

26 Everett, p. 156.

27 Ibid, p. 162.

28 Ibid, pp. 165–6.

29 History of Macroom Golf Club at www.macroomgolfclub.com.

30 *The Irish Times*, 27 October 1925. The soldiers were three lieutenants, described as intelligence officers, and their driver, who disappeared in the Macroom area in April 1922. Their bodies were found in a boggy area some miles away in December 1923: they had been shot dead. Everett wrote in her memoirs, and Lady Ardilaun presumably believed, that they were tortured in the castle before they were taken away and shot.

31 Ibid, 9 September 1909. Iveagh did not take up the offer.

32 House of Commons, 9 March 1905.

33 *The Irish Times*, 23 March 1906.

34 cf House of Commons debate on private members' bill, 25 May 1906.

35 Dennison and MacDonagh, p. 38.

36 Ibid, p. 44.

37 Ibid, pp. 67–9. Individual publicans and bottlers, often the same person, had always advertised Guinness but the company itself had never indulged in brand advertising up to this point.

38 *The Irish Times*, 15 August 1913.

39 Ibid, 16 August 1913.

40 Dennison and MacDonagh, pp. 47–8.

41 Ibid, p. 117.

42 Ibid, pp. 139–41.

43 Padraig Yeates, *Lockout: Dublin 1913*, Gill & Macmillan, Dublin, 2000, p. 5.

44 Ibid, p. 145.

45 *The Times*, 22 September 1913.

46 *The Irish Times*, 8 November 1913.

47 *The Times*, 14 November 1913.

48 Ibid, 25 November 1913.

49 Dennison and MacDonagh, pp. 147–8.

50 House of Commons, 29 April 1915.

51 Martelli, p. 306.

52 Letter dated 14 April 1915, Parliamentary Archives, London.

53 Ibid, Bonar Law papers, April and May 1915.

54 House of Commons, 29 April 1915.

55 House of Commons, 4 May 1915.

56 Dennison and MacDonagh, p. 159.

Chapter Nine: A New World Order

1 *Daily Telegraph*, 20 April 1868, quoted in Peter Galloway, *The Most Illustrious Order of St Patrick*, Phillimore & Co, Sussex, 1983, p. 32.

2 Galloway, p. 44.

3 Martelli, p. 357.

4 Galloway, p. 49.

5 Patrick Buckland, *Irish Unionism 1885–1923, A Documentary History*, Belfast, HMSO, 1973, p. 147.

6 R.B. McDowell, *Crisis & Decline: The Fate of the Southern Unionists*, The Lilliput Press, Dublin, 1997, pp. 38–9.

7 *The Irish Times*, 11 October 1911.

8 Ibid, 29 November 1913.

9 House of Commons, 11 February 1914.

10 McDowell, p. 49. Robinson subsequently changed his surname to Dawson.

11 Page L. Dickinson, *The Dublin of Yesteryear*, Methuen, London, 1929, p. 14.

12 Brian Bond and Simon Robbins (editors) *Staff Officer: The Diaries of Lord Moyne 1914–1918*, Leo Cooper, London, 1987, p. 98. The "diary" was written after the war from recollections, notes and letters which Walter, who later became Lord Moyne, had sent to his family.

13 *The Irish Times*, 12 July 1916.

14 Bond and Robbins, p. 99.

15 *The Times*, 2 October 1918.

16 McDowell, pp. 64–6.

17 House of Commons, 30 March 1920.

18 *Southend Observer*, 15 November 1922, quoted by Wilson, p. 186.

19 McDowell, pp. 104–5.

20 House of Commons 16 February 1922.

21 *The Irish Times*, 23 January 1922. The League wound itself up a year later after partition was confirmed by the British parliament. The rival Irish Unionist Alliance advised its supporters not to vote in the first Free State elections and became the Dublin advisory committee of the Southern Irish Loyalists' Relief Association, which was based in London.

22 *The Irish Times*, 16 June 1922.

23 His old friend David Plunket, now Lord Rathmore, was 80 at that stage and died in August 1919.

24 Lloyd George papers for May 1919. Parliamentary Archives, London.

25 *The Irish Times*, 20 October 1928.

26 Michelle Guinness, p. 186.

27 Dennison and MacDonagh, pp. 162–3.

28 Ibid, p. 164.

29 Ibid, p. 168.

30 Martelli, p. 297.

31 *Iveagh* v *Revenue Commissioners*, IR 1930, p. 386 ff.

32 Ibid, 9 April 1932.

33 Martelli, p. 302.

34 Quoted in *Irish Independent*, 16 October 1927.

35 Interestingly, *The Irish Times* did not report this proviso, although other newspapers, such as the *Irish Independent* and *The Times* in London, did.

36 House of Lords, 8 December 1953.

Chapter Ten: Guinness is Good for You

1 Dennison and MacDonagh, p. 175.

2 Quoted in Michelle Guinness, p. 133.

3 Ibid, p. 157 for the whip version of the story; Mulally, pp. 50–1 for the candlestick.

4 *The Times*, 12–24 July 1895.

5 *The Irish Times*, 22 November 1900.

6 Quoted in Michelle Guinness, p. 241.

7 *The Irish Times*, 8 April 1905.

8 *The Times*, 25 June 2003.

9 Ibid, 16 July 1903.

10 Martelli, op. cit., pp. 311–12.

11 *The Irish Times*, 5 March 1902.

12 *The Times*, 6 January 1906.

13 Ibid, 3 August 1908.

14 Ibid, 27 July 1932.

15 George Martelli, *The Elveden Enterprise*, p. 87.

16 Jonathan Guinness, op. cit., p. 43.

17 Dennison and MacDonagh, op. cit., p. 180.

18 It is tempting to see shades of Guinness in one of the fictional portraits of ad agency clients in Sayers' first novel *Murder Must Advertise*, which has very funny descriptions of the creative cynicism of copywriters. One was a staid and somewhat righteous client, an old-fashioned and religiously minded firm which made boiled sweets and non-alcoholic liquors and disapproved of women in the agency smoking and showing more arm and neck than the company's directors thought seemly.

19 Dennison and MacDonagh, op. cit., p. 182.

20 Ibid, p. 179.

21 Dáil Éireann, 20 October 1932.

22 Dennison and MacDonagh, p. 213.

23 *The Times*, 24 March 1932.

24 *The Irish Times*, 18 April 1932.

25 Dennison and MacDonagh, p. 255.

26 Ibid, p. 256.

27 *The Irish Times*, 2 October 1934.

28 *Connacht Tribune*, 13, 20 and 27 August and 17 September 1938.

29 Dáil Éireann, 3 May 1939.

30 *The Irish Times*, 22 July 1939.

31 House of Lords, 28 March 1935.

Chapter Eleven: Adventures and Misadventures

1 Robert Rhodes James, ed., *Chips: The Diaries of Sir Henry Channon*, Weidenfeld & Nicolson, London 1967, p. 397. Fritzi was Prince Friedrich Georg Wilhelm Christoph of Prussia, an Anglophile grandson of Kaiser Wilhelm II. Brigid was Lady Brigid Guinness, daughter of the second Earl of Iveagh and younger sister of Channon's estranged wife Lady Honor Guinness.

2 Cf Piers Paul Read, *Alec Guinness: The Authorised Biography*, Simon & Schuster, London, 2003.

3 Charlotte Mosley, "Guinness, Bryan Walter, second Baron Moyne (1905–1992)", *Oxford Dictionary of National Biography*, Oxford University Press, September 2004; online edition, January 2007.

4 *The Irish Times* and *The Times*, 28 August to 2 September 1933.

5 *Connacht Tribune*, 29 September and 6 October 1934.

6 *The Irish Times*, 27 October 1934.

7 Ibid, 19 November 1934.

8 Quoted in Michael de Cossart, *Ida Rubinstein*, Liverpool University Press, 1987, p. 20. Brooks' portraits of Ida can be seen on the Smithsonian Institution's website, www.si.edu.

9 De Cossart, p. 73.

10 Piers Brendon, *Winston Churchill: A Brief Life*, Secker & Warburg, London, 1984.

11 Rhodes James, p. 397. The ellipsis in this quote is in the book, which is a heavily bowdlerised version of Channon's diaries. Publication of the full version has been prohibited by his family until 2017. Being a "viveur" was a compliment in Chips' book: the "curious" Guinness money traits probably meant being careful with money. But Chips' estimate of Walter's wealth may have contributed indirectly to the story that he spent a third of his fortune on Ida Rubinstein, since his will was probated for £2 million, rather than the £3 million of Chips' estimate. However, that was but a small part of Walter's growing fortune, most of which was contained in the Moyne trusts.

12 House of Commons, 4 May 1925, Vol. 183, cc602-704.

13 *The Times*, 22 January 1931.

14 Martin Gilbert, *Winston S. Churchill, Volume V, 1922–1939*, Heinemann, London, 1976, p. 561.

15 Mary Soames, *Clementine Churchill*, Cassell, London, 1979, p. 266.

16 The case is the subject of several books, notably *White Mischief: The Murder of Lord Erroll* by journalist James Fox, which was made into a film of the same name in 1987 by Michael Radford and featuring Greta Scacchi, Joss Ackland and Charles Dance. After his acquittal, Delves Broughton returned to England and killed himself with a morphine overdose in a Liverpool hotel in 1942.

17 Soames, op. cit., p. 266.

18 Ibid, p. 264.

19 *The Times*, 23 May 1935.

20 Ibid, 11 April 1936.

21 Lord Moyne and Kathleen Haddon, "The Pygmies of the Aiome Mountains, Mandated Territory of New Guinea" in *The Journal of the Royal Anthropological Institute of Great Britain and Ireland*, Vol. 66 (Jul.–Dec. 1936), pp. 269–90.

22 *The Times*, 26 May 1936.

23 Gilbert, *Winston S. Churchill Companion, Volume V*, p. 1155.

24 Soames, op. cit., p. 278.

25 "Colonel" Barker was neither an officer nor a gentleman but a woman who pretended to be a man and had "married " a girl from Brighton.

26 Diana Mosley, *The Pursuit of Laughter*, Gibson Square, London, 2009, pp. 59–63.

27 Jonathan Guinness, p. 56.

28 Like his Uncle Ernest, Murtogh Guinness had a fascination with mechanical things and built up a collection of 700 mechanical music machines and automata which he kept in the two side-by-side townhouses in which he lived in New York. He bequeathed them, plus an endowment to maintain them, to the Morris Museum in Morristown, New Jersey, on his death in 2002.

29 *The Times*, 2 May 1998.

30 *The Times*, 12 October 1935.

31 *Daily Telegraph*, 8 August 2002.

32 Bryan Guinness, *Potpourri from the Thirties*, Cygnet Press, London, 1982, p. 12.

33 Mary S. Lovell, *The Mitford Girls*, Little Brown & Co, London, 2001, p. 145.

34 Rhodes James, p. 38.

35 Ibid, p. 106.

36 Gore Vidal, *Palimpsest*, André Deutsch, London, 1995, p. 195.

37 Quoted in Geoffrey Wansell, *Terence Rattigan*, Fourth Estate, London, 1995, p. 147.

38 *The Times*, 21 February 1945.

39 Vidal, p. 195.

40 Wansell, pp. 172–4.

41 *The Times*, 13 April 1937.

42 Ibid, 3 January 1939.

43 Martelli, *The Elveden Enterprise*, pp. 121–2.

44 UK National Archives, file KV2/163 document 44a.

45 *The Irish Times*, 8 December 1954.

46 Charlotte Mosley (ed.), *The Mitfords: Letters between Six Sisters*, Fourth Estate, London, 2007, pp. 282–3.

47 *Daily Telegraph*, 12 August 2003.

48 cf Efraim Karsh and Rory Miller, "Freya Stark in America: Orientalism, Antisemitism and Political Propaganda" in *Journal of Contemporary History*, Vol. 39, No. 3 (July 2004), pp. 315–32.

49 House of Lords, 26 February 1942.

50 Bernard Wasserstein, *Britain and the Jews of Europe 1939–1945*, Oxford University Press, 1979.

51 Haman was the biblical Persian minister hanged for trying to kill all Jews.

52 Wasserstein, p. 117.

53 House of Lords, 9 June 1942. On behalf of the Labour Party, Arthur Elveden's brother-in-law Lord Listowel disowned Wedgwood's remarks.

54 Transcript of Eichmann trial, session 59.

55 Quoted by Ian Black in "The Assassins", *The Guardian*, 5 November 1994.

56 Chaim Weizmann, *Trial and Error*, New York, 1949, p. 438.

57 House of Commons, 7 November 1944.

58 Michael J. Cohen, "The Moyne Assassination, November, 1944: A Political Analysis" in *Middle Eastern Studies*, October 1979, p. 370.

59 Quoted by Black, op. cit.

60 Cohen, op. cit., p. 361.

61 De Cossart, p. 205.

62 J. Bowyer Bell, "Assassination in International Politics: Lord Moyne, Count Bernadotte, and the Lehi" in *International Studies Quarterly*, March 1972, p. 66. Bowyer Bell is best known in Ireland for his history of the IRA, *The Secret Army*, which was prompted by his researches into militant Zionist groups which modelled themselves on the IRA of the War of Independence.

63 *The Times*, 26 June-1 July 1975.

64 Bryan Guinness, *Personal Patchwork*, Cygnet Press, London, 1986, p. 214.

65 *The Irish Times*, 8 December 1944. The difference between Chips Channon's estimate that Walter was "worth" £3 million and his will leaving £2 million may explain the belief among some that he had spent a third of his fortune on Ida Rubinstein. However, his will took no account of the trusts he had set up before his death, and he was "worth" very much more than the probated amount.

66 Quoted in *The Times*, 5 July 1975. Hacohen's article criticised the Israeli ceremonies for appearing to legitimise Moyne's assassination.

67 *The Times*, 20 February 1945.

68 *The Independent*, 23 May 1998; *The Times*, 4 May 1998.

69 Mulally, op. cit., p. 163.

70 *The Irish Times*, 2 December 1941.

71 Ibid, 13 November 1943.

72 Ibid, 20 November 1943.

73 Ibid, 15 January 1944.

74 Ibid, 10 August 1946.

75 Ibid, 9–16 March 1951.

76 *The Times*, 22 December 1949.

Chapter Twelve: The Seventh Generation

1 Dennison and MacDonagh, p. 261.

2 *The Times*, 1 November 1946.

3 Jonathan Guinness, p. 91.

4 Tony Millns, "The British Brewing Industry 1945–95", in R.G. Wilson and T.R. Gourvish, *The Dynamics of the International Brewing Industry Since 1800*, Routledge. London, p. 154.

5 Jonathan Guinness, p. 65.

6 *Time*, 26 March 1951, Quoted in Mulally, p. 63.

7 House of Lords, 30 June 1954, Vol 188, cc293–9.

8 Millns, p. 153.

9 Tony Corcoran, *The Goodness of Guinness*, Liberties Press, Dublin 2005, p. 95.

10 Flood, p. 74.

11 *The Times*, 6 and 11 July 1953.

12 *The Irish Times*, 29 September 1979.

13 *The Times*, 16 June 1955.

14 Michelle Guinness, pp. 157–8.

15 *The Times*, 16 June 1955.

16 Ibid, 27 April-2 May 1966.

17 Ibid, 21 May 1958.

18 *Daily Telegraph*, 30 January 2007.

19 *The Times*, 5 January 1959.

20 Jonathan Guinness, p. 77.

21 Sarah Curtis, editor, *The Journals of Woodrow Wyatt Vol 1*, Macmillan, London, 1998. The entry is for 25 January 1986, in which he described Paul Channon's appointment as Secretary for Trade and Industry as "scraping the barrel". He

went on, unfairly: "He's a shallow, uninteresting man with no ballast or authority, merely the Guinness millions behind him. I've never liked him though his wife is jolly."

22 *The Times*, 13 March 1963.

23 *The Irish Times*, 15 October 1966.

24 Ibid, 19 December 1966.

25 Ibid, 5 January 1967. Suki Potier was later linked with the Rolling Stones' Brian Jones who was found dead in his swimming pool in 1969. She married a Hong Kong businessman, Robert Ho, and they were both killed in a hit-and-run accident in Portugal in 1981.

26 Ibid, 17 January 1967.

27 Hunter Davis, *The Beatles*, Columbus, McGraw-Hill Book Co., 1968, p. 357.

28 *The Independent, Daily Telegraph, The Irish Times*, 22 November 1989.

29 *The Times*, 5 May and 16 October 1978; *The Irish Times*, 5 and 6 May 1978.

30 *The Observer*, 25 November 1979.

31 *The Times*, 8 August 1978. She was the daughter of Maureen's daughter, Caroline Blackwood, and her second husband, composer Israel Citkovitz. Caroline was married to the poet Robert Lowell at the time of the death; she had previously been married to the artist Lucian Freud.

32 *The Guardian* and *The Times*, 5 September and 6 December 1986. Gottfried von Bismarck was found dead in a London flat in October 2007 from an overdose of cocaine.

33 *The Guardian*, 27 August 1986.

34 Philip Murphy, "Boyd, Alan Tindal Lenno ", *Oxford Dictionary of National Biography*, Oxford University Press, September 2004, online edition, January 2008.

35 Jonathan Guinness, p. 97.

36 Dennison and MacDonagh, p. 202.

37 H.D. Kay, *Biographical Memoirs of Fellows of the Royal Society*, vol. 14, p. 302.

38 Probate Office, London.

39 Jonathan Guinness, p. 76.

40 *The Times*, 30 December 1957.

41 *The Times*, 16 August 1975.

42 Interview with Liam Cosgrave.

43 Derek Wilson, "Guinness, (Arthur Francis) Benjamin, third earl of Iveagh (1937–1992)", *Oxford Dictionary of National Biography*, Oxford University Press, September 2004, online edition, October 2006.

44 *The Times*, 3 August 1992.

45 *The Times*, 7 February 1984.

46 *The Irish Times* and *The Times*, 22–25 May 1984.

47 *The Times*, 19 December 1984.

48 Jonathan Guinness, pp. 105–8.

49 *The Irish Times,* 6 February 1981.

50 Ibid, 13 December 1980.

51 Jonathan Guinness, p. 120.

Chapter Thirteen: Success and Scandal

1 James Saunders, *Nightmare: The Ernest Saunders Story,* Hutchinson, London, 1989, pp. 1–10.

2 Ibid, p. 53.

3 Jonathan Guinness, pp. 163–4.

4 Saunders, p. 70.

5 Jonathan Guinness, p. 148.

6 *The Times,* 11 July 1985.

7 Ibid, 29 July 1985.

8 David Donaldson QC and Ian Watt FCA, "Guinness PLC: Investigation under Sections 432 (2) and 442 of the Companies Act 1985", Department of Trade and Industry, London, The Stationery Office, 1997, p. 34.

9 *The Times,* 18 July 1985.

10 Jonathan Guinness, p. 166.

11 Donaldson and Watt, p. 42.

12 Saunders, p. 140.

13 *Daily Telegraph,* 30 January 2007.

14 Ibid.

15 Saunders, p. 158.

16 Donaldson and Watt, p. 278.

17 Jonathan Guinness, p. 229.

18 *The Irish Times,* 12 September 1986.

19 Donaldson and Watt, p. 205. Guinness eventually recovered all but $3 million of this investment.

20 *The Guardian,* 13 June 1990.

21 Ibid, 13 March 1990.

22 Jonathan Guinness, op. cit., p. 358.

23 Publication was delayed until all the court cases and appeals were completed.

24 *The Scotsman,* 14 April 1986, cited by Jonathan Guinness, p. 211.

25 Donaldson and Watt, p. 56.

26 Ibid, pp. 133–5.

27 Ibid, pp. 214–35.

28 Ibid, p. 269.

29 Ibid, p. 279.

30 *The Economist*, 9 June 1990.

31 Jack Lyons died in February 2008 at the age of 92.

32 *Financial Times*, 28 August 1990.

33 *The Guardian*, 14 March 1990.

34 *The Independent* and *The Times*, 17 May 1991.

35 *The Guardian*, 16 February 1993.

36 Ibid, 18 December 1996.

37 *Times Law Reports*, 1 February 2002.

Epilogue

1 Mosley, pp. 693–4.

2 Richard Davenport-Hines, "Blackwood, Lady Caroline Maureen Hamilton-Temple", *Oxford Dictionary of National Biography*, Oxford University Press, 2004. Their sister, Natalia, had died of a heroin overdose in 1978 (see Chapter 12).

3 *The Guardian*, 18 February 1995.

4 *Daily Telegraph*, 30 January 2007.

5 Rhodes James. Diary entry for 12 May 1937.

6 *Financial Times*, 18 February 2005.

7 Ibid, 25 July 2007.

8 Ibid, 10 May 2008.

9 Ibid, 11 June 2007.

10 Ibid, 22 August 2008.

11 Iveagh Wealth Fund Factsheet, March 2009.

12 *The Times*, 10 May 2004.

13 *The Observer*, 7 January 2001.

INDEX

Index

Index

387

Index